# The Power of God

MICHEL RENÉ BARNES

# The Power of God

## Δύναμις in Gregory of Nyssa's Trinitarian Theology

The Catholic University of America Press
Washington, D.C.

The paper used in this publication meets the minimum requirements of American National Standards for Information Science—Permanence of Paper for Printed Library materials, ANSI Z39.48-1984.

∞

*Library of Congress Cataloging-in-Publication Data*

Barnes, Michel R.

The power of God : Δύναμις in Gregory of Nyssa's Trinitarian theology / Michel René Barnes.

p. cm.

A revision of the author's thesis (Ph.D.)—University of St. Michael's College.

Includes bibliographical references and index.

1. Trinity—History of doctrines—Early church, ca. 30–600. 2. Power (Christian theology)—History of doctrines—Early church, ca. 30–600. 3. Dynamis (The Greek word) 4. Gregory, of Nyssa, Saint, ca. 335–ca. 394—Contributions in doctrine of the Trinity.

I. Title.

BT109.B37 1998

231′.044′ 092—dc21

98-20197

ISBN 0-8132-0929-3 (alk. paper)

For CCC and DeeDee

*sanza de li occhi aver più conoscenza,*
*per occulta virtù che da lei mosse,*
*d'antico amor sentì la gran potenza.*

*Dante,* Purgatorio

# Contents

# Preface and Acknowledgments

THERE IS SOMETHING EXCITING yet fragile about having one's first book published. A work of intense intimacy is turned out onto the public world where strangers pass judgment. Happily, the passage of the writing from private to public is also an opportunity for debts to be acknowledged, which begins the act of repayment, an act that can never be completed. The book before you is a revised version of the doctoral dissertation I wrote at the University of St. Michael's College, Toronto, co-directed by (alphabetically) Joanne McWilliam and John Rist. The dissertation contained material from my Th.M. thesis, directed by John Egan, S.J. My debt to these generous scholars and teachers has to be acknowledged immediately, since their efforts made this moment possible. For the second phase of this writing, namely the book form, I am grateful to The Catholic University of America Press, David McGonagle, Susan Needham, and my anonymous reviewers.

I have had the benefit of a good education. Probably the most decisive event in my adult life was my four years at St. John's College, Santa Fe, New Mexico (sister to the older campus in Annapolis, Maryland). Fr. Michael Ossorgin, now passed on, introduced me to "the Greeks"—from Homer to Aristotle. It was a gentle but deeply enthusiastic introduction. The same gentleness was there when Fr. Michael introduced some of us to the treasures of the Orthodox tradition (a completely different set of "Greeks") and brought our souls back home (even if, as in my case, home was the Catholic Church). But some vision is not gentle: Dennis Higgins taught me to see the beauty in truth, a better Thomist than he ever imagined he could be, a title he would never claim. I can still feel the pure ripping thrill of finally understanding Euclid's proposition I.47, and it was Higgins who enabled that. There was more Aquinas (and Aristotle) with Thomas Slakey, who strengthened the Catholic mind that had been given back to me. After I had been taught to see and hear the beauty and good in the truth, Robert Bunker taught me to trust my own voice.

If St. John's College was so significant for me, it is also because of the friendships I made there: Karl Bohlmann, Galen Brenningstahl, Mark D. Jordan, Jan Malcheski, and Joan Paine (now Mother Susanna). Among these friends I first read the Fathers and with these friends I translated Clement of Alexandria's *Miscellanies.* Nothing from me could travel without their names being present and their memories recalled.

I went to Toronto expecting to do medieval theology. But in my first church history course with John Egan, S.J., I discovered where my interests truly lay: patristics. It was John who introduced me to the study of the early church and who taught me how to read their works carefully, and I miss him greatly since his death in January of 1998. I have to thank another professor at Regis, Fr. Tibor Horvath, S.J., for his courses in hermeneutics and for being one of the best graduate teachers I ever worked with. There can be in a doctoral program a moment when (and it always seems "suddenly") the graduate student makes the drive to be a scholar his or her own. I remember very clearly when this happened to me: it was in a doctoral course I took with a visiting scholar, Maurice Wiles. Whatever academic career, whatever academic presence I have, began not when I entered the doctoral program but in that class, when suddenly everything about the discipline began to matter.

It was this event that led me to John M. Rist, who taught in the Philosophy and Classics Departments, University of Toronto. Our relationship started off slowly, with me leaving him notes as I tried to puzzle out middle and neoplatonism. Eventually we talked face to face. Professor Rist gave me the desire to do the work as best as it could be done. At the time I was deeply grateful to Professor Rist for his intellectual support. Now, as I direct graduate students, I find more reason to be thankful for the dedication he lavished on me: I am grateful for the comments he offered on my chapters and the frequent, easy-going conversations we had. But I am especially grateful for him (in philosophy and classics) taking me (in theology) under his wing when he was under no formal obligation to do so and when I was already so largely "formed" in my interests.

The class I took with Canon Wiles was where I first met Daniel H. Williams. We were both doctoral students with an intense interest in the fourth century and both nursing a suspicion that things then had not been quite what the history books were telling us. We began, in that class, a professional collaboration and a personal friendship that remain among the great gifts my job has brought me. This book reflects, in bits and pieces here and there, the hundreds of conversations Daniel and I have had over the years. I must also thank those among my professional colleagues who have helped me with encouragement and kind words over the years: Robert Gregg, Dennis Groh, Joe Lienhard, S.J., Fred Norris, and Bishop Rowan Williams (the external reader of my dissertation). These colleagues have made "Early Christianity" a kind and exciting field to work in. I have a good job, in all its parts, and much of the pleasure derives from the good of working with people such as these. I must also mention my interdisciplinary friend, Tomas Brand.

As many of my readers will already know, a significant part of writing a dissertation or a book is the simple act of surviving. With their love, patience, and support, Jan and our daughter Jess have done as much as anyone could to help me stay human. There are no words to describe your sacrifices, or my debt. I will not forget. Finally, I acknowledge with gratitude the gift I was given in my family: my mother, Renée Ponchin, and my now deceased father, Lewis, as well as my brother René, have supported me for as long as I can remember with their love, encouragement, and humor (not to mention the money). Thank you.

Thank you all.

Portions of this book have appeared previously in press, under revised forms, as "One Nature, One Power: Consensus Doctrine in Pro-Nicene Polemic," *Studia Patristica* 29 (1997): 205–23; and as "Eunomius of Cyzicus and Gregory of Nyssa: Two Traditions of Transcendent Causality," *Vigiliae Christianae* 52.1 (1998): 59–87.

# Abbreviations

| | |
|---|---|
| ANF | The Ante-Nicene Fathers |
| CCL | Corpus Christianorum, Series Latina |
| CSEL | Corpus Scriptorum Ecclesiasticorum Latinorum |
| GCS | Die griechischen christlichen Schriftsteller |
| GNO | Gregorii Nysseni Opera |
| *JTS* | *Journal of Theological Studies* |
| M | Migne, Patrologia Graeca |
| NPNF | A Select Library of Nicene and Post-Nicene Fathers, Second Series |
| *NoM* | *Nature of Man* |
| *OAM* | *On Ancient Medicine* |
| *ONF* | *On the Natural Faculties* |
| SC | Sources Chrétiennes |
| *VC* | *Vigiliae Christianae* |

*All other titles, including journal titles, are not abbreviated.*

# Chronologies

*Select Chronology of the Fourth Century*

| | |
|---|---|
| 318–325? | Eusebius of Caesarea writes *Preparation for the Gospel* and *Proof of the Gospel* |
| 325 | Council of Nicaea |
| 330–335? | Asterius of Cappadocia writes his *Syntagmation* in support of Arian theology |
| 330–335? | Marcellus of Ancyra writes against Asterius' *Syntagmation* |
| 336–337 | Eusebius writes *Against Marcellus* and *Ecclesiastical Theology* |
| 341 | "Dedication" creeds at Antioch |
| 341 | Athanasius and Marcellus arrive in Rome |
| 343/42? | Council of Sardica |
| 355 | Eusebius of Vercelli presents creed of Nicaea at Council of Milan; Athanasius promotes Nicaea |
| 357 | Synod of Sermium issues proclamation (the "Blasphemy") attacking *homoousia* |
| 357/58 | Phoebadius writes *Against the Arians,* attacking Sermium, 357 |
| 358 | Council by Basil of Ancyra condemns Aetius, circulates critical Letter(s) |

| | |
|---|---|
| 359 | Council of Rimini and Seleucia (Antioch) |
| 359/60 | Gregory of Elvira writes *On the Faith,* attacking Rimini, 359 |
| 359 | Aetius' *Syntagmation* |
| 359–360? | Marius Victorinus writes *Against Arius* |
| 359/60 | Constantinople: Eunomius delivers an "Apology" *(Apologia)* |
| 360 | Council of Constantinople: Homoian creed promulgated as Imperial norm |
| 360–361? | Hilary of Poitiers writes *On the Trinity* |
| 361 | Synod of Antioch: radicals split from eastern Homoians |
| 362 | Synod of Alexandria: *Ep. Antioch* |
| 363–364 | Gregory of Elvira rewrites *On the Faith,* removing modalist indiscretions |
| 363 | Eunomius publishes enlarged *Apology* |
| 364 | Basil of Caesarea publishes his *Against Eunomius* |
| 378 | Ambrose of Milan writes books I and II of *De Fide* |
| 379/78 | Gregory of Nyssa writes *On the Soul and Resurrection* |
| 379 | Book I of Eunomius' *Second Apology (Apologia Apologiae)* |
| 380 | Gregory writes *On the Nature of Man* and book I of his *Against Eunomius* |
| 380–383 | Gregory and Eunomius write additional books in their mutual polemic |
| 380 | Gregory of Nazianzus delivers *Theological Orations* in Constantinople |
| 380 | Ambrose of Milan writes books III through V of *De Fide* |

| | |
|---|---|
| 381 | Council of Constantinople: Gregory of Nazianzus presides over first session |
| 381 | Ambrose's Council of Aquileia attacks Palladius and western Homoianism |
| 381 | Theodosius issues Imperial edict supporting those who believe Trinity of "one majesty, one power . . . three persons in divine unity" |
| 381–383? | Gregory of Nyssa writes "short" treatises on the Trinity, including his *On "Not Three Gods"* |
| 383 | Eastern Emperor presented with Competing Creeds focusing on Holy Spirit |
| 385? | Gregory of Nyssa writes *Great Catechism* (or *Catechetical Oration*) |
| 385–392? | Gregory writes *On the Life of Moses* |
| 400–404 | Augustine writes books I through IV of *On the Trinity* and his *Third Tractate on John* against western Homoians |
| 410–416? | Edited western Homoian documents circulate as "Arian Sermon" |
| <412 | Augustine writes books VI and VII of *On the Trinity* exegeting 1 Cor. 1:24 |

## *Master Chronology*

| | |
|---|---|
| c. 540–c. 480 B.C. | Heraclitus |
| 500/499–428/27 | Anaxagoras |
| fl. c. 450 | Parmenides |
| c. 495–c. 435 | Empedocles |
| 430–420 | *On Ancient Medicine* |
| 428/27–348/47 | Plato |
| 384–322 | Aristotle |
| c. 135–c. 50 | Posidonius |

| | |
|---|---|
| 106–43 | Cicero |
| 85 | Antiochus of Ascalon—“Middle Platonism” begins |
| <100 | Wisdom of Solomon |
| <100 | *On the Cosmos* |
| c. 15 B.C.–c. A.D. 50 | Philo |
| A.D. 52–57 | Paul, 1 Corinthians, Romans |
| c. 100 | Epistle to the Hebrews |
| 101–177 | Atticus |
| 2d century | *Chaldean Oracles* |
| fl. mid 2d century | Numenius |
| 129–210 | Galen |
| fl. c. 200 | Alexander of Aphrodisias |
| 150–211/15 | Clement of Alexandria |
| c. 155–230/40 | Tertullian |
| late 2d century | *Discourse on the Eighth and the Ninth* (NH VI.1) |
| d. 235 | Hippolytus |
| c. 185–c. 254 | Origen |
| 204/5–270 | Plotinus—“Neoplatonism” begins |
| d. c. 311 | Methodius |
| 234–305 | Porphyry |
| c. 242–327 | Iamblichus |
| c. 264–339 | Eusebius of Caesarea |
| c. 335–394/95 | Gregory of Nyssa |
| c. 325–394 | Eunomius of Cyzicum |
| <350 | *The Concept of Our Great Power* (NH VI.4) |
| c. 339–397 | Ambrose of Milan |
| c. 411–485 | Proclus |
| fl. 1st half 6th cent. | Simplicius |

The Power of God

# Introduction

## *Approaching the Question*

THERE IS AN IMPORTANT, but largely unexplored, summary by Gregory of Nyssa of his trinitarian faith in the work *On the Holy Trinity.* There Gregory says that he believes in "three Persons . . . one Goodness, one Power, one Godhead. . . ."[1] Anyone expecting the familiar and "orthodox" formula of "three Persons, one essence (or nature)" must come away surprised by Gregory's chosen expression of his faith: the "three Persons" one expects is certainly there, but instead of "one essence" or "one nature," or even "same in essence," the language of unity is found in the terms "Goodness, Power, Godhead." This book is about why language such as "one Goodness, one Power, one Godhead" could and did express Gregory's pro-Nicene faith, although my own inquiry focuses on that middle term, *power*—δύναμις. The reason why Gregory would use *power* in a trinitarian formula in the early part of the 380s is fundamentally a simple one: *power* was a scripturally-based term, authoritative in the tradition, given content and nuance by philosophy, and—by the fourth century—having a rich history in trinitarian theology. The expression "one power" was a traditional doctrine in Christian trinitarian writing that captured well

1. *On the Holy Trinity,* ed. Fridericus Mueller, vol. 3:1a, *Antirheticus Adversus Apollinarium. Opera Dogmatica Minora. Gregorii Nysseni Opera* (Leiden: E. J. Brill, 1958), 5.18 ff. Hereafter, *Gregorii Nysseni Opera* will be cited as *GNO.*

Throughout this volume, references generally follow the form "volume, page and line."

what the specifically Nicene doctrine of one nature or essence meant among its supporters in the second half of the fourth century.[2]

I say that Gregory's reason for using *power* in a trinitarian formula is fundamentally a simple one, but I must admit that his reasoning will not seem simple to us today. Gregory knew the theological language of *power* and understood its rich history of meaning and authority in Christian doctrines of the Trinity. That knowledge has, I think, been largely lost to us, and understanding Gregory's theology requires us to recover an understanding of *power,* its received meanings, and its authority for doctrines of the Trinity as they derived from both Christian tradition and pagan philosophy. The first goal of this study, then, is a recovery of *power* as a technical term.

To this task may be added another. Gregory's trinitarian theology has not often been the subject of contextual study; that is, Gregory's trinitarian theology has not often been examined precisely in terms of the historical context of its development and writing. While one might expect the study of late pro-Nicene polemics (against late "Arianism") and the study of the Cappadocian doctrine of the Trinity to overlap significantly and commonly, this has not been the case until very recently, and even so remains the case for only a few Cappadocian (or Arianism) scholars.[3] Instead, Gregory's theology has been understood primarily in terms of themes or overarching categories that operate (in all the important ways) free from the actual historical context in which he wrote. Amazingly, the study of Gregory's trinitarian theology has been largely the domain of either systematics or comprehensive studies of the doctrine of the Trinity, both of which necessarily treat Gregory's theology *en passant.*[4] As a result, Gregory's trinitar-

2. In his recent *Dieu et le Christ selon Grégoire de Nysse: Étude systematique du "Contre Eunome" avec traduction inedité des extraits d'Eunome* (Bruxelles: Culture et Vertité, 1994), Bernard Pottier correctly notices that the term δύναμις is central to Gregory's argument in *Against Eunomius;* he also knows that *power* is not to be understood in its Aristotelian sense. But Pottier never gives the reader any evidence of why *power* should be recognized as a significant term in theology or philosophy (except in a passing reference to the emperor Julian at the very end of the book).

3. The most significant of these scholars are (chronologically) Ronald Heine, *Perfection in the Virtuous Life* (Cambridge: Philadelphia Patristic Foundation, 1975); Mariette Canévet, *Grégoire de Nysse et l'herméneutique biblique* (Paris: Études Augustiniennes, 1983); and Frederick Norris, *Faith Gives Fullness to Reason: The Theological Orations of Gregory of Nazianzus,* trans. Lionel Wickham and Frederick Williams (Leiden: E. J. Brill, 1990).

4. Nothing can confirm this judgment so easily as a glance at Margarete Altenberger and Friedhelm Mann, eds., *Bibliographie zu Gregor von Nyssa* (Leiden: E. J. Brill, 1988), which will show

ian theology generally and his use of *power* specifically now have to be carefully situated within the context of pro-Nicene polemic in the second half of the fourth century.

The final problem that complicates the task of understanding the role of *power* in Gregory's pro-Nicene trinitarian theology is the burden of scholarly disputes in this century over the role of philosophy in the development of Christian doctrine. These disputes have been lively in scholarship both on Gregory and on the development of the doctrine of the Trinity and have meant that scholarly judgments of "orthodoxy" regularly turned upon an ancient author being free from the influence of philosophy. Scholarship in the early part of this century was much concerned either with indicting Gregory as a "Hellenizer" or with defending him against such a charge. The division of Gregory's writings into "dogmatic" or "mystical" has its roots in the modern defense of Gregory against the charge by von Harnack of being a Hellenizer (and also, to a lesser extent and in a different way, against similar charges by Cherniss).[5] The defense of Gregory has been played out through examining his use of philosophical sources. Scholars like Daniélou[6] and Jaeger[7] attempted to interpret Gregory's use of philosophy as a case of Gregory transcending philosophy. It was thought that in his dogmatic, that is, apologetic, writings, Gregory wrested from the philosophical categories of the pagan milieu a Christian ontology while in his mystical writings, Gregory wholly transformed the psychologi-

---

that scholars have not commonly asked the question: What is the specific historical context of *On 'Not Three Gods'* . . . or *On the Holy Trinity?*

5. Adolf von Harnack slighted Gregory's trinitarian theology, calling it semi-Arian, while Harold Cherniss slighted Gregory's anthropology, calling it Platonic, not Christian. See Harnack's *History of Dogma,* trans. Neil Buchanan (reprint, Gloucester: Peter Smith, 1976), 3.4, 86–87; and Cherniss's *The Platonism of Gregory of Nyssa* (1930; reprint, Berkeley: B. Franklin, 1970), 61–63. The older judgment that Gregory's trinitarian theology is somehow corrupt still has some small presence today; see, for example, Cornelis P. Venema, "Gregory of Nyssa on the Trinity," *Mid-America Journal of Theology* 8 (1992): 72–94.

6. In *Platonisme et théologie mystique: Doctrine spirituelle de Grégoire de Nysse,* 2d ed. (Paris: Aubier, 1953), Jean Daniélou does not hesitate to point out similarities between Gregory's position and pagan philosophical sources, but he does this in the complete confidence that Gregory is not corrupting Christianity.

7. Werner Jaeger distances his opinion from Daniélou's (by portraying himself as between the two extremes of Cherniss and Daniélou), while at the same time he emphasizes the distance from Origen's theology to Gregory's (that is, restating a cherished opinion of Daniélou's). See Jaeger's *Two Rediscovered Works* (Leiden: E. J. Brill, 1954), 120–21.

cal language of the day into a Christian existentialism. In descriptions such as these, the polemical character of Gregory's theology once again recedes in importance. Moreover, for most of this century, the important accounts of Gregory have consistently described his opponent Eunomius of Cyzicus as a stand-in either for Arius or for Origen, or as the personification of an excessive attachment to philosophy,[8] thereby depriving Gregory's theology of historical context. A careful reading of Gregory's works in their historical context requires operating free from stereotypical or reductionist understandings of the theology Gregory sought to refute and against which so much of his own theology was developed.[9]

Just as the presence of philosophy in Gregory's doctrines has been used as an indication of the heterodox character of his theology, so too in scholarly evaluations of Arianism, the influence of philosophy has been seen as an indication of heresy. This kind of judgment has figured significantly in studies of Arius and Eunomius.

There are three features of Arius' theology that have supported judgments on his debt to philosophy: his use of ἀγέν(ν)ητος and other terms that seem technical;[10] his apparent relegation of the Son to the role of an "intermediary," which was considered by scholars to be a feature of either cosmological philosophy or pagan polytheism;[11] and his use of "logic,"

8. Caricaturing Eunomius in this way does much to support a defense of Gregory from the very same charges—at the hands of Harnack, Cherniss, etc.—of an excessive attachment to philosophy.

9. Although one might suspect that such evaluations of Eunomius have ceased to appear in the most recent scholarship, there is evidence to the contrary: see, first, Panayiotis Papageorgiou, "Plotinus and Eunomios: A Parallel Theology of the Three Hypostases," *The Greek Orthodox Theological Review* 37 (1992): 215–31, who reduces Eunomius' understanding of "hypostasis" to Plotinus' on the basis of Eunomius' embrace of the "Plotinian" supposition that the cause is greater than its effect; see as well, Pottier, *Dieu et le Christ selon Grégoire de Nysse,* where Eunomius' theology is reduced to "metaphysics," for example, page 11.

10. See, for example, T. E. Pollard in his *Johannine Christology and Arianism* (Cambridge: Cambridge University Press, 1970), 188–91.

11. Éphrem Boularand, for example, believes that Arius had "un motif très précis" for the Son in creation: God used the Son as His instrument in the creation of the world, "d'une sorte de démiurge intermédiare entre sa solitude et l'univers des créatures. Nous voilà en plein platonisme" (*L'hérésie d'Arius et la "foi" de Nicée,* vol. 1 [Paris: Éditions Letouzey et Ané, 1972], 75,) L. Barnard argues in "The Antecedents of Arius," *Studies in Church History and Patristics* (Thessalonika: Analekta Blatadon, 1978), 181, that the doctrine of the Son as "an instrument in the work of creation" can be found in Theognostus (whom Gregory of Nyssa cites as a precedent for Eunomius' doctrine

or the dialectical nature of his argument. Many of the "philosophical" features attributed to Arianism are also found in Eunomianism. The traditional understanding is that Eunomian theology is Aristotelian in origin (excepting Eunomius' theory of language, which Gregory of Nyssa associates with Plato's *Cratylus*). Eunomius' writings, like those of Arius, are thought to be characterized by a use of syllogistic argument, that is, dialectic, that allows their opponents to describe their theologies as Aristotelian in nature.[12] The most influential of such judgments were those of J. de Ghellinck[13] and E. Vandenbussche.[14] Both scholars begin with the ancient polemical descriptions of Aetius and Eunomius as practitioners of "theological technique," a description that appears already in Epiphanius, Sozomen, and Socrates.[15] At the present time the traditional understanding has largely been superseded by an emphasis on Eunomius' platonic roots, either Neoplatonic[16] or Middle Platonic,[17] with an authoritative minority suggesting Stoic influence.[18] Recently two opposed revisions of Eunomian scholarship have interpreted Eunomius, on the one hand, as a Christian of a "Neo-Aristotelian" background battling both pro-Nicene

---

to this effect). Despite Barnard's comment, there has been almost no scholarly treatment of Eunomius' emphasis on the Son as demiurge.

12. Basil's discussion of Eunomius' philosophical sources may be found in *Against Eunomius* I.5.

13. J. de Ghellinck, "Quelques appreciations de la dialectique et d'Aristote durant les conflicts trinitaires du IV siecle," *Revue d'histoire écclesiastique* 26 (1930): 5–42.

14. E. Vandenbussche, "La part de la dialectique dans la théologie d'Eunome le Technologue," *Revue d'histoire ecclesiastique* 40 (1944–45): 47–72. More recently see Milton Anastos, "Basil's *Κατὰ Εὐνομίου*, A Critical Analysis," in *Basil of Caesarea: Christian, Humanist, Ascetic,* ed. Paul J. Fedwick (Toronto: Pontifical Institute of Medieval Studies, 1981), 1:67–137.

15. See Epiphanius, *Panarion* 76.2.13; Sozomen, *Ecclesiastical History* IV.26; and Socrates, *Scholastici Ecclesiastica Historia* II.35.

16. See, especially, Jean Daniélou, "Eunome l'Arien et l'exegese néoplatoncienne du *Cratyle*," *Revue des études grecques* 69 (1956): 412–32. One also thinks of Newman's judgment: "Plato made Semi-Arians, and Aristotle Arians." John Henry Newman, *The Arians of the Fourth Century,* 4th ed. (London: Basil Montagu, 1876), 335 n. 1.

17. In *A History of Neo-Arianism,* 2 vols. (Cambridge: Philadelphia Patristic Foundation, 1979), Thomas A. Kopecek argued not only for Middle Platonic, as opposed to Neoplatonic, sources to Eunomius' theology but also for philosophical sources that are mediated through the Christian tradition (in pointed if not quite acknowledged opposition to Daniélou).

18. See Lionel Wickham, "The Syntagmation of Aetius the Anomean," *Journal of Theological Studies,* 19 (1968): 532–69; and John Rist, "Basil's 'Neoplatonism': Its Background and Nature," in *Basil of Caesarea,* ed. Paul J. Fedwick (Toronto: Pontifical Institute of Medieval Studies, 1981), 1:137–200, esp. 185–88.

and gnostic Christianity,[19] and, on the other, as an anti-metaphysics Christian.[20]

Strangely, even in so superb a work as R. P. C. Hanson's *The Search for the Christian Doctrine of God,* where sensitivity to historical context is unsurpassed, the effects of the old accusations of "Hellenization" can still be seen in cases where Hanson "brackets out" the significance of philosophy. For the purposes of this study, the most important example of such a bracketing is Hanson's conclusion that Gregory's trinitarian theology "is not greatly affected by his philosophical ideas, and the fact that those who have written about these latter ideas have tended to a large extent to ignore the former supports this view."[21] I will argue to the contrary that Gregory's trinitarian theology makes substantial use of philosophical ideas; indeed, I will show that the utility of a term like δύναμις for trinitarian speculation lies in large degree in its philosophical background. Gregory's debt to philosophy in this regard is not unique among pro-Nicene polemicists; yet what distinguishes Gregory's use of "one power" and related trinitarian formulae is the fact that he consciously develops and justifies the trinitarian sense of the doctrine "one power" by explicitly understanding *power* in its philosophical sense. The integral role that a technical understanding of power plays in Gregory's polemics provides a basis for pro-Nicene theology to reach the mature, definitive form it will take in his theology. Unless we uncover the philosophical sense(s) of the term, we will not be able to recognize *power* as the significant term it was in theology (both Christian and pagan), nor will we be able to appreciate its role in the trinitarian controversies of the fourth century.

## *Back to the Beginning:* Power *in Greek Philosophy*

The need to recover the significance of *power* in Christian theology leads to a somewhat surprising solution: in order to truly understand

19. Raoul Mortley, *From Word to Silence,* 2 vols. (Bonn: Peter Hanstein Verlag Gmbh., 1986), 2:128–59.

20. Maurice Wiles, "Eunomius: Hair-splitting Dialectian or Defender of the Accessibility of Salvation?" in *The Making of Orthodoxy: Essays in Honour of Henry Chadwick,* ed. Rowan Williams (Cambridge: Cambridge University Press, 1989), 157–72.

21. R. P. C. Hanson, *The Search for the Christian Doctrine of God* (Edinburgh: T. & T. Clark, 1988), 723.

Gregory's reasoning in the fourth century after Christ, we must turn to the fourth century before Christ. The beginnings of what I call the "technical" sense of *power* lie in the literature of the medical authors who lived a generation or two before Plato. Among the medical authors—belonging predominantly to the Hippocratic school—*power* means the affective capacity (or capacities) of any given existent distinctive to the identity of that existent.[22] This sense of power is developed in the Hippocratic literature through associating power with the concept of nature (φύσις): power is the affective capacity of the nature, or nature as affective capacity. Already the reader can sense the kind of unity presupposed in the Hippocratic play between power and nature. And already the reader can imagine the kind of play *power* and *nature* might have in Christian discussions of God's existence—"God's nature, God's power." The presence of power causality in discussions of the divine is a general feature of classical theologies. The role of power in Gregory's discussions of the Trinity shows the presence that "power theology" had generally in the era. More than this, Gregory's doctrine of the Trinity, like his theology overall, shows the influence of the medical understanding of power specifically; Gregory makes no secret of his debt to medical thought, and he regularly makes this thought central to his arguments (as, for example, in *On Virginity*). For any understanding of the technical notion of power, it is useful to return to the medical source of this sense. For an understanding of Gregory's use of *power,* it is necessary to return to the medical origins and use of the term.

For the early Hippocratics, δύναμις means the causal capacity of a material entity. In their cosmology, everything that exists is composed of indi-

22. The medical origins of the technical sense of δύναμις may be said to be a recent discovery. In earlier scholarship the origin of δύναμις as a philosophical term was found in Pythagorean doctrine, primarily on the basis of "fragments" thought to be pre-Socratic in origins but which are now dated to a time after Aristotle (and are perhaps neo-Pythagorean). The most important example of this earlier judgment will be found in Jean Souilhé's classic work, *Étude sur le terme Δύναμις* (Paris: Librairie Felix Alcan, 1919), which proceeds from a presumption of Pythagorean origins for δύναμις. Souilhé (and others like A. E. Taylor) built a description of the "Pythagorean" origins of δύναμις too elaborate and too definite to be supported by textual evidence. Similarly, W. Grundmann built his account of the philosophical sense of δύναμις on Philolaus' "Pythagorean" fragment in his article on δύναμις for the *Theological Dictionary of the New Testament,* II, 284–317; see, for example, page 286. Some early geometrical sense of δύναμις is not to be discounted entirely, since both Plato (*Theaetetus* 148 B) and Aristotle (*Metaphysics* 1019b 34) use δύναμις to mean a mathematical root or square root.

vidually subsistent affective qualities or powers: the fundamental level of existence is an irreducible unit of powers. It is mixtures of powers that produces everything that we perceive to exist, for it is the existence of specific *powers* in a mixture that determines the identity or nature of an existent, and it is the action of these powers upon other mixtures that determines all the causal relations that we perceive and know. For the Hippocratic philosophers, the concept of power(s) describes everything that really exists.

Two specific doctrines are particularly important for both Hippocratic philosophy and the later Christian appropriation of power [δύναμις] causality. The first doctrine is that these powers are organized or understood as opposites, insofar as one power (or collection of powers) acts to destroy, drive off, or reverse the action of another specific power (or collection of powers). The second significant doctrine is a distinction that is made between the unique power of an existent that is distinctive or peculiar to a thing and thereby identifies the nature of that existent (power in its proper sense) and the power that belongs to a thing as one of a number of powers and that is not unique to the existent (*power* in its secondary sense). For example, there is a difference between fire's δυνάμ(ε)ις of hot and fire's δυνάμ(ε)ις of dry or ever-moving. Hot is distinctive to fire's nature; it reveals fire's nature because it is unique to fire. Other elementals have the power of dry or ever-moving (air, for example). The power hot is the power of fire insofar as fire is fire. This kind of power is always singular. The power dry, like the power ever-darting, belongs to fire but not only to fire. This kind of power is understood to exist always in the plural. The first kind of power is connatural to the existent, for wherever this kind of power is, the existent must necessarily also be (wherever there is heat there is fire). The second kind of power may be understood as natural in the broad sense of that term, but the presence of one of this kind of power does not necessarily indicate the presence of a specific existent: the presence of ever-moving alone does not necessarily indicate the existence of fire the way the presence of the hot does.

However, the role played by the concept of power in classical philosophies and theologies is not due simply to the Hippocratic use of the term. There is another important stage in the development of the technical sense of *power,* which owes to Plato. In the Hippocratic writings power causality remains wholly materialistic. Plato takes this understanding of cause, strips it of explicit material associations, and develops it to describe immaterial causes: virtues in the soul, faculties of knowledge in the mind, and the Good. The action of virtues in the soul and knowledge in the mind are both described as power causalities, for example. One of the most important examples for theology of this development occurs in the *Republic* when Plato compares the action of the sun to the action of the Good. This passage marks Plato's clear appropriation of medical causal language in an application that leaves behind the explicit materialistic context of that language.[23] Gregory's application of *power* to trinitarian doctrine follows Plato not only in using power causality to describe immaterial causal relationships but also in using an explicit analogy between a material power and an immaterial power. Moreover, a passage like the *Republic*'s provides an important insight into Gregory's understanding of the kind of cause God is: He is a Power in the ontological sense the medical philosophers gave to *power;* namely, the power that belongs to something insofar as it exists and not simply insofar as it has office.

Finally, apropos of Plato and power, it is worth remarking that the specific branch of Plato scholarship that has typically been influential among patristic scholars has generally not been of the sort to recognize the importance of power for Greek philosophy generally and for Plato's thought in particular, except through the association of δύναμις with Aristotle's philosophy. To my knowledge, this monograph marks the first written appearance in patristic scholarship of a "medical" understanding of Plato's thought. This study proceeds with the understanding that medical philosophy is an important and bona fide component of ancient Greek and Hellenistic philosophy, a judgment that some readers may find new. Therefore I have taken special care to provide as self-contained and thorough an account as possible of power in Plato's philosophy. An alternative account like this of Plato's philosophy is needed to replace previous scholarship that is no longer credible but continues to influence patristic studies.

23. To my knowledge no one has previously considered the influence of Hippocratic philosophy on the "transcendentalism" of *Republic* 509 B, especially in light of the use of δύναμις there.

### *Power and Christian Polemic*

*Power* named first and foremost the affective capacity of something that exists; that affective capacity was understood to exist insofar as the existent was itself—the affective capacity existed insofar as the existent was what it was. Power, then, was linked both to the identity of an existent and to the real or actual existence of an existent. To put all this a slightly different way: the concept of power was an understanding of affective capacity as fundamentally linked to the identity and existence of an existent. For Christians the concept *power,* in the specific senses given to it in pagan philosophy, had a certain appropriateness in describing God and especially for speaking of God as Trinity. First of all, God acted: God had, to put it in the jargon, an affective capacity. God acted in history upon individuals and nations. Perhaps most importantly, God acted as the maker of the world, of the cosmos. If one understood God as one who acts, then the term *power* was quite appropriate (as Philo's works, as well as Wisdom of Solomon, Rom. 1:20, and Heb. 1:3, attest). For Christians there is a further, intensely fundamental act on God's part: His production or generation of a Son, a Word, a Wisdom, a Power—whatever title one picks to name this product and the associated relationship of origin and continuity. In the patristic era, any trinitarian theology is necessarily a theology of God's productivity. It is equally true to say that questions in patristic trinitarian theology are necessarily questions about God's productivity.

Different understandings of the originating relationship between the first and the second Persons found expression in different ways of relating the second Person to God's power. For example, the Son can be described as God's very power, as "one with" God in just the way an affective capacity is one with an existent. (In the fourth century, Athanasius spoke this way.) Or, the Son can be described as "God's power" (among powers), thereby implicitly relativizing the sense of *power* so that it does not mean that specific affective capacity that uniquely identifies the existent but one of the several secondary powers an existent possesses. (In the fourth century, Asterius was famous—infamous?—for teaching something like this.) Finally, the power of the first and second Persons might be described as being one and the same, so that the Father and Son are said to have the same "one power." (Nicenes of the second half of the fourth century taught this doctrine.) If *power* is being used in its philosophical sense—indicated by the use of associated philosophical language like *nature*—then to say that the Father and Son have one and the same power is to say that they have one and the same nature. If *power* is being used in its more common political sense—sometimes indicated by associated political or volitional language—then what is meant by "the Father and Son have one and the same power" is that they have the same intention when they each act. The use of *power* in trinitarian doctrines is thus open to a variety of understandings: most of these understandings may be found in Christian literature from the late second and early third centuries and again in Christian literature of the fourth century.

The first two chapters of this book make clear the philosophical sense of *power* that will later be appropriated by Christians, either directly from philosophical sources or indirectly through Jewish sources (such as Wisdom of Solomon). The third chapter establishes the presence of power language and thought in the trinitarian literature of the late second and early third centuries. Establishing this presence is important first because it reveals the different power doctrines in Christian trinitarian theology. Yet the existence of power doctrines at this early time is not, in itself, important for this study (except insofar as the fact of power-based trinitarian theology is established). What is most important about the existence of power doctrines in the trinitarian literature of the second and third centuries are the precedents, the options, this literature establishes for trinitarian theology in the decisive debates of the fourth century. This is the subject of the fourth chapter. The different trinitarian power doctrines of the fourth century restate the positions of the previous centuries, positions that are by then traditional and potentially authoritative. The least one can say about fourth-century power theologies is that they are all traditional (which is not to say that they are all equally credible or successful). When Gregory and others use power-based trinitarian language, they are using doctrinal language that owes its content and authority not only to its philosophical origins but to its Christian descent as well. What distinguishes Gregory's use of *power* from that of his pro-Nicene peers is the degree to which he explicitly links the scripturally-based *power* language (such as 1 Cor. 1:24) of traditional trinitarian doctrine to the power causality it connotes in philosophy.

Christian theologies of power in the fourth-century controversies divide over whether the Father's power that is operative in the generation of the Son is God's connatural power or another kind of power, the political or moral power. In Eunomius' trinitarian theology, the power—δύναμις—of God operative in the generation of the Son is the political or moral power and not God's connatural power. Gregory, by contrast, understands the power of God operative in the generation of the Son to be God's connatural power and not another kind of power, the political or moral power. One finds, in this particular analysis, a neat divide between the theologies of Gregory and Eunomius in their understandings of the concept *power.* Eunomius' subordinationist theology has no use for divine productivity described in terms of power causality, while Gregory gradually identifies pro-Nicene theology with an account of divine productivity described precisely as power causality.

Although Eunomius' theology has been portrayed as outside the sensibilities of mainstream fourth-century Christian thought, in fact much of his language was borrowed from his predecessors and undoubtedly was recognized as such by his contemporaries.[24] As I show in chapter five, Eunomius' primary description of God is that of a being that by nature neither is produced nor produces. His primary description of the Son is as a being that is produced and produces. The Son's relationship with God is determined by his unique status as the single effect of God's activity and as the obedient instrument or servant of that activity (a description with its own cosmological connotations). The Son's relationship with the cosmos is described in terms of His role as creator; the Son can fulfill this role because He receives from God the δύναμις to create.

Both Eunomius and Gregory agree that the kind of unity that holds between the divine nature and divine productivity determines the kind of unity that holds between the first and second Persons because the act of generation or production is the act through which the product's nature is

24. See my "The Background and Use of Eunomius' Causal Language," *Arianism After Arius: Essays on the Development of the Fourth Century Trinitarian Conflicts,* ed. M. R. Barnes and D. H. Williams (Edinburgh: T. & T. Clark, 1993), 217–36.

determined. If God's productive capacity is not inherent in His nature, then a common nature cannot be communicated to the product. Eunomius and Gregory also agree that statements on the status of God's productive capacity are dramatized in doctrines of the Son as the creator God—they also share the understanding that the Son is the creator. Eunomius believes that the moral, nonnatural unity between God and his creative capacity is dramatized in the Son's reception of the delegated capacity to create; Gregory believes that the Son's capacity to create reveals the common power or faculty and thus the common nature the Son shares with the Father, given that the capacity to create is not something that can stand apart from the divine nature. Eunomius is thus led to emphasize God's transcendence in contrast to not only the Son but also the capacity to produce the Son, while Gregory is led to emphasize the transcendence of the divine productive capacity in common with the divine nature, so as to ensure the fully natural, fully transcendent source of the Son and thus His own transcendent nature. Eunomius' theology leads him to take creation as the fundamental term for divine production to the point where Eunomius will describe the Son Himself as created, while Gregory's theology leads him to take generation as the fundamental term for divine production, even to the point where Gregory will describe creation as one sense of generation.

Gregory's theology of divine power is treated in chapters six and seven. Gregory understands δύναμις as the capacity to act that is distinctive to a specific existent and that manifests the nature of that existent. Gregory argues that if the Father and Son manifest the same δύναμις then they must also share the same φύσις. Gregory supports this argument through analogies with physical examples of the unity between a δύναμις and a φύσις: the most important of these examples is the relationship of heat to fire, a use that shows well the debt Gregory's thought owes to the ancient elemental sense of power and its associated causality. Gregory's theology never surrenders this analogy, although, it is true, he does not always describe heat as the δύναμις of fire. The etiology associated philosophically with *power* is given a Christian context in scriptural references, of which the most important is 1 Cor. 1:24. This biblical passage, like John 5:19 (with which it is often associated), plays an important part in the polemics between those sympathetic with Nicene theology and those against it.

*Gregory's Trinitarian Theology in Its Pro-Nicene Context*

One important result of this study is to make clear the importance of the issue of divine productivity in fourth-century trinitarian controversies. *Father-Son* language cannot be approached simply as naming relations: the argument is over divine productivity. In both Gregory's and Eunomius' minds, the debate over the divine nature of the Second Person is not simply an argument over whether *Son* implies "same nature" or not, but over the necessarily prior question of the character of divine productivity. Both Gregory and Eunomius understand the type of nature the Son receives (and thus is constituted of) to be determined by the kind of productive capacity characteristic of God.

Both Eunomius and Gregory ask the question: does God possess a "natural" productive capacity? A "natural productive capacity" is one that can reproduce the nature of the productive existent. If a productive capacity is not a natural one, then the capacity cannot reproduce the nature of the productive existent. A productive capacity that reproduces the nature of the existent must exist within the nature of the productive existent; a productive capacity that does not reproduce the nature of the existent must exist outside the nature of the productive existent. If God has a natural productive capacity, He can produce a "Son" with the same nature; if God does not have a natural productive capacity, whatever "Son" means it cannot mean a product with the same nature as God. Not surprisingly, Gregory and Eunomius argue their doctrines of divine productivity using models and language available in etiologies of the day. Each of these theologians tends toward precedents and language that support his understanding.

The question of divine productivity is not encompassed entirely in the doctrine of natural generation. For both Gregory and Eunomius, judgments on divine productivity translate into not just trinitarian or christological doctrines but doctrines about creation. Is creation a function of divinity, or should one understand the act of creation as somehow (yet necessarily) removed from what divinity is in itself? If productivity is natural to God, then creating itself (a kind of productivity) has its source in God; if productivity is not natural to God, then creating must in some way have its source exterior to God. It goes almost without saying that Gregory's understanding is that God is naturally productive and that God creates. Eunomius understands that God is not naturally productive, and creation is the function of something exterior to God's nature. Gregory and Eunomius are arguing to arrive at doctrines of the "Son" that will win the day. The argument over interior or natural productivity versus exterior or accidental productivity is carried on in terms of whether divine productivity is a capacity that can be delegated by the true God (for it is not natural) or whether divine capacity is such that it cannot be delegated (any more than nature can be delegated).

The last point I want to make is this: in Gregory's view, the inherent productivity of the divine nature (enacted by the Father, manifested in the Son) is a subject matter not very different from that of divine goodness. Denying a real Trinity is fundamentally the same as denying the intrinsic goodness of God: *giving* is the highest good, and *existence* is the highest gift. If the Father does not—indeed, as Eunomius argues, *cannot*—generate existence as full as His own, then the limits of God's goodness have been reached. Gregory's distinctive emphasis on divine infinity is well known to his modern readers, and I need not elaborate on what it would mean to him to imagine that—of all properties—God's goodness had a limit.

### *Operations and Power*

Perhaps the most commonly known characterization of Gregory's (and of Cappadocian) trinitarian theology is the doctrine that the unity of nature (among the Three) is proved by the unity of their activities. If the Father, Son, and Holy Spirit all perform the same activities, then they must have the same nature (which produces or enables these activities). This doctrine is so well known among theologians and scholars that its logic seems obvious and is taken for granted. Yet the logic of the doctrine is not as commonsensical as it might seem. Two questions—two very different kinds of questions—about the logic of the doctrine arise immediately. First, how do we understand the relationship between activities and natures so that the link between them is guaranteed? Secondly, is the doctrine—and the logic of the doctrine—as we find it in Gregory's writings actually articulated in, and sufficiently summarized by, the language of "nature-activities"? In fact, the answer to both these questions reveals the significance of power-based theology for Gregory.

How, then, does one understand the relationship between activities and natures so that the link between the two is guaranteed? The link between the two is not obvious. A bicycle and a horse both perform the same "operation" of transportation, but they have completely different natures: unity of activity does not prove unity of nature. Obviously Gregory's reasoning must pivot on designating a certain class of "activities," not just any one. The presumption is that there are some functions which are distinctive to the nature or identity.[25] If we know that some functions belong only to a specific nature, then the discovery of the function necessarily means the existence of the nature. But the logic of the argument is carried in the idea that each nature has a function which is distinct to it. The name of the function unique to a nature is, of course, *power*. Which brings us to the second question: is the doctrine—and its logic—as articulated by Gregory best stated in "activities" language? The answer is no. The notion of an activity by itself does not bring one to the intrinsic link between being something and doing something; only the notion of power does that. Undoubtedly Gregory sometimes uses "activity" language to make this case, but the logic (and frequently the actual argument in the text) does not stand separate from the concept of power. There are other reasons for activity—ἐνέργεια—appearing in Gregory's writings. When Gregory's theology is examined in its polemical context, the status of ἐνέργεια takes on an entirely different sense than one finds in the common received understanding.

The utility of *power* for Gregory's polemical theology is due in large part to its traditional christological associations. Gregory understands a formula like "one nature because one power" to be a suitable and credible statement of the unity among the Persons, but he also recognizes that the same exegetical tradition that gives *power* authority in a polemic may tend to limit the use of the title to cases involving the second Person. The limitations on power language are not philosophical, but exegetical: *power* is pre-

25. Identifying such functions as a class is the subject of Plato's *Protagoras* 320 D ff.

dominantly a term used in a christological context, with—in the Greek-speaking church at least—little clear reference to the Spirit. When Gregory needs to enlarge his argument to include the divinity of the Holy Spirit, he will turn to a term with a more pneumatological scriptural base: ἐνέργεια, operation or activity. By the early 380s, "activity" is a term frequently associated with the Holy Spirit in polemical disputes over divinity. Ἐνέργεια is as scriptural and as philosophical a term as δύναμις and often appears with δύναμις in causal sequences. If ἐνέργεια has been read by modern scholars with the understanding that it has a broad and equal application to the Trinity, this is because a supplemental metaphysics has supplied a context that relates ἐνέργεια to the common φύσις. Modern scholarly readings of ἐνέργεια as a general trinitarian title, with equal application in demonstrating the divinity of all three Persons, depend upon the Aristotelian metaphysics of scholasticism (or rather, the modern scholastic privileging of the Aristotelian metaphysics in medieval thought).[26] The falling away of δύναμις as a general trinitarian term depends, I imagine, upon the truncated influence of its supporting metaphysics.

*Power*, δύναμις, has had an Aristotelian connotation because it forms one half of that distinctively Aristotelian insight of potentiality versus actuality, actuality here being either ἐνέργεια or ἐντελέχεια in the Greek. It is this insight which we moderns have been taught to see as Aristotle's distinct contribution to classical philosophy. Moreover, given the preponderance of Aristotelian philosophy in Catholic theology for the last seven hundred years, it should come as no surprise that *power* has often been understood this way in important Catholic histories of doctrine. However, my observation has been that non-Catholic (indeed, non-Christian) intellectual thought is just as bent to this connotation of *power*. A more accurate account of the orthodoxy of this reading of Aristotle and the signifi-

26. I note that the significance of the concept of *power* for medieval theology and philosophy has been treated recently in works by Lawrence Moonan, *Divine Power: The Medieval Power Distinction up to its Adoption by Albert, Bonaventure, and Aquinas* (Oxford: Clarendon Press, 1994); Irven Michael Resnick, *Divine Power and Possibility in St. Peter Damian's De Divina Omnipotentia* (Leiden: E. J. Brill, 1992); and P. L. Reynolds, "The Essence, Power and Presence of God: Fragments of the History of an Idea, From Neopythagoreanism to Peter Abelard," *From Athens to Chartres—Neoplatonism and Medieval Thought: Studies in Honour of Edouard Jeauneau* (Leiden: E. J. Brill, 1992), pp. 351–80.

cance of his philosophy in modern reconstructions of classical philosophy cannot single out scholasticism for blame; indeed, scholasticism's vitality in the era of Enlightenment scholarship may be better seen as a religious manifestation of a reading of Greek philosophy that was culture wide and epoch deep: Zeller, I think, owed nothing to Suarez. The automatic association of δύναμις with Aristotle is due, then, to an ahistorical reading of Aristotle and a misunderstanding of how Aristotle was read. In the eras of middle and neoplatonism, the potentiality-actuality distinction is a distinctly minor application of these terms.[27]

Clearly, one's awareness of the importance of *power* as a term in transcendent causality is linked to the philosophical tradition from which one reads (or in which one was trained). As I have just indicated, the understanding of Plato and Aristotle typical of most of the 19th and 20th centuries was tone deaf to the term. However, another tradition of scholarship, typified by Souilhé and Cornford,[28] had a very lively sense of the concept's significance. The insensitivity which some traditions in modern philosophy have shown to the concept is, I think, fundamentally the artifact of choices once consciously made but now forgotten. The concept of force was very important to Spinoza, Leibniz, and Hegel, but with Kant it lost its credibility. Kant excluded force from categorical status because he regarded it as one of the pure but derivative concepts of the Understanding.[29] After that, although the concept *Kraft* was important for right-wing Hegelians, left-wing Hegelians such as Jean Hippolyte found Hegel's very project of explicating the Concept of Force to be beside the point. Indeed, Heg-

27. A. C. Lloyd's "Activity and Description in Aristotle and the Stoa", *Proceedings of the British Academy,* LVI (1970), 227–40, and "Neoplatonic Logic and Aristotelean Logic," *Phronesis,* 1 (1955–56), 58–72 and 146–60, provide helpful accounts of how Aristotle's use of δύναμις and ἐνέργεια was understood in later Greek thought. A more extensive treatment of a Neoplatonic understanding of δύναμις and ἐνέργεια may be found in Stephen Gersh's *From Iamblichus to Erigenia* (Leiden: E. J. Brill, 1978). J. N. Findlay's comments may serve to summarize the more common understanding of δύναμις and ἐνέργεια: ". . . the Neoplatonists, while they sometimes defer to the Aristotelian subordination of potency to act, really invert Aristotle altogether, as every eidetic philosophy must do . . . true δύναμις is also true ἐνέργεια, and a higher ἐνέργεια than the limited ἐνέργεια of species or instance." "The Logical Peculiarities of Neoplatonism," in *The Structure of Being: A Neoplatonic Approach,* ed. R. Baine Harris (Norfolk: International Society for Neoplatonic Studies), p. 7.

28. Souilhé's work has already been cited; for Francis M. Cornford, see his *Plato's Theory of Knowledge* (reprint, Indianapolis: Bobbs-Merrill Company, 1957).

29. See G. R. Mure, *A Study of Hegel's Logic* (Oxford: Clarendon Press, 1950), p. 122 footnote.

el's subtlety on the doctrine of force and its manifestation struck the Marxist oriented Hippolyte as "empty and forced."[30] On the other hand, I was intrigued to find that contemporary phenomenology had rediscovered the concept of power or force. For example, Gadamer's interpretation of Hegel's "inverted world" takes seriously the Concept of Force and its Manifestation from Hegel's *Logic.*[31] Moreover, when one reads John Sallis' account of Plato's philosophy,[32] one finds a fully developed appreciation of the concept signified by δύναμις, even if it is very much tied up with Heideggerian philosophy.[33] Still more intriguing is the fact that those recent scholars of Plato who have uncovered his debt to the cosmologists and Hippocratics are, by and large, sympathetic to the analytic school of philosophy.

### *Summing Up*

Finally, I have to acknowledge one aspect of my account of Gregory's theology that differs substantially from many previous scholarly treatments of Gregory and the Cappadocians. For a variety of prominent scholars Gregory's theology has been the field of engagement for contesting the influence of philosophy upon Christian theology. Was Gregory substantially influenced by philosophy or not? Is this influence a sign of corruption or not? Often both sides of this debate agreed that the substantial influence of philosophy on Christianity was intrinsically a bad thing, a corrupting influence, and the argument turned upon Gregory's status *vis a vis* philoso-

30. *Genesis and Structure of Hegel's Phenomenology of Spirit,* trans. Samuel Cherniak and John Heckman (Evanston: Northwestern University Press, 1974), p. 124 ff. Hippolyte concludes his discussion of Hegel's treatment of Force in the *Phenomenology* by emphasizing that the doctrine of force and manifestation finds its meaning in the grander concept of Hegel's dialectic. Hippolyte's feelings that Hegel's treatment of Force is not proportionate to the final worth of the concept seems to be due to Hippolyte's own final judgement that the true sublation (and meaning) of Force is in the Concept of Dialectic itself. Hegel's movement into the Law of Phenomena leaves the Concept of Force too much in the phenomenal realm, without anchoring it in the realty of thought. I would like to suggest, tentatively, that recent interest in the concept of *power* or force may be linked (particularly in British scholarship) to a renewed interest in Hegel, or what may be characterized as returning theological appreciations of Hegel that are basically "right-wing" in their judgements.

31. Hans-Georg Gadamer, "Hegel and the Dialectic of the Ancient Philosophers," in *Hegel's Dialectic,* trans. P. C. Smith (New Haven: Yale University Press, 1971), p. 15.

32. *Being and Logos* (Pittsburgh: Duquesne University Press, 1975).

33. One also thinks of Paul Weiss' "The Dunamis," *Review of Metaphysics,* 40 (1987), 657–74.

phy. Those who argued that Gregory was fundamentally free of philosophy (however much he used or transformed that philosophy) found in Gregory's opponents—in heretics generally—the site of the corrupting influence of philosophy.

I will argue that Gregory's theology is indeed influenced by philosophy. I suppose it would be more accurate to say that I assume that this is the way Christians thought about the key issues of their faith—all Christians, or at least all educated Christians, of whatever doctrinal sympathies. It speaks only to the continuing influence of the limitations of Christian sensibilities of the nineteenth or the early twentieth centuries to try to divide orthodox from heretical Christianity on the basis of the imagined role of philosophy in the theology of either. Such a presupposition is no longer credible, whether it is advocated in the pages of a work influenced by Harnack or Meyendorf. Whatever orthodox Christianity was and is, its relationship to philosophy was (and remains) much more complicated than rejection.

As I remarked at the beginning of this introduction, it may seem strange to propose that in order to understand trinitarian theology of the fourth century *after* Christ, one has to return to the thought of the fourth century *before* Christ, yet obviously I think that this is so. Such a return enables us to recover a sense of what the words mean and what the logic of the thought is. In the case of the trinitarian doctrine of "one nature because one *power*"—which is what Nicene theology is understood to be when it is finally received as the theology of the universal church at the end of the fourth century C.E.—the story begins in the fourth century before Christ, and so this book begins at the beginning.

# 1 The Origins and Significance of Δύναμις in Preplatonic Philosophy

## *Character-Power Physics*

SCHOLARLY ACCOUNTS OF THE EARLIEST philosophical use of *power*—δύναμις—have, until recently, set the term within the context of the Presocratic cosmologists. These accounts describe the use of δύναμις in what is commonly called Presocratic "character-power" or "quality-thing" physics. Mourelatos describes this understanding as follows: "What we call a quality was for all Presocratics a characteristic which could not be considered separately from that of which it was a characteristic."[1] Each perceived characteristic was thought of as a thing or material in itself: an object was "hot" because of the presence of the Hot, which was itself an object or material. Each character-power was the active substance that made the Hot (the Cold, etc.) precisely that.[2]

1. Alexander P. D. Mourelatos, "Heraclitus, Parmenides, and the Naive Metaphysics of Things," in *Exegesis and Argument* (Assen, Neth.: Van Gorcum and Company, 1973), 16–48, esp. 27.

2. This active state suggests one translation for δύναμις, namely, active power. Mourelatos calls the δυνάμεις character-powers on page 18 of "Heraclitus, Parmenides, and the Naive Metaphysics of Things"; Cornford uses the expression quality-things in *Plato's Theory of Knowledge*, 234–38, as does Jon Moline in *Plato's Theory of Understanding* (Madison: University of Wisconsin Press, 1981), 85–86. An excellent review of the vagaries of translating δύναμις is given by A. L. Peck in his introduction to (and translation of) Aristotle's *Parts of Animals* (London: William Heinemann, Ltd., 1937), 30–32. In *Philosophy and Medicine in Ancient Greece* (Baltimore: Johns Hopkins Press, 1946), W. H. S. Jones says that δύναμις "has in the scientific writings of the fifth century B.C.E. a special and technical signification, which for modern minds at least is not easy to understand" (93). Jones's definition of δύναμις looks too much toward Plato's use of the term in the *Phaedrus:*

A good illustration of this notion of character powers or substantial qualities may be found in water's observed response to temperature. If one understands water as "wetness" per se, then a change in the temperature of a "unit" of water should produce a change in the quantity of the water, since some "thing" (that is, the Hot, the Cold) is being added to the "wetness." And this is precisely what happens: water expands when it boils and evaporates, or, water expands when it freezes. A jug designed to hold one unit of water breaks when a "unit" of the Hot or the Cold is added.

The notion of "character-power" may be found in Greek literature before its attachment to δύναμις. Lloyd remarks that many natural phenomena, but "especially those associated with movement of some sort . . . ," were personified in Homer and Hesiod.[3] Opposites of a general nature, such as Night and Day, and archetypal entities, such as Strife, Heaven, Pain, and the Ocean, appear very early in Greek literature, such as in Hesiod's *Theogony.*[4] Mourelatos makes a good case for interpreting these archetypes, especially the Opposites, as character-powers.[5] However, these character-powers are not referred to as δυνάμεις; as Souilhé notes, the word δύναμις occurs only three times in Hesiod, and in all cases in a physical or military sense that suggests nothing of character-power physics.[6] But the idea of "character-power" was there in this form of literature.[7]

The earliest use of δύναμις in Greek literature seems to be related to the verb, δύναμαι, meaning "to be able" (or "can [do]"). Souilhé has an extensive catalogue of early literary use of δύναμις. He finds the word in the works of, for instance, Homer, Lysias, Andocides, and, on rare occasions, Hesiod, and in the historians Herodotus, Thucydides, and Xenophon. The sense of the word among these authors is that of physical, military, or

"A δύναμις is a property of a body considered as having the power to act or to be acted upon, or as Plato puts it in the *Phaedrus* (270 C–D). . . ."

3. G. E. R. Lloyd, *Polarity and Analogy* (Cambridge: Cambridge University Press, 1966), 201.

4. Ibid., 160.

5. Mourelatos, "Naive Metaphysics," 30–31.

6. Souilhé, *Étude,* 7. For all its limitations, Souilhé's study has never been surpassed or duplicated as a close textual commentary on the occasions of δύναμις in Greek texts up to Aristotle. Though I must reject Souilhé's theory of Pythagorean origins for the philosophical sense of δύναμις, I accept his catalogue of the early non-philosophical uses of δύναμις since whatever errors have crept into his work on that subject will not affect my study one way or another.

7. Not only Mourelatos, "Naive Metaphysics", 30–31, but Lloyd, *Polarity and Analogy,* 41–48 and 201–4.

political force, a meaning that remains expressed in the English cognate "dynasty." According to Souilhé, only Xenophon, on rare occasions, uses δύναμις as a synonym for φύσις: Aristophanes, for example, uses δύναμις in a sense indistinguishable from Homer's.[8] There is an interesting "enlargement" of the sense of the word towards a sense of "ability" or "possibility," which may be found in Pindar.[9] Souilhé notes, but does not take seriously, the fact that there are very few attestations of δύναμις among the Greek cosmologists. Like many scholars of his generation and afterwards, Souilhé was overly influenced by fragments of later origin purporting to be the doctrines of the Pythagoreans and Presocratic cosmologists. A significant body of scholarship from the first half of the twentieth century builds an elaborate account of the Pythagorean use of δύναμις on the strength of what is now regarded as a spurious account from Philolaus.[10]

The most important early use of δύναμις as a philosophical term is in the texts of the Hippocratic Corpus: several of these works, including *On Ancient Medicine* and *Regimen* I, are dated no later than the generation before Plato.[11] The writings of the Hippocratic Corpus[12] are important sources, both directly and indirectly, for the various meanings attached to δύναμις by later philosophers, including, as my next chapter will show,

8. Souilhé, *Étude,* 10.

9. Ibid., 37.

10. The most obvious examples of this error are found in Souilhé, *Étude,* 23–25; John Burnet, *Early Greek Philosophy* (1892; reprint, A. and C. Black, Ltd., 1930), and A. E. Taylor, "Forms and Numbers: A Study in Platonic Metaphysics," in *Philosophical Studies* (London: Macmillan and Company, 1934), 91–150, esp. 97–99, and "The Words Εἶδος/Ἰδέα in Pre-Platonic Literature," in *Varia Socratica* (Oxford: James Parker and Company, 1911), 178–267, esp. 263.

11. There are no certain dates for the origins of *On Ancient Medicine* and *On the Nature of Man;* as I will describe, one enduring project of Hippocratic medicine was ascertaining which of the "Hippocratic" texts were indeed by Hippocrates. We can say that both these texts were written after Empedocles (ca. 495–435 B.C.E.) and before Plato (ca. 429–347 B.C.E.) though perhaps no more than the generation just before Plato. *On Ancient Medicine* is hereafter referred to as *OAM;* all references to this work are from the *Collected Writings of Hippocrates,* ed., trans., and comm. W. H. S. Jones (1923; reprint, Cambridge: Harvard University Press, 1972), Loeb Classical Library, vol. 1; *The Sacred Disease* and *The Art* are in vol. 2, and *On the Nature of Man* (hereafter cited as *NoM*) and *Regimen* I are in vol. 4. In *Philosophy and Medicine,* 94–95, Jones gives an analytical list of every use of δύναμις in *OAM.*

12. For a history of Greek medicine, see E. D. Phillips, *Greek Medicine* (Southampton: Thames and Hudson, 1973); for an excellent account of Hippocratic medicine and of the rise of "the Hippocratic Corpus" as a body of work, see Wesley D. Smith, *The Hippocratic Tradition* (Ithaca: Cornell University Press, 1979), esp. chap. 3.

Plato. This is an important point for any treatment of the intellectual history of patristic theology and needs to be emphasized since medicine's influence upon patristic theology has largely remained unacknowledged in patristic scholarship generally, and in scholarship on Gregory in particular.[13] In the case of scholarship on Gregory, what treatment there has been of the influence of medicine on Gregory's thought has falsely cast Greek medicine as something distinct from, if not opposed to, Greek philosophy. Moline's sense of medicine as "the oldest, most familiar, and philosophically most sophisticated science [in Plato's time]" is almost entirely missing from contemporary patristic scholarship.[14] As this chapter's account of δύναμις in Hippocratic causality will show, these medical writings are the source of the insight that what exists, affects, as well as the first clear and certain use of δύναμις to refer to this existential capacity to affect.

## *The Early Context for the Use of Δύναμις*

The earliest[15] certain use of δύναμις occurs in Parmenides' *Poem,* in the context of fundamental opposites:

> But once all things had been named Light and Night and these according to their meanings [or powers, δυνάμεις] have been attributed to these things. . . .[16]

13. In this chapter I will indicate in passing (for example, in the notes) thematic similarities between Hippocratic medicine and Gregory's thought. More direct observation of medicine's influence on Gregory's theology will wait until chapters 6 and 7.

14. Moline, *Plato's Theory of Understanding,* 83. Several good descriptions of philosophy and medicine in both the classical and Hellenistic eras are available: Ludwig Edelstein, "The Relation of Ancient Philosophy to Medicine" in *Ancient Medicine,* ed. Owsei and C. Lilian Temkin (1967; reprint, Baltimore: Johns Hopkins University Press, 1987), 349–66; Michael Frede, "Philosophy and Medicine in Antiquity," in *Essays in Ancient Philosophy* (Minneapolis: University of Minnesota Press, 1987), 225–42; Mohan Matthen, "Empiricism and Ontology in Ancient Medicine," in *Method, Medicine and Metaphysics,* ed. R. J. Hankinson (Edmonton: Academic Printing and Publishing, 1988), 99–121.

15. Parmenides is thought to have lived 515–450 B.C.E. This fragment actually has a late attestation: it is given by Simplicius, *Physics* 180:9–12. The authenticity of δύναμις in this fragment is supported by the lack of any obvious technical use of or emphasis on the term; its very ambiguity or vagueness suggests that Simplicius is not introducing the term for his own purposes (though I have no doubt that Simplicius found Parmenides' use of the term familiar). I regard as spurious the Presocratic passages using δύναμις reported *via* "Aetius."

16. Αὐτὰρ ἐπειδὴ πάντα φάος καὶ νὺξ ὀνόμασται
καὶ τὰ κατὰ σφετέρας δυνάμεις ἐπὶ τοῖσί τε καὶ τοῖς,
πᾶν πλέον ἐστὶν ὁμοῦ φάεος καὶ νυκτὸς ἀφάντου
ἴσων ἀμφοτέρων, ἐπεὶ οὐδετέρωι μέτα μηδέν.

The fact that the first clear philosophical use of δύναμις is by Parmenides and that subsequent use of δύναμις occurs in a post-Parmenidean context is worth noting and emphasizing; indeed all the extant medical works that use δύναμις are written after Parmenides. Two of Parmenides' doctrines become fundamental assumptions in the philosophies of his successors: first, the idea that there is a kind of being or existence that is fundamental or true being and that is to be distinguished from the appearance of existence;[17] second, that true existence is distinguished from the appearance of existence by the unchanging and unchangeable nature of the for-

---

(Leonardo Tarán, *Parmenides: A Text with Translation, Commentary, and Critical Essays* [Princeton: Princeton University Press, 1965], 161). While Tarán's translation emphasizes literalness, Cornford's translation in *Plato and Parmenides,* 47, is both more accessible and more sensitive to the role of δύναμις: "But now that all things have been named Light and Night and the names corresponding to their several powers [δυνάμεις] have been assigned to these things. . . ." Tarán argues (162) that δύναμις is to be understood as synonymous to σήματα, a term that occurs earlier in 8:55.84. Souilhé, *Étude,* 26, also understands δύναμις here to mean (an) opposite character power, but he links Parmenides' use to Pythagoras *via* Alcameon. Similarly, in "Hippocratic Medicine as a Historical Source for Aristotle's Theory of the *Dynameis,*" *Studies in History of Medicine* 4 (1980): 112, V. P. Vizgin notes that the term δύναμις "is very rarely found in early philosophers. Thus, the word δύναμις is used to designate qualitative opposites in Parmenides (B 9, DK) where they characterize the two essential forms, light and darkness. But in medical writings, starting from Alcmaeon, the word is the designation of a leading idea . . ." (8). In short, Vizgin regards Parmenides' use of the term as insignificant and then supplies an imaginary literary history of the medical use of δύναμις that fills in the blanks from "Alcmaeon" (that is, "Aetius") to *OAM.*

Kahn and Mourelatos both understand δύναμις to mean an "opposite character-power," though Kahn emphasizes "opposite" and Mourelatos emphasizes "character-power." These translations are closer to Mario Untersteiner's understanding that δύναμις means φύσις in his *Parmenide* (Firenze: La Nuova Italia, 1958), clxxxiv n. 65, than to Tarán's. Though Tarán does not describe his translation in this way, he attributes to Parmenides a use of δύναμις very close to the use of the term by Plato in the *Cratylus,* a text I will treat in the next chapter. For more on Parmenides' primary opposites, see G. S. Kirk, J. E. Raven, and M. Schofield, ed., tran., comm., *The Presocratic Philosophers,* 2d ed. (Cambridge: Cambridge University Press, 1983), 254–62.

17. The presence of this distinction between real and illusionary existence before Parmenides is shown through a fragment of Heraclitus: "The real constitution [φύσις] of things is accustomed to hide itself." Kirk, Raven, and Schofield, *Presocratic Philosophers,* 192, no. 208. The same kind of distinction in post-Parmenidean philosophies may be illustrated by two quotations. The first is from Democritus: "By convention are sweet and bitter, hot and cold, by convention is color; in truth are atoms and void . . ." (Fragment 9, ibid., 255–56, no. 303). The second is from the Hippocratic work, *Regimen* I: "So of all things nothing perishes, and nothing changes into beings that did not exist before. Things change merely by mingling and being separated. . . . Whenever I speak of becoming or perishing I am merely using popular expressions; what I really mean is mingling and separating. The facts are these. Becoming and perishing are the same thing; mixture and separation are the same thing; increase and diminution are the same thing; becoming and mixture are the same thing . . ." (*Regimen* I, IV 11–15, 25–30, Loeb, vol. 4, 234–35). I will return to both of these passages.

mer. Philosophers as varied as Anaxagoras, Democritus, and Plato share these two assumptions, though with very different applications.

Parmenides' belief that true being was distinguished from the illusion of existence by its eternal nature was consistently influential among subsequent philosophers. Even philosophers who did not believe in the absolute unity of true being, such as Empedocles, nonetheless accepted that the fundamental criterion of true being was that it did not come to be or pass away but rather was unproduced and unending: ἀγένητος.[18] The teachings of post-Parmenidean philosophers on fundamental being differed about the identity of this being, namely, whether it was the four elementals, an indefinite number of elementals or humors, or an indefinite number of atoms. Yet these post-Parmenidean philosophies all agreed on the character of true existence, namely, that it was unchanging. These Parmenidean assumptions provide the context for a philosophical use of δύναμις; within this Parmenidean context the importance of δύναμις is that it is used to add or to make explicit a third criterion for true being: being acts upon other being. This last insight is a feature particular to the philosophies of the early Greek medical writings (the Hippocratic Corpus)[19] and of Plato.[20]

18. The key passage for this description of being is the well-known fragment 8:1–5 of the *Poem:* "Being is ungenerated and imperishable, whole, unique, immovable, and complete. It was not once nor will it be, since it is now altogether, one continuous. For, what origin could you search out for it? How and from where did it grow?" Tarán, *Parmenides,* p. 85, slightly altered. See *Parmenides,* p. 82 for the Greek text and attestations. I will later discuss Eunomius' doctrine on God as ἀγέννητος (the difference between ἀγέννητος and ἀγένητος is irrelevant). The teachings on ἀγένητος by Parmenides have some direct relevance to the development of Christian doctrine although historically the two events are separated by more than five hundred years: from a literary point of view, most of the fragments attributed to Parmenides date from the Common Era. Fragment 8, lines 1–4, which describe Being in α-privative terms (including ἀγέννητος), appears in the writings of Clement of Alexandria and Eusebius of Caesarea, as well as those of Pagan authors such as Simplicius, Plutarch, and Sextus. The appearance of these fragments at this time is testimony to the interest in ἀγέννητος in the Common Era and the contemporary awareness of the direct relevance of Parmenides' thought.

19. However, it must be emphasized that the medical writers did not understand the distinction between true and apparent existence as a critique of sense data; indeed, medical writings such as *On Ancient Medicine* insist on the primacy of observation over hypothesis, and variations on this claim recur throughout the history of Greek medicine. As I describe below, the important distinction for the medical writers may be expressed as either that between the real unit (which is a cause) and the mixture (which is the subject of change), or as the distinction between discrete simple substrata and the compounds formed by these discrete substrata.

20. There is, of course, a tension between the second and third transcendental "insights," namely, that *being is unchanging,* and that *being acts.* Without trying to solve or belittle the prob-

*Elemental Being and Causes*

Whatever Parmenides may have meant in his teachings on being, after him (and until Plato) statements about true being were statements about kinds of material being. There were different opinions about what these kinds of being were in themselves: some evidently called them elementals [στοιχεία], others spoke of atoms, while others (the medical writers) called them humors. In the Hippocratic writings, an existent was understood both to be (that is, to exist) and to be specifically what it is because it was constituted from or built up of material parts (usually called humors [ἰκμάς or χυμός]): real existence was to be found in these parts,[21] while existence as normally recognized (that is, as objects or things) was due to the presence of these existent parts in the objects or things. The true existence of these parts lent (as it were) existence to an object or thing, and the characteristics of these parts lent characteristics to the object or thing made up of these parts. These parts were understood to "lend" existence because they fulfilled Parmenides' criteria for being: they were irreducible, indestructible, and eternal.

The humors and elementals differed conceptually from the atoms of Leucippus and Democritus in one important respect: the theory of atoms was used to explain away the reality (true existence) not only of all specific objects but of observable causal activity, while the medical writers meant, above all, to insure the reality of observable causal relations (in the broad way they conceived these relations). At stake in the reality of these causal relations was the reality of medical therapy. Democritus' theory of atoms led him to conclude that "[b]y convention are sweet and bitter, hot and cold, by convention is color; in truth are atoms and void. . . ."[22] The theories and observations of the Hippocratic writers led them to the opposite

lem of this tension, it may be helpful for the reader to understand the medical distinction between humors and powers as an attempted solution to this problem, where humors refers to (material) *being as unchanging* and powers refers to *being as acting.*

21. Plato's report in *Phaedrus* 270 C–D of this Hippocratic doctrine makes clear the epistemological content of the division into parts and powers. I will return to this passage from Plato in the next chapter.

22. Fragment 9, Kirk, Raven and Schofield, *Presocratic Philosophers,* 255–56, no. 303, cited above.

conclusion: sweet and bitter, hot and cold, etc., were no illusions; these forces (by which I mean δυνάμεις) really existed, indeed the relationships among these forces were the laws of reality.[23] Implicit in this use of δύναμις is the understanding that anything that is has δυνάμ[ε]ις; the medical writers (probably including Empedocles) find δύναμις to be a sign of existence, and indeed Plato will later (in the *Sophist*) make this understanding explicit. Whether Parmenides aligned the δυνάμεις with being or appearance (scholars disagree),[24] the Hippocratic and Platonic understandings of the concept definitely aligned δύναμις with being and not with mere appearance.[25] One example from Plato will illustrate both the understanding of δύναμις as "not mere appearance" and Plato's common thought with the Hippocratics. In the dialogue *Cratylus* (394 B) Plato refers to physicians who can recognize the δύναμις of a drug, however camouflaged it may be by the addition of (foreign) colors or smells: no matter how a drug appears, its capacity to affect remains (the same).

### *Δύναμις in the Hippocratic Writings*

The most important use of δύναμις in early Greek philosophy is as the name for characteristics or properties which may be understood as being active, that is, their presence has effects upon anything nearby. A δύναμις is the distinctive affective capacity (or capacities) of any specific exis-

23. As again the passage from *Regimen* I, IV 11–15, 25–30 illustrates.

24. Mourelatos argues that "The main features of the cosmology of the 'Doxa' are these. Things in our familiar sensible world are a mixture of two 'opposites' (ἀντίος) or 'forms' (μορφή), Light and Night. Each of these two opposites is cognate with a series of 'powers' (δυνάμεις), e.g., 'shining' and 'nimble' for Light, 'obscure' and 'heavy' for Night." "Naive Metaphysics", p. 28. See also Lloyd's confident reading of Fragment 9 of the *Poem* quoted above as an example of a cosmological doctrine of equal opposite primary substances in his *Polarity and Analogy*, p. 217.

25. Harold Miller's opinion on the relative being of δύναμις is that any "entity . . . could be known in two aspects: as active and thus manifesting its essential nature, it is δύναμις; as passive but having the potentiality of action, it is substance. . . . the concept of δύναμις is far more basic than substance for the simple substances are identified, characterized, and known in essence only through their specific δυνάμεις." "*Dynamis* and *Physis* in *On Ancient Medicine*," *Transactions of the American Philological Association*, LXXXIII (1952), 184–197; here, p. 192. Much about this statement by Miller is wrong: the anachronistic and vague use of essence, passive, and potentiality, and the quick assumption that this sense of δύναμις is used consistently and clearly. But Miller's basic insight is correct: for the Hippocratics, at least, δύναμις is the fundamental level of existence. Vizgin has a similar opinion: "One might say that the notion of 'nature' for him [the author of *OAM*] is substantially covered by the notion of power." "Hippocratic Medicine", p. 8.

tent,[26] that is, those causal capacities that belong to an object because it is specifically what it is: the hot (heat) is the δύναμις of fire, for example, and anything which lacks the δύναμις of the hot is not fire. The activity or effect peculiar to a δύναμις is that it reproduces itself or gives its *nature* to whatever it is near to or added to: the best example of a δύναμις reproducing itself or giving its *nature* is the hot (or more accurately, the hot [thing]) of fire transforming wood into (the hot of) fire.

The effect of a δύναμις is identical with the δύναμις itself; a δύναμις acts by manifesting itself, thereby replacing (or dominating) the previously manifested δύναμις. A hand becomes cold because of the presence of the cold, just as soup, blood or sea water are each salty because of the presence of the salty. (Salt is salty because of the presence of the salty, though the mineral salt includes the presence of the dry and the earthen.) Effects of this sort are the manifestation of what has been added either through the addition of a power that was not there before but has been inserted or brought in through material spread, or through an addition to what was there before, changing the preponderance of a power from "recessive" (we would say) to "dominant." The first kind of account, which claims an insertion or spread, usually presumes that an elemental consists entirely of one power: fire is simply the hot, for example, and the hot is fire.

The second kind of account, based upon an addition to what is already there, usually presumes that elementals are composed of two (or more) powers: fire was considered by some to be composed of the powers the hot and the dry, for example. The Hippocratic authors are decidedly of the second school and are engaged in various kinds of polemics against teach-

26. Souilhé, *Étude*, pp. 36–41, argues that what is common to all the writing of the *Hippocratic Corpus* is the teaching that each δύναμις or power produces a specific effect which identifies its causal power. The general sense of δύναμις in *OAM* 14, Jones, Loeb 1:37, is that each of the different powers ". . . produces an effect or change of one sort or another"; this sense recurs in the other Hippocratic texts which use δύναμις to explain causality (i.e., *NoM, The Sacred Disease, The Art,* and *Regimen* I). The author of *OAM* 22, pp. 56–57, defines a δύναμις as "an intensity and strength of the humours. . . ." which I take to be an attempt to distinguish conceptually the causal capacity of humors from the humor *per se* without attributing to the powers a material existence separate from a humor. Miller gives this definition for δύναμις in *OAM:* ". . . a δύναμις is a simple real entity which is characterized and identified by its specific activity and whose specific essential nature is revealed to the senses by its activity." P. 191 of "*Dynamis* and *Physis* in *On Ancient Medicine.*" Souilhé, *Étude*, p. 36, agrees.

ers of the first school, namely Empedocles (according to *On Ancient Medicine*).[27] There are several other important doctrinal differences between the Hippocratic school and Empedocles (as *OAM* portrays him). Empedocles limits the number of elemental causes to four and accounts heat the most important of these,[28] while the author of *OAM* wants to increase the number beyond four and to dethrone heat as the most important.[29]

27. The accepted interpretation of *OAM* is based on the explicit intention of the author (who is anonymous): his purpose is to deny the method of those who give medical treatment on the basis of an hypothesis concerning man's *nature.* The specific hypothesis that the author opposes is threefold: first, that of all the powers of which man is made, the most important are the Hot and the Cold, and of these two, the Hot is the most important. Second, that all powers may be found in *nature* individually, that is, not in combination. And finally, that illness is caused by the presence of a power that is "too strong." This scheme seems to be associated with the school of Empedocles. See *OAM* 20:6, 53, and G. E. R. Lloyd, "Who Is Attacked in *On Ancient Medicine?*" *Phronesis* 8 (1963): 108–26. Anaxagoras, too, rejects a tendency in Empedocles to limit not only the number of significant elements but the number of elements themselves. So we know from Aristotle: *Physics* Alpha 4, 187a23, for example: "Anaxagoras again posited an infinity of principles, namely the homoeomerous substances and the opposites together, while Empedocles posits only the so-called [four] στοιχεία" (Kirk, Raven, and Schofield, *Presocratic Philosophers,* no. 485, 368–69, slightly altered). However specific the target of *OAM* may be, it remains an attack against all who would ruin the art of medicine by basing it on hypothesis rather than observation. Within this context the author makes particular use of δύναμις since it is the δύναμις that is observed.

28. It is important to remember the strong religious understanding attached to fire consistently throughout the history of Greek thought. Heraclitus, for example, described fire as the fundamental element underlying all existence: "All things are an equal exchange for fire and fire for all things . . ." (Kirk, Raven and Schofield, *Presocratic Philosophers* no. 219, 198). More than this, for Heraclitus fire has divine "directive capacity" and "embodies the rule of measure in change which inheres in the world process, and of which the Logos is an expression" (ibid. 199). The soul, in particular, is composed of fire (ibid. 204). This association of fire with the divine persists. A. A. Long and D. N. Sedley comment on fire's "special status" in the Hellenistic era within the quartet of elements: "It is the element par excellence . . ." (*Hellenistic Philosophers* [Cambridge: Cambridge University Press, 1987], 1: 286.) For the Stoics not only was fire a permanent feature of the universe, but indeed god was a fire (278) that "is designing, [and] causes growth and preservation" (275). Likewise, the *Chaldean Oracles,* to give another example, speak of a creative fire: "All things have been created from One fire" (Ruth Majercik, ed., tran., comm., *The Chaldean Oracles, Fragment* 10 [Leiden: E. J. Brill, 1989], 53). When Gregory of Nyssa speaks of the intellect as being like fire (as he does in *On the Making of Man*), or when he explains the Father's generation of the Son through the analogy of a fire having choice and thus producing flame (as in *Against Eunomius* 3:6), he builds upon a sense of fire that was already old and authoritative at the time he wrote.

29. See *OAM* 15:25 and 16:1–2, 1:42–43. On pages 5–8, Vizgin argued that the thought of *OAM* represents a complete rejection of the doctrine of the four elementals, and the building of an alternative cosmology from a different set of experiences. Vizgin's argument is not strong for the "rejection" of the four elementals by the author of *OAM;* Vizgin pushes this argument more than he should because he has set his account of *OAM* within a grander thesis of the existence of two opposing Pre-Aristotelian traditions of elementary qualities—the first being that of the four elementals, the second that of the humors. To dramatize this opposition Vizgin portrays *NoM* as a pure representative of the first cosmology and *OAM* as a pure representative of the second.

The standard examples of δυνάμεις or powers,[30] then, were hot, cold, wet, dry, sweet, sour, acidic, and salty.[31] In each case, when these are added to something else (by contact or mixture), they make that something else like themselves: hot makes something hot, wet makes something wet, or the salty makes something salty. This pure illustration of *like from like* causality is not the only kind of causality understood in the powers, but it seems to have been the kind of causal activity that was typical of a power,[32] and it may be understood as the "first sense" of δύναμις as a cause.[33]

30. I take these examples from *OAM* 1.3, but esp. 14:30–33; 15:15–18; and 17:8–11. I focus upon *OAM* because of its extensive use of δύναμις, which makes the work congenial to my purposes in this study. However, a number of scholars have shown that *OAM* was understood as the most important statement of Hippocratic doctrine, the work by which other "Hippocratic" works were judged or interpreted. For a summary of the arguments on the importance of *OAM*, see Smith, *The Hippocratic Tradition*, 208–10. Therefore, my own emphasis on this work parallels the attention it received in medicine in the centuries preceding Galen.

31. Traditionally, scholars have given a chronological and conceptual priority to the first four of these powers, primarily on the basis of reports such as Aristotle's in *On the Parts of Animals.* There are two widespread scholarly assumptions at work in such accounts of powers that must be recognized. The first influential assumption in scholarship is that at an early stage in Greek philosophy—a stage for which we have no textual evidence—the powers hot, wet, cold, and dry were identified with the elementals fire, water, earth, and air, and that over time these powers were separated from their "host" elementals. The second influential assumption is that the "Empedoclean" (as Aristotle identifies it) use of four powers is the older "established" or "traditional" doctrine of powers and that the medical doctrine of an indefinite number of powers, which includes "organic" traits such as salty or bitter, is a reaction to the older doctrine (ignoring the possibility that the medical use may be equal or prior in age and authority to the "Empedoclean" number). There are scholars who believe that Alcmaeon of Croton taught a list of δυνάμεις that differed from the contemporary list of the Pythagoreans principally in recognizing an indefinite number of Opposites (as opposed to the Pythagoreans, who posited only ten). For these scholars Alcmaeon is the authority for the medical doctrine of an indefinite number of powers. There are, however, problems with the literary sources for our knowledge of Alcmaeon's doctrines, especially for his use of δύναμις.

32. Peck, *Parts of Animals*, 31, says, for example, that the "original usage of the term [δύναμις] seems to have been strong substance of a particular character." In *Plato and Parmenides*, Cornford says that in ". . . the fifth century the hot, for example, was conceived as an active power (δύναμις) residing in bodies and enabling them to act on our senses. . . . A portion of the hot present in a body is the power which makes us feel hot and heats other, colder, bodies" (47). (Cornford gives a more detailed account of δύναμις in *Plato's Theory of Knowledge*, 234–39.) Moline quotes Cornford's remarks in *Plato and Parmenides* (as well as Vlastos and, indirectly, Peck) to support his own account of Plato's dependence upon the medical use of δύναμις (*Plato's Theory of Understanding*, 85).

33. Plato depends upon the *like from like* causality associated with a δύναμις in his account of virtues, for example, but his other uses of the term invoke its more generalized connotation of active cause. (I discuss Plato's use of power and δύναμις in the next chapter.) The Hippocratic authors assume the *like from like* causality of a power and, for polemical reasons, dwell upon the multiple and differing effects a power can have.

*Powers and Opposites*

As the above examples suggest, each individual power was understood as one among a number of opposite powers. Opposition described the fundamental relationship, especially the causal relationship, among primary existents or beings, as, for example, among the elementals (στοιχεία) or the powers. "Opposites are," as G. E. R. Lloyd put it, "among the principles or elements on which the cosmological theories of . . . Presocratic philosophers are based."[34] A specific opposite acted by destroying, forcing out, or replacing (accounts varied from philosopher to philosopher) its opposed correlate. As an opposite, a specific power likewise acted upon its opposite or contrary by destroying, forcing out, or replacing it: hot acted specifically upon cold, for example.[35] Accounts of the action of a power seemed to have developed from the understanding that a specific power acted only upon its particular opposite, to the understanding that a power affected a range of related opposite powers: hot acted upon the cold (its opposite), as well as the wet, for example, cold and wet being conceived as related opposites as hot and dry were related.[36] The arguments about opposites among later philosophers like Empedocles, Anaxagoras, and early Hippocratics such as the author of *OAM* may usefully be understood as arguments over

34. Lloyd, *Polarity and Analogy,* 16.

35. Or good upon evil. See D. G. Bostock's "Medical Theory and Theology in Origen," in *Origeniana Tertia,* ed. Richard Hanson and Henri Crouzel (Rome: Edizioni dell'Ateneo, 1985), 191–99, where Bostock gives a good description of the role of the medical doctrine of opposition in Origen's Christology. Bostock concludes that "It is possible . . . that Origen's definition of evil has been influenced by medical thought. What is certain is that both Galen and Hippocrates [*sic*] believed that evil was removed by the use of contraries, and that Origen echoed this belief. He was well aware that the science of medicine consisted in the knowledge of contraries, and he applied the principle of healing by contraries to his theology. [As Origen says] 'All the contraries were adopted by my Lord and Savior, so that he might cancel out the contraries with one another . . .'" (197).

36. As, for example, in *Regimen* I 4:2–4, Jones, Loeb 4:233: "Fire has the hot and the dry, water the cold and the moist. Mutually too fire has the [that is, takes the] moist from water, for in fire there is moisture, and water has the [that is, takes the] dry from fire, for there is dryness in water also." The thought of the second sentence is that since fire (the hot and the dry) removes the wet from water, that wetness must go somewhere, and it goes to the fire. Fire does not remove and absorb the cold of water since fire is primarily the hot, which cannot absorb its primary opposite, cold; fire can absorb the opposite of its secondary feature, dryness, however.

which powers are related,[37] to what extent, and how.[38] However, the developments in thought that increased the range of existents a specific power could effect never eliminate the original association of δύναμις with a causality that acted upon a contrary.

The division of fundamental being into relations of oppositions has consistently been described by scholars as the first and oldest form of Greek philosophical thought. This is, as Lloyd points out, how Aristotle describes the philosophies of his predecessors.[39] The most important such description by Aristotle is his report in *Metaphysics* Alpha 5 of a Pythagorean table of ten opposites, which he contrasts with Alcmaeon of Croton's table of an indefinite number of opposites.[40] By combining this account of ancient doctrines of the division of being into sets of opposites with Aristotle's identification of some of these opposites with powers in *On the Parts of Animals,* some modern scholars have concluded that Alcmaeon, if not Pythagoras, used the word δυνάμ[ε]ις to describe these opposites. Unfortunately, Aristotle does not say that either the Pythagoreans or Alcmaeon called these contraries "δυνάμεις" or any other term we might recognize as meaning power in the sense under discussion here.[41]

37. An example of this kind of grouping of powers is found in *OAM,* where the author argues that transformation of the power sweet changes it into the related power acidic (as when sweet wine turns to vinegar). Powers are understood in a continuum of degrees of opposition: a power moves toward its opposite by specific degrees, each of which is incrementally less like the beginning state and more like the end. Gregory provides an example of this tendency to organize powers into combinations of related and incremental oppositions when he describes the medical doctrine of opposites "meeting" (and coexisting) in members of other pairs. The hot and the cold meet in the wet, for example. See *On Virginity* XXII. Lloyd's *Polarity and Analogy,* 20–23, has a helpful summary of the role of opposition in Hippocratic thought.

38. See Lloyd, *Polarity and Analogy,* 48–56, for a summary of these arguments. Some arguments of Plato's may usefully be understood in this light as well.

39. *Polarity and Analogy,* 15–18.

40. Ibid., 16.

41. The text that attributes the term "δυνάμεις" to Alcmaeon is from Aetius. See Kirk, Raven, and Schofield, *Presocratic Philosophers,* no. 310, 260: "Alcmaeon maintains that the bond of health is the equal balance of the powers ["δυνάμεις"], moist and dry, cold and hot, bitter and sweet, and the rest, while the supremacy of one of them is the cause of disease." This fragment is a tenuous source from which to draw any conclusions beyond the obvious observation that "Aetius" recognizes the moist and dry, cold and hot, bitter and sweet, etc., as "δυνάμεις", an attribution that may owe only to *Parts of Animals* or a Hippocratic text like *On Ancient Medicine.* Perhaps Alcmaeon did indeed speak of the moist and dry, etc., as "δυνάμεις", but neither Aristotle's nor Aetius' report is proof of that. The best argument for an early use of δύναμις for the elemental

*Powers in Hippocratic Mixture Physics*

For the author of *OAM* everything that exists above the level of the powers (δυνάμεις), exists as a mixture.[42] The author of *OAM* rejects identifying elementals with a single power (an opinion he associates with Empedocles) and teaches the presence of many different, even opposing, powers in any elemental. The author argues his point by showing that his doctrine that things exist as something more than a simple elemental or a simple power better corresponds to human experience and gives a better account for the action of those things that are causes. (The paradigmatic account of cause and effect is medicine; the paradigmatic case is diet.) The important assumptions in *OAM* about the existence of powers in mixtures may be summarized in two related observations:

1. There are levels of unity or entity associated with the mixture(s) of powers, where we recognize "things" or "objects." Different levels of existence are associated with kinds of unity.

2. Effects travel between these levels in either direction, producing changes in the members of the mixture (that is, the powers) or in the recognized entity (that is, the object, or a nature). Changes among powers are primarily conceived in terms of relative concentrations (that is, more or less of a δύναμις compared to another δύναμις), especially between opposite powers, where the preponderance of one power negates the effects of another.

To expand on the first point: every object may be considered as "*one*" at different levels of entity or in different senses of the term. When we speak of an object we speak of a perceived unity, but as the unity breaks down (physically, or in abstraction), existence is attributed to another, more primary, level. To put this observation in language more native to the author of *OAM,* when we understand that whatever seems to be *one* actually exists as a mixture, then we recognize that existence at the funda-

opposites is one that acknowledges the tentative and hypothetical nature of the conclusion: there are a number of authors who clearly use δύναμις with this sense, and these authors do so with an apparent confidence that their audience will recognize the connotation.

42. This question of things understood as powers simply versus powers in mixture may refer back to an earlier complete identification of each elemental with a specific power.

mental level, namely, at the level of the powers, produces as an effect of their association another level of existence. All that we usually recognize as objects or things exists at this level of entity; such objects are, in fact, examples of this level of entity. Bread is a good example because we recognize a piece of bread as an intact object, whether it happens to be a loaf or a slice, and, more important, even though we know it was produced by a mixture and still consists of a mixture. Still, the unity and entity of any object is understood to depend to the existence of entities—the powers—at a "lower" level. This dependence is one aspect of the second point listed above.

The teaching of the "Empedoclean" school of medicine,[43] as the author of *OAM* presents it, is that things (not just simple things like elementals but complex things like foods) that are composed only from a single power exist in the real world and that illness occurs when one of these powers is too strong for the body to assimilate.[44] Treatment seems to center around doses of the "hot" foods (because of the unique status of the hot), but it is not clear if powers in opposition also play a part. On the other hand, the author of OAM teaches that powers never exist in isolation but rather always in mixtures; when no one power in the body "dominates" (in a metaphor borrowed from the political sense of δύναμις)[45] the others, the body

43. Moline, *Plato's Theory of Understanding,* 87 and 95, speaks with great confidence and emphasis on the role of δύναμις in the philosophy of Empedocles. For example, Moline speaks of Empedocles as the "earliest philosopher to develop very explicitly a connection between δύναμις or powers and εἴδη or forms . . ." (87). Moline (84–87) follows Peck, Cornford, and Vlastos in assuming the use of δύναμις among Presocratics such as Empedocles and Anaxagoras. Moline's own treatment of the sense of δύναμις among the Presocratics emphasizes a common understanding: the medical authors (and to a lesser extent, Empedocles) are important for his study because they associate δύναμις with εἶδος, and thereby provide Plato's contemporaries with a prior understanding of εἶδος. I agree that the character-power causality associated with δύναμις in Hippocratic writings figures prominently in Plato's thought; however, more caution needs to be shown in attributing the use of δύναμις to specific Presocratic cosmologists.

44. *OAM* 14:20–45.

45. The common scholarly judgement is that this "political" understanding of δύναμις goes back to the physician and philosopher Alcmaeon of Croton, an approximate contemporary of Pythagoras. (See, for example, Phillips, *Greek Medicine,* pp. 20–21, and notes. Phillips should not be singled out for this opinion though; it is a commonplace in modern scholarship.) Aristotle mentions Alcmaeon several times; the most interesting such reference is *Metaphysics* Alpha 5, 985b23 ff., where Aristotle contrasts the Pythagorean list of ten fundamental contraries with Alcmaeon's understanding of fundamental contraries as being more general in character and indefinite in number. The source for thinking that Alcmaeon understood these opposites as δυνάμεις

is in health. Illness is when one power exists out of proportion to the others and spoils the balance of health. The treatment of any illness consists in restoring the balance of health by adding to the body the power opposite to that in excess:

Since the hot will give up its heat only when mixed with the cold, and the cold can be neutralized only by the hot. But all other components of man become milder and better the greater the number of other components with which they are mixed. A man is in the best possible condition when there is complete coction [*sic*] and rest, with no particular power [δύναμις] displayed.[46]

The argument in *OAM* against the "Empedoclean" teachings is twofold. First, powers do not exist in isolation (or in a pure mixture) in the world; each appears in combination with another; there are, for example, no foods composed entirely of one power. "For they [the Empedocleans] have not discovered, I think, an absolute hot or cold, dry or moist. . . ."[47] Secondly, if it is merely the presence of a strong power (for example, in a food) that causes harm, why does not the same food injure everyone? And why is it that all concentrated foods (for example, spicy foods) do not injure the same person?[48] Both "Empedoclean" and "Hippocratic" (of *OAM*) philosophy seem to speak about the excess assertion of a power causing illness, but "Empedoclean" doctrine speaks of the isolation of powers in things (that is, foods), while the author of *OAM* denies that powers ever exist isolated, even in a sick body. For the Empedocleans, sickness is due to the presence of a strong (as opposed to a weak) power, while for the Hippocratics, sickness results from a preponderance of one power suppressing another power or disturbing a mix of other powers. The author of *OAM* clearly understands this question of how powers exist as being fundamental in a

---

is Aetius, and I have already indicated my reservations about Aetius as a source for Alcmaeon's doctrines.

46. *OAM* 20:49–56; Jones, Loeb 1:50–53.

47. The complete passage reads: "For they have not discovered, I think, an absolute hot or cold, dry or moist, that participates in no other form [ἄλλῳ εἴδει κοινωνέον]. But I think that they have at their disposal the same foods and the same drinks as we all use, and to one they add the attribute of being hot, to another, cold, to another, dry, to another, moist, since it would be futile to order a patient to take something hot, as he would at once ask, 'What hot thing?'" (*OAM* 15:4–22; Jones, Loeb 1:40–41). This is an important passage for the understanding of Plato as well as of Hippocratic medicine.

48. *OAM* 20:23–48; Jones, Loeb 1:54–55. This point is developed in the next section.

sense not narrowly "medical" but rather including physics or cosmology. For this author, to fail to talk in terms of mixtures or combinations, is to fail to talk about the real world.[49]

The basis for this critique of the "Empedocleans" is empirical: no one has experienced anything that is entirely or absolutely "hot," "bitter," "cold," or any other power-quality. Everything known, as evidenced in the medical area of food, possesses several different qualities: ". . . the truth being that one and the same thing is both bitter and hot, or acid and hot, or salt and hot, with numerous other combinations, and cold [also] combines with other powers."[50] Again the favorite illustration of an object with many powers is bread, since it is both produced by, and contains, many different qualities.[51] Bread serves as a good example of powers existing in the world in a mixture since it is a clear illustration of how every object consists not of one power but of many.

### *Power and Nature as a Formula*

In the Hippocratic writings a number of noteworthy terms are used in association with power. The most important of these is *nature*—φύσις—which refers to the character of a union of powers.[52] The nature is the principle of unity in a mixture, meaning its ability either to successfully assimilate new members (that is, powers), or to suffer from the assimilation.

49. *OAM* 15:5–15; Jones, Loeb 1:40–41, quoted above.

50. *OAM* 17:8–15; Jones, Loeb 1:44–47.

51. "For a thing which has been exposed to fire and to water, and has been made by many other things, each of which has its own individual property and nature [ἰδίαν δύναμιν καὶ φύσιν], has lost some of its qualities and has been mixed and combined with others" (*OAM* 13:32–35; Jones, Loeb 1:3637). The author continues by remarking upon the different kinds of breads—for example, bolted or unbolted flour, winnowed or unwinnowed wheat, thoroughly kneaded or not thoroughly kneaded, etc. and concludes: "The properties [δυνάμεις] too of each variety are powerful, and no one is like to any other. . . . For each of these differences produces in a human being an effect and a change of one sort or another . . ." (*OAM* 14:7–12; Jones, Loeb 1:36–37). Vizgin understands this passage to mean that the primary means of moderating powers is by cooking (especially boiling and baking) ("Hippocratic Medicine" 6), and from the point of view of diet therapy, he is correct. But Vizgin is so intent on drawing the distinction between the "dynamic" "culinary" theory of *OAM* and the "substantial" "tactile" theory of *NoM* and the cosmologists that he ignores statements in *OAM* on the importance of a balanced mixture, as at *OAM* 14.

52. Miller defines φύσις in *OAM* as "composed of an indefinite number of simple real constituents, each of which he [the author of *OAM*] conceives primarily as a δύναμις." "*Dynamis* and *Physis*" 189.

This use of *nature* can be illustrated from *OAM:* for example, chapter 13 speaks of the case of a man whose nature is not strong but weaker than the average and who is thus more affected by "strong" foods than most, while chapter 14 recognizes that there are some foods that are too strong for human nature, in general, to assimilate.[53] When *nature* or φύσις is used of powers individually, it means a concrete or material principle of identity.[54]

Previous scholars have emphasized the epistemological function power(s) served in relation to the concept of the nature of some thing.[55] For

53. There is a bias specific to *OAM* against treating *nature* as an important concept in its own right that is not common to all the Hippocratic writings. The author of *OAM* regards the judgments of those who write κατὰ φύσιν (for example, Empedocles) as short-sighted, and he contrasts their subject-matter and methods with his own (as a physician). There is no such attitude in *Nature of Man,* as the title would indicate: the polemical target of *NoM* is whoever teaches that the nature of man is composed of only one elemental. The term φύσις in *NoM* is more easily understood to mean principle of identity or internal disposition than is usual with *OAM. NoM,* for example, describes how the components that make up a living thing disperse when that organism dies (in a Greek version of ashes to ashes, dust to dust) by saying that ". . . each component must return to its own nature when the body of a man dies, moist to moist, dry to dry, hot to hot, and cold to cold. Such too is the nature of animals, and all other things. All things are born in a like way, and all things die in a like way. For the nature of them is composed of all those things I have mentioned above. . . . [that is, the moist, dry, hot, and cold]" (*NoM* 3; Jones, Loeb 4:10–11; translation slightly altered, although in each case *nature* is φύσις. *OAM* never uses *nature* in this broad, inclusive sense. Vizgin says that *NoM* never uses χυμός or ἰκμάς (humors) in his account of organic causality ("Hippocratic Medicine" 2 n. 2).

54. William Heidel offers an extensive account of the concept *nature* among the Presocratics, including the Hippocratics (whom he equates simply with Hippocrates), in his essay "Περὶ Φύσεος: A Study of the Conception of Nature Among the Pre-Socratics," reprinted in *Selected Papers,* ed. Leonardo Tarán (New York: Garland Publishers, 1980), 79–133. His general description of φύσις is somewhat different than my own, but when he speaks of Hippocratic writings, we tend to agree.

55. Souilhé argues, with some influence, that the relationship between φύσις and δύναμις is that between subject and causality, that in itself φύσις is without effect and that in itself δύναμις is without ground. "Due to the δύναμις, the mysterious φύσις, the substantial εἶδος or the primordial element, is made known, and is made known by the action of the δύναμις (*Étude* 56). (See Cornford's appropriation of this judgment in *Plato's Theory of Knowledge,* 235: "This [understanding of δύναμις and φύσις] explains why it was possible, especially at a later date, to pass from the known to the unknown, from the appearance to the reality, and how easy it was to identity nature [φύσις] with the δύναμις.") Souilhé (as well as Cornford and Miller) did not treat the possibility that the power reveals the nature as a visible part reveals the invisible whole rather than simply as the visible reveals the invisible. Souilhé over-interpreted his sources and presumed too heavily on the hypothesis of Pythagorean origins and geometrical context of the original philosophical use of δύναμις. While the author of *OAM* is clearly concerned to build upon a set of specialized terms with recognized meanings (that is, to develop or preserve a technical language), this is the last and almost least of his concerns: explicit definitions appear only at the end of his work, and then only for δύναμις and σχῆμα, the latter of which has played no part in the treatise

example, Miller describes the relationship between the two concepts in these terms: "It is the activity of the δύναμις, and it alone, which makes known, by reason of its observable manifestation, the real nature [that is, the *physis*] of the entity. To know the δύναμις is therefore to know the essential nature of the entity."[56] Miller's judgment represents the scholarly consensus on this topic,[57] and I have little to add, except to emphasize aspects of Hippocratic doctrine that provide some insight into Christian arguments using the same conceptual language and related methods.[58]

What we might then call "Hippocratic epistemology" followed a method of taking what seems to be one and dividing it into its constituent elements, a method later reported and endorsed by Plato: "Then see what Hippocrates and true reason say about nature. Surely it is in the following way that we must inquire into the nature of anything. In the first place we must see whether that [which we wish to understand] . . . is simple or complex. In the next place, if it is simple, we must inquire what power [δύναμις] nature has given it. . . . If, on the other hand, it is complex, we

before that point. Souilhé's belief that the origins of δύναμις as a philosophical term were in Pythagorean geometry led him to assume, and find, a degree of systemization and comprehensiveness that is simply not there in the literature. (One might add that it is not yet there in the geometry of the era either; Souilhé assumes that geometry was always as systematic as Euclid made it.)

56. The Hippocratic texts are not quite as neat and explicit as Miller is in their description of the epistemological relationship between the power and a prior material substrata (or, alternately, between the power and a principle of identity). Above all, their account in this matter is primarily functional (or, as we would say in theology, economic): what is most knowable, like what is most real, is whatever acts or affects, a class usually identified with the powers. What does not act is known either through mediated action (that is, the δύναμις) or through supposition (following conceptually from the existence of δυνάμεις).

57. Miller, "*Dynamis* and *Physis*," 191. Vizgin offers a similar judgment: "As for the medical writers, they hold that nature makes itself seen only through bodies acting, that is, through their forces, and that only when one understands powers and knows the ways of influencing them, can one govern the organism as a whole." ("Hippocratic Medicine" 11). Jones' account of δύναμις defines δύναμις through reference to the φύσις: "A really existent entity, any truly real thing, manifests its nature (φύσις) to our perceptive faculties through its δύναμις, or perhaps its δυνάμεις." (*Philosophy and Medicine*, 93).

58. One interesting example of Gregory's use of φύσις with δύναμις occurs in his *Refutation of the Creed* (of Eunomius). Gregory offers his account of names: "But things are named . . . in conformity with the nature and power inherent in each. . . . [A]s, for instance, in the case of fire, the element itself is one thing in its nature, while the word which denotes it is another (for fire itself possesses the powers of shining, of burning, of drying and heating, and of consuming whatever fuel it lays hold of, but the name is but a brief word of one syllable) . . ." (*GNO* 2, 305:23–28; NPNF 5:278).

must enumerate its parts, and note in the case of each what we noted in the case of the simple thing. . . ."[59] In other words, knowledge of the object as a whole (the φύσις) is found by investigating the object in its constituent parts or elements. Each of these constituent parts consists of a number of powers, which are themselves associated with some material substrata (for example, στοιχέια, χυλός), and some organizing principle (for example, the φύσις, or the εἶδος). Plato says that this method will bring one to a knowledge of the nature of the subject at hand; the medical writers would agree but expect this knowledge of the nature to remain in terms of cause: *OAM,* for example, refers to nature (φύσις) only as an organization of causes,[60] or a source of modification to a cause,[61] or simply a recipient of a cause.[62] Plato may have had higher expectations. Certainly any kind of definition of nature would, strictly according to the Hippocratic method, remain at the level of "a mixture of this or that kind of powers. . . ." The Hippocratics did not consider the nature to be more "real" than a power; indeed, as Miller and Vizgin have put it, the power is the fundamental category of existence.

59. *Phaedrus* 270 C–D, Jones's translation, slightly altered, in *Hippocratic Writings,* 1: xxxiv. There is a long-standing debate over exactly which text in the Hippocratic Corpus Plato is taking this method from. This debate is motivated by the opportunity to use Plato's declaration that this method is from Hippocrates to discover a text that is by Hippocrates and not simply from his school (that is, "Hippocratic"). Jones refers to Galen's understanding that Plato was referring to *NoM* (*Hippocratic Writings* 1:34–35), though Jones follows Littre and thinks that Plato's passage resembles *OAM* 20 more. Moline summarizes previous scholarship in some detail (*Plato's Understanding* 217 n. 40). These scholarly arguments have largely turned not on the doctrine of division into powers but on the relative priorities of medicine and nature in *OAM* and in Plato's thought. Moline finally agrees with Louis Bourgey, who "regards the *Phaedrus* passage, not as reporting on a definite work of Hippocrates, but as reflecting the general teaching of Hippocrates as it was commonly known" (*Observation et experience chez les médecins de la collection hippocratique* [Paris: Librairie philosophique J. Vrin, 1953]). D. S. Hutchinson, in "Doctrines of the Mean and the Debate concerning Skills in Fourth-Century Medicine, Rhetoric and Ethics," *Method, Medicine and Metaphysics,* 23, thinks that Plato was paraphrasing *Regimen* I, though he is cautious about accepting that this means that *Regimen* is indeed by Hippocrates. I agree with the caution of Bourgey, Hutchinson, and Moline. Bourgey's point seems to me to be demonstrated by the wide range of resemblances scholars have found.

60. *OAM* 22.

61. In *OAM* 11, the author begins by describing how the different eating habits of people alter the way in which a forced fast affects people (for example, someone accustomed to a large breakfast and a small or late lunch will hardly feel the effects of missing lunch). *OAM* 12 treats the description in 11 as analogy that allows the author to conclude that a weak nature suffers the effects of errors more quickly and severely than a strong nature.

62. As, for example, in *OAM* 9. These three distinctions are my own.

The medical tradition seems to have been more content in its limitations than Plato's report of the "Hippocratic method" suggests. The Hippocratic understanding of the method presumes that what lies "behind" the powers is unknowable, except in terms of the powers themselves or a strictly materialist description (that is, as when *nature* or φύσις means a way of being built). It may be that this early agnostic realism of the Hippocratics is largely a product of their practical concerns, but it seems not to have remained simply this in later medical writings. By Galen's time the agnostic realism is systematized: Galen's own account of any organic being begins with the powers, not the essence or nature.[63] Indeed, Galen makes what now seems a cryptic remark that knowledge of the power takes place in ignorance of the essence.[64] Some scholars (for example, May) take this remark as Galen's "humble" acknowledgement of his own limitations or the sorry state of medicine in the early Common Era. I take his comment as an implicit acknowledgement of a distinction between power and essence, and of the expectation among some of his contemporaries that the proper object of knowledge is the essence, an expectation unknown to *OAM*, alien to the older Hippocratic tradition, and furthermore an expectation Galen does not share (unlike May). Galen notes this ignorance of

63. Galen's sequence is δύναμις, ἐνέργεια, and ἔργα. I give the background of this sequence in my article, "The Background and Use of Eunomius' Causal Language" (217–36). I take this occasion to alert the reader that in all that follows, the word *essence* consistently translates "οὐσία." There is no English word that can successfully capture all the senses conveyed in every use of οὐσία, but so as long as the reader understands that I am not invoking or implying anything more by the word *essence* than my analysis here describes, an arbitrary but common translation like *essence* will do.

64. D. J. Furley and J. S. Wilkie cite the passage in their commentary to Galen's *On Respiration and The Arteries* (Princeton: Princeton University Press, 1984): ". . . so long as we are ignorant of the true essence of the cause which is operating, we call it a faculty [δύναμις]." Furley and Wilkie cite the passage for what it says about what Galen includes as δυνάμεις and they conclude, first, that "in the case of the homoeomerous parts of the body, to know the true essence of the cause would be to know the exact proportions of the warm, the cold, the moist and the dry. . . ." They add that "there is no reason to suppose that any further and unknown cause is supposed by him [Galen] to underlie the four qualities, so they should not be called faculties [that is, δυνάμεις]" (64). Margaret May has a different interpretation of this remark by Galen. She is puzzled by what she sees as Galen's tendency to multiply powers: "Whenever an action is necessary, there appears a faculty [that is, δύναμις] to take charge of it" (*Galen: On the Usefulness of the Parts of the Body,* 2 vols. [Ithaca: Cornell University Press, 1968], 50). "But let it not be imagined" she adds, "that Galen was unaware of the fact that he was really explaining nothing [by multiplying all these δυνάμεις]." May then quotes the famous "ignorant of the true cause" passage.

the essence, but he does not lament it.[65] Similar expectations are debated in the trinitarian controversies of the fourth century.

I would like to develop a slightly different aspect of the relationship between power and nature, namely the use of the phrase "power and nature" (δύναμις καὶ φύσις) to designate the entire existent, the object as it exists, or the fundamental components of reality.[66] The first use in Greek philosophy of the phrase "δύναμις καὶ φύσις" occurs in the Hippocratic writings *OAM, NoM,* and *The Sacred Disease;* the phrase is of particular importance for this study since it is regularly used in the early trinitarian controversy to describe the unity between the first and second Persons, and it a special feature of Gregory of Nyssa's trinitarian theology.

"Power and nature" is used in *OAM* when the author wants to speak of all the aspects of an existing thing. For example, *OAM* says, "For a thing, which has been exposed to fire and water, and has been made by many other things, each of which has its own power and nature, has lost some of its qualities and has been mixed and combined with others."[67] A similar use occurs in *NoM* in which that author argues that where both the power and the nature differ, there must be different things or entities: "How could they [blood, phlegm, bile] be like one another. . . ? For they are not equally warm, nor cold, nor dry, nor moist. . . . From the following evidence you may know that each of them has its own power and its own nature [and that they are not one and the same]."[68] When the author of *The Sacred*

65. The remark by Galen has to be handled with care; too much can be made of it. In *On the Doctrines of Hippocrates and Plato* Galen insists (contrary to the opinion of Aristotle, Posidonius, and Chryssipus) that there are three essences in the soul. These essences are indeed known by their respective powers, but Galen is confident enough of their existence to argue at length against his opponents. On the other hand, in *Blood in the Arteries,* 2, Galen says that "the living differs from the nonliving by its participation in faculties [δυνάμεις], not by superiority of substance [οὐσία]," an opinion that shows, first, that "ignorance" of essence is not complete and second, that following the Hippocratic method and outside the polemical context (of contested psychologies) power was a more important concept than essence for Galen.

66. Jones remarks in his 1943 translation of *NoM* that "recent research" makes it likely that ". . . in the medical writers δύναμις is often used with ἰδέα or φύσις to form a tautological phrase meaning 'real essence.'" p. 7, note 1.

67. *OAM* 13; Jones, Loeb 1:35–37. See also *NoM* 5, where δύναμις is also used with a related meaning in a phrase with ἰδέα. The author of *NoM* uses the phrase ἰδέα καὶ δύναμις in his proof that the humors bile, phlegm, and blood are not one and the same. Δύναμις is used similarly with εἶδος in chapter 15 of *OAM,* for example.

68. *NoM* 5; Jones, Loeb 4:12–15.

*Disease* wants to claim that "there is no need to put the disease [in question] in a special class and to consider it more divine than the others," he says that each disease has a nature and a power of its own, meaning that they all exist in the same way as one expects a disease (and everything else) to exist.[69] The association of power with nature reinforces the understanding that a power is an intrinsic "natural" feature of any existent thing; the movement of powers into and out of a mixture is the coming to be and passing away of a thing.[70]

What should be noted about these three occurrences of "nature and power" is that in each of them *power,* like *nature,* is used in the singular. One expects a reference to the nature to be in the singular, not so much power. For example, the *OAM* passage says of fire and water that each has its own "nature and power," yet the author has already argued that neither fire nor water nor anything else has only one power. Similarly, the argument in *NoM* is that the humors are different from one another because they each have a different "nature and power." The same kind of argument is made in *Sacred Disease* to show that all diseases belong to the same class of existents (natural, not divine). My interpretation of these passages is that the use of the singular of power in the phrase "nature and power" expresses an understanding of the affective capacity of the existent as a whole or as a unit.[71]

69. *The Sacred Disease* 21; Jones, Loeb 2:182–83.

70. To carry this thought further, in the medical writings a power is always understood as "real" and not an "illusion." Parmenides' opinion on δύναμις, as most scholars interpret fragment 9:2, places δύναμις among the δόξαι (though what exactly this placement means for the reality of δύναμις depends upon one's understanding of the role of δόξα in Parmenides' thought). Miller thinks, as I have already quoted, that in *OAM,* φύσις or nature is understood to be "composed of an indefinite number of simple real constituents, each of which . . . [is conceived] primarily as a δύναμις." I am less certain that the humors do not have a claim to the status of "real constituents"; they seem not to fit this category because they seem not to be "simple" (they have two or more powers). The interpretive problem is that the judgment that simplicity must have meant unicity depends upon a very speculative reconstruction of the development of "abstraction" among the Presocratics and Hippocratics as a whole. However, even with the limitations of our knowledge, it is certain that, beginning with the Hippocratic writings, a power was considered to have true existence because a power was the basis for all experience: conceptually, the power is that which cannot be doubted because it is the cause of existence as experienced. Only a body of doctrine that radically doubted experience (that of Parmenides? the Atomists?) could judge the powers to be not real or to be an illusion. (Such doubters would not include Plato.)

71. I believe that Aristotle reveals the same use of the singular in *On the Parts of Animals* 646b–650a, 110–33, as I discuss in the next chapter.

*The Action of Multiple Powers Described*

*OAM* and the medical writers have two generalized accounts of power causality. The first account describes the action of a power as the manifestation of the power itself: the hot in fire causes a log to be hot, and, when the balance of powers is right and the log (or the mixture that the log is) is composed of all the powers of fire, it will be transformed into fire. A log bursts into flame because the powers in the igniting (actually spreading or contributing) fire have been transferred to the log through the action of a sort of material spread: all the powers that make up fire (that is, the hot, the dry, the ever-moving, etc.) are added to the log and become the dominant form of the log.[72]

The second sort of causality associated with power occurs when a power produces an effect (product) that has a different nature from the originating power (that is, when the presence of the power is not manifested in the product). This occurs when the causal or originating power in question cannot dominate the subject of its presence. A good example of such a case is the action of fire upon clay. The hot and the dry powers of fire cannot dominate the cold and the wet of the clay (or, as we might put it, fire does not cause clay to ignite). Instead what happens is a partial dominance: the hot temporarily dominates the cold (when the clay is "fired") but eventually recedes, losing to the δύναμις cold. However, the dry power of fire does replace or dominate the wet power of clay, so that the wet clay becomes dry earthenware or pottery. In every causal relation where the action/presence of a power does not result in the manifestation of the added power, it is either because that power enters a mixture that is so thoroughly combined that no one power can dominate sufficiently to

72. Accounts of why fire becomes the dominant form of the log (that is, ignites it rather than the fire being transformed by the log into a stationary cold thing) vary among philosophers. Many philosophers would say that the dominance of fire is simply an expression of the unique, fundamental status of fire relative to all other existents (including the other elementals). Other philosophers would modify that judgment to say simply that fire is an elemental composed of a very strong power. Still other philosophers would say that fire produces fire (in the log) when the power in the first fire reaches a certain concentration or density: a small fire will not, after all, turn a large log into fire (unless there is a supplementary presence of fire-related powers at hand, for example, a heavy preponderance of the dry, or of the 'ever-moving'—that is, friction.)

be manifested or, more significantly, because of the influence of the other, secondary, powers.

It may be helpful to think about the mechanics of manifestation by making a distinction between primary and secondary powers in an elemental. The *primary power* of an elemental is that power with which the elemental is most identified in experience; in earlier times when elementals were described in terms of only one characteristic, the primary power was that single characteristic with which the elemental was traditionally identified.[73] *Secondary powers* may be recognized by either of two criteria. First, secondary powers specific to an elemental are those which are judged to have the least influence on other objects. Second, any power which is the primary power of some specific elemental is a secondary power when found in another elemental. An illustration will, I hope, help make my "primary–secondary" distinction clear: the primary power of fire is the hot, the secondary power is the dry (and any other of the powers). The dry fulfills the criteria for "secondary" power since traditionally the dry was considered a weak power compared to the hot; furthermore, the dry was first considered the "primary" characteristic of air.

The "primary–secondary" distinction is useful in describing the development of the power concept in Hippocratic thought. The medical writers saw that the variety of causal effects was not well explained by the old understanding that elementals consisted of one power or that other existents were composed of a single elemental. *OAM* and *NoM* are filled with polemical examples of the failure of the old understanding. The observed effects of causes were best explained by understanding causal capacities to exist in combinations and to act in concert. The most important implication for this understanding of an inherent multiplicity in causality was that the dominance and manifestation of the primary power depended upon the action or presence of the secondary power. A sufficient threshold of the secondary power allows the primary power to be dominant and mani-

73. The characterization of one power in a mixture as "primary" has an analogue in the language of *OAM* 17:44–47. When the author argues that the hot is not the sole cause of fever but rather the hot (or cold) in combination with other powers (for example, bitter, salt, etc.), he allows that the hot is present as the "directing factor" (or "leader").

fested: wood that is dry enough burns (that is, is hot). But when the presence of the secondary power is insufficient, the primary power is not dominant or manifested: wet wood will not burn, though it will become/show the dry.

An awareness of the roles that all the powers play in any causal relation allows us to recast our understanding of one of the major arguments appearing in *OAM*. The author's argument against a causality based on the preeminence of the hot has been understood by most modern scholars only as an attempt to replace one favored power with another favored power. Vizgin, for example, understands the argument in *OAM* as one round in a running debate between "the elementalists" (that is, the Presocratic cosmologists) and "the botanicalists" (the Hippocratics); the former favor the tactile elements, especially the hot, while the latter favor the culinary "order of [the] tactile."[74] I would like to suggest a very different understanding of the argument in *OAM* against the universal primacy of the hot.

The point that is repeatedly emphasized in *OAM* is that no power acts alone since no power exists alone in isolation. Previous philosophers or physicians have described a causality that presumed the existence of the hot in isolation from other powers and the action of the hot in isolation from other powers. For the author of *OAM*, to show that the first of these "isolations" is not real (that is, does not occur in the world) is to show as well that the second isolation does not occur. The substance of his argument is to show that the hot does not exist in isolation but always in combination: the hot and the astringent, the hot and the insipid, the hot and the flatulent,[75] the hot and the bitter, the hot and the acidic, or the hot and the salty.[76] The statement in *OAM* of alternative preferred powers (that is,

74. Vizgin, "Hippocratic Medicine," 5. He describes the two opposing schools of thought on pages 3, 5, and 7–10. Vizgin also notes on page five that this emphasis on the culinary (rather than the tactile), and the attendant language of *humors,* is not found in *NoM* but is rather a distinguishing feature of *OAM*. The reader is warned of a major typographical error in the text. The passage reads: "Unlike the author of NH [meaning *NoM*], the author of the treatise 'Of the Ancient Medicine' belongs to physicians of the *medical* trend. 'Empirical' does not mean here. . . ." (Emphasis added). "Empirical" in fact appears nowhere prior to this point. The sentence should read: ". . . the author of the treatise 'Of the Ancient Medicine' belongs to physicians of the *empirical* trend. . . ."

75. *OAM* 15; Jones, Loeb 1:40–41.

76. Ibid. 17; 1:44–47.

the astringent and the insipid, etc.) comes only as a conclusion in the demonstration that no one power has the same effect in all possible combinations with other powers.

> . . . surely it will make a difference whether he [the doctor] administers the hot astringent thing, or the hot insipid thing, or that which is cold and astringent at the same time . . . or the cold insipid thing. For I am sure that each of these pairs produces exactly the opposite of that produced by the other. . . . [77]

The critique is this: if the hot in two different combinations with two different powers produces two different (indeed, opposite) effects, then the hot alone does not determine or produce those effects: the combined action of the specific powers in a given mixture does. Though the author may follow this conclusion with a statement on the "powerfulness" of the astringent and the insipid, he cannot claim that in different combinations these powers behave any differently than the hot does in combination.[78] If his argument gives new status to any class of powers, it is not to the class of "botanical" or "culinary" powers since they are as subject to the critique of combination as the old status powers. Rather it is the class of ancillary or "secondary" powers that gains new status or significance since they determine the causal effect of powers in combination as much as the "leading" (that is, primary) power.[79]

### *The Power and Multiple Effects*

The final point to be considered regarding the understanding of the concept of power connoted by the term δύναμις among the medical writers is that they are the earliest source for a judgement that was later to become a truism in the philosophy of the Common Era, and which figured significantly in the trinitarian controversies, namely that a single cause can

77. Ibid. 15; 1:40–41, emphasis added. The text then continues: "For it is not the heat which possess the greatest power [δύναμις], but the astringent and the insipid, and the other qualities I have mentioned. . . ."

78. See Lloyd's discussion of the ways in which the author of *OAM* is vulnerable to his own criticisms in *Polarity and Analogy*, 69–70.

79. To return to the terminology of *OAM* 17; Jones, Loeb 1:46–47: "Heat, too, is present, but merely as a concomitant, having the strength of the directing factor which is stimulated and increases with the other factor, but having no power greater than that which properly belongs to it" (Jones's translation, slightly altered).

have multiple and even opposite effects.[80] For the medical writers this judgment was a point of dispute; their proofs in its favor figure prominently in their polemics against (what they perceived as) the old monistic type cosmologies.[81] For the Hippocratics the existence of multiple and opposite effects resulting from a single cause is the best evidence that everything exists in or as a mixture not only because, as one might expect, it shows that the agent (the cause) is itself composed[82] but because the nature[83] of the recipient of the cause determines what the effect of the cause will be as much as the nature of the cause.

The argument in *OAM* for the proposition that the effect of any special part in a mixture is determined by the other members in the mixture begins with the claim that a single characteristic effect for a specific part occurs only when that part exists in true isolation or purity (that is, never, according to the author). Indeed, the argument by the author of *OAM* for the multiple effects of a cause is explicitly cast as one against a monistic position. "For they have not discovered" he says, "an absolute hot or cold, dry or moist. . . ."

80. For example, Origen gives the example of the multiple effects of the sun: "So, too, if the sun were to utter a voice and say, 'I melt things and dry them up,' when being melted and being dried up are opposites, he would not be speaking falsely in regard to the point in question, since by the one heat wax is melted and mud dried." *On First Principles* III.1.11, Butterworth, p. 175. This kind of argument figures significantly in the Christian theology of the fourth century, first, as in the works of Eusebius who uses it to prove that God is one despite His multiple operations, and second, in the work of Gregory, who uses it to prove the Trinity is one, despite the activities of the different Persons. One typical example of Gregory referring to this principle may be found in *Against Eunomius* I:27, where Gregory speaks of the multiple effects of fire: "Copper melts, clay hardens, wax dissolves, other living things if they fall into it are destroyed, but the salamander comes to life; tow is burnt, amianthus [asbestos] is washed by flames as if by water. . . ." "Contra Eunomium I", trans. Stuart. G. Hall in *El Contra Eunomium I,* ed. Mateo-Seco and J. Bastero (Pamplona: Ediciones Universidad Navarra, S. A., 1988), 91.

81. This includes not simply true monist positions, which described all existence as one because it was composed of a single element, e.g., fire, but also those cosmologies which taught the existence of unmixed single elementals, or which (still) equated those elementals with one trait, e.g., that fire was only the hot (and not the hot and the dry, etc.). By this latter criterion, Empedocles is a "monist" (or a "Neo-monist", meaning that his monism attempts to preserve the insight—as he understood it—of his predecessors, but without preserving literally some of the doctrines or language) and indeed the author of *OAM* complains that Empedocles unrealistically postulates the existence of pure, simple elementals. As I have already described, the problem of what constitutes real being or the final discrete substrata was a point of dispute between the Hippocratic writers and non-medical cosmologists (and, according to Vizgin, between authors in the Hippocratic tradition as well).

82. As, eg., fire can have multiple effects because it is both hot and dry.

83. By *nature* I mean specific composition.

And if one hot thing happens to be astringent, and another hot thing insipid, and a third hot thing causes flatulence (for there are many kinds of hot things, possessing many opposite δυνάμεις), surely it will make a difference whether he administers the hot astringent thing, or the hot insipid thing, or that which is cold and astringent at the same time . . .[84]

As a result of this observation, the Hippocratics can offer this easy objection to the monists, namely that multiple effects show the composed nature of the agent: there is no simple hot thing, or wet thing, but only mixtures of the hot, cold, wet and dry, in different combinations. However, a more fundamental critique of the monists lies in the insight that the traditional argument for simple causal elementals presumed that a causal relation was defined entirely by the transmission of a force from an active cause to a simple, passive, and uniform patient which thus reproduced the agent.

The author of *OAM* offers the examples of wine or cheese as illustrations of this new insight.[85] He notes that people speak of the power of wine and its effect upon a drinker, but wine has, in fact, different effects upon different drinkers. A more telling judgement follows from the observation that "strong" cheeses do not affect everyone in the same way or to the same degree: some people can eat a large quantity of a strong cheese without feeling any discomfort while others are made sick from eating just a little. The ultimate effects of wine and cheese are determined by the nature of the mixture (that is, the body) they act upon (by being ingested).

The importance in medicine of the doctrine that the nature of the patient plays a role in determining the specific effect of the agent is indicated by the repeated arguments in its favor in the fifth century B.C.E. Wesley Smith refers, for example, to a passage in the *Regimen* that treats the same question:

The same power [δύναμις] does not belong to all sweet things nor to all particulars of any class. For many sweet things are laxative, many binding, many drying, many moistening. . . . [86]

The argument also appears in Diocles' *Hygiene to Pleistarchus,* as we know from the fragment quoted by Galen in his work *Faculties of Food:*

84. *OAM* 15 1–21; Jones, Loeb 1:40–41.
85. *OAM* 20 24–48; Jones, Loeb 1:54–55.
86. *Regimen* II 39; Smith, *Hippocratic Tradition,* 185.

Those who suppose that foods which have like kinds of humors or smells or heat or anything else of the kind all have the same faculties (δυνάμεις) are mistaken. One could point out many dissimilar results which come from such similar things. One must not suppose that everything which is laxative or diuretic, or which has some other δύναμις does so because it is hot, cold, or salty since the sweet and bitter and salty, etc., do not in all cases [prove] to have the same δυνάμεις. Rather, one must consider that the whole nature (φύσις) is responsible. . . .[87]

The theory of multiple effects was sophisticated enough to recognize that while a given cause might produce many different, even opposing, effects, each set of effects was nonetheless distinctive to the specific cause. Heat, for example, might have the opposite products of melting ice and hardening clay, yet these effects were associated with heat and heat alone; the effects of heat's opposite, cold, were quite different from the effects of heat. The author of *OAM* insists that the effects of opposite causes will always remain opposites, providing that one constituent power in the mixture of each cause is opposite (to the other causal mixture). The quotation cited above from *OAM* 15 makes precisely this point and bears repeating: even if we speak of a hot thing, the author notes, "there are many kinds of hot things, possessing many opposite powers" and therefore:

Surely it will make a difference whether he [the doctor] administers the hot astringent thing, or the hot insipid thing, or that which is cold and astringent at the same time . . . or the cold insipid thing. For I am sure that each of these pairs produces exactly the opposite of that produced by the other. . . .[88]

The medical critique recognizes that the patient determines the effect of a cause (for example, heat melts ice but hardens clay),[89] and that therefore the grounds for understanding causality as consisting, as it were, of movement in one direction (as, to use a political analogy, from ruler to subject) is false.[90] The "old" causality conceives of a causal relationship as involving,

87. Smith, *Hippocratic Tradition*, p. 183. Galen's citation also shows that the argument Diocles was making was beyond controversy in Galen's own era, since Galen produces the passage not for the sake of the argument on cause and effects but to show, in Smith's words, that Diocles "did not succeed in creating a science in Galen's sense."

88. *OAM* 15 15–24; Jones, Loeb 1:40–41.

89. The use and validity of an analogous argument from physical examples to medical examples is addressed explicitly in *OAM*. Lloyd treats the uses of analogy in *OAM* in *Polarity and Analogy*, 354.

90. The unity of the powers which constitute an object is described by the author of *OAM* in the political language usually attributed to Alcmaeon. When powers exist in "harmony," they form

as it were, two entities, the agent and the patient. The agent acts upon the patient by transforming the nature of the latter into the same nature as the former. A good illustration of this is again the action of fire upon wood: fire converts wood into fire. The "new" causality, by contrast, conceives of a causal relationship as involving three entities, the agent, the patient, and the distinctive nature of the patient. This may again be illustrated by the example of fire: fire may indeed turn wood into fire but only because of what wood itself is, since fire does not turn clay into fire but into pottery.

I do not wish to insist upon this artificial and arbitrary "counting" of the objects involved in a causal relation.[91] A more accurate way of describing the new insight is to note that while the character of the causing entity (insofar as this nature or character was distinguished from the causing thing itself) was always a factor in describing the efficacy of any causal activity, what the medical writers add is the insight that the nature or character of the affected entity is also important. When abstracted from its lingering materialism, the medical critique of the monists is the source for Plato's definition in the *Sophist* of the mark of reality, including both the capacity to affect and the capacity to be affected.[92]

---

a simple whole. But if the powers are not in harmony and fall into isolation in an undiluted mixture, some powers become too strong and there is disorder, ταραχή, in the body: "[A] vast number of . . . things [that is, foods], possessing properties of all sorts, both in number and in strength . . . when mixed and uncompounded with one another are neither apparent nor do they hurt a man. . . . And from such foods, when partaken plentifully of by a man, there arises no disorder at all or isolation of the powers [δυνάμεις] resident in the body, but strength, growth and nourishment arise from them, for no other reason except that they are well compounded, and have nothing undiluted and strong, but form a single simple whole" (*OAM* 14:3857; Jones, Loeb 1:3839). This word ταραχή for disorder or confusion is a political term used by Herodotus and Thucydides (Liddell & Scott, *Intermediate Greek Lexicon*, 792) to describe the confusion of an army or fleet, or "political tumult."

91. An equally legitimate way of describing the difference between the old and new causalities is to say that the old account thought of three entities involved in any causal relationship: the agent, the agent's distinctive character (which, at some stage of thought had been identified with the agent), and the patient. The new causality expanded the number of relevant entities in any account causal to four: the agent, its distinctive character, the patient, and the patient's distinctive character. What is important is the new recognition that the character of the patient counts in any given causal relationship.

92. Vizgin, "Hippocratic Medicine," 11, offers the same opinion (for once, more tentatively than I do) by quoting Solmsen's earlier comment that "as far as antecedents for Plato's 'power to act and to suffer' matter, the medical writers may well have approximated this conception more closely than the Presocratic physicists" (Friedrich Solmsen, *Aristotle's System of the Physical World* [Ithaca: Cornell University Press, 1960], 360).

*Conclusion*

For the early Hippocratics power—the technical sense of δύναμις—meant the causal capacity of a material entity. In their cosmology, everything that exists is composed of individually subsistent affective qualities or powers. The fundamental level of existence is an irreducible unit of powers. It is the mixture of powers that produces everything else that is perceived as existing, for it is the existence of specific powers in a mixture that determines the identity or nature of an existent, and the action of these powers upon other mixtures that determines all the causal relations that we perceive and know. For the Hippocratic philosophers, the concept of power(s) describes everything that exists.

Two specific doctrines are particularly important for both Hippocratic philosophy and the later Christian appropriation of δύναμις causality. The first doctrine is that these powers are organized or understood as opposites, insofar as one power (or collection of powers) acts to destroy, drive off, or reverse the action of another specific power (or collection of powers). The second significant doctrine is a distinction in the relationship between the nature or identity of an existent and the power(s) of an existent that is made according to whether the power is understood as the peculiar or distinctive power of a thing or whether the power is one of a number of powers of a thing. For example, there is a difference between fire's power of hot and fire's powers of dry or ever-moving. Hot is distinctive to fire's *nature;* it reveals fire's nature because it is unique to fire. Other elementals have the power of dry or ever-moving (for example, air). The power hot is the power of fire insofar as fire is fire. This kind of power is always used in the singular. The power dry, like the power ever-darting, belongs to fire but not only to fire. This kind of power is understood to exist always in the plural. The first kind of power is connatural to the existent, for wherever this kind of power is, the existent must necessarily also be (wherever there is heat, there is fire). The second kind of power may be understood as natural in the broad sense of that term, but the presence of one of this kind of power does not necessarily indicate the presence of a specific existent: the presence of ever-moving alone does not necessarily indicate the existence of fire the way the presence of the hot does.

In the Hippocratic writings, this kind of causality remains wholly materialistic. As I will describe in the next chapter, Plato's accomplishment is to take power or δύναμις causality and to apply it to immaterial causes. One of the most important examples for theology of this development occurs in the *Republic* when Plato compares the action of the sun to the action of the Good. Gregory's application of power or δύναμις causality to trinitarian doctrine follows Plato not only in using power causality to describe immaterial causal relationships but in using an explicit analogy between a material power and an immaterial power.

# 2 The Role of Δύναμις in Plato's Philosophy

## *Introduction*

IN THIS CHAPTER I TURN to Plato's use of δύναμις in his philosophy. I understand Plato's use of δύναμις to be indicative of the significant influence medicine had upon him; indeed, Plato's thought may properly be understood as his application of Hippocratic causality in general, and (where relevant) the medical use of δύναμις in particular, to new subject matters. One of the most important of the new subjects is that of virtue. Plato also uses Hippocratic language to describe different kinds of knowledge. These are both discourses about soul. Δύναμις also figures in Plato's discussion of an ordered universe, not, as one might expect, by way of a doctrine of the demiurge but through Plato's recounting of Anaxagoras's teaching of a δύναμις governing the cosmos. Questions about the cosmos are not separate from questions about soul, for each serves as a model of Plato's expectations for the other. More pointedly, questions of soul and cosmos are joined in Plato's overriding quest for a teleology. Plato's use of Hippocratic method and the medical sense of δύναμις as a mark of existence seem separate from the larger concern for teleology, but by the later dialogues (and in some works of Aristotle's), even these are brought within the perimeter of an account of a teleological cause in being.

I emphasize Plato's concern for teleological causes for two reasons: first, I believe that it is an accurate and helpful account of what is central to and common to the philosophy of Plato's writings, apart from my specific concerns here; and second, Plato's description of teleological cause for both ontology (that is, the role of the Good over Being in *Republic* 509 B) and cosmology provides the specific means by which δύναμις is used in a theological context by all forms of Hellenized religion—Pagan, Jewish, and Christian. Through his concern for teleology, Plato transforms δύναμις and the Hippocratic causality it describes into a "theological" term of causality.[1]

Furthermore, Plato's use of the same concepts and language to describe both psychological causality and material causality is an opportunity to recognize that the usual rigid distinctions made in trinitarian scholarship between "psychological" language and "ontological" language are more the products of modern distinctions between disciplines than reflections of ancient thought and usage. Finally, to my knowledge, the claims of recent Platonic scholarship for the importance of the Hippocratic writings on Plato's philosophy have not previously been recognized in patristic scholarship, and this study marks the introduction into the field of Patristics of these accounts of Plato's philosophical "roots," with their accompanying interpretations of Plato's philosophical doctrines.

### *Plato and His Predecessors*

Plato's understanding of causality is, in the early dialogues, similar to the causality associated with δύναμις in the medical writings.[2] Each cause

1. It is important not to underestimate Plato's task but to remember that the quest for a "teleological" cause is pursued, not simply in the realm of cosmology but also in more simple, day-to-day realms. Socrates' desire for an explanation of his body being in prison—beyond an anatomical one—should be taken not simply as a metaphor for the "real" question of teleological cause at a cosmological level but as a case of the real limitation of Presocratic etiology. There seems to have been no Presocratic conceptual apparatus to support accounts of any teleological causality outside the realm of politics (political power being a clear and undeniable case of action resulting from a will for something). Aristotle still must argue in *Parts of Animals* that in sexual reproduction, the seed has a specific product as its end since others (Aristotle singles out Empedocles) deny even so simple a case of nonpolitical action towards an end. (I treat Aristotle's argument later in this chapter.) William Arthur Heidel observes the complete lack of teleological causality in the accounts of the Hippocratics and the Presocratics generally: ". . . even where a modern scientist would involuntarily slip into modes of expression which imply final causality, the pre-Socratics, though at a loss for a satisfactory explanation, offer no such suggestion." ("Περὶ Φύσεος: A Study of the Conception of Nature Among the Pre-Socratics," in *Selected Papers,* ed. Leonardo Tarán [New York: Garland Publishers, 1980], 93).

2. The chronology of the dialogues is a perennial topic in Plato scholarship. The place in that chronology of most of the dialogues that I will refer to in this chapter is reasonably clear, or at least uncontested. (Among these dialogues, only the place of the *Cratylus* is disputed; some scholars think of it as pre-*Phaedo;* others regard it as a work of the early "Middle Period.") The only

possesses the characteristic or quality it produces, or else it could not produce that characteristic. A number of scholars have recently claimed that both the causality of the forms and that of the virtues are based on the causality of the quality-powers.[3] Teloh, for example, has argued that the cases of "self-predication" (that is, statements such as "justice is just" and "holiness is holy") are important examples of the Presocratic causal principle in use.[4] Thus, Plato continues to think of causes in terms of "like from like" and cannot imagine a quality being produced that did not exist previously in the cause. Brentlinger suggests that the immediate source of this causality for Plato is Anaxagoras and that in many important respects Plato's physics follows that of Anaxagoras.[5] According to Brentlinger, Plato shares with this physics the understanding that a quality is a material "stuff" and the possession of this material quality by any object is due to a "part" of this material quality being in the mixture of the whole. Any object's quality is "like" its cause in that each quality is a manifestation of the presence of the material quality itself—colors, shapes, sizes, weights, etc.—as a part of the whole mixture. All qualities, according to Anaxa-

---

sequence that is relevant to my argument is that "virtue" dialogues such as the *Protagoras* and *Charmides* predate the *Phaedo;* that the *Phaedo* predates *Republic* IV–VI and the *Timaeus;* and that the *Republic* predates the *Philebus.* This skeleton of a sequence is commonly accepted by contemporary scholars.

3. A previous generation of scholars, working in the first half of this century, already understood many of Plato's doctrines, including his use of εἶδος, as showing the influence of Hippocratic literature in general and of the Hippocratic concept of δύναμις in particular. The most important of these was Souilhe, whose work *Étude sur la terme Δύναμις* offered a thorough text-based study of the term. The weakness of this study for understanding the development of the philosophical senses of δύναμις is that Souilhé accepted as authentic texts that now lack credibility, and, under the influence of these texts, he failed to follow through on the implications of an observation he had made, namely that δύναμις appeared only very rarely in the "writings" of the Presocratic cosmologists. On the other hand, Souilhé's "errors" sometime parallel the "errors" of Hellenic readers of the same texts who typically worked from doxographies. Souilhé's study had great influence among a number of scholars, Cornford being one of the most important of these. H. C. Baldry, "Plato's 'Technical Terms,'" (*Classical Quarterly* 31 [1937], 141–150) is another important work that describes Plato's use of εἶδος / ἰδέα in terms of the prior medical use of δύναμις. On the other hand, the importance of δύναμις was not universally recognized, and one can read numerous treatments of Plato's thought without encountering any mention of the term. For reasons that escape me, it is indeed these latter works that seem to have provided the foundations for modern estimations and appropriations of Plato.

4. Henry Teloh, *The Development of Plato's Metaphysics* (University Park: Pennsylvania State University Press, 1981), 34–45.

5. John Brentlinger, "Incomplete Predicates and the Two-World Theory of the *Phaedo,*" *Phronesis* 17 (1972): 61–79, esp. 66–69.

goras, exist in all things, and the manifestation of any particular quality is a result of a numerical preponderance of parts.[6]

Even when Plato moves away from this material theory of causality, he retains the notion that each cause possesses the quality it produces. The most famous instance of this is in the *Phaedo* 100 A–C,[7] where Socrates gives his own account of causality, formulated explicitly against the limitations of Anaxagoras' theories.[8] In this account, anything "beautiful" is such because it participates in "the beautiful itself." The same sort of explanation applies for the qualities "small," "greatness," "two-ness," etc.[9] The language remains that of immanent physics: the term for participation is κοινωνία, a word used, as noted before, by the author of *OAM* and a number of other Presocratics.[10] The causality of the *Phaedo* remains one where the cause, that is, a form, possesses the very quality of the characteristic it produces.[11]

6. Ibid., 63–66.

7. The interest of patristic scholars in the *Phaedo* has remained limited to its treatment of the immortality of the soul. Charalambos Apostolopoulos, for example, has argued in his *Phaedo Christianus* for the influence of Plato's dialogue upon Gregory of Nyssa's dialogue, *On the Soul and Resurrection.* The weakness of Apostolopoulos' work is his assumption that the *Phaedo* is only about a doctrine of the soul. A more thorough and rounded account of how the *Phaedo* was understood in Antiquity appears in *The Greek Commentaries on Plato's Phaedo,* by L. G. Westerink, I:7–27. Brentlinger, Moline, and Teloh find *Phaedo* 99–104 very important for a correct understanding of the continuity between Plato's causality of the forms and the Presocratic causality of the character-power/quality-thing (usually expressed in terms of δύναμις). My attention to this text indicates my agreement with their reading. The other Platonic text emphasized by recent scholars who recognize δύναμις as an important concept in Plato's thought is *Protagoras* 330–331: see, for example, the works of David Savan, "Self-Predication in *Protagoras* 330–331" and Jerome Wakefield, "Why Justice and Holiness are Similar: *Protagoras* 330–331." The attraction of *Protagoras* 330–331 is its use of δύναμις in a "self-predication" (e.g., holiness is holy, beauty is beautiful) causality.

8. If the frequency of Plato's references to this doctrine of Anaxagoras is any indication, Plato was greatly drawn to and greatly disappointed by a doctrine whose influence he could never entirely shake. One important—for this study—mention of Anaxagoras' doctrine, as Plato understood it, is in *Cratylus* 400 B: ". . . do you not believe the doctrine of Anaxagoras, that it is the mind or soul which orders and holds the nature [φύσις] of all things? . . . [If this were true] then there would be an admirable fitness in calling that power [δύναμις] which causes and holds all nature [φύσις] [mind or soul]. . . ." Fowler, Loeb, pp. 60–61. See also *Philebus* 28 D–29 A for a late remembrance by Plato of this doctrine.

9. See, for example, *Phaedo* 101 A. The scholarly debate over whether these forms of qualities are considered truly transcendent in this dialogue is irrelevant to the present point.

10. The passage in *OAM* reads: "For they have not discovered, I think, an absolute hot or cold, dry or moist, that *participates in no other form* " (*OAM* 15; Jones, Loeb, 1:40–41 [emphasis added]). See also Baldry, "Plato's 'Technical Terms,'" 147–49.

11. Teloh treats Plato's argument of *Phaedo* 102 A–105 C in some detail in *The Development of Plato's Metaphysics,* 109–14, stressing the anti-Parmenidean character of Plato's arguments. The

## *Plato's Critique of Presocratic Causality*

Plato's physics differs, however, from the Presocratics in at least one important feature. What the Presocratics, including the author of *OAM*, formulated as a question of the final discrete substrata—whether atoms, seeds, or humours—Plato will conceive of as a teleological failure. For Plato, any causality that ends with a material cause does not, and cannot, provide a teleological explanation for either any causal sequence or essence. This critique appears as early as the *Phaedo*,[12] and at least as late as the *Timaeus:*

> [The four elements] are thought by most men not to be the second [cause], but the prime cause of all things, because they freeze and heat, and contract and dilate, and the like. But they are not so, for they are incapable of reason or intellect; the only being which can properly have mind is the invisible soul, whereas fire and water, earth and air, are all visible bodies.[13]

---

Eleatics found the existence of contrary qualities in natural phenomena to be, as Teloh puts it, "a problem." Plato's account of "participated forms" is intended to solve the problem of "inconsistent phenomena." (Teloh does not mention the anti-monistic tendency of Hippocratic writings such as *NoM* and *OAM*.) Moline's interpretation of Plato's "beautiful by beautiful" argument is slightly different than Teloh's: Moline finds in this argument Plato's appropriation of a Hippocratic power causality: "It would not be wrong, then, to say that Plato was something of a behaviorist in his conception of forms as δυνάμεις, or quality-things, communicating their own characteristic behavior to their participants. . . . Plato evidently employs this model to explain every appearance presented to us by a sensible thing, even ones such as beauty (*Phaedo* 100 C4) and largeness (*Phaedo* 102 B). Beauty is a beautifying quality-thing and largeness an enlarging one. . . . [Simmias'] largeness enlarges him as heat would warm him. Plato has but one model on which he explains anything one says about a particular, a model on which the behavior of a particular is viewed as being more exactly the behavior of one of the δυνάμεις mixed into the particular as a constituent" (*Plato's Theory of Understanding,* 92). However, Moline does not acknowledge that *power* is not used in the *Phaedo* in reference to either elemental or self-predicating causality (unlike, say, in the *Protagoras*); indeed, what is striking about the dialogue, from the point of view of causality, is the absence of δύναμις (with the one exception noted below). The dialogue serves as a good indication of the way in which this kind of causality could be discussed without δύναμις being mentioned, and to that extent, the dialogue probably represents the influence of cosmological rather than Hippocratic thinking on causality. Plato does, after all, cite Anaxagoras and not Hippocrates in this dialogue. Moline's interpretation of δύναμις in the *Phaedo* is correct insofar as the dialogue shows the overlap between the cosmological (non-δύναμις based) account of powers and the medical (δύναμις based) account of character-powers.

12. *Phaedo* 97 C–99 C.

13. *Timaeus* 46 D–E, *The Collected Dialogues of Plato,* Edith Hamilton and Huntington Cairns, eds., 4th ed. (New York: Pantheon Books, 1966), p. 1174. Hereafter referred to as Hamilton.

Plato's attempt to develop a teleological causality has two important accomplishments. First, qualities are related to the entities possessing them in a "logical" (as opposed to a material or spatial) manner. This means that whereas before an entity was understood as a specific collection of qualities (as, for example, in *OAM*), for Plato it is understood in terms of an immaterial unit in association with other immaterial units. (This immaterial unit was, over time, conceived of as a form, a monad, or a number.) Such an association of immaterial units serves as the foundation for determining both what a power or quality-thing is and for recognizing a principle of unity within a mixture of powers. The second accomplishment of Plato's teleological causality is the transfer of moral qualities from the material or cosmological realm to the psychic. The first accomplishment diminished the importance of the old use of δύναμις, while the second one provided a new, important sense.

The critique of the old theory of causation and predication is presented in the dialogue *Phaedo* where the theory of forms is offered as an alternate causality. Presocratic physics is there characterized as one that explains the existence of an entity, or the attribution of a quality to an object, in terms of the physical association of material qualities. The number two is explained in this system as one and one being close together. Thus the cause of qualities or object compounds is material. This is true of qualities whether they are attributes of relation or simple predications: "hot," "white," "tall," (or "taller"), "heavy," (or "heavier") are each said of an object because of the presence of a material quality that is the "hot," "white," "tall," or "heavy." The association and withdrawal (when a quality is lost) of these qualities is understood as simple material proximity.[14]

Plato's critique of this causality does not deny the material causes of qualities or objects, though there remains something unsatisfactory for

14. Again the passage from *Regimen* I illustrates this understanding well: "So of all things nothing perishes, and nothing changes into beings that did not exist before. Things change merely by mingling and being separated. . . . Whenever I speak of becoming or perishing I am merely using popular expressions; what I really mean is mingling and separating. The facts are these. Becoming and perishing are the same thing; mixture and separation are the same thing; increase and diminution are the same thing; becoming and mixture are the same thing . . ." (*Regimen* I, IV 11–15, 25–30; Jones, Loeb 4:234–35).

Plato about the material account. What first makes such an account unsatisfactory is that it does not describe entities, qualities, or activities in any teleological system. Anaxagoras had said that it is Νοῦς that governs the cosmos,[15] but, according to Socrates in the *Phaedo,* all he offered were mechanistic explanations.[16] What must be added is a causality that explains the entity "for its own sake," by which was meant, in terms of the good. This teleological explanation will give an account that is based upon what the entity is, rather than what it is made up of. (This critique is repeated at length and developed in the *Timaeus,* as I describe below.) Thus, Socrates is sitting in a room waiting for his execution, not because the muscles in his legs are pulled in a certain way, but because of Socrates' belief that he should accept the authority of the law.[17] The activities of Socrates' bodily parts are not causes in the important sense for Plato but rather that by which a cause acts. For an "ontology" this means that a true explanation of any entity, its activities and attributions will be in terms that explain why an entity is exactly what it is, or which explains attributions in terms of the entity rather than explaining the entity in terms of its attributions.[18]

Such an explanation is dependent upon there being some necessary connection between an entity and its attributions which is more than any necessity imposed by its material parts. An explanation of necessity that is based on the material will disregard the entity *per se* since the explanation would account for all instances of the quality regardless of what entity it is attributed to. To give an example of such a material explanation: if the explanation of snow melting is kept at the level of the opposition of the Hot and the Cold, that is, that any Cold cannot co-exist with any Hot, then

15. When Plato refers to this doctrine, he frequently says that Anaxagoras taught that the cosmos was governed by a δύναμις; Plato says this, for example, in the *Cratylus* 400 B: the "power [δύναμις] which causes and holds all nature [φύσις]"). A related use of δύναμις (attributed to "our predecessors," though the context makes it clear that Anaxagoras is meant) can be found at *Philebus* 28 D–29 A. The most significant use of δύναμις in the *Phaedo* occurs at 99 C, where after referring to Anaxagoras (at 97 C ff.), Plato speaks the doctrine of a δύναμις that governs the universe. I return to Plato's (and Anaxagoras') use of δύναμις in reference to the ordering of the universe later.

16. *Phaedo* 97 C–99 C.

17. Ibid. 98 C–E.

18. I am not happy about using the word *ontology,* much less *metaphysics,* and I have tried to keep both words to a minimum: all I mean by either is "an account of what exists."

snow is reduced to an instance of the Cold.[19] The principles that describe snow, and snow melting, are cosmological since it is cosmology that provides us with the only set of relations that are necessary. Such a cosmological explanation does not provide us with any account of the whole entities that we perceive, nor of why the discrete and permanent elemental powers have gathered into those entities. If the unity of an entity, which is for Plato the "whatness" of an entity, is not caused by the material mixture, then it must be caused by something else: an immaterial simple.

A second reason why Plato rejects the old etiology of material qualities added to a mixture lies ironically in his own acceptance of one tenet of the Presocratics, namely, that a cause must be what it produces.[20] Plato is forced to reject the sufficiency of the Presocratic account of cause and attribution not only because it is not teleological but because it introduces a paradox into the very activity of causation. The paradox is the production of the same effect (or product) by two opposite causes. The solution to the paradox is that of participation in the forms. The search for a teleological ontology or metaphysics is not successful in the literal terms of the *Phaedo,* but the attempt to remove the paradox of causation is. The theory of forms preserves the received understanding of a cause possessing the character it produces.

The paradox and its solution are set out by Socrates in two examples: the first is that of a particular man being taller than another man by a given unit ("taller by a head") and shorter than another man by the same unit ("shorter by a head").[21] The same unit makes the man taller and shorter. The second example perhaps makes the problem more clear: the number 2 is produced by the sum of adding 1 to 1; but 2 is also produced by dividing 8 by 4, or by subtracting 5 from 7. Addition and division/subtraction are opposite processes, and yet they produce the same result (or effect).[22] But what produces the same effect cannot be called opposites. Or, alternately, if causes are considered to be what they produce, then the act

19. I use these examples because Socrates uses the same ones in his argument at *Phaedo* 103 D.

20. Socrates offers three examples of a rational account of causality in *Phaedo* 100 E: it is by beauty that beautiful things are beautiful; it is by largeness that large things are large; and by smallness small things are small.

21. See *Phaedo* 101 A–B.

22. Ibid. 101 C.

of addition that yields 2 is identical to the act of division that yields 2. Opposites thus admit of, or are identical to, their own opposites.[23] Such a conclusion clearly puts not only the doctrine of "causes are themselves what they produce" in trouble, but also the equally, if not more, important doctrine that "opposites are not the same." This statement of opposition is very important for Plato in the *Phaedo,* and he returns to it frequently.

On the other hand, that opposites produce or are their own opposites is a basic tenet of any theory of quality-powers in a material mixture, such as that of the medical writers and Anaxagoras. In such theories, opposites are combined "all in all." The exclusion of cosmological opposites occurs at a level too small ever to be seen. Plato has no quarrel with such a theory as long as it describes the association of material qualities; as Socrates admits, it is clear that on a *material* level, opposites do produce opposites.[24] But Plato distinguishes between descriptions of associations, which would include statements such as (1 + 1 = 2), (7 − 5 = 2), and (8/4 = 2), and statements that define. Since 2 is not defined by any of these three descriptions, there is no production but only a statement of association. Such a conclusion, however, makes clear the metaphysical limitations of a theory of material causes: if it attempts to define, then it is a system of paradoxical causes; as long as it describes associations, it cannot define any entity. Some other category of causes must provide the definition of 2 and all other definitions.

Thus Plato admits that our perception of any given entity is the perception of a collection of entities in mixture whose preponderant manifestations are those that we recognize and call the entire collection by. For example, what we call "white" is as well "black," though it is mostly "white."[25]

23. Ibid. 97 A–134.

24. The argument that opposite things produce opposite things occurs at *Phaedo* 70 E–71 B; Plato summarizes this judgment at 103 B and then distinguishes the action of an opposite thing from the action of the opposite itself: "We maintain that the opposites themselves would absolutely refuse to tolerate coming into being from one another" (Hamilton, 84).

25. *Protagoras* 331 D–332 A; Lamp, Loeb, 161. This passage is a good illustration of Plato's debt to Anaxagoras: "Well, at any rate, he said, justice has some resemblance to holiness; for anything in the world has some sort of resemblance to any other thing. Thus *there is a point in which white resembles black,* and hard soft, and so on with other things which are regarded as most opposed to each other; and the things we have spoken of before as having different δυνάμεις [331 D6] and not being the same kind as each other . . . these in some sense resemble one another and are of the same sort" (translation slightly altered and emphasis added). This passage also gives evidence

But this conditional recognition is not a sufficient explanation for our perception of an entity as a whole, since our intellect acts to distinguish one entity from its opposite. Each act of knowledge of an entity presumes a knowledge of the entity exclusive of its opposite. The intellect knows units, though it does not find them in the material world. It finds mixtures that seem like units and calls these mixtures after the units they seem most to be. The units after which material entities are called are the forms.[26] In the *Phaedo,* a form is the entity insofar as it exists without internal contradiction, that is, without the presence of its opposite. Since material entities are necessarily composed of contradictory parts, the forms are immaterial. That it neither contains nor produces its opposite is *the most important* description of the nature of a form in the *Phaedo.*[27]

---

of a point I made earlier: a common task among the early Presocratics was the organization of elementals into opposites, but by the time of Empedocles and *OAM,* the task has developed into finding a continuum between apparent opposites.

26. In *Plato's Theory of Understanding* (88–97), Moline develops the old argument that Plato's use of εἶδος depends on and develops out of the prior medical use of the term: this dependence on the medical tradition allows Plato to assume a common understanding of *eidos* that he can then build on. In chapter 15 of *On Ancient Medicine,* for example, powers that coexist in a mixture with other powers "participate" (κοινωνέω) in other forms. And later it is said that "If a humour that is sweet assumes another form (εἶδος), not by admixture, but by a self-caused change, what will it first become . . . ? I think acid" (*OAM* 24; Jones, Loeb 1:62–63). In both these passages, the identity of a power as a specific, particular power is described in terms of the existence of a form. Each change in a power is also a change of form; and coexistence of many powers is a participation in many forms. In "The Words εἶδος and ἰδέα in Pre-Platonic Literature," Taylor argued that εἶδος meant "substantial quality" (216), a claim that was disputed by later scholars, notably Jones, *Hippocratic Writings,* 1:10, and Baldry, "Plato's Technical Terms," 143. In the only passage of *OAM* where εἶδος is used with a sense of "the visible" (7:14), it means appearance as opposed to reality. Jones (71 and 93) and Taylor (214) believe that this use supports a conclusion that εἶδος moved from an earlier sensual or epistemological sense to a more metaphysical or constitutive sense.

There is a related use of ἰδέα in the Hippocratic authors. In the argument at *NoM* 5; Jones, Loeb 4:1215, ἰδέα refers to the visual traits, the "appearance" of the elementals. The different humors are distinguished from one another by their different appearances and their different powers: blood is unlike bile, both to sight and to touch. These differences are evidence of the real distinction between blood and bile, evidence that the author uses to refute those—"like Melissus"—who teach that by nature the human body is composed of only one element (and that this single component is the source of its unity). Appearances, then, are important as accurate indications of differences in natures or identity.

27. In *Against Eunomius* I, Gregory applies a similar kind of reasoning to argue for the generation by God the Father of a common nature in the Son, against Eunomius' claim of dissimilar natures between God and Son. As for Plato an immaterial form cannot produce something opposite to itself, so for Gregory an immaterial God cannot produce something opposite to himself. Gregory's argument, like Plato's, is couched in the language of elementals and quality-powers: "As heat and cold are by nature opposites—one might take as examples for the argument fire and ice,

## *Δύναμις in Plato's Account of Virtues*

In his early dialogues Plato uses δύναμις to discuss both definitions and the causal nature of virtues. For the early dialogues a virtue is understood as a δύναμις of the soul that produces an act or a condition with the same identifying characteristic as the virtue; for example, justice both produces acts that are "just," and is itself "just."[28] Virtuous acts are understood primarily in terms of their causes; a virtue is not so much an act as it is the capacity that produces an act.[29] Thus, in a didactic analogy to the virtue of courage, Socrates offers the definition of quickness that it is the "δύναμις that gets a great deal done in a little time."[30] This example makes clear that the definition of a virtue that is sought is not of the act itself—that is, quickness does not mean doing something fast—but rather of the capacity or faculty that produces the characteristic act or state. The causal principle of virtue is that of the Presocratic quality-powers: a cause can produce as an effect only what the cause is already. This is brought out clearly in the early *Protagoras,* where if the virtue justice produces acts that are just, then justice itself is just. In the early dialogue *Laches,* Plato will explore the nature of courage by analogy to speed, a physical δύναμις; in

---

each of which is what the other is not—and as the physical manifestations of each of these is quite different from each other,—it is characteristic of ice to make cool, of fire to warm. . . . If, then, goodness is attributed to the unbegotten being, and the begotten is, as they say, distinct in nature from the begotten, then surely the characteristic of the unbegotten will also differ from what characterizes the begotten. . . . Since the Father's being is held to be good, while that of the Son, because he is not like the Father in terms of being, so the heresy believes, is consequently found on the opposite side, what conclusion follows? What is opposed to the Good exists, and *from the Good itself what is contradictory* in nature *got existence*" (*GNO* 1:175:30–177:29; Hall, 110, emphasis added).

If Apostolopoulos' thesis on the literary influence of the *Phaedo* on Gregory's *On the Soul and Resurrection* is accepted, then one may see Gregory's argument in *Against Eunomius* I (written not more than a year after *On the Soul*) as theologically influenced by the *Phaedo*'s description of production by the forms. Gregory's use of this argument for the Trinity by analogy to the forms is, to my knowledge, a first. There is a general precedent in Philo, and doubtless he influenced Gregory, but Philo's argument, like many Christian arguments in the time between Philo and Gregory, centers on the *Logos,* a concept missing from Plato's and Gregory's arguments.

28. See, for example, *Meno* 78 C; *Lesser Hippias* 375 E2 ff.

29. *Laches* 191 E–192 C.

30. Ibid., 192 B. In order to emphasize the significance of δύναμις for Plato's thought and to illustrate the wide range of senses the term carried in his writings, I will often insert the Greek term in English translations.

Book I of the *Republic* Plato speaks of the causality of virtue in the language of the causality of heat and cold.[31] This, as Teloh points out,[32] continues the character-physics of the Presocratics and, more importantly (though Teloh does not point this out), the Hippocratics.

In an important passage in the *Charmides*,[33] Plato groups the δύναμις of wisdom with that of the hot, of speed, and of senses like hearing and sight, and of relations such as "greater than," "heavier than," and "less than." A definition of wisdom as the "science of itself and other sciences" is offered, and Plato discusses this as an example of self-predication, where the δύναμις has the object to which it is applied.[34] Thus, science is not the act of knowledge but the object of the act of knowledge. The question of whether powers can be applied to themselves is discussed in the dialogue predominantly in terms of cause or production. But the examples of production cited are the same as those in the *Phaedo:* the reified or monadic relations that are understood to be the paradoxes of opposite effects solved by the doctrine of the forms. This inherently relational sense of δύναμις is made explicit by examples of powers such as hearing and its object sound, and sight and its object color. In these examples there seems to be no suggestion of productivity but a causality of completed activity. There is also no suggestion in the dialogue of any difference between the δυνάμεις that are productive and those that are relational.[35] While in Hippocratic philos-

31. *Republic* 335 D.

32. *Development of Plato's Metaphysics,* 44.

33. Wisdom is introduced at 165 E, and there follows a lengthy discussion of the wisdom of wisdom, as it were. Δύναμις language is introduced at 168 B that is quickly (at 169 A) associated with Hippocratic-type examples of δύναμις causality: "But in the case of hearing or sight, or in the δύναμις of self-motion, and the δύναμις of heat to burn. . . ." The question of self-predication reads: ". . . whatever has its own δύναμις applied to itself will also have the οὐσία to which its δύναμις was applicable, will it not? For instance, hearing is, as we say, just a hearing of sound, is it not? . . . So if it is to hear itself it will hear a sound of its own; for it would not be otherwise. . . . And sight, I suppose . . . if it is to see itself, must have a color, for sight can never see what is colorless" (*Charmides* 168 D; Lamb, Loeb, 62–63).

34. Plato writes: ". . . this science is a science of something, that is, it has a certain δύναμις whereby it can be a science of something . . ." (*Charmides* 168 B; Lamb, Loeb, 6061). This understanding that science possesses what is to be known seems very similar to Aristotle's understanding that art has within it the work of art that art produces.

35. There is an unresolved ambiguity in the early dialogues as to whether virtues are themselves δυνάμεις of the soul, or whether virtues are psychic states that "have" δυνάμεις. Part of the ambiguity derives from Plato's own uncertainty as to whether a power can truly be fundamental. The question of fundamentality may be expressed in two ways: (1) Can powers really exist alone,

ophy, character-powers were self-predicable (that is, the hot was hot), Plato seems to be suggesting in the *Charmides* that some powers are not self-predicable, that is, there are some δυνάμεις that produce an effect that they themselves are not.[36]

In the *Protagoras* Plato gives an extended discussion of virtues as δυνάμεις by building upon the analogy between human virtues and physical, primarily animal, abilities.[37] This analogy is an important one for Plato. Physical abilities such as flight, speed, or strength that are peculiar to different animals are called δυνάμεις. In the myth of the *Protagoras* these powers are attributed to particular classes of animals in a special sense that precludes applying the δυνάμεις generally. Thus, the δύναμις of speed applies to a rabbit but cannot be applied to a human in the same sense, no matter how fast a runner. Another example of this sort is strength: strength is a power only of a particular class of animals, for example, bears, and the ability cannot be attributed to humans. Each δύναμις has a sense that is properly applied to a specific class of animals only, with no univocal meaning shared among other classes. However, the function that each specific δύναμις has in the definition of the appropriate creature(s) is analogous between classes. For instance, speed can only be attributed to certain classes of creatures, but the function of speed in the definition of a rabbit is analogous to that of strength in a bear, or virtue in a human.

### *Δύναμις in a Teleological Cosmology*

The reason for this univocal attribution is that δύναμις is properly understood only within a cosmological sense. That is, the necessity that binds

---

or are they necessarily associated with some other, prior, matter? This is the form of the critique of δύναμις in *OAM* (and perhaps the late Presocratics, for example, Anaxagoras). (2) Can a power alone give an adequate or true account of itself to the mind? Plato's use of a power/essence dichotomy, as in the *Cratylus*, and his developed theory of transcendent forms seem to suggest a negative answer—even in a relatively early dialogue like the *Cratylus*. Powers are not self-sufficent or self-explanatory but require a prior principle. The form theory of the *Phaedo* makes this clear, and so the forms provide what the pseudo-teleology of Anaxagoras fails to give.

36. This kind of discussion is important for Christian trinitarian theology because pro-Nicenes like Gregory will assume that God cannot produce (that is, generate) what He is not and so argue that anything produced by God must be what He is. Whatever ambiguity Plato may have exploited in this dialogue finds no place in the argument for the common nature between a δύναμις and its product.

37. The myth begins at 320 D.

each δύναμις to a particular limited class of animals is cosmological in origin. In myths this cosmological origin is expressed by the rationale of "compensation" (which is an "intentional" version of balance).[38] Each power is possessed as a balance to its opposite: for example, speed is the opposite of strength, and these two are never found together. Speed may be understood as a positive version of "unstrength," just as strength is a positive version of "unspeed" (as distinguished from opposites such as speedy/slow, strong/weak).[39] The cosmological principle of balance also requires that there is a limit to both the number of different powers to be distributed and the incidence of each power. Both the understanding of opposite powers balancing and the limited number of possible attributions of a power serve to suggest the material nature of these δυνάμεις.

The mythic or cosmological explanation of the delegation of powers according to a principle of compensation portrays the previously discussed problem of associated powers. To the extent that the myth was believed, it solved the problem of explaining why certain powers either are or are not associated with one another and are characteristic of particular things. The *Protagoras* myth could have had some appeal for Plato, since it offers a primitive teleological explanation of associated powers; some attributes—the δυνάμεις—serve to identify and distinguish classes of creatures that

38. This geometrical principle of balance or equality is found in nearly all the Preplatonic cosmologists. See, for example pages 105–10 of Kahn's "Anaximander's Fragment: the Universe Governed by Law," in *The Presocratics,* ed. A. P. D. Mourelatos (New York: Anchor Press, 1974), 99–117. The expression "balanced opposites" is, according to Kahn (*Anaximander and the Origins of Greek Cosmology,* 187), found in Parmenides' description of "The two symmetrical forms which together fill the cosmic sphere": "The All is full at once of Light and Night, both equal, since neither has any part in the other" (*fragment* 9, Cornford's translation in *Plato and Parmenides* 47). Empedocles places great emphasis on his doctrine of balance between the character–powers Love and Strife, for he describes these two as being "equal in length and breath" (fragment B17:20). It remains an evident law of thought through to Aristotle's time, as when he says, "The opposites must always be in a state of equality" (*Physics* 204b13).

39. In *Protagoras* 332–33, Plato develops a list of at least seven opposites: wisdom/folly, temperance/foolishness, strength/weakness, swiftness/slowness, beauty/ugliness, good/evil, and shrill-voiced/deep-voiced. His point is that each thing has only one opposite. I assume this point is a kind of axiom attached to the polarity cosmology described in the previous chapter. Plato continues to dwell on this axiom in various ways over his writings since he is not sure how the relation holds among immaterials. By Gregory's time the idea that each thing has only one opposite is a commonplace, but no less powerful for that: I have already cited Gregory's argument at GNO I:176–77, where he assumes that in the immaterial realm what is not truly good (that is, is not God) must be its opposite.

other characteristics—for example, shapes, size, color—do not.[40] This is the working premise of the *Cratylus.* But what begins in the *Protagoras* as a myth about material abilities becomes, in Plato's hands, logical categories. In the *Protagoras* Socrates is asking whether the virtues differ from one another in a way similar to the way one lump of gold differs from another or whether they differ as one sense differs from another, for example, sight from hearing. This latter difference is for Plato not just one of quantity but one of kind. As Savan points out, the δύναμις of sight is seeing, and the δύναμις of justice is just acts, so δύναμις in this regard means the essential or identifying act of any given thing.[41] Teloh goes further and remarks that the conclusion that justice, holiness, etc., each has a δυνάμεις allows Socrates to obtain from Protagoras[42] the conclusion that justice, holiness, etc., are themselves things (πρᾶγμα).[43] What has a δύναμις is necessarily a thing. So the δύναμις is the identifying (or fundamental) act of a thing, which by virtue of its affectiveness denotes an existent. This is very close to the "mark" of what really exists in the *Sophist,* as we shall see. However, though a δύναμις specifies some existent thing, it does not seem to specify only simple things, that is, only objects with one identifying act. Justice and holiness turn out to be the same thing, virtue, just as seeing and hearing are parts of the same head.

In his own cosmology Plato replaces the intentionality expressed in Protagoras' mythic drama of Prometheus handing out δυνάμεις with a teleology based on transcendent principles. The forms of Middle Period dialogues are often described in the language of final causality.[44] More importantly, there is a recurring discussion of the activity of a Cosmological Νοῦς or Ψυχή that is the source of order and activity for all nature. In discussing this transcendent Mind/Soul, Plato makes a consistent use of δύναμις that is common to all periods of the dialogues.[45]

40. This list of distinguishing characteristics, that is, color, shape, comes from Plato himself: "In a δύναμις I cannot see any *color or shape* or similar mark such as those on which in many other cases I fix my eyes in discriminating in my thought one thing from another" (*Republic* 477 D, emphasis added; Shorey, Loeb, 523).

41. "Self-predication," 132.

42. At *Protagoras* 330 B–E.

43. *Development of Plato's Metaphysics,* p. 45.

44. Ibid., 133–38.

45. The expectation that Plato uses δύναμις in the *Timaeus* to describe the Demiurge is not borne out: the three occasions—*Timaeus* 28 A5–B1, 41 C3–5, 46 E3–7—when the two terms are used in proximity, the term δύναμις is extraneous to any description of the Demiurge and there

One of the earliest examples of this use of δύναμις is in the *Phaedo* where Plato again uses δύναμις to refer to that principle that ". . . causes things to be now placed as it is best for them to be placed, [and] . . . the good which must embrace and hold together all things."[46] This, again, is in a discussion inspired by Anaxagoras' claim that Mind governs the Cosmos.[47] Δύναμις in this passage is a cause that provides not only material order or harmony in nature but is also a final cause that provides the good of each object. The analogy to the soul and the body is not as clear as it will be in the *Cratylus,* but the relationship is supplied by the central question of the dialogue: the immortality of the soul. The immateriality of this δύναμις is evident from the Anaxagorean reference and the doctrine of the forms introduced shortly thereafter. This immateriality qualifies the δύναμις of the Mind/Soul to be the first principle of the Cosmos since, as mentioned earlier, only an immaterial cause can offer a satisfactory teleological causality.

In the *Cratylus,* Plato uses an analogy to describe the relationship of the Mind/Soul to nature. He suggests that as the soul is the δύναμις which

---

is no suggestion of a link between the two terms. Similarly no other passages in Plato seem to offer the basis for describing the cosmic capacity to create as a demiurgic power. (Aristotle offers nothing as well.) Scholarly descriptions of the Demiurge as a "power" cannot be trusted. R. G. Bury, for example, notes that "the role of the . . . 'Demiurge' is similar to that of the Anaxagorean 'Nous' . . . ," though only with some important qualifications: the Demiurge did not produce *ex nihilo,* he does not continue to act directly, etc. (I do not know from where Bury learns what Anaxagoras thought the *Nous* did or did not do.) Then Bury adds: ". . . later on [in the *Timaeus*] we hear of . . . 'the Divine Power' . . ." and in the *Philebus* "many phrases . . . echo the language of the *Timaeus,* describing the Efficient cause as a 'Demiurgic' power (27 B) . . ." (R. G. Bury, *Plato with an English Translation,* in *Timaeus, Cleitophon, Critias, Menexenus,* and *Epistles,* intro., comm., and trans. R. G. Bury, vol. 7, The Loeb Classical Library [Cambridge: Harvard University Press, 1929], 7–8). Δύναμις does not occur in any of these passages.

46. *Phaedo* 99 C; Hamilton, 80.

47. I have already mentioned the *Phaedo* reference (at 99 C) to the doctrine of a δύναμις which governs the universe, given in a lengthy discussion of Anaxagoras' doctrine of a Νοῦς that gives purpose to all things (at 97 C ff.): after Plato lists (and discounts) various material cosmologies (for example, the earth is held up by vortexes or a column of air), he refers, in contrast, to the teaching of a δύναμις which disposes all things "in the best possible way." The reference is so oblique (as Burnet suggests in his still useful textual commentary on *Plato's Phaedo,* 107–8) that it seems to assume that the listener/reader will know and recognize the connection between δύναμις and Anaxagoras' teaching. There are, however, no extant fragments of Anaxagoras' where he refers to the cosmic mind as a δύναμις. Plato does not use δύναμις for his own doctrine on the ordered universe (for example, he never speaks of the demiurge as being or having a power), and I am willing to accept that Anaxagoras did indeed formulate his doctrine using δύναμις.

causes life in the body, so the Mind/Soul is the δύναμις which causes order and holds all nature (φύσις).[48] This analogy is made with Anaxagoras in mind, for he is offered as the proof-text for the activity of the Mind/Soul.[49] That the cosmic Mind/Soul was a δύναμις seems to have been part of the received cosmology of the day. Though there are no extant texts from the Presocratics where the Mind/Soul is referred to as a δύναμις, Plato describes it as such in this dialogue and others with no self-consciousness and with none of the proferred definitions that characterize many of his doctrinal debuts or neologisms.[50]

## *The* Cratylus *and the Linguistic Sense of Δύναμις*

The use of *power* in the psychology of virtues is not the only important early use of δύναμις. In the *Cratylus,* Plato applies a δύναμις causality to the "action" of words (and their components) upon the mind. This "linguistic sense" of δύναμις is a special feature of the *Cratylus* (with a few later references). The use of *powers* in the *Cratylus* is of special interest for this study due to its role in the Eunomian controversy, and this dialogue will be considered in detail before moving on to the psychological sense and other uses that were more characteristic of Plato's philosophy.[51]

In the discussion on naming in the *Cratylus,* δύναμις is used with three specific senses. First, there is the δύναμις or sense or meaning of the word or name itself.[52] (In the *Cratylus* all words are names of some thing. Thus,

48. *Cratylus* 399 E–400 B.

49. Ibid., 400 A.

50. Grundmann argues in his article on δύναμις for the *Theological Dictionary of the New Testament,* 2:284–317, that the "oldest example [of δύναμις as a cosmic principle] is to be found in a larger fragment of the Pythagorean Philolaos [namely, It is necessary to consider the works [ἔργα] and the being [οὐσία] of number according to the power [δύναμις] which is the decad]" (286). Grundmann makes this judgment because he considers the fragment to be authentically Pythagorean, an opinion that most scholars no longer hold. The "oldest example of δύναμις as a cosmic principle" must therefore be either Anaxagoras *via* Plato, or Plato.

51. Gregory was the first to suggest that Eunomius borrowed his theory from that dialogue at *Against Eunomius* 2, *GNO* 1:344:13. The question whether Eunomius was influenced by the *Cratylus,* either directly or indirectly by way of a commentary, has played a central role in modern scholarship on the Eunomian controversy where the *Cratylus* has been presented as the basis for determining philosophical influences on Eunomius. See Daniélou, "Eunome l'Arien et l'exégèse néoplatonicienne du *Cratyle.*"

52. This sense of δύναμις appears regularly in Gregory's *Against Eunomius,* especially book 2, which is the work most concerned with refuting Eunomius' theory of language. For example, at *GNO* 1:265:20, Gregory says that all divine attributes or titles of God have the same δύναμις. One

"word" and "name" are interchangable translations for the Greek ὄνομα.) Second, a name refers to the δύναμις of the object named, δύναμις here meaning something like its intelligible presence. And third, each part of a word, the letters and syllables, has a δύναμις, that is, that by which it signifies. Aside from these linguistic applications of δύναμις, there is in the dialogue the recurring psychological sense of *power* common to all three periods of dialogues.

At the beginning of the *Cratylus,* Plato considers the problem of synonyms. The sort of synonym that is discussed specifically is that of proper nouns, names such as Hector or Astyanax (which both name the same person). However, the question is understood more generally as having to do with all cases where two or more different words refer to the same one thing. In this regard, words from different languages, such as *cat* and *le chat,* are considered to be synonyms. Their variety of syllables makes such words appear different, but only to the "uninitiated." Just as the physician can recognize specific drugs even if they are mixed with coloring or perfume, so too, according to Plato, the "man who knows about names" is not fooled by the camouflage of different sounds or spellings. Thus, Astyanax, Hector, and Archepolis all mean King, just as the words Agis, Polemarchus, and Eupolemus all mean General. Plato calls what is recognized in each of these names, despite their camouflage, the δύναμις of a word. Continuing the medical analogy, as the power of each drug remains the same despite the additions, so too the power of each name remains the same despite variations in spelling.[53] What remains about a drug is its medical property or its effect, and what remains about a name is its sense or meaning, or that by which the meaning is communicated.[54] The active or productive sense evident in the medical example applies in the case of definitions: the meaning or reference that is shared by many synonyms produces the same effect

---

particularly interesting play upon the linguistic sense of δύναμις occurs in *Against Eunomius* 2:4; *GNO* 2:147:23–148:4. At 147:23, Gregory turns from a long description (which begins at 146:27) of the Son as the Δύναμις of God, by which the Father has all works (ἔργα), to the δύναμις of Eunomius' argument (at 148:4), thereby implicitly contrasting God's saving Δύναμις with Eunomius'.

53. Moline remarks in *Plato's Theory of Understanding,* 67, that "Plato's theory of the power of words is modeled upon Greek theories of nutrition. . . ."

54. This medical sense of δύναμις remains: Gregory refers to the destructive δύναμις of a poison in *Against Eunomius* 2; *GNO* 1:390:21.

in each case, that is, knowledge of the thing named. (That the δύναμις of words has effects upon the mind is found again in the *Philebus,* 24 C2.)

This is another application of the causal principle of material participation or transmission discussed in other early dialogues. In the *Phaedo* (102–3) Plato discusses this principle in the context of names: particulars, he says, are named after the form. Brentlinger puts it this way: ". . . the linguistic dependence of the names of the particulars upon the names of the qualities in them, is founded on the ontological dependence of the qualities of particulars upon the quality of the pure quality present in them."[55] An example of this in the *Cratylus* is the etymology of the name Poseidon. The φύσις of the sea acted (ἐγένετο 402 E2) upon Poseidon (in his unnamed state) as a restraint upon his feet. Poseidon is named after this δύναμις of restraint that is an effect or quality of the sea (402 E4).

Plato gives two descriptions of the knowledge provided by a name. In the first description a name refers to the δύναμις of the object named.[56] Δύναμις in this usage seems to be most properly translated as distinctive property, function, or defining characteristic. For example, Plato remarks on the appropriateness of the name Apollo because it "aptly indicates" the four powers of the god: his abilities in music, prophecy, medicine, and archery.[57] Later, the list of δυνάμεις properly signified by the name Apollo includes "ever-darting, "purifying," and "accompanying."[58] There is a similar use of δύναμις in the *Symposium.*[59]

55. Brentlinger, "Incomplete Predicates and the Two-World Theory of the *Phaedo,*" 68.

56. In *Against Eunomius* 2, *GNO* 1:305:24, Gregory says that things are named according to the φύσις and δυνάμεις of the thing; he means by this statement that some names refer to the thing as a unity, that is, words that name the φύσις (for example, fire), while other names refer to the multiple characteristics or properties of a thing, that is, words that name the δυνάμεις (for example, shining, burning, drying, heating, etc.).

57. *Cratylus* 404 E–405 A.

58. *Ibid.,* 405 E–406 A, Fowler, Loeb, p. 76.

59. *Symposium* 202 E. The practice of finding etymologies for the names of the gods by analyzing their characteristic functions (or δυνάμεις) is emphasized by Eusebius of Caesarea in *Preparation of the Gospel* III in his quotations from Porphyry, who, in the fashion of the *Cratylus,* finds the origins of the names of Gods in their distinctive powers. (Eusebius introduces the quotations from Porphyry by referring to the *Cratylus* at 103 C.) In *La preparation evangelique,* ed. and trans. Édouard des Places, SC 228 (Paris: Les Éditions du Cerf, 1976), 210, III, II, 5, Hera is called after the δύναμις of ether. At 212, III, II, 7, Hestia is derived from the δύναμις of earth, just as at 214, III, II, 14, Themis is called after the δύναμις of prophecy. Eusebius' point in adducing these

The second description in the *Cratylus* of the knowledge provided by names is that they refer to the οὐσία of an object. After Plato establishes the existence of primary "fundamental" names out of which other names are built, he describes names as imitations and discusses what names should properly imitate.[60] Those aspects of objects, such as color, shape, or sound, he says are not proper objects of imitation in a name. For this reason, painting, graphic design or sketches, and sound imitations such as bird-calls are not names. On the contrary, names imitate the οὐσία of an object.[61] The contrast of οὐσία with aspects such as color, shape, or sound suggests that οὐσία means "essential quality," or the "thing *per se*." (However, in the *Charmides,* οὐσία seems to refer to the secondary characteristics.) The relationship between the οὐσία of an object and its aspects such as color, shape, sound, etc., may be in parallel to the dialogue's earlier contrast between the δύναμις of a name, which remains constant and is that

---

etymologies is to show that the pagan Greeks understood the gods as corporeal: early civilizations (like the Cretans), for example, understood Zeus as a man, mortal even if heroic, while the Greeks identified their gods with elemental forces; Zeus was identified with fire. Eusebius' purpose in this argument is not only to stress the Christian doctrine of the immaterial nature of God (and to turn the charge by pagan apologists back upon them that Christians had a crass theology) but to stress that it is the "rational and immortal mind in man's nature" that most resembles God as an image and likeness. The mind is judged to be like God because it, as in the case of God, is immaterial and incorporeal, intelligent and rational, and capable of virtue and wisdom. Gregory offers versions of Eusebius' argument in his *On the Soul and Resurrection* and *On the Making of Man;* in the first work Gregory is not concerned with any trinitarian interpretations of this image and likeness, while in *On the Making of Man* he is.

60. Aristotle's summary of the senses of στοιχεία in *Metaphysics* Delta 3, 1014a25 ff., is worth quoting, for it can help a modern reader to see the unity among the varied uses of the term: "By an element we mean 1) the first constituent of which a thing is composed and which is indivisible in kind into other kinds; for example, the elements of speech are those of which speech is composed and into which it is ultimately divisible, while they can no longer be divided into other parts of speech distinct in kind from them. And even if they are divisible, but the parts are of the same kind, they are called 'elements'; for example, a part of water is water, while a part of a syllable is not a syllable. Similarly, those who speak of the elements of bodies mean the parts into which the bodies are ultimately divided, while those parts are no longer divisible into other parts differing in kind; and whether such parts are one or more, they are called 'elements'. . . . 2) Also, by a transfer of meaning men call 'an element' that which, being one and small, is useful for many things; and so the small and the simple and the indivisible is called 'an element'. Hence it comes about that the most universal objects are elements, in view of the fact that each of them, being one and simple, belongs to many or to all or to most; and on this account, unity and the point are thought by some to be principles" (trans. Hippocrates P. Apostle in *Metaphysics* [1966; reprint, Bloomington: Indiana University Press, 1973], 76).

61. *Cratylus* 423 E ff.; Fowler, Loeb, 137.

which informs, versus the syllables, letters, and sounds that make up any particular word and that may obscure its true meaning.

Imitation occurs at the level of the letters themselves. Despite having rejected examples such as bird-calls as names, Plato's notion of imitation remains alliterative rather than symbolic, for the act or material of imitation occurs at a phonetic level, that is, the letters, symbols, etc., of a word.[62] And despite his earlier rejection of painting as naming, Plato uses the painting of portraits to describe imitation by sounds. Just as the pigments in paints resemble the colors of the original, so too the sounds of the letters make phonetic resemblance possible, as this quotation illustrates:

> . . . names can never be like anything unless those elements of which names are composed exist in the first place and possess some kind of likeness to the things which the names imitate.[63]

Words are images of the things they name, "painted" in the resembling sounds of the letters out of which words are made. For instance, the letters δ and τ are appropriate imitations of the stationary nature referred to in the words δεσμεύω, "to bind," and στάσιμος, "stationary." The appropriateness of the imitation of specific essence by sounds is determined by the ability of a letter to suggest that "essential quality" in pronunciation. The appropriateness of a letter, or its capacity to imitate, is called the δύναμις of the letter.[64] The δύναμις of the letter γ stops the tongue and is thus appropriate to imitate things of a halting nature. The aforementioned letters δ and τ have the power to imitate "binding" and "rest." Just as the pigments of the paints carry the color(s) the original possesses, the δύναμις of a letter imitates the δύναμις of the object.[65]

By describing words as imitations of the essence, Plato clearly means that the ontological status of words is less than that of the essence or object. Imitations, by definition, lack the reality of the originals. Though the no-

62. *Ibid.*, 429 B9; 139.

63. *Ibid.*, 434 B1–7, p. 171.

64. One finds a general form of this description of the δύναμις of letters in Basil's *Epistle* 235: when we learn to read, Basil says, "we must first believe that the letter a is said to us; then we learn the characters and their pronunciation, and last of all we get the distinct idea of the δύναμις [meaning *sense*] of the letter" (NPNF 8:275).

65. The language of "likeness" predominates in this part of the *Cratylus:* ὅμοια at 433 C, 434 A5, and 435 E1; μιμήματα at 434 B7 and μιμέομαι at 434 B2; and εἰκών at 433 C6 and 439 A5, to name but the most obvious cases.

tion of imitation initially suggests what is common to the original and image, the notion also requires a fundamental difference between the two. This is made explicit in the discussion of the portrait where Socrates points out to Cratylus that a portrait with all the properties of Cratylus would not be a portrait after all. In the same way, a word with all the properties of the object named would not be a name, but the thing itself. What is additional to an object, though missing in a name, is not the aspects of an object—color, sound, etc.—but something important to real knowledge, something loosely called ἀλήθεια. In Stoic logic δύναμις will be given as one of the criteria of ἀλήθεια.[66]

*Power and Means of Knowing*

In the *Cratylus* Plato also applies the same causal principle to the act of naming as he earlier applied to names themselves. If the intellect (here, διάνοια) gives names, or more precisely, if the intellect produces names, then the intellect must have the quality of names or naming as itself. Using Plato's language, we could say that naming is a δύναμις of the intellect, as the soul is the cause and power of life to the body, or the Cosmic Mind is the cause and power of order in all nature. If the intellect is a cause of names, then there is something common between the intellect and the names it produces. This commonality may be best expressed if we understand "the intellect produces names" as a parallel expression to "the beautiful produces beautiful [things]." (That the "naming" act of the intellect—the διάνοια—is a power is indicated even in the late dialogue *Critias* where

66. The Stoics apparently included a linguistic sense of δύναμις (i.e., meaning or function), along with οὐσία (essence or substance) and σύστασις (constitution or structure), in their logical criteria for distinguishing between "truth [ἡ ἀλήθεια]" and "the true [το ἀληθές]". Louis Roberts, "Origen and Stoic Logic", describes these two distinctions so: "The difference in essence is that the true is incorporeal, because it attaches to the proposition. Truth and the true differ in constitution because truth implies knowledge of a number of truths, while the true is something simple. And they differ in meaning because truth pertains to knowledge, while the true does not." The use of these two categories by Origen helps to understand the point of the distinction: "He [Origen] constantly uses truth to refer to the reality of the 'mystery' of the world of ideas, to what he considers the substantial character of the *Logos*, and 'true reason' as such. The true he takes as a property of a proposition." *Ibid.*, 437. Anthony Long also describes the distinction and the three criteria in his "Stoic Distinction Between Truth and the True" in *Les Stöiciens*, 297–315. For more on δύναμις as a term in Stoic logic, see J. Moreau, "Immutabilité du Vrai. Necessité logique et lien causal," in *Les Stöiciens*, 347–360, especially 352.

Plato uses both the terms διάνοια and δύναμις to denote the meaning of a word, as Souilhé points out.)[67]

Such an interpretation seems close to Plato's own thought in the Middle Period dialogue, the *Republic.* In Book 5, Plato calls the intellect—still meaning διάνοια—a power of the mind, and makes the general proposition that for each power—δύναμις—of the mind there is a separate object of knowledge. (Similarly, in the *Timaeus,* mind and true opinion are related to separate objects of knowledge.)[68] Thus, the objects known by that power διάνοια are ontologically different from those known by that power νόησις or the power ἐπιστήμη.[69] Each power or δύναμις knows its "own" objects, and each object is appropriate to a particular power because of something common to both the power and its set of objects of knowledge.

Plato does not specify what each noetic power has in common with its object(s) of knowledge nor how objects of knowledge of one δύναμις differ from objects of knowledge of another δύναμις. Brentlinger suggests that the objects differ from one another as degrees of reality.[70] This seems to correspond to the divided line discussion in the *Republic,* and Brentlinger interprets *Timaeus* 29 B as supporting his suggestion. In the *Cratylus* Plato seems to apply a scheme of degrees of reality to cognition: there is the example of knowing the "true meaning" of a word that both exists, despite different spellings—perhaps independent of any spelling—and is distributed among its synonyms. This cognition is directly analogous, as Plato remarks, to that of medical knowledge perceiving the true, that is, causal, identity of a medically-active object despite the camouflage of added colors or odors.

### *Active and Passive Powers*

In his early dialogues the basic understanding that Plato has of δύναμις is that of an affective capacity. All entities have a δύναμις which is in relation to, or is applied to, some specific object or state. The relationship between the δύναμις and object is generally one of productive cause and effect, though in some cases the sense is that of agent and instrument.

67. *Étude,* 131–32.

68. *Timaeus* 51 D.

69. *Republic* 477 E–478 A.

70. Brentlinger, "The Divided Line and Plato's Theory of Intermediates," *Phronesis* 8 (1963): 146–66, esp. 158–59.

Examples of the first sense, that is, cause and effect, are: the hot and heat, speediness and getting things done quickly, and justice and just acts. Examples of the second sense, that is, agent and instrument, are: hearing and sound, and sight and color. Plato does not make any explicit distinction between these two sorts of relationships, but he does wonder whether δύναμις can be divided into classes, according to the object or recipient of their act. This question occurs in the early dialogue *Charmides* where Plato asks whether any δύναμις possesses the object of its activity. Those powers that possess their product would fall into the category of productive cause and effect, while those powers that do not possess the object of their activity correspond to the category of agent and instrument.

Despite the importance of the concept *power* in Plato's early thought, it is not until his Middle Period dialogue, the *Republic,* that Plato gives a specific definition of *power:*

> Shall we say that δυνάμεις are a class of entities by virtue of which we and all other things are able to do what we do or they are able to do? I mean that sight and hearing, for example, are powers. . . . [71]

The definition plays upon the non-philosophical sense of the verb δύναμαι, as in δυνάμεθα and δύναται, meaning "can do" or "are capable." Though the definition begins with common usage, Plato shifts to the technical philosophical language quickly:

> In a power I cannot see any color or shape or similar mark such as those on which in many other cases I fix my eyes in discriminating in my thought one thing from another. But in the case of a power I look to one thing only—that to which it is related and what it effects, and it is in this way that I come to call each of them a power. . . .[72]

The affective or productive sense of *power* is emphasized in two distinct uses that tend to be associated with dialogue periods. In the early dialogues, *power* has a productive sense—which is characteristic of the psy-

71. Φήσομεν δυνάμεις εἶναι γένος τι τῶν ὄντων, αἷς δὴ καὶ ἡμεῖς δυνάμεθα ἃ δυνάμεθα καὶ ἄλλο πᾶν ὃ τί περ ἂν δύνηται, οἷον λέγω ὄψιν καὶ ἀκοὴν τῶν δυνάμεων εἶναι. . . . *Republic* 477 C ff. The translation is by Shorey, Loeb, p. 523, slightly altered. Shorey draws attention to the history of δύναμις, and refers to Souilhé's work. To communicate the richness of δύναμις he translates it as "faculties, powers, abilities". Rather than stumble over such ambiguities, I simply use δύναμις or power.

72. *Republic* 477 C–D, Shorey, Loeb, 523–524.

chic virtues. In the later dialogues, the productive sense is used in the discussion of material causes and characteristic effects, including examples that are typical of either the Presocratic Cosmologists or the Hippocratics. Neither the early nor the late periods of dialogues exclude the "dependent" sense of *power,* though its use is not as common as in those dialogues of the Middle Period.

Plato expands on his understanding of dependent powers by suggesting that such powers exist in pairs. Plato applies the word δύναμις to both the affective capacity and to that which is affected. Each active power then is related to a (symmetrical), corresponding passive power, without which the active power either has no effect or cannot act. Thus, the power of sight depends upon the "power of being seen," etc.[73] Powers are not causes absolutely but are such only when matched with the corresponding instrument or receptor. Plato is not able to explain exactly how these two powers are connected, except to say that the gods "yoked" them together. This is restated in the *Theaetetus,* which was written shortly after the *Republic.* (Some scholars say immediately after.)

> Of each kind there are any number of instances, but they differ in that one kind has the power of acting, the other the power of being acted upon. From the intercourse and friction of these with one another arise offspring, endless in number, but in pairs of twins. One of each pair is something perceived, the other a perception, whose birth coincides with that of the thing perceived. [74]

Though this text deals with the process of perception, this is still clearly a more sophisticated attempt to say that powers are "yoked" together. It is also a definite development from the pairing-off in the *Charmides.* There, only the active member of the pair is described as a power, for example, sight, hearing—while the second member—color, sound—is described as an essence. This difference of terminology suggests that there is a difference in kind-of-being between the two, even if essence—οὐσία—is not used in any special technical sense (as seems to be so). By the time of the *Republic* and the *Theaetetus,* Plato had seen that the pair are of the same kind of being—γένος τῶν ὄντων—and that the unity of the pairs of powers must

73. *Republic* 507 E.
74. *Theaetetus* 156 D, Hamilton, 861.

be reflected in a corresponding terminology. The need for this unified terminology is expressed in the *Theaetetus.*[75]

It is in this context of the *Theaetetus* discussion of the interaction of powers in sensation that Plato offers an important new term. When the (active) power of a sense meets the (passive) power of the object perceived a third entity (or entities, since Plato speaks of "twins") is "born."[76] These twins are that which is perceived, twin-1 as it exists in the sense organ and twin-2 as it exists in the sensed object. Both these twins are called by the same name, quality or ποίημα. *Theaetetus* 182 A is generally regarded as the debut of this term, and Plato's initial description of the term is interesting.

> That any one of these things [whiteness, hotness, other perceptions] is something that moves in place, simultaneously with a perception, between agent [the object perceived] and the patient [the sense organ]; and that the patient [the sense organ] becomes perceptive, and not a perception, while the agent [the object perceived] comes to have a quality rather than to be a quality. [77]

"Quality" means the perceived characteristic produced by the intercourse of the two powers and is to be distinguished from the material quality-power after which the quality is named. Thus, the object comes to "have" a quality, rather than "to be" a quality: a quality, say whiteness, is something different from white, the quality-power. The sense organ becomes perceptive and not a perception; the reception of the quality is not the transformation of the sense organ into the affecting material quality-power. This is important. Perception is no longer conceived of as a spread of a material quality-power whereby the sense organ becomes what it perceives. What one attributes to the object in terms of perception, for example, the quality of whiteness, is not the same as what one attributes to the object in terms of its existent parts, for example, the power white. Plato distinguishes this perception, whiteness, from the material object and the sense organ that together produce it. Neither the material object nor the sense organ is "whiteness." The old question from the *Charmides* of whether a power applied to itself has the object of that power is now answered "No." The power is material; its "object of perception" is not.

75. *Theaetetus* 156 B ff.

76. *Ibid.*

77. *Theaetetus* 182 A–B, Hamilton, 886.

### *Power and Identity in Natural Causes*

In those dialogues that deal with the objects of natural science—for example, the *Timaeus,* parts of *Sophist* and *Philebus*—δύναμις means either that which produces characteristic effects or those characteristic effects themselves. For example, in the *Timaeus* when Plato describes the four classes of "fiery" liquids, he says:

> . . . there is the oily [sort of liquid], which is smooth and divides the visual ray, and for this reason is bright and shining and of a glistening appearance, including pitch, the juice of the castorberry, oil itself, and the other things which possess this δύναμις. . . .[78]

The next class of liquids are those which "expand the contracted parts of the mouth" and by this power cause sweetness, as, for example, honey.

In the first example quoted, *power* refers to the characteristic of being "smooth and divid[ing] the visual ray" etc., while the second use of *power* suggests the capacity that produces a characteristic. Similar uses can be found elsewhere in the dialogue, where *power* refers in one case to the characteristic effect(s) of the four elements and then to the elements themselves. In the *Philebus* δύναμις is applied to the characteristics of fire and the other elements (29 B), while elsewhere in the *Philebus* δύναμις is the capacity to cause—τῆς αἰτίας δύναμιν.[79] These examples show that, as in the Hippocratic use of δύναμις, the distinction between the productive capacity and its characteristic effect(s) is neither strong nor consistent. Plato's "failure" to distinguish the two depends upon his retention of the understanding that a cause contains its effects; this axiom is developed explicitly in the dialogue. Plato emphasizes the continuity between cause and effect generally, whether between a power and its object, or being (whatever the term used) and power, for—as with the Hippocratics—it is this continuity that serves as the foundation of knowledge.

### *The Return to a Teleological Cosmology*

Plato returns to the description of the cosmic Mind/Soul as a δύναμις, and the analogy to the human body, in the *Philebus,* one of his last dia-

78. *Timaeus* 60 A–B, Hamilton, 1185.
79. *Philebus* 30 D, Fowler, Loeb, 269.

logues. In this dialogue, Plato reworks the Prometheus myth—the same myth used in the *Protagoras*—and gives a system of cosmological causes of being: the Limited, the Unlimited, the mixture of the two, and the cause of this mixture. Unlike the forms of Middle Period dialogues, there is no statement in *Philebus* that these causes are transcendent to the material world. Instead, the images are those of immanence, of causes working from within. Plato moves easily from applying statements learned from "looking inwards" to our interior δύναμις[80] (as in the early psychological dialogues) to the cosmos as a whole and vice versa. The ability to make such comparisons depends upon the organic unity between our interior self, that is, our souls, and the Soul of the cosmos. The analogy between humanity and the cosmos is a proportion—our material parts are to the Cosmic Element-powers as our soul is to the Cosmic Mind or Soul. The language of *power* applied in earlier dialogues describing the capacity of the soul to affect material parts is retained: the causality of the Mind that orders the cosmos is called a power.[81] Plato acknowledges that this doctrine of Cosmic Mind is not his originally but comes from a predecessor, Anaxagoras.[82]

Plato's criticisms of accounts of being based on mixture physics in dialogues like the *Sophist* and *Philebus* express a common point: any account of existence that never gets beyond being as elemental parts (for example, powers, atoms, etc.) cannot be an account with a teleology. Teleological existence, which means teleological causality, can only be attributed to a unity, as Plato says in the *Sophist:*

> Whenever a thing comes into being [οὐσία], at that moment it has come to be as a whole; accordingly, if you do not reckon unity or wholeness among real things, you have no right to speak of either being, or coming-into-being as having any existence.[83]

Anaxagoras and the other Presocratics (excluding Parmenides, whose

80. *Philebus* 58 D.

81. *Philebus* 30 D, 31 A.

82. *Philebus* 30 D. Plato's argument from the relation between the psychological and the cosmological, and the suitability of δύναμις to describe both realms, illustrate a point worth noting in passing. They make clear an important feature of much of Greek philosophy in general and of Platonism in particular: unlike modern sciences, there is no firm division in methodology or language between those different subjects of discourse, such as cosmology or psychology.

83. *Sophist* 245 D, Hamilton, 989.

failure is of a different nature) failed to describe a teleological system and fell into materialism because they attributed fundamental existence to discrete autonomous parts. For Plato, the first effect of the teleological cause, the Good, is unity: its first product, οὐσία (or whatever name this "cause of unity" is known by). He makes this point regularly through the different periods of the dialogues. In the famous passage from the *Republic* (509 B), the Good produces the οὐσία, which is the cause of intelligibility and existence. (I return to this passage shortly.) In the *Philebus,* he says:

> Every instance of generation is for the sake of some being [οὐσία], or another, and generation in general is for the sake of being in general.[84]

In this case, οὐσία is understood to be a particular thing in the material world; it is the "reason to be" for δύναμις. The effect of the Good is to provide a principle of unity and/or substantial definition that is the necessary connection among specific powers and secondary characteristics or effects such as qualities. Plato states this in the *Philebus,* where the activity of the Good is expressed in terms of beauty, that is, measure and proportion. Due to beauty, compounds and mixtures are held together as one since ". . . any compound, however made, which lacks measure and proportion, must necessarily destroy its components and first of all itself; for it is in truth no compound, but an uncompounded jumble.[85]

Beauty here means measure and proportion, valued states suggestive of Presocratic element-powers. The activity of harmonizing is the most important power of the Good because it enables existence at all levels: this harmonizing causes essence (οὐσία), which in turn produces compounds and entities. Without beauty, as here defined, mixtures would never make up entities but would remain indistinguishable muddles. Thus, the early questions of how and why disparate qualities become entity-mixtures are re-addressed. Unlike the apparent solution of the transcendent forms, the answer here is in terms of ends or essences that are nonetheless material. The hot, the cold,[86] or any attribute that can be said to be more or less, etc., is called "indeterminate" (often misleadingly translated "infinite").[87] The

84. *Philebus* 54 C, Fowler, Loeb, 354–355.

85. *Philebus* 64 D–E, Fowler, Loeb, 388–389.

86. *Philebus* 24 A–25 A.

87. The "Indeterminate" consists, for instance, of those quality-powers that admit of "more or less," etc. (which Brentlinger calls the "indeterminate," and Teloh the "dyadic," attributes).

names of these "indeterminates"—hotter, colder, shorter, taller, etc.—are all united linguistically: they all possess the same δύναμις or meaning,[88] namely, "they do not allow any definite quality to exist; they always introduce in every instance a comparison . . . and thus they create a relation of more or less, doing away with fixed quality."[89]

*Power Causality in Aristotle's Treatment of the Presocratics*

Plato's reworking of the Presocratic understanding of δύναμις through the discovery of a purposefulness in production (whether that production is of the whole cosmos or just some small part of it) is the Platonic doctrine of production and becomes normative for teleologies after his, as we see in Aristotle. Aristotle continues Plato's project of developing a teleological content for the old character-power cosmologies.[90] One noteworthy example of the continuation of the teleological sense of power may be found in Aristotle's work, *Parts of Animals,* where the term occurs in a number of significant passages and where many of the themes present in Presocratic and Platonic accounts of causes are incorporated into Aristotle's own causality. One important use of δύναμις by Aristotle is in his argument for teleological causes in biological processes, primarily in the teleological nature of reproduction. Aristotle compares the formation of a fetus to the building of a house, for in both "the process is for the sake of the actual thing [οὐσία], the thing is not for the sake of the process."[91] Aristotle's

88. *Philebus* 24 C2. Despite the obvious translation of "meaning" for δύναμις, there is nonetheless an effectiveness or activity attributed to the δύναμις.

89. *Philebus* 24 C.

90. The title of Vizgin's article, "Hippocratic Medicine as a Historical Source for Aristotle's Theory of the *Dynameis,*" suggests that his subject is the influence of medicine upon Aristotle's philosophy. Yet Vizgin has very little to say about Aristotle's "Theory of the *Dynameis*": Vizgin refers only to the *Meteorology* (without noting the uncertainties in its authorship), and even that only briefly. The relationship between the Hippocratics and Aristotle that Vizgin explores is that between the two Presocratic accounts of substrata (the first tactile and focused on the elementals, the second culinary and focusing on the humors) and Aristotle's two approaches to the problem of quality: in the first "qualities are attributes of some essences, [and] they depend absolutely on the latter, and are unthinkable without a substratum, while according to the second approach they [qualities] appear as independent acting powers free of any material substratum" (1). The first approach is found in the *Metaphysics* and the *Categories,* the second in the *Meteorology.* After giving this summary of Aristotle's theories of quality (as he understands them), Vizgin has nothing else to say about Aristotle.

91. *Parts of Animals,* 640a18–20; Peck, Loeb, 60–61.

description of teleology is strikingly reminiscent of Plato's description of teleology in the *Philebus:* "Every instance of generation is for the sake of some being [οὐσία] or another, and generation in general is for the sake of being in general."[92] In short, Aristotle's account of teleology in *Parts of Animals* sounds typically "Aristotelian," but in fact it represents Aristotle's continuance and development of a key Platonic doctrine.

In his discussion of teleological causes in biological processes, Aristotle refers to Empedocles, for the latter's failure to appreciate the reality of this teleology caused him to overstate the role of gestational accidents[93] in determining the nature or character of the product: Empedocles, Aristotle says, "was unaware that the seed which forms the animal must begin with the appropriate δύναμις."[94] This power in the sperm[95] contains, or is the form (Aristotle calls it λόγος), that gives definition or specific being to the living organism reproduced and that produces an offspring of the same specific kind of being as the parent:[96] power is the causal capacity, in this case, of the seed.

92. Ibid. Aristotle's Greek reads: "ἡ γὰρ γένεσις ἕνεκα τῆς οὐσίας ἐστίν, ἀλλ' οὐχ ἡ οὐσία ἕνεκα τῆς γενέσεως." Plato's Greek reads: ". . . ἑκάστην δὲ γένεσιν ἄλλην ἄλλης οὐσίας τινὸς ἑκάστης ἕνεκα γίγνεσθαι, ξύμπασαν δὲ γένεσιν οὐσίας ἕνεκα γίγνεσθαιν ξυμπάσης." *Philebus* 54 C, Fowler, Loeb, 354–55.

93. Empedocles evidently taught that life developed in four stages. The first stage consisted of arms and legs that existed without a body. The second stage was an era of creatures with many faces, or part animal, part human. The third stage was that of whole-natured forms: genderless humans resembling those described later by Plato in the *Symposium.* The fourth stage is the world as we know it. For an account of Empedocles' theories, together with the relevant fragments, see Kirk, Raven, and Schofield, *Presocratic Philosophers,* 1963, 303–5.

94. *Parts of Animals,* 640a24–25, Peck, Loeb, 60–63.

95. That a seed has a δύναμις is a commonplace in the Hellenistic era and a favorite image in some pro-Nicene polemic.

96. This argument for the continuity of nature between parent and offspring is an early argument for *X from X* causality, applied in a biological context. The argument proceeds from a materialism that is, of course, irrelevant to later theology, namely, the material bits of sperm that communicate the defining end and that determine the common nature between parent and child: "men are begotten by men, and therefore the process of the child's formation is what it is because its parent was a man" (*Parts of Animals,* 640a25–26; Peck, Loeb, 62–63). Aristotle's further example of a cause reproducing its nature in its product is art, a surprising example from the perspective of later religious controversies. Yet Aristotle's explanation of why art is such an example is helpful for understanding the reproduction he sees at work: the cause of an artifact is the art itself, say sculpting, that contains in itself what the marble block is to become. When the marble block becomes just that, through the efficacy of the art, then the art has reproduced its own content in the artifact (see ibid., 640a31–33). This understanding of the causality at work seems to resemble Plato's understanding of the causality in the faculties of virtues I have described.

Aristotle's next use of δύναμις occurs in a context that suggests that Empedocles is again the foil, though he is not mentioned by name. Aristotle offers a list of the three kinds of composition found in a body,[97] or, in other words, the three kinds or levels of parts that make up any body.[98] The first kind of part in a body is that of general material existence: "First of all we may give composition out of the στοιχεία, the Earth, Air, Water, and Fire, though perhaps it is better to say δυνάμεις instead of στοιχεία. . . ."[99]

The sense of powers in this passage is reasonably clear: δυνάμεις is another name for the στοιχεία, the elementals, out of which everything that exists is composed. If one assumes an Empedoclean background for this doctrine of elementals, then Aristotle's understanding of the role of these powers in composition may be elaborated upon beyond the little he says in this section. Empedocles taught that whatever exists is composed of a combination or mixture of tiny bits of four elementals: fire, earth, water, and air, the same four Aristotle regularly emphasizes. These four elementals are eternal and cannot be destroyed: they do, however, pass into

97. The second and third kinds of composition are those of "uniform" (ὁμοιόμερον at *Parts of Animals,* 646a21; Peck, Loeb, 106–7) substances or parts in animals, such as bone or flesh, and "non-uniform" [ἀνομοιόμερον at ibid., 646a23, 108–109] parts of the body, such as face, hand, etc. In short, the uniform parts are those constructed for a single task, while the nonuniform parts are constructed for multiple tasks: a uniform part like a piece of bone does just one thing (that is, makes up into a bone), but a nonuniform part, like a hand, does several things (for example, open, close, etc.). Aristotle's subject may perhaps be better understood as divisions of types of unity or levels of organization in any body, with the additional awareness that Aristotle wants to discuss these levels of unity or organization within a materialist context. He does not want to separate these levels of organization from their material ground.

98. Montgomery Furth provides a helpful description of these divisions in his article, "Aristotle's Biological Universe: An Overview," in *Philosophical Issues in Aristotle's Biology,* ed. Allan Gotthelf and James G. Lennox (Cambridge: Cambridge University Press, 1987), 22–52, esp. 30–37. Furth finds Aristotle's use of Earth, Water, Air and Fire to be indicative of an "Empedoclean infrastructure" (30) in the first level of composition. He also notes that "these four elements, then, are the most basic to figure in the explanation of biological phenomena; sometimes in the biological works they are called *δυνάμεις* (potencies, powers, strong substances)" (31).

99. *On the Parts of Animals* 646a12–20, Peck, Loeb, 106–107, Peck's translation slightly altered (though he leaves δυνάμεις untranslated after describing the difficulties in translating the term on pp. 30–31 of his introduction). Aristotle adds that this list gives some of the δυνάμεις but not all—a complete list is given elsewhere. The editor of the text understands this as a reference to Aristotle's list in Book 2 of *Generation and Corruption.* That list has two features to note: first, the Empedoclean association of the four elementals is explicit; and second, the elementals are never called δυνάμεις.

and out of different mixtures or combinations. Δυνάμεις, then, is the term Aristotle offers for the elementals in mixture(s), from which all other material things take their existence.

My understanding is that Aristotle's use of the plural of *powers,* δυνάμεις, in this context is not an accident; in its received use, the term δυνάμεις names the several elementals that, in mixture, make up the foundation of material existence.[100] On the other hand, δύναμις, the singular of power, is not just a name for only one of these elementals: it is rather the name for the affective capacity of any existent as a cause, as one finds Aristotle saying later in *Parts of Animals,* when he says that the transformation (in digestion) of food into nutrition occurs through the "δύναμις of the hot."[101] Aristotle's discussion of the role of uniform and non-uniform parts in the composition of an animal may seem to contradict my judgement, since there he distinguishes uniform parts as those parts where the powers are separated out into kinds, while in non-uniform parts the powers appear in combinations.[102] Yet in the elaboration of this distinction, Aristotle does not say that the uniform parts have only one power (singular) but that uniform parts are those where the powers (plural) are separated out.[103] What is true is that each of the δυνάμεις has a δύναμις through which it (the elemental) brings about effects and actions [ἔργα καὶ πράξεις].[104]

100. As I have described above, the incidence of δυναμ[ε]ις in Preplatonic texts is limited to "philosophies" which understood true being to consist of discrete material substrata. Indeed, the concept δύναμις figures most in accounts which emphasize the multiplicity or multiple nature of the material substrata. The author of *On Ancient Medicine,* for example, is clear on the fact that there are many δυνάμεις, and he chides Empedocles for emphasizing the Hot over the others in (diet) therapy, as though one could find any food which was just the Hot. Similarly, Parmenides uses δυνάμεις to refer to Night and Day, multiple powers, even when his philosophy otherwise seems monistic. Radically monistic philosophers, such as Heraclitus, do not use δυναμ[ε]ις. The scholarly opinion that the origin of δυναμ[ε]ις as a philosophical term lies with Alcmaeon, as his term for the Opposites (which he thought were indefinite in number) is an expression of the implicit awareness that the elementals—and δυναμ[ε]ις—must be plural.

101. "Everything that grows must of necessity take food. This food is always supplied through liquids and solids, and the concoction and transformation of these occurs through the δύναμις of the hot." *Parts of Animals,* 650a5–6, Peck, Loeb, 132–133, translation slightly altered.

102. *On the Parts of Animals* 646b 18–23, Peck, Loeb, 110–111.

103. *Ibid.* "In the uniform parts, then, such δυνάμεις are found apportioned out separately; one of the parts, for example, will be soft, another hard. . . . In the non-uniform parts, on the other hand, these δυνάμεις are found in combination, not singly. For example, the hand needs one δύναμις for the action of compressing and another for that of grasping."

104. *Ibid.,* 646b13, 110–111.

Δυνάμεις—the plural—remains a term for material or quasi-material entities, while δύναμις—the singular—is a term for a virtually abstracted property, namely, the capacity to affect (considered broadly).[105]

There is something fundamentally traditional in the sense of δυνάμεις (that is, the plural term) in these passages from Aristotle, and though the sense of δύναμις (that is, the singular term) here is not identical or limited to the specific "Aristotelian" sense communicated by δύναμις, there is an opening in the use of δύναμις to an understanding of immaterial causality. Aristotle has moved away from the narrow application of δύναμις (i.e., as contrasted with ἐντελέχεια) found in *On Generation and Corruption,* which I take to be an earlier work.[106] The understanding of δύναμις in *On the Parts of Animals* is closer to Aristotle's use and understanding of the notion in his late work, *On the Soul.*

## *The Understanding of Power as Transcendent Cause*

To finish my account of the Platonic sense of *power,* I will set aside my chronological treatment of Plato's writings and return to a text I mentioned earlier: *Republic,* Book 6, and the passage at 509 B:

> . . . say that the objects of knowledge not only receive from the presence of the good their being known, but their very existence and essence is derived to them from it, though the good itself is not essence but still transcends essence in dignity and surpassing power."[107]

105. Δύναμις is thus the ground for the phenomenological manifestation of any existent, as modern phenomenologists like to point out. For example, in his *Being and Logos,* 495–497, Sallis frequently refers to the role of δύναμις in Plato's thought, and he interprets *Sophist* 247 D–E through a historical summary of the senses of δύναμις. Sallis' understanding of the fundamental sense of δύναμις is stated more than once in the book: "Being as such, δύναμις in that fundamental sense . . . is the power of bringing something forth into manifestness, the power of letting it show itself. Being as such, δύναμις, is just showing as such" (497; cf. 512).

106. There are two relevant schools of thought about the sequence of Aristotle's writings and the development of his thought, which I can distinguish or summarize according to the question of Aristotle's biological writings (since I am here treating those writings). The first school thinks that Aristotle moved away from his early biological interests, the second school thinks that he moved into biological interests. I am not competent to offer an argument for either judgement, but I find the second description more sound to at least this extent: there is nothing "immature" about Aristotle's biological writings.

107. (*Republic* 509 B; Shorey, Loeb, 106–7): Καὶ τοῖς γιγνωσκομένοις τοίνυν μὴ μόνον τὸ γιγνώσκεσθαι φάναι ὑπὸ τοῦ ἀγαθοῦ παρεῖναι, ἀλλὰ καὶ τὸ εἶναί τε καὶ τὴν οὐσίαν ὑπ᾽ ἐκεί-

While this text is not one of Plato's last works, his readers in the Hellenistic period considered it to be his "last word," as it were, on the relationship between the good, being, and power.[108] The importance for theology of *Republic* 509 B and the medical causality behind it lies in its authoritative account of a first cause that produces effects that bear its mark but not its nature. *Republic* 509 B describes a causal relationship in which δύναμις causality does not simply reproduce itself but produces a product that depends upon its cause while being, in identity or nature, unlike the cause.[109]

The statement that the Good exceeds being in dignity and power comes as the conclusion of an argument by analogy that is filled with references to δυνάμεις of various sorts. Socrates' analogy follows this form: just as seeing depends not only upon the power of seeing in the eye and the power of visibility in something (to be) seen, but also upon a light (that is, the sun) for the eye to see and a view to be seen, so too the mind and its object depend upon something else (that is, the Good) to enable the mind to know and its object to be intelligible.

> This reality, then, that gives their truth to objects of knowledge and the power [δύναμις] of knowing to the knower, you must say is the idea of the good, and you must conceive it as being the cause of knowledge, and truth insofar as known.[110]

---

νου αὐτοῖς προσεῖναι, οὐκ οὐσίας ὄντος τοῦ ἀγαθοῦ, ἀλλ᾽ ἔτι ἐπέκεινα τῆς οὐσίας πρεσβείᾳ καὶ δυνάμει ὑπερέχοντος.

108. For a good account of the interpretation of *Republic* 509 B in the Hellenistic era, see John Whittaker's "ΕΠΕΚΕΙΝΑ ΝΟΥ ΚΑΙ ΟΥΣΙΑΣ," in *Vigiliae Christianae* 23 (1969): 91–104. I will give examples of Plotinus' interpretation below, but a good illustration of the Christian interpretation of the *Republic* passage is from Eusebius of Caesarea: "Herein Plato says most distinctly that the intellectual essences receive from 'the good', meaning of course from God, not merely the property of being known, but also their existence and essence. . . . So far he [Plato] does not regard the ideas as coessential, nor yet suppose that they are unbegotten, because they have received their existence and their essence from Him who is not an essence, but far transcends essence in dignity and power, whom alone the Hebrew oracles with good reason proclaim as God, as being the cause of all things" (*Preparation for the Gospel* 11:21; Gifford 3:2, 542).

109. Thus Gregory uses two kinds of δύναμις causality: the usual Hippocratic *X from X,* like from like, causality to describe the generation of the Son; and the dissimilar product causality of the Hippocratics, given a transcendental status in *Republic* 509 B, to describe the relationship between Creator and created. For this distinction between causalities to hold in the case of God and to work as a means of distinguishing productive acts, δύναμις must be one with the divine life, that is, transcendent.

110. *Republic* 508 E, Shorey, Loeb, 102–105.

Furthermore, just as the sun causes generation, growth, and nourishment—all the things necessary to life—but is not itself alive, so too the Good causes existence and being in what is (to be) known but is not itself being—indeed, the good is beyond being, and as the cause of being exceeds being "in dignity and power," a conclusion one of Socrates' audience (Glaucon) finds extravagant.[111]

There is much that is familiar about the analogy and its conclusion: the description of reciprocal powers that together bring about a completed action, the political resonances in "dignity" and "power," as well as moral connotations to power (that is, δύναμις and "the good"), and an association of δύναμις and οὐσία, power and essence. Yet what is most provocative, if not quite as Glaucon saw it, is the specific kind of causal relation chosen: the sun is chosen for the analogy because it is a cause that does not resemble its effects.

This type of causal relation is not outside the realm of Hippocratic power physics, as I showed in my previous chapter, but in the *Republic* argument it is offered as something at once familiar and unsettling. From the beginning Socrates offers the sun as an example of a cause that is unlike its effects in nature; given the sun as a paradigm of cause, the fact that the good is unlike its effects is foregone. Yet the language of this conclusion is specific: the Good is beyond "being" in "power" and "dignity." That a cause is beyond its effect in power is almost tautologous (for something is a cause because it has a power first, and something is an effect because it receives the power), and the example of the sun has been chosen precisely because it has a power that the other powers (sight, being seen) lack. The statement that this cause is beyond the "dignity" of its effect is strange since this is not something that one could say about any causal relationship: one torch does not exceed another torch in dignity. Yet the political roots of this causal language are worth remembering here, and there is some difference precisely in "dignity" and in "power" between the king and his subjects.

111. In *Being and Logos,* 405–12, Sallis gives a helpful account of the dialogue's argument by analogy: aside from its simplicity, the virtue of Sallis's account is that he keeps the sun description in mind while interpreting the cryptic 509 B passage. The weakness of Sallis's comments lies in his failure to bring in the received character of Plato's understanding of δύναμις until his discussion of *Sophist.*

What happens in the *Republic* argument is that "dignity and power" are used to express the difference in natures between the causes (sun, the Good), and their effects, just as the Hippocratics used *power* and *nature*—δύναμις καὶ φύσις—to express the same distinction, but to a very different purpose. The differences in causal natures serve as a way of illuminating the unique and superior nature of the Good.

Clearly I understand the passage to express the intersection of Plato's new causality of forms and the older but still paradigmatic causality of powers. These two etiologies are brought together in Plato's writings typically for one purpose: to help clarify the new causality of forms.[112] What the analogy establishes is that participation can be a one way relationship: *x* participates in *X*, but *X* does not participate in *x*. Sight and appearance participate in sunlight, but sunlight does not participate in sight or appearance; knowing and existence participate in the Good, but the Good does not participate in knowing or the kind of existence described.

### *Transcendent Power*

For my study of power the most important aspect of the passage that concludes at *Republic* 509 B is that power is applied at that point of the argument to the transcendent cause of existence and intelligibility. In the *Republic* discussion, Plato outlines different kinds of powers and sets the Good among them. Thus the Good may be beyond essence (or being, οὐσία) but it is not beyond δύναμις, a description that is consistent with Plato's references to the Cosmic Mind as a δύναμις. When later Platonists, particularly the Neoplatonists, distinguish the Good from other existents and deny it traits or properties, the Good is still spoken of as having a power. Examples of the understanding that however transcendent the Good may be, it is still a power (and thus still a cause) are found in Plotinus' writings. For example, when Plotinus is describing the generation of the Intellect by the First Principle, he says that the Intellect ". . . comes from a great δύναμις, the greatest indeed of all, and [the Intellect] arrives at being and substance: for that Principle is beyond being. That is the productive δύναμις of all things. . . ."[113]

112. My judgment depends upon Moline's argument in *Theory of Understanding*.

113. *Ennead* V 4, 2, 36–39, Armstrong, Loeb vol. 5:148–149. This argument is preceded by a very

Elsewhere the Good is spoken of as being without intellect and without activity (ἐνέργεια),[114] but it remains a power that gives power, as in *Ennead* 5:6, in what I take to be a reminiscence of the *Republic* discussion: "... that which gives [Intellect] light is nothing else but is simple light giving Intellect the δύναμις to be what it is."[115]

These statements by Plotinus give a good indication of the understanding in the Platonism of Gregory's era that the Transcendent is not beyond being a cause: an undynamic (or, to coin a term, α-δύναμις) or fruitless Good, is a very unplatonic thing to imagine, apophatic-like statements about the First Principle or statements of delegation notwithstanding. This point is worth emphasizing because an example like Philo (once again) misleads the modern reader into expecting, and assuming, a theological separation between the Transcendent and causality, so that, for example, the power is thought not be divine in the same way or as truly as the essence is. Yet Gregory understands the divine power to be unknowable and transcendent to the rest of existence, for in his writings the title "transcendent" is applied most frequently to the divine power and not to the divine essence.[116] Indeed, as I have already suggested, one important way in which Gregory's doctrine of God differs from Eunomius' is that Gregory consid-

---

interesting use of the analogy of fire: Plotinus argues that in everything there are two movements (sometimes he calls these two δυνάμεις, here he calls them two ἐνέργειαι), an inward and an outward movement. The inward movement is that of identity, the outward that of relation. Thus: "... as in fire there is a heat which is the content of [fire's] substance [οὐσία], and another which comes into being from that primary heat when fire exercises the activity which is native to its substance in abiding unchanged as fire." V 4, 2, 30–34, Armstrong, Loeb vol. 5:146–147. This theory of a double motion appears in Victorinus' account of the Trinity and—to reach very far afield—provides the content of Hegel's very important understanding of *Kraft*.

114. *Ennead* I 7, 1, 19–21, Armstrong, Loeb vol. 1:270–271: "For because it [the Good] is 'beyond being,' it transcends activity [ἐνέργεια] and transcends mind and thought." An important distinction in Plotinus' thought between δύναμις and ἐνέργεια—at least in relation to the One/Good—is that while the Good is described as being beyond or without ἐνέργεια, it is not described as being beyond or without δύναμις.

115. *Ennead* V 6, 4, 19–20, Armstrong, Loeb vol. 5:210–11. I speak of this as a reminiscence of the *Republic* VI discussion, though Armstrong does not.

116. For example, at *Against Eunomius* 1; *GNO* 1:212:10, Gregory argues that Eunomius improperly "... gives priority to the term 'Unbegotten' over all the terms for God, those, that is, which refer to his transcendent power ..." (Hall's translation, 128). And in Gregory's *Refutation of the Creed* of Eunomius, he speaks of the various titles that "... represent to us the transcendent power ..." (*GNO* 2:365:13; NPNF 5:119).

ers the divine capacity to generate, which Gregory calls the δύναμις, to be fully God and wholly transcendent, while Eunomius considers the divine capacity to generate, which Eunomius calls the ἐνέργεια, not to be fully God and transcendent.

*Conclusion*

This chapter, like the one before it, establishes the importance of power or δύναμις in Greek philosophy. I have treated Plato's understanding of power in detail for two reasons. The first is to provide a thorough account of the different kinds of understandings of power that are characteristic of Greek philosophical thought generally. The second reason is to establish the importance of *power* as a philosophical term for Plato and, through him, classical and Hellenistic philosophy generally. Just as Luke's account (in Acts) of the arrival of St. Paul in Rome implies that, in reaching Rome the Gospel has reached all the known world, so too when power is understood to be important for Plato's thought, it will be understood to be important for virtually all later philosophers in the era under study.

The most important feature of Plato's development of the concept power is his "abstracting" of power from its use in Hippocratic mixture physics. For the Hippocratics a power is a material cause, a stuff or a structure in stuff. Plato takes the causality described in mixture physics and applies it to a wide range of causes that are not conceived of as matter acting upon matter. The action of virtues in the soul and knowledge in the mind are both described as power causalities, for example. Plato does not reject all of the old material causality; rather, he develops it in the areas in which he is convinced that the old cosmology is unsatisfactory: sensation is still understood as matter acting upon matter, for example, but the idea that purpose can be provided by a material cause is rejected decisively.[117] Plato's rejection of the old material description of power causality is exemplified in his account of the Good in *Republic* 508 B–509 B. For Plato's

117. It is interesting to note that although what is distinctive to Plato's psychology is his development of power causality away from the action of matter, the dominant interpretation of Plato's psychology in Gregory's era is precisely that he understood causes in the soul to be based in material parts of the body.

philosophy, this passage marks his clear appropriation of medical causal language in an application that leaves behind the explicit materialistic context of that language. For Gregory, the *Republic* passage provides an important insight into the kind of cause God is: He is a Power in the ontological sense the medical philosophers gave to *power,* namely, that power belongs to something insofar as it exists and not simply insofar as it has office.

# 3 Δύναμις as a Theological Term among Pagans and Christians in the Early Common Era

IN THE LAST CHAPTER I SHOWED how δύναμις received its foundational theological content and application in Plato's use of the term in *Republic* 509 to describe causality associated with the Good. The purpose of this and the next chapter is to bridge the period between Plato and Gregory of Nyssa by treating important theological uses of δύναμις by pagan philosophers and Christians in the early Common Era. I make no claim that these chapters constitute an exhaustive treatment of such uses of δύναμις, but they will provide evidence of the continuing role of our key concept in the theologies and philosophies of the Common Era. Some of these uses of δύναμις simply illustrate the developing understanding and application of *power* as a concept associated with the transcendent. Other of these uses will have a substantial influence on the development of Christian trinitarian theology in general and Gregory's doctrine in particular. I will, however, defer specific accounts of interaction between pagan and Christian doctrines to those moments in my argument where the intersection of the two sources figures directly in understanding the text at hand.[1] This chapter will offer illustrative or representative cases of δύναμις in the writings of early Common Era pagan authors. Just as the previous two chapters moved from the physical to the transcendent, so too in this

1. For example, in his argument against Eunomius, Gregory associates a certain understanding of power with Philo. Rather than describe Gregory's characterization of Philo in this chapter, I will discuss this issue when I treat that part of Gregory's argument against Eunomius.

chapter, I will begin with medical applications of δύναμις and move to the metaphysical, then to the psychological, and finally to transcendent or theological uses. The transcendent or theological use of δύναμις in hellenistic philosophies can then serve as an introduction to the Christian use of δύναμις in trinitarian theology. Most of this chapter will be devoted to treating Christian sources, but even so the treatment of δύναμις in trinitarian theology cannot be exhaustive. Instead, I will focus on late second century appearances of δύναμις in trinitarian theology and then on the use of δύναμις (or *power*) by authors who figure indirectly and directly in the fourth-century controversies. My focus on second-century appearances of δύναμις in trinitarian theology is intended to show the basis of the "traditional character of δύναμις-based trinitarian theology." The late second century gives clear examples of the significance of the concept of *power* for trinitarian theology.[2]

In this chapter I will treat three Christian authors, all of whom write at the turn from the second to the third century: Tertullian, Hippolytus, and Origen.[3] Only the treatment of Origen can be considered to be a nearly complete study: the survey of Tertullian and Hippolytus is intended to highlight their contributions to a tradition of what I am calling "power theology." Their contributions differ. Tertullian provides good examples of the two kinds of doctrines of divine power that will play in trinitarian theology through the third and fourth centuries and that will have a deci-

2. Two Nag Hammadi codices that might date from the late second century show a significant use of *power:* VI.1, *The Discourse on the Eighth and the Ninth,* and VI.4, *The Concept of our Great Power.* If *The Teaching of Silvanus* (VII 4) predates Clement of Alexandria and Origen, it would show the moment in Christian reflection when Wisd. 7:25 crosses into trinitarian and christological discourse. *The Teachings* describes a "two power" understanding of the relationship between the Father and the Son, in which the Father is the inward or internal power and the Son is the outward or expressed power. More work needs to be done on discerning the chronologies of literary-theological strata in *The Teachings of Silvanus* in order to be clear about what, precisely, dates from the second and third centuries and what reflects a later fourth-century hand.

3. When discussing Hippolytus, the *Against Noetus,* and Tertullian, two methodological questions appear for determination. First, is the *Against Noetus* by Hippolytus? I think so, for at least the reasons given by Allen Brent in *Hippolytus and the Roman Church in the Third Century* (Leiden: E. J. Brill, 1995). The second methodological question is how to sequence Hippolytus and Tertullian. Quasten thinks that Hippolytus borrowed from Tertullian, but Kelly thinks that Hippolytus' trinitarian theology is more "primitive" than Tertullian and so predates him. I will treat Tertullian first and then Hippolytus primarily because of the possibility of influence of Hippolytus upon my final figure in this chapter, Origen.

sive role in the early trinitarian controversies of the fourth century. In particular Tertullian's strong statement of the unity of power and substance (or nature) illustrates this understanding of power theology as it figures in patristic trinitarian discussions generally. It also illustrates Tertullian's understanding of this unity, which has specific repercussions later in Latin pro-Nicene theology.

For this study the virtue of Hippolytus' expression of power theology lies in two areas (aside from his serving as a noteworthy case of the intersection or coexistence of eastern and western theologies). Hippolytus' use in *Against Noetus* of the two forms of power theology already seen in Tertullian confirms their widespread presence in Christian theology.[4] What is distinctive to Hippolytus' expression of the two doctrines of power is, first, that his use suggests, on the basis of literary evidence, an early association between the doctrine "one power, one nature" and polemics; and second, a resemblance between the Christian application of "power" in trinitarian theology and a pagan application of the same in triadic theology (that is, in the *Chaldean Oracles*).

The use of δύναμις with such terms as φύσις and οὐσία to describe God's nature, as well as doctrines on the "number" of God's δυνάμεις, are recognizable exegetical positions in the theology of Origen, and the terms of the debate over δύναμις and related language are clearly carried over from the works of this theologian, as I will show. Obviously, doctrines on God's δύναμις are not unique to the theologies of Alexandria; however, it is through the Alexandrian theologies of Origen especially that an emphasis on δύναμις becomes a fundamental feature of trinitarian theology of the Greek-speaking participants in fourth-century trinitarian debates. For Alexander, Athanasius, and Arius, the argument over alternative exegesis is carried on within that local tradition. For Eusebius, Asterius, and Mar-

4. An equal case study of the early presence of the two forms or doctrines of power theology can be made of Clement of Alexandria's trinitarian theology. See, for example, F. Sagnard's comments in *Clément d'Alexandrie Extraits de Théodote*, Sources Chrétiennes, vol. 23 (Paris: Éditions du Cerf, 1948), appendice A; William McFadden's "The Exegesis of 1 Cor. 1:24, 'Christ the Power of God and the Wisdom of God' until the Arian Controversy" (Ph.D. diss., Pontifical Gregorian University, 1963), 18–32; and Rowan Williams's *Arius: Heresy and Tradition* (London: Darton, Longman, and Todd, 1987), 124–31.

cellus, the same argument is carried on in the language of the Alexandrian tradition they have appropriated (or, in the case of Marcellus, refused to appropriate). The sign that Origen's theology is indeed the source of the use of δύναμις as a trinitarian term by the principals in the Nicene controversy is their justification of this title through an exegesis of Wisd. 7:25, Heb. 1:3, and 1 Cor. 1:24.[5]

My discussion of fourth-century sources in the next chapter will follow through on the doctrines of divine power documented here in chapter three. Chapter four is designed primarily to reveal the presence of a broadly based "power" trinitarian theology in both the East and West prior to the decisive development of one-power doctrines in Gregory of Nyssa's own theology of divine power. But Gregory's use of δύναμις can only be understood precisely in terms of a broadly based pro-Nicene polemic that emphasizes power (δύναμις, *virtus/potestas*), while the strength of the earlier fourth-century trinitarian uses of power theology lie in part in the traditional character of δύναμις-based trinitarian theology. While any curious reader of these texts will be drawn to questions regarding origins and precedents in Jewish and early Christian literature from the turn of the Era, such questions are deferred, or rather referred to treatments that already exist of the significance of δύναμις in the Jewish understanding of divinity and in primitive Christianity.[6]

## *From the Physical to the Transcendent*

Evidence of the role of power in the philosophical thought of the early Common Era may be found in the same field where we first discovered the technical sense of δύναμις developing: medicine. Again, as we would ex-

5. Wisd. 7:25(a) reads: "For she is a breath of the power of God, and a pure emanation of the glory of the Almighty. . . ." Hebrews 1:3 reads: "He reflects the glory of God and bears the very stamp of his nature, upholding the universe by his word of power." 1 Cor. 1:24 reads: ". . . but to those who are called, both Jews and Greeks, Christ is the power of God and the wisdom of God" (RSV translations).

6. One still thinks, for example, of Pierre Biard's *La Puissance de Dieu* (Paris: Bloud and Gay, 1960), although it sometimes sacrifices historical sensitivity to pursue the broad theme of "power." Examples of work more directly significant to this study would include Alan F. Segal, *Two Powers in Heaven* (Leiden: E. J. Brill, 1977); Jarl E. Fossum, *The Name of God and the Angel of the Lord* (Tübingen: J. C. B. Mohr, 1985); and David Winston, *Logos and Mystical Theology in Philo of Alexandria* (Cincinnati: Hebrew Union Press, 1985).

pect, δύναμις appears as a term for a source or cause. One major work by Galen of Pergamum (129–99 C.E.) is entitled *On the Natural Powers,* or as it is usually translated, natural "faculties." In this treatise on organic causality, Galen's subject is "from what faculties [δυνάμεις] these effects [of organic life] themselves, as well as any other effects [ἔργα] of nature which there may be, take their origin."[7] Even this simple declaration of intent is heavy with the technical senses Galen gives to the components of the generalized causal sequence.

> Now, of course, I mean by an effect [ἔργον] that which has already come into existence and has been completed by the activity [ἐνέργεια] of these faculties [δυνάμεις]—for example, blood, flesh, or nerve. And activity is the name I give to the active change of motion, and the cause of this [change] I call a faculty [δύναμις].[8]

In Galen's understanding, a faculty is the causal capacity associated with and distinctive of each "part" or organ of a body. The eye, then, has the faculty of sight. This system is more sophisticated and nuanced than it might seem at first blush since it is tied to the discovery of discrete or integral parts or organs in the body. If one discovers (through anatomy, for example) that a supposedly simple organ (that is, the stomach) is actually composed of several distinct parts (for example, the stomach, upper intestine, lower intestine), then one must attribute a distinct capacity or function to each part. Alternately, if one discovers that a function that originally seemed simple (for example, digestion) is actually composed of distinct stages or component acts (for example, a patient can break down food but gains no nourishment from the mash), then by the same logic Galen would conclude that there are distinct parts or organs in the "stomach." (This conceptual link between material part and causal capacity will reappear in Galen's psychology.) What we would normally call the faculty or power in any organ, such as nutrition in the stomach, is in Galen's etiological system actually the activity [ἐνέργεια] of the power; the power itself is prior to the act, prior to and separate from the material motion. As May puts it, "Whenever an action is necessary, there appears a faculty to take charge of it."[9]

7. *On Nat Fac.* 1:2.2; Brock, 5.

8. *Ibid.*, 1.2.7 Brock, 13.

9. Margaret T. May, *On the Usefulness of the Parts of the Body,* 2 vols. (Ithaca: Cornell University Press, 1968), 50.

Activities begin and cease, but the power exists so long as the material integrity of the organ remains intact.[10]

The same causal sequence appears in the works of the Neoplatonist Iamblichus (245–326) of Chalcis. Of anything that is to be known Iamblichus says "[w]e attain to a perception of them through their activities, of which the powers are the immediate mothers; for a power is median between an essence and an activity, put forth from the essence on the one hand, and itself generating the activity."[11] Iamblichus also uses this sequence in his account of the soul, as both Festugière and Dillon point out: the soul is abstracted into its essence, its powers, its activities, etc. Later, in the fourth century, when the Emperor Julian (usually considered an "Iamblichean") gives his description of the Sun God, he announces that he must "describe his substance [οὐσία] and his origin, and his powers [δυνάμεις] and his activities [ἐνέργεια]. . . ."[12] The same causal sequence appears in Hilary of Poitiers's description of the way in which God is known through His capacity to act:

> . . . since power [*virtus*] is the very reality of the nature, and the operation is the capability of the power, the unity of the Father's power in itself is known through the capability of the nature, for insofar as anyone has known God in the power of nature, to that extent he has known God the Father in the capability of the nature. . . .[13]

10. I have argued elsewhere that ἐνέργεια's connotation as a cause of temporary duration, compared to δύναμις's connotation as a cause of permanent duration (as reported by Clement of Alexandria at *Strom.* 8.9.33), figures in Eunomius' own emphasis on ἐνέργεια as the apt descriptive term for the kind of causality that God, the unbegotten essence, has. See "The Background and Use of Eunomius' Causal Language," in *Arianism After Arius: Essays on the Development of the Fourth Century Trinitarian Conflicts,* M. R. Barnes and D. H. Williams, eds. (Edinburgh: T. & T. Clark, 1993), 217–36; here, 228–29.

11. *In Alcibidiadem* 4.12–16, in John Dillon's *Iamblichi Chalcidensis in Platonis Dialogos Commentariorum Fragmenta,* 75. In his commentary on this passage (232 ff.), Dillon calls the causal sequence "typically Neoplatonic" and while finding the sequence in the era of Middle Platonism (for example, in Tertullian's *de Anima*), nonetheless says that "the more elaborate applications of it [the sequence] seem not to appear before Iamblichus." Here Dillon overlooks Galen. A. J. Festugière believes the origins of this language to be from Aristotle's *de Anima;* see his *La Révélation d'Hermès Trismégiste,* 4 vols. (1949–1954; reprint, Paris: Société d'Editions des Belles Lettres, 1983), 3:153–66. Although Festugière notes that Alexander of Aphrodisias and Tertullian know of the series, he treats only Iamblichus and Julian. P. L. Reynolds treats a variation of the sequence in "The Essence, Power and Presence of God," 351–80.

12. *Hymn to King Helios* 132B, in *The Works of the Emperor Julian,* vol. 1, W. C. Wright, ed. and trans., 4 vols. The Loeb Classical Library (1913; rpt., Cambridge: Harvard), 357.

13. ". . . cum uirtus naturae res esset et operatio ipsa uirtutis sit potestas, per uirtutis potestatem naturae in se paternae unitas nosceretur: cum in quantum se quisquam Deum cognouisset in

Where Hilary learned this sequence, whether from a Latin or from a Greek source, early at home in Gaul or later in exile in the East, is not known. What is clear is that this passage shows the same causal sequence, with the same presupposed technical senses for the key terms, that we find in the previously mentioned pagan authors whose thoughts show a platonic school (whether Middle or Neo-) bent.

One possible source for Hilary's knowledge of the sequence is Tertullian's *On the Soul.* There Tertullian, like Iamblichus after him, speaks of the soul in terms of its nature, its powers (*vires*), activities (*efficaciae*), and its works (*operae*).[14] Whether Tertullian has to be regarded as a source of this terminology for the West or not, he is evidence of the psychological application of the concept of power. Here, again, Galen represents both our clearest and our most authoritative source for the role of power in accounts of the soul. In his *On the Doctrines of Hippocrates and Plato*[15] Galen describes the opposition in psychological schools (Aristotle and Posidonius on the one hand, Hippocrates, Plato, and Galen on the other) precisely in terms of judgments on the existence of multiple powers (faculties—δυνάμεις) or multiple essences (οὐσία) or parts (μέρη) in the soul. Aristotle and Posidonius teach that the soul is one essence with three powers; Hippocrates, Plato, and Galen teach that the soul is three essences each of which (Galen will agree with his opponents) possesses its own power. The issue, as Galen presents it, is whether the rational and irrational (etc.) exist as wholly different "essences" in the soul, specifically associated with a specific "part," or whether the rational and irrational (etc.) are both powers of the same essence.

Galen's use of δύναμις in this psychological context is not just an idiosyncracy. The role of "power" in Stoic psychology has received substantial treatment by scholars recently, most notably by Inwood.[16] Moreover, as we

---

naturae uirtute, in tantum Deum Patrem cognosceret in potestate naturae . . ." (*de trin.* 9:52.10–14; CCL 62).

14. *De Anima* 14.3 and 5–13. However, the Latin terminology is sufficiently different from Hilary's that it is difficult to believe that he took the sequence from Tertullian.

15. *On the Doctrines of Hippocrates and Plato* VI 2, 5; Phillip De Lacy, ed., trans., and comm., 3 tomes, in *Corpus Medicorum Graecorum,* vol. 4, 1, 2 (Berlin: Akademie-Verlag, 1978, 1980, 1984), 1: 369. This work is hereafter referred to as *On the Doctrines.*

16. Brad Inwood, *Ethics and Human Action in Early Stoicism* (Oxford: Clarendon Press, 1985). See also André-Jean Voelke, *L'idée de volonté dans le stoïcisme* (Paris: Presses Universitaires de France, 1973), although this is not to suggest that Inwood and Voelke agree.

shall see in chapter six, "power" figures significantly both in Gregory's own psychology and in his first attempt at refuting Eunomius' theology. Gregory's early argument will turn on an analogy between the human mind and God. The psychological sense of δύναμις is traditional, and so is the theological.

In the late second and the beginning of the third centuries, one finds a wide variety of works that use *power* (δύναμις) in a theological or transcendental context. To take just one example, the *Chaldean Oracles*[17] (late second century) evidently used δύναμις to describe productive capability and relationships of identity within the triadic first principle or God. The Father, the *Oracles* says in one fragment, "did not enclose his own fire in his intellectual Power."[18] Or again, "Power is with Him [the Father], but Intellect is from him."[19] And again, "For the first Transcendent Fire does not enclose its own Power in matter by means of works but by means of Intellect."[20] As is obvious, the *Oracles* teach a triad of divinity: Father, Power, and Intellect. The doctrine that Power is with the Father but Intellect is from him suggests that Father and Power have a relationship of unity that is different in kind than the relationship of unity between Intellect and Father or Intellect and Power. One such difference is productivity: Father and Power together produce Intellect.[21] It is a characteristic feature of the theology of the *Chaldean Oracles* that the grammatical gender of the titles for the first and second Gods is transposed into gendered figures: the Father is obviously male, while the Δύναμις, feminine in gender, is identified with the female Rhea, whose productivity is described in terms of her fertileness.[22]

17. John Dillon has suggested that the *Chaldean Oracles* influenced Gregory of Nazianzus' trinitarian theology, which makes similarities between language in the *Oracles* and in our Gregory's writings suggestive of an influence relationship (but only suggestive). See Dillon's "Logos and Trinity: Patterns of Platonist Influence on Early Christianity," in *The Philosophy in Christianity*, Godfrey Vesey, ed. (Cambridge: Cambridge University Press, 1989), 1–14.

18. Frag. 3, *The Chaldean Oracles*, ed., trans., and comm. Ruth Majerick (Leiden: E. J. Brill, 1989), 49.

19. Ibid., frag. 4.

20. Ibid., frag. 5, 51.

21. One telltale feature of the thought of the *Chaldean Oracles* is that the identifying trait of each God (Father, Power, Intellect) is shared in a secondary sense among the three. Thus the fragment speaks, for example, of the "Intellectual Power." This understanding is taken over by Porphyry and Marius Victorinus.

22. I know of no case in Christian literature where the grammatical gender of δύναμις is transposed into a female character. Marius Victorinus seems to give such a reading, however, to *Sophia* in his treatment of the Holy Spirit.

Most scholars have assumed that in the *Chaldean Oracles,* the sexual basis for unity between the Father and the Δύναμις (Rhea) is the fundamental conceptualization of the "cause" of unity between the two, so that the question of whether or not δύναμις might itself conceptually support a doctrine of unity between the first and second Gods has not been addressed.

In a related passage from another author, Iamblichus faces the problem of how the transcendent can act without materiality or passion. His solution is to postulate powers that (first) shield the divine from the passion of material activity and at the same time (secondly) act upon everything while simultaneously "passing through" all things "without contact." The Divine Power(s), then, functions both as boundary and intermediary between the divine and material existence. The divine acts in the material world through its power(s), which allows the divine to forego direct contact with materiality, instead remaining "impassible and undefiled."

Proclus reports that Numenius of Apameia (fl. 150) made a distinction among doctrines that teach birth among the divinities: some teach that the divine essence is itself mixed with matter, while others teach that the divine essence itself is not mixed with matter, but only the δυνάμεις and ἐνέργεια of the divine οὐσία mix with matter.[23] Proclus attributes the latter belief to Numenius himself. In other words, Numenius believed that divine begetting cannot mean that the existent (or essence) enters matter but that in begetting, only the divine power or an activity can enter matter. We note first the general presupposition that divine begetting involves matter in some way, a dark presupposition that also looms on Eunomius' conceptual horizon whenever he talks about God's production of the Son. However, the most remarkable aspect of this quotation from Numenius is the opposition it sets between the divine οὐσία, on one hand, and the δυνάμεις and ἐνέργεια, on the other. The fact that in this passage Numenius groups δύναμις and ἐνέργεια together, such that δύναμις (like ἐνέργεια) stands over against οὐσία (not grouping power with essence) shows a distinctive understanding of the ontological status of δύναμις, one which Eunomius

23. *Numenius Fragments,* Édouard des Places, ed. and trans. (Paris: Société d'Éditions, 1973), fragment 50, 93–94.

and Numenius will have in common.[24] This set of distinctions, with its implicit boundaries of unity, situates all divine activity on the side of what is not divinity in itself, leaving the real divinity (οὐσία) unengaged. The divine οὐσία stands above and apart from matter, but its δύναμις or ἐνέργεια can join with matter. This is Eunomius' own doctrine of the Incarnation in (as will be seen) Eunomius' own preferred language. God, the divine οὐσία, must be understood to stand above and apart from matter, but the product of God's ἐνέργεια joins with matter. Divinity itself cannot be joined to matter, although an activity (ἐνέργεια) of the Divine can enter matter and work there. This is Numenius' understanding of what divine generation means; it is Eunomius' understanding as well. The context of divine generation is the same for each author; the specific terminology is the same; the doctrinal conclusion is the same. Problems with passion in the "generation" of the Son by the Father, and recourse to distinctions in causality to solve those problems, are two similarities shared by second- and third-century pagan theologian-philosophers and fourth-century Christian theologians. As we shall see in chapter seven, the question of passion in the "generation" of the Son by the Father will become a major topic of dispute in the trinitarian controversies of the second half of the fourth century.

### *Tertullian's Doctrine of "One Power, One Substance"*

When we turn to Christian theology, power theology appears in the Latin tradition with the same doctrinal function and ambiguities we can observe in Greek authors. We find, first of all, that Tertullian uses *power* (often *potestatis,* but also *virtus*) in doctrinal formulations in which the sense is "one power, one substance." This understanding and use of the term appears particularly in the *Against Praxeas,* when Tertullian, having insisted upon the distinctness of the Divine Persons, draws back to affirm their substantial unity. Tertullian's definition of this unity in diversity is almost too famous to need be quoted here:

24. Chapter 6 will show a further similarity between Eunomius' and Numenius' understandings of divine productivity and doctrines of creation.

. . . three, however, not in condition, but in degree; not in substance, but in form; not in power [*potestatis*], but in aspect; yet of one substance, and one condition, and of one power inasmuch as He is one God. . . .[25]

This formula of unity is repeated again shortly:

All along did He therefore strenuously aim at this conclusion, that while they were of one power [*virtus*] and essence, they should still be believed to be two.[26]

A second doctrinal sense of a "power" trinitarian theology also appears in Tertullian's writings, namely, where "power" identifies the second Person. There are a number of passages in which Tertullian states the identity of titles for the second Person: Power, Word, Wisdom, Son, and, in at least one important case, Spirit. A few times the title Power is drawn from 1 Cor. 1:24, but it is Luke 1:35 that serves as the most significant scriptural description of the Son as Power.[27] Despite being well known to scholars, Tertullian's interpretation of the Lucan passage deserves to be noted here, for it is a distinctive reading of the text.

Tertullian understands Luke 1:35 to be a description of the entrance of divinity into human nature. The Lucan passage is as much a first description of the Incarnation as John 1:14. The "Spirit of God" that comes over Mary, and the "Power of the Most High" that overshadows her, are each identified by Tertullian as the Word Himself. Luke is not here describing the impregnation of Mary by the Father (via the Holy Spirit) but the Son's arrival into humanity. The Son is the "Spirit of God," and the Son is the "Power of the Most High." (The Most High is God, the Father.)

The alternative understanding—that the "Spirit of God" is God and the "Power of the Most High" is God—is precisely what Tertullian's opponents are arguing. (The Lucan passage itself is probably introduced initially into the debate by Praxeas.) The polemical context requires Tertullian to emphasize the reference to the Son in the passage and opens up the way for him to identify the Son as God's "Power." Moingt has argued that Tertullian's understanding of the Trinity as *unius potestatis* is not like that of either the Apologists or the Nicenes, for although ". . . . il [Tertullian] con-

25. *Against Praxeas* (*Adversus Praxean*) 2, CSEL 47.230.2–3; ANF 3.598.

26. Ibid., 22; CSEL 47.271.2; ANF 3.618.

27. Luke 1:35, it should be observed in passing, uses *virtus* just as 1 Cor. 1:24 does. The connection between the two texts could only seem obvious to Tertullian.

nait bien la notion révélée que le Fils est la virtus Patris, mais ne s'en sert pas pour expliquer l'unius potestatis."[28] In literal terms, Moingt's opinion that Tertullian never offered a doctrine of "the Son is the Power of God" based on 1 Cor, 1:24 is wrong. But substantially, Moingt is right, for Tertullian never takes the next, seemingly obvious, step of deducing that "if the Son is the Power of God, then He must be eternally united with God (as power is co-existent with substance)." The Son's title of "Power" is never developed for its implications of unity: the closest Tertullian comes is at *On the Flesh of Christ* 14, where he argues that if He is the "Spirit of God" and the "Power of the Most High," then the Son can hardly be regarded as lower than the angels.[29] Positioning the Son vis à vis the angels is an enduring central concern of Latin christology: *virtus/virtute* language places some burden on this argument since (like δύναμις in Paul's "powers and principalities") Tertullian uses *virtutes* to mean angels, and the Son must be distinguished from these "powers".[30]

Amid the Luke 1:35 inspired argument in *Against Praxeas* that Son, Power, Word and Spirit are all synonomous titles for the second Person, Tertullian offers a delicately phrased articulation of the *X from X* doctrine.[31] The argument runs so: Any product of God that is from Himself has the same quality as He it is produced from and to whom it belongs. Therefore Spirit and Word are God because each is from God but is not exactly the same as Who each is from. Whatever is from God is God, and, although existing in itself, is not God Himself but as God because from the same substance as God Himself. Tertullian's wording is somewhat tortured even while his intent is clear: whatever comes from God personally is God in substance but exists in itself, still "God" but in existence in relation to

28. See Joseph Moingt, *Unité et processions,* vol. 3 of *Théologie trinitaire de Tertullien,* 4 vols. (Paris: Aubier, 1966–1969), 838, note 2. Moingt identifies two senses of the phrase *God's power:* the first, that of the single power of the Father, Moingt finds in Tertullian; the second, that the Son is this power, Moingt does not find in Tertullian. (See also pp. 838–839, including notes 2 and 3.) In his dissertation on the pre-Nicene use of 1 Cor. 1:24, McFadden reports only one clear reference by Tertullian to 1 Cor. 1:24: namely, at *Against Praxeas* 19:2, where Tertullian uses 1 Cor. 1:24 to show that the Wisdom mentioned in Prov. 8 is the Son, since the Son is "the Wisdom and Power." See "The Exegesis of I Cor 1:24", 63–68, especially 65 and 67.

29. *On the Flesh of Christ* (*de Carni Christi*) 14, CSEL 70.226.32; ANF 3.534.

30. *Against Praxeas* 19, CSEL 47.261.3.

31. *Ibid.*, 26, CSEL 47.278.9–16.

its producer. Power, Wisdom, Word, and (with great ambiguity) Spirit[32] are the attribute(s) of the divine substance and, when considered in themselves, are God but, when considered as attributes, are from God. Part of the difficulty with following Tertulian's thought here is that he collapses the distinction between product and property, or rather, Tertullian understands Power, Wisdom and Word to be a certain class of products that exist in their producer as properties, and conversely, as properties that exist as products. The relationship between God (the Father) and the second Person can only be described in the play between such categories (as property and product). The Son is a product of the divine substance, but that generation is of the kind that the identity of the product is "to stand in relation to the substance," to exist because of what the substance is. Tertullian is expressing a "genetic" understanding of an *X from X* causality as finely as he can: the Son is what the Father is but not as the Father is (and so, not the Father).

Tertullian's power theology then attempts to express the natural unity that exists between God and the Son while maintaining their real distinction. Power is understood as a kind of existence that is co-extensive with the nature or substance. Anything that exists (including the divine substance or God) exists in or with power, and any complete statement of "one nature" must include the assertion of "one power" (and vice versa). The doctrine of "one power, one nature" is not understood by Tertullian to mean that the Father and Son have no mutual distinction; over against "Praxeas," Tertullian must insist that identifying the Son as divine through describing the Son as a property of that divinity does not collapse the Son into the Father. When we turn to Origen next, we shall see that he finds more ambiguity in the description of the Son as "the Power of God" and as "X from X". Those reading Tertullian in the fourth century who were sympathetic to Nicaea would have found in him a strong identification of power with nature, so strong in fact that a not quite so sophisticated reader as Phoebadius might have failed to be able to distinguish power from substance with any real clarity.

32. Remembering that Power is Wisdom is Word, but that sometimes (even in the same sentence) Spirit is equivalent to these titles and sometimes refers to the divine substance itself.

*Power Theology in Hippolytus'* Against Noetus

Hippolytus' understanding of the unity between Father and Son is expressed as a "one Power" doctrine. "He [the Son as speaking in Scripture] has revealed two persons [πρόσωπα], but a single Power." This formula appears in *Against Noetus* as Hippolytus seeks to balance his statements of divine unity and divine diversity. The Father and Son are distinct at the level of persons (and in the economy) but one at the level of power or nature. Almost the exact same language will be used at the conclusion of this section of the work; after asserting that the Father, the Son, and the Holy Spirit really are "three," Hippolytus says:

> But if he [Noetus] wants to learn how God is shown to be one, he must know that this [God] has a single Power; and that as far as Power is concerned, God is one: but in terms of the economy the display [or manifestation] is triple. . . .[33]

Hippolytus' first statement that the Scriptures reveal "two persons but a single power" occurs as he is offering an exegesis of John 10:30, "I and the Father are one," a passage that was to have a rich life in the coming trinitarian controversies of the late fourth century. Hippolytus refers to this text in order to prove the diversity of persons: the Gospel says "are one," that is, "we are one," not "we am one" or "I am one." The saying as a whole is taken to be a description of diversity in unity: "I and the Father are"—diversity; "one"—unity. The scriptural expression of these two realities is then restated by Hippolytus in alternate language that grounds the truths revealed in Scripture. Hippolytus' restatement follows the same sequence as John: "He revealed two persons"—diversity; "but a single power"—unity.

Further expressions by Hippolytus of a power theology appear in the second half of the work; these tend to follow the character of a passing reference made already at *Against Noetus* 4.11: "He was Word, he was Spirit, he was Power," a formula that unifies these titles (including Spirit) in a manner reminiscent of Tertullian and that at least one editor has seen as a reference to Luke 1:35 (as it was for Tertullian).[34] In these later references

33. *Hippolytus of Rome: Contra Noetum,* 8.2; trans. Robert Butterworth, S.J. (London: Heythrop Monographs, 1977), 64–65.

34. Namely, Butterworth in his translation, *Contra Noetum,* 54.

to power, the concept is understood as being specifically descriptive of the second Person, that is, the Word, who is then identified by the title "Power," which is to say, "the Power of the Father."[35]

Hippolytus' trinitarian doctrine of a "two stage" Logos is too well known to need to be restated here except to remark that his theology of the second Person as the Power of the Father rests upon a similar two-stage model. When Hippolytus wishes to show that the separate existence of the Power or Word in its second, that is, separate, stage neither diminishes nor multiplies the divinity, he turns to an *X from X* account of divine generation that is explicitly cast in terms of a Power doctrine.

> [The generation of the Son] is like light from light, or like water out of a spring, or like a sunbeam out of the sun. For there is a single Power that comes out of the All. But the All is the Father, and the Power out of him is the Word.[36]

Here Power is identified with the Word that "comes out of," a concept that parallels the earlier economic formula of "manifestation." The "All" is to the "Power" as the "Father" is to the "Word."[37] Through the *X from X* language, we can know both that the causal relationship between Father and Son (or All and Power) is like that of "light from light" (*X from X*); and that the relationship of natures or identities is like that of "light from light." In the references to Power that follow the *X from X* formula, Hippolytus moves to identify Power with the second Person, who has come from the Father: the Word is the Power of the Father. Yet, as is typical of Hippolytus, the shift to attributing "Power" solely and specifically to the Word serves not only to describe the identity of the Word but to restate the unity in the Godhead: He is the Father's Power[38] whose sending makes the Father known. Offhand we might expect Hippolytus' vocabulary in these passages to simply revolve around the title "the Word," but from *Against Noetus* 11.1 to 16.1, the author moves back and forth between Power and Word as

35. McFadden, "Exegesis of 1 Cor. 1:24," 60, relates Hippolytus' identification of titles in *Against Noetus* to a similar statement in his *Commentary on the Canticle of Canticles.* The *Commentary* also represents the only time Hippolytus clearly cites 1 Cor. 1:24.

36. *Contra Noetum* 11.1, 70–71.

37. McFadden, "The Exegesis of 1 Cor 1:24," 62 n. 18, finds a parallel reference to Christ as the "Power of the All" in *Acta Philippi* 132.

38. *Contra Noetum,* 11.4 and 16.1. Butterworth seems to regard ἐξουσία (at 12.2) as a functional synonym to δύναμις.

identifying titles. In short, Hippolytus declines to be satisfied with simply a "Word" theology. I believe that this is because of the continuing presence of the *X from X* causality articulated at 11.1.

There are thus two doctrines of "one power" in Hippolytus' theology. In the first doctrine of one power, this formula articulates an understanding of divine unity within a specific context of arguing for the reality of divine personal diversity. In the second doctrine of one power, the formula articulates the identity of the second Person (the "Word") in such a way as to define the personal identity of the Word (who He is) and to relate that identity to the unity of the Divine. If we follow Butterworth's literary analysis of *Against Noetus,*[39] then the first doctrine of one power is polemical in intention or origin, an articulation shaped by the design to assert the reality of the divine persons while at the same time affirming the substantial unity. Obviously Hippolytus' argument that God is one in power is polemically motivated, since it is a doctrine offered against Noetus' trinitarian theology. Butterworth's judgment is that everything in the first half of *Against Noetus* (that is, up to Chapter eleven) is formally polemical, that is, governed by a rhetorical stance over against another position. All the material in the second half of *Against Noetus,* by contrast, is catechetical in intention or origin, which means that the doctrine of identifying the Word with the Power of God takes on a polemical role only accidentally. It is, as a doctrine in itself, another way of talking about the Trinity, a way that self-consciously speaks to those who already have right belief rather than speaking to those who are in error.

In Tertullian's *Against Praxeas* we have seen a similar polemical use of the "one substance, one power" doctrine. Both Tertullian's and Hippolytus'

39. In Chapter three of *Contra Noetum,* Butterworth proposes a schema for the literary structure of *Against Noetus* in which the two "one power" doctrines may be situated. All the treatments of δύναμις in which God is said to have one power are in the first part of the text ("A"), which Butterworth describes as "hostile" in intention and controlled by polemics. All the identifications of Δύναμις with the Λόγος occur in the second part of *Against Noetus,* ("B"), which Butterworth describes as "friendly" and instructionally-oriented. Assuming, first, that Butterworth's literary division is true to Hippolytus' intentions, and, second, that the work was widely read and with at least as much literary integrity as it has today (!), then can we, with any confidence, imagine that the two-fold structure of the work, and the dual genres of doctrinal articulation, were obvious to a fourth-century reader? Would a fourth-century reader have recognized that initial one-power formulations were polemically designed while the later "Word is Power" formulations were instructionally designed?

works are written against what they take to be modalist trinitarian theologies, and in both cases the assertion of "one substance (or nature), one power" functions as the limiting case understanding of the primary polemical teaching of the real diversity of persons in God. In other words, both Tertullian and Hippolytus are primarily arguing against an understanding of God that does not allow for the real and separate existences of the Father and Son. In the process of refuting the modalist position, each theologian comes to the point where the affirmation of diversity cannot stand alone but has to be coupled with a proper understanding of the unity between these real and separate existences ("persons"). The doctrine of "one nature, one power" is not simply *a* way of arguing for divine unity; the doctrine is, in the context of both Tertullian and Hippolytus, *the best* way to argue for divine unity in support of the doctrine of real diversity in that divine unity. Pro-Nicenes, then, have a precedent for articulating a doctrine of "one nature, one power" in order to argue for divine unity in a theological climate in which divine unity has been pushed too far and has ended up as modalism.[40]

I believe that I can take the point about the literary positioning of the doctrine of "one nature, one power" one step further. After Hippolytus announces that "as far as the Power is concerned, God is one," he adds that "in terms of the economy the display [of the Power] is triple—as will be shown later when we give an account of the truth."[41] This "account about the truth" is the second, catechetical, half of the work. The doctrine in the catechetical section that treats Power as a title identifying the second Person (the Word) is not to be taken, then, simply: the identification of Power with the second Person is a matter of the manifestation of that one Power. The Power is one but in the economy its manifestation is triple. In fact, when one reads that later account of the truth, the economic manifestation of the Power is spoken of only in terms of its manifestation as the second Person, the Word, the Power of God.

Power properly speaking is one in the divine nature, but in the economy it is attributed to each of the three Persons inasmuch as the economy

40. Whether contemporary scholarship has arrived at a point where it can confidently announce that that precedent was a matter of conscious or common knowledge among late fourth-century Nicenes is another matter.

41. *Contra Noetum* 8.2, 64.

is a manifestation of the divine nature and power. The Son is constituted as uniquely manifesting the divine nature and power, and as the unique manifestation of God (as distinguished from the Father and the Holy Spirit) appropriates the title Power in a special way. Obviously, the Son is not going to be conceived as more God than the Father: to the contrary, the Son is described by Hippolytus as an Image, the revealing of the divinity. Power, as we have seen in philosophical sources, is nature as it reveals itself in affect. Such an understanding is a fairly apt description of the economic identity of the Word. The two doctrines of power expressed in the first and second parts of *Against Noetus* are not, then, alternative doctrines. The first doctrine expresses an understanding of how the divine power exists in itself, namely, as one, as the nature is one. The second doctrine expresses an understanding of how divine power is expressed in the economy, namely, especially as the Son or Word. In the economy the concept (in the shape of the title) of Power is appropriated in a unique way by the Person who manifests that power.[42]

## *Origen:* Δύναμις *and the Wisdom Tradition*

Origen's use of *power*—δύναμις—is based upon an exegesis of 1 Cor 1:24, Heb. 1:3, and, especially, Wisd. 7:25. His unique contribution to trinitarian theology is to develop a new "Wisdom" account of the Godhead based on these texts.[43] Origen's emphasis on δύναμις as a trinitarian term is an expression of the fundamental role Wisdom theology played in his thought. The most important example of the role of Wisdom theology in

42. The easiest way to draw out the similarity between this understanding and that of, for example, the *Chaldean Oracles*, is by contrasting the two. The *Chaldean Oracles* begins by associating a trait (for example, Power, Intellect) with a specific person of the triad but presumes that this trait is also a characteristic of all of the triad. Hippolytus, in *Against Noetus*, begins by associating Power with the one divine nature but presumes that Power is also a special characteristic of a specific Person of the Trinity.

43. One of the best treatments of Origen's development of a Wisdom Christology is A. H. B. Logan's "Origen and Alexandrian Wisdom Christology," in *Origeniana Tertia* (Rome: Edizioni Dell'ateneo, 1985), 123–29. Logan's initial observation is that Origen is the first Christian to understand Wisd. 7:25 in a Christological sense. Logan refers to the apparent Christological interpretation of Wisd. 7:25 in *The Teachings of Silvanus*, which he thinks "represent[s] an Alexandrian Christian Wisdom tradition which prepared the way for theologians like Clement and Origen" (128). See also Robert M. Grant, "The Book of Wisdom: Reflections on the History of the Canon and Theology," *Studia Patristica* VII (1963): 462–72.

Origen's thought is his appropriation of the Wisdom of Solomon as a *bona fide* text of revelation. Although the Wisdom of Solomon was not in the Hebrew canon and was used only minimally by Christians before him, Origen found in that work an account of God's nature comparable to the account in John 1.

Origen understood Wisd. 7:25 specifically as a description of the generation of the second Person from the First.[44] He uses this passage, together with 1 Cor. 1:24 and Heb. 1:3, as the scriptural authority for developing an account of the union between the first and second Persons based upon the title, δύναμις. Both Wisd. 7:25 and 1 Cor. 1:24 refer to the "Power and Wisdom" of God, which Origen interprets as titles of the second person that describe the nature of His union with God. Similarly, both Wisd. 7:25 and Heb. 1:3 are seen as descriptions of the generation of the second Person. The use of these three scriptural texts together in mutual support of a common exegesis of *power* becomes an indication of the influence of Origen on all sides in the trinitarian controversies: Eusebius of Caesarea, Athanasius, and Gregory of Nyssa, for example, all support their understanding of the second Person as power with references to the three texts, as well as interpreting each text via the other two. It is the Wisdom of Solomon that takes precedence in Origen's own treatment of the second Person as the power and wisdom of God. However, as the trinitarian controversy develops, the Wisdom passage recedes in importance, in part due to the association of Wisd. 7:25 with the favored Arian proof text, Prov. 8:22, an association that first occurs in Origen's *On First Principles* 2. 1. Eusebius of Caesarea's very definite emphasis on Wisd. 7:25 is at least a clear indication of his debt to Origen; but it may also be an early indication of his non-Nicene theology.[45]

For the purposes of this study, there are three works by Origen where his use of δύναμις is an important influence in trinitarian theology gener-

44. The Greek for Wisdom 7:25 is: ἀτμὶς γάρ ἐστιν τῆς τοῦ θεοῦ δυνάμεως καὶ ἀπόρροια τῆς τοῦ παντοκράτορος δόξης εἰλικρινής· διὰ τοῦτο οὐδὲν μεμιαμμένον εἰς αὐτὴν παρεμπίπτει.

45. A good example of this association of the three scriptural texts occurs in Athanasius' *Defence of the Sentences of Dionysius* 8–15: Athanasius begins with a reference to the Hebrews text as proof that Christ was the Word of God, then moves (in 9) to what is at least a reference to Wisd. 7:25 and may also include 1 Cor. 1:24. In chapter 15, there are distinct references to both 1 Cor. 1:24 and Wisd. 7:25.

ally, and on the use of the term in the early trinitarian controversies surrounding the Council of Nicaea especially: *On First Principles, Commentary on the Gospel of John,* and the *Dialogue with Heraclides.* For thematic reasons I will discuss Origen's *Dialogue with Heraclides* first, then *On First Principles,* and finally his *Commentary on the Gospel of John.*[46]

The reference to δύναμις in the *Dialogue with Heraclides* is the briefest of the discussions in the three texts but in some ways the most interesting. In their conversation,[47] Origen asks Heraclides about his understanding of Christian belief on the nature (and number) of God(s):

> *Origen:* The Father is God?
> *Heraclides:* Completely.
> *Origen:* The Son is different from the Father?
> *Heraclides:* How could the Son exist if he were the same as the Father?
> *Origen:* Though the Son is distinct from the Father, he is also God?
> *Heraclides:* He is also God.
> *Origen:* And in their unity there are two Gods?
> *Heraclides:* Yes.
> *Origen:* We confess two Gods?
> *Heraclides:* Yes. The power is one.[48]

This brief passage has not received the attention it deserves. Quasten, for one, correctly emphasizes it, but his interpretation of "δύο θεοί, μία δύναμις" is misleading: "It is the same formula of later theology," he says, "Two persons but one nature." Leaving aside the question of "later theology," what is frustrating about Quasten's statement is his leap from "one power" to "one nature." Quasten is on to something, but he doesn't give it away. He supplies the "one nature" phrasing that a modern reader might expect but without explaining how "one power" functions as a virtual synonym for "one nature."[49]

46. Another important occasion of Origen's use of Wisd. 7:25 and Heb. 1:3 is his *Commentary on Hebrews,* which now remains only as fragments from Pamphilus' *Apology for Origen,* translated by Rufinus.

47. The apparent context for this work is that Origen was sent to examine the Bishop Heraclides, whose orthodoxy was in doubt.

48. *Dialogue with Heraclides* 2: 15–27, in *Entretien d'Origène avec Heraclide,* ed. and trans. Jean Scherer. Sources Chrétiennes, vol. 67 (Paris: Les Éditions du Cerf, 1960), 56–59.

49. Scherer sees a dependence of Origen's μία δύναμις formula on 1 Cor 1:24, and he notes the precedent in Hippolytus' δύο πρόσωπα ἔδειξεν δύναμιν δὲ μίαν of *Against the Heretics* 13, and the subsequent use in Ambrose *In Luc* II, 66, "*esti personis duo, potestate unum sunt.*"

In the dialogue, the formula "two Gods, one power" serves as doctrine that both Origen and Heraclides can agree upon. Origen has taken pains to establish the real distinction between the Father and the Son and that both Father and Son are αὐτός θεός. The equal reality and divinity of the two being agreed upon, Origen then accepts Heraclides' statement of divine unity: there is only one power. Unlike other formulations based on power (for example, Wisd. 7:25, Heb. 1:3, and 1 Cor 1:24), this statement does not identify the power with the Son, or with any one Person at all. Power is that common ground of both Gods. It is only in this passage that Origen does not associate δύναμις with either the Father or the Son individually, or with the Father and the Son in a mechanism of generation or participation (that is, power from power).[50]

Origen's most extensive treatment of the generation and nature of the Son using Wisd. 7:25, Heb. 1:3, and 1 Cor. 1:24 is found in *On First Principles.*[51] Origen begins with the understanding that in these three texts, "Wisdom" is synonymous with "Word" in John 1:1.[52] The Word is thus God's Wisdom, understood as having a separate existence, not simply existing as wisdom exists in human minds.[53]

Origen understands Wisd. 7:25 to provide five definitions of God and each indicates a characteristic of God's Wisdom: power, glory, eternal light, operation, and goodness. Power stands apart from the rest of the list of attributes because Wisdom has been described not as a breath of glory,

50. Johannes Quasten, *The Ante-Nicene Literature after Irenaeus,* vol. 2 of *Patrology* (Westminster: Newman Press, 1953), 63, understands "one power" to be a description of the divine nature, rather than a description simply of moral or political unity, because of the contrast drawn between the two Gods and the one power: Quasten expects a symmetry of degrees of existence between the two formulas, and the understanding "one authority" (= δύναμις) balances existents (two Gods) with an accident (or, at best, a quality or a kind of relation, that is, authority).

51. See, for example, *On First Principles,* 1.2.5, where Origen refers to both Wisd. 7:25 and Heb. 1:3; Heb. 1:3 appears also at 1.2.7 and 1.2.9 with Wisd. 7:25. 1 Cor. 1:24 is used at 1.2.2 and 1.2.9.

52. Thus Origen says, "For wisdom opens to all other beings, that is, to the whole creation, the meaning of the mysteries and secrets which are contained within the wisdom of God, and so she is called the Word. . . . In the beginning of his gospel, when by an appropriate declaration he [John, the evangelist] defines the Word to be God: 'And the Word was God, and he was in the beginning with God'" (*On First Principles* 1.2.3, 63–71, G. W. Butterworth, trans. [New York: Harper Torchbooks, 1966], 16–17). See also comments in *Traité des Principes Tome I (Livres I et II)*, commentary by H. Crouzel and M. Simonetti, SC, vol. 253 (Paris: Les Éditions du Cerf, 1978), 114–17. Citations to the English translation will henceforth be to Butterworth.

53. See *On First Principles* 1.2.2, which mentions wisdom. Crouzel makes the same point about the separate existence of God's power; see SC, vol. 253, 48 n. 54.

eternal light, operation, or goodness but as a breath of the power of God. Origen then gives his own definition of power:

> Therefore one must understand God's power [as that] by which He has strength, [as that] by which he both begins and holds together and governs all things visible and invisible, [as that] by which he is sufficient for all things, whose providence he wields, in all of which he is present as if united [to them].[54]

Both Origen's list of divine attributes and his definition of power deserve some comment in light of the later debate associated with Nicaea over God's power(s). The list from Wisd. 7:25 associates power with other titles that are not obviously philosophical; rather, the list has a doxological quality to it, where power is the same kind of title as eternal light or glory. Nothing about the list suggests, for example, that power names an attribute of existence that is as fundamental as essence or nature. It is not clear whether power is an attribute that one uses exclusively of God or whether all existents, or even all rational beings, may be said to have power. Terms such as glory and eternal light do seem to suggest that power applies only to God's nature. The same thing is true of Origen's definition of power. Thus, in this reading, power does not seem to name that by which all rational existents "establish and preserve," except that in the case of God, His power "establishes and preserves all things visible and invisible." Though Origen's definition combines the sense of δύναμις as capacity with the sense of δύναμις as political power, power, in his definition, seems to be a uniquely divine attribute.

However, there is one parallel to Origen's definition that indicates a different context for Origen's use of δύναμις. Simplicius says that the Stoics defined a δύναμις, meaning *power* as faculty, as a "sort of disposition of the soul which can produce and regulate a set of activities as discrete events." This definition seems close to Origen's understanding that δύναμις is that "by which he [God] both begins and holds together and governs all things . . . " In short, the use of *power* here includes the psychological sense of faculty.[55] Origen's paradigm for his term starts out as doxological but

54. *On First Principles*, 1.2.9, 275–79.

55. Williams understands Origen's doctrine of "production from the will" as an expression of his "profound concern for the simplicity, immateriality and indivisibility of the divine nature" that leads Origen to emphasize "the analogy between God and the human mind; so it is not

ends up as psychological. This interpretation is confirmed by Origen's own language, for he soon introduces the mechanism of will, saying that from the first power there proceeds a breath that "proceeds as will proceeds from the mind," and takes on an existence of its own:

> . . . the will of God comes itself to be a power of God. There comes into existence, therefore, another power, subsisting in its own proper nature . . . a kind of breath of the first and unbegotten power of God.[56]

God's will, Origen says, is always complete and sufficient. The desire in that original power is never without the object of that desire: the mirror—as the Wisdom text tells—of that first power, a(nother) power. The use of will begins as an analogy, but ends, in Origen's argument, as more than that since the second power is nothing but the instant satisfaction of the will (or, as Origen also calls it, and I have followed, desire): God's will produces, by its own transformation, the object of its desire. Or, as Crouzel puts it, ". . . ce vouloir qui procède du Père constitue existentielle le Fils. . . ."[57] Not only is there no other way for God to produce except through desire but there is no other reason for God to produce.[58] The transition from understanding "from the will" as an analogy to understanding it literally parallels the change in Origen's understanding of power from a doxological title to a psychological cause. The more literally one takes the description "from the will" the more δύναμις is understood to name the kind of causality present in generation.

There are thus two powers: the first is the unbegotten power from which arises the second power.[59] The power that is the second Person is

---

surprising that what proceeds from God, his Word or Wisdom, should be conceived on the analogy of a mental operation." Williams properly includes among the terms of this psychological analogy δύναμις and ἐνέργεια, but improperly suggests that the terms reveal the "Aristotelean sequence of potency and act" (*Arius*, 138–39). Rather the terms are used with the sense, and in the sequence, of faculty and operation, as I will show.

56. *On First Principles* 1.2.9; Butterworth, 23.

57. Crouzel, SC, vol. 253, 41 n. 36.

58. I use the word the vague word "produce" here intentionally in an attempt to avoid the textual question whether the pre-Rufinus text used begotten or created in these passages. The importance of the distinction between those two words is a value from a later time.

59. Origen adds another layer of distinctions to the title Power in his *Commentary on John*. Origen asks whether Christ is called Power (and Wisdom and Justice) absolutely or only "for us" (though for Origen these two senses are not necessarily mutually exclusive). Origen's conclusion is that Christ is both the power of God absolutely and the power of God for us. What Origen

not the very power of the first Person. The Wisdom text itself provides the grounds for the conclusion that the product of the first power is a power like the first (if the commonplace of "like produces like" were not enough): Wisdom, the passage says, is an unspotted mirror of God's power, an image of God's goodness. Origen develops the image metaphor:

It is written thus: "And Adam begat Seth after his own image and after his own kind." This image preserves the unity of nature and substance common to a father and a son. For if "all things that the Father doeth these also the Son doeth likewise," then in this very fact that the Son does all things just as the Father does, the Father's image is reproduced in the Son, whose birth from the Father is as it were an act of his will proceeding from the mind.[60]

Thus Origen emphasizes the unity of activity between Father and Son as the basis for the "imaging" of the Father in the Son.[61] This unity of activity does not mean that the Son's resemblance is limited to a kind of moral resemblance. Origen is here assuming the kind of argument that will later find its most developed form in the Cappadocians: unity of action is a sign or criterion of a common nature.[62] Furthermore, the unity of activity

means by the expression "for us" is indicated, I believe, in his comparison of Johannine and Pauline titles of Christ. Origen recognizes a certain equivocal sense to the term *power,* since all things possess power in some degree; but everything that has power has it through participation in Christ, the Power of God. The sin of Simon Magus, Origen says, was his claim to be the very power of God "which is called the Great," that is, that in which all other powers participate (*Commentary on John* 1:23, 241–42). These other powers include spiritual and godly beings, namely, the pre-existent souls and angels. Scriptural references to Christ as the "Captain of the powers" indicate both Christ's superior claim to the title Power, as well as the equivocation (or participation) inherent in the shared title, Power. See *Commentary* 1:26, 291–92.

60. *On First Principles,* 1.2.6; Butterworth's translation, 19. Crouzel points out that this passage figures in the controversy over Origen's use of the terms οὐσία, ὑπόστασις, and ὁμοούσιος; see Crouzel, SC, vol. 253, 40–41 n. 35. See also G. Christopher Stead, *Divine Substance* (Oxford: Clarendon Press, 1977), 211.

A second point to be noticed about this passage is Origen's reference to John 5:19; the entire verse runs: "Jesus said to them, 'Truly, truly, I say to you, the Son can do nothing of his own accord, but only what he sees the Father doing; for whatever he does, that the Son does likewise.'" The first portion of this verse is cited by anti-Nicene apologists such as Eunomius as evidence of the Son's dependence upon, and inferiority to, the Father.

61. As Crouzel puts it, the Son is the image by his action (SC, vol. 253, 41 n. 36).

62. Like Origen, Gregory uses the relationship between Adam and his son (although Gregory names Abel) as an analogy to the relationship between God and the Son. Gregory says that ". . . the essential nature of Adam and Abel is marked by the same characteristics, we must certainly agree that one essence is in both, and that the one and the other are exhibited in the same nature" (*GNO* 2:30:14–16; NPNF 5:143). Gregory's statement on the unity between the Father and the Son is stronger than Origen's. Origen finds the "reproduction of the image of the Father" in the actions

between Father and Son indicates that the will is the source of the Son, or rather, the mode of his generation, since will is the source of all activity (at this level of being).[63] That is, the origin of the Son is in the act of God's will proceeding from His mind. Finally, against the Gnostics,[64] production by the will insures that the Son's generation does not involve a splitting up or a spreading out of the divine essence since the means of production is immaterial (an argument that returns in the Nicene controversy).

### *Origen's Doctrine of Production from the Power*

In Origen's theology, the origin of that second power in the first is a guarantee of that second power's eternal existence; "since God always had both the power and the will, there was never the slightest reason or possibility that he should not always have had this good thing that he desired. This proves that there always existed that breath of the power of God, having no beginning but God himself."[65] Production from the will provides

---

of the Son rather than in the begetting by the Father, while Gregory finds only the "mark" or evidence of the same nature in the "identical characteristics."

63. Rowan Greer, *The Captain of Our Salvation,* Beiträge zur Geschichte der Biblischen Exegese, vol. 15 (Tübingen: J. C. B. Mohr, 1973), 47.

64. Origen's reference to Simon Magus's sin in claiming to be the "Great Power of God" deserves a further note in light of questions of Gnostic influence. Origen's mention of Simon Magus and the "Great Power" motif marks his own experience of Gnostic associations with power language. Indeed, his mention of power and Simon at *Commentary on John* 1:33, 241–42, reflects what many scholars recognize as one of the most, if not the most, distinctive uses of *power* in the era from the close of the New Testament period until the demise of Gnosticism. Jarl E. Fossum, for example, introduces the use of *power* as a "Name of God" with the case of Simon Magus in *The Name of God and the Angel of the Lord* (Tübingen: J. C. B. Mohr, 1985), 162–74. Fossum's point is to argue that Simon's title does not simply name him as a "carrier of a power" but rather "Simon is the Great Power and no 'carrier' of it" (172). Fossum shows that the title "Great Power" was recognized as the same kind of title as Messiah, and, like the phrase "I am," as a claim to divinity. Fossum also mentions the role of this title in (Christian) Gnostic literature, such as the Acts of Peter, the Gospel of Peter, and the Pseudo-Clementine literature (which is now considered to address Eunomian theology). Another important Gnostic reference to the "Great Power" is in the *Nag Hammadi Codex* VI, 4: *The Concept of Our Great Power,* ed. and trans. Frederik Wisse and Francis Williams, in *Nag Hammadi Studies,* vol. 11 (Leiden: E. J. Brill, 1979), 294–323. This text, which in the Coptic dates from the mid-fourth century C.E., includes many of the features of power found in the Christian authors discussed in this chapter, including a distinction between the power and powers (VI, 4, 38, 7), where the one power is superior to the multiple powers (VI, 4, 47, 10). Perhaps more significantly, this text contains a reference to the errors of the Anomians. See *The Concept of Our Great Power,* 292, for a discussion of the term *Anomoians* as a means of dating the codex, and 305 for the reference to *Anomoians* itself.

65. *On First Principles,* 1.2.9; Butterworth, 23. This argument is picked up later by Athanasius to show the eternal existence of the second Person; the argument from the eternal wisdom and

the same guarantee that the Son's generation is eternal, for God was never without His will. God's will alone is sufficient for production, and requires no other agent: "And on this account my own opinion is that an act of the Father's will ought to be sufficient to ensure the existence of what he wills; for in willing he uses no other means than that which is produced by the deliberation of his will."[66]

The power that the second Person is identified with is thus not the very power of God—that is, the power God has in his own existence—but a second produced or generated power: a power from a power. All sides in the early stage of the Nicene controversy could (and did) comfortably describe the production of the second Person from the first as an *X from X* causal relationship.[67] Expressions like light from light or wisdom from wisdom occur in virtually everyone's writings. Clearly, in themselves, they do not specify that the cause reproduces its own nature or identity in the product. The value of *X from X* expressions turned upon the understanding one had of the meaning(s) of the two X's: were the two X's used in exactly the same sense, or were they used as a kind of homonym? Was X said of the cause in the same way that X was said of the effect? Clearly Nicenes and pro-Nicenes would answer yes to these questions, while anti-Nicenes and non-

power of God allows Athanasius to move away from the title of "Son," which can suggest a beginning and which seemed too biological or materialist a description of the nature of the union. E. P. Meijering thinks that in *On First Principles,* Origen argues that insofar as God's productive capacity exists, it must be productive. See Meijering's "Athanasius on the Father as the Origin of the Son" in his collection *God Being History* (Amsterdam: North Holland, 1975), 89–102. Meijering's particular point is that Origen used this notion that a cause is always productive insofar as it exists in his argument for the eternity of the Son and the Cosmos. Meijering paraphrases Origen's thought thus: "Since God has always been almighty there must have always been a creation, a product of his almightiness" (90). Meijering concludes that ". . . Origen postulates eternal products of God's creative power" (99). Meijering then compares the opinions of Origen, Athanasius, and Arius on the questions of God's eternal power and the eternity of the world. On the first point Athanasius agreed with Origen but identified this power with the eternal Son. On the second point Athanasius believed as the Arians did that the world (for Athanasius, excluding the Son) had a beginning in time, that is, was not eternal. Crouzel makes the same point, that Origen used the notion of a productive cause to argue for the eternity of the Son, when he refers to Origen's conclusion that "There was no time when he [the second Person] did not exist." See Crouzel, SC, vol. 253, 48 n. 55, and also 48–50 nn. 55–61.

66. *On First Principles* 1.2.6; Butterworth, 19. See Crouzel's note to this effect in SC, vol. 253, 41–42 n. 37.

67. Normally *X from X* expressions can be understood as examples of "like from like" causality. However, to say "like from like" in the trinitarian controversy is still too ambiguous.

Nicenes would answer no.[68] Differences in the argument over what exactly an *X from X* expression meant may have come down to preferred examples of such a relationship. Fire from fire seems to have been less open to an equivocal interpretation of the two appearances of "fire" than the "wisdom" in wisdom from wisdom.[69] Radiance examples figure prominently in Athanasius' arguments, for example, although Eunomius has no problem explaining the occurrences of "light" in *light from light* as homonyms.

As the previous chapters have shown, the kind of cause that reproduces itself in an *X from X* causality is called a power, δύναμις. True *X from X* relationships, in which a cause reproduces itself (or its nature), are examples of a power causality.[70] The earliest and most significant examples of such a causal relationship are those associated with elementals such as fire (the hot) and ice (the cold). The effect of fire is to make more fire: *X from X*. The most positive interpretation (from a Nicene point of view) of Origen's statement in *On First Principles* that the second Person is a power from God's power is that this is meant as a statement of an unequivocal *X from X* relationship, in which the power reference in "power from power" is offered not simply as an example of a like from like relationship but as a reference to the kind of causality in a true *X from X* relationship. The

68. Eunomius made the homonym argument explicitly and tied it to a theory of language in which a name referred to the essence of a thing. In *In Search of Asterius* (Göttingen: Vanderhoeck, 1990), 128, Wolfram Kinzig thinks that Asterius held a similar theory of language, but the reason for his assertion has to do with the similarity between Asterius' and Eunomius' interpretations of *X from X* expressions, rather than any clear evidence in Asterius of a linguistic theory.

69. Those French Augustinians who reject de Régnon's paradigm argue that the incidence of such examples from the material world in Greek pro-Nicene writings indicates that Greek trinitarian theology has a materialistic understanding of the common *ousia*. In particular, these scholars accuse Greek pro-Nicenes of failing to understand the difference between the expression "essence from essence" and all other *X from X* expressions.

70. I will use the terms "generic" and "genetic" to distinguish between the use of *power* simply as one example of an *X from X* relationship, and the use of *power* in an *X from X* expression where *power* is used as a paradigm of all true *X from X* relationships. The theology of Marius Victorinus provides a clear example of a distinction being made between *power from power* as a genetic case of an *X from X* causality and other expressions that are generic examples of *X from X* causality. Victorinus' understanding of *X from X* expressions is that they are in fact examples of power causality. "The Logos, the Word, is Light from Light, Spirit from Spirit, and substance from substance, [not separated by time, but] insofar as one is the cause of the other, so that by power they are always together. For the shining of the light is not separated but is always in the light" (*Against Arius* 1A, Mary T. Clark, trans., in *Marius Victorinus: Theological Treatises on the Trinity,* The Fathers of the Church, vol. 69, [Washington, D.C.: Catholic University of America Press, 1981], 141).

problem with such an interpretation of *X from X* statements in *On First Principles* is that elsewhere (that is, *Commentary on John*), Origen refers to "power from power" as one example among many such *X from X* expressions, and the sense of such expressions is clearly that the effect *is like* the cause and not that the effect *is the same* (kind of thing) as the cause.[71]

This latter understanding of *X from X* causality is a weaker statement of unity than if Origen had simply identified the Son with the power God has insofar as He exists; his is the kind of δύναμις theology that one later finds in the theology of Eusebius and Asterius and, by implication, Arius. The strength of such an identification would have been the preempting of any need to search out the language of production models for proofs of unity: the existence of God's own power is apparently a given, just as it is a given in the case of any existent. As it is, Origen's theology emphasizes the importance of, first, the kind of generation that produces the second Person, but secondly, and more importantly, the very fact of the second Person's production or generation. The second Person is understood fundamentally as a generated existent. While accounts of production may differ in the degree of union they offer between producer and product, by definition they all presuppose a logical priority in the cause or producer.[72]

We must note, despite its seeming obviousness, that Origen's account of the relationship between the first and second Persons emphasizes the

71. McFadden erroneously takes all *X from X* expressions as claims to common nature because he understands all such expressions to refer to relationships of true power causality; see "Exegesis," 42–43. As a result of his failure to distinguish between an equivocal use of X in *X from X* expressions (such as one finds in Asterius and Eunomius) and the univocal use of X in *X from X* expressions (such as one finds in Athanasius and Gregory), McFadden interprets all *X from X* expressions as statements of consubstantiality.

72. Williams, *Arius,* 138, takes care to explore Origen's argument that the Son is eternal because God's power was always effective (and thus, its products must always have existed). This causal relationship is restated in terms of relative predication: if God was always a Father, He must have always have had a Son. Thus, Williams says, "the necessity for creation depends upon the prior fact of God's defining himself as Father," and he emphasizes the role of Origen's doctrine that God creates by His own will in His Wisdom as a means by which Origen "avoids any suggestion of an automatic [that is, involuntary] creation." Yet the reference Williams gives on page 297 for making this comment, *On First Principles* 1.1 (=2).9 ff., is that of Origen's account of a power from a power, etc. In short, Williams identifies the capacity that is the source of God's eternal creative act with the capacity that is the effect of God's eternal creative act. Williams is wrong to make this identification without working through his understanding of the content of Origen's *power from power* (*X from X*) argument, since (as he noted on page 134) Origen gives a very different interpretation to the argument *power from power* in his *Commentary on the Gospel of John.*

fact of the second Person's generateness. The nature of the second Person is described primarily in terms of the nature of his production by or from the First. Wisd. 7:25 and Heb. 1:3 are both understood to be accounts of the generation of Wisdom, Power, or Breath. It is this feature of Wisd. 7:25 and Heb. 1:3 that has highlighted their use by Origen for scholars.[73] 1 Cor 1:24, by contrast, does not use *power* and *wisdom* in the context of a production account; yet the effect of its exegesis *via* the Wisdom and Hebrews texts is as a support for a production account. In general, this is Origen's interpretation of 1 Cor 1:24. Athanasius, on the other hand, will use Power and Wisdom in 1 Cor. 1:24 precisely because they are terms describing the second Person's unity with the First that do not describe this relationship as a causal relationship. Although Origen's acceptance of production language as fundamental to Christology cannot be confused with, say, Eunomius' identification of the first Person with unproduced (ἀγέννητος) and the second Person with produced (γέννητος), yet Eunomius' theology may be said to express a legitimate insight into the character of earlier trinitarian theology: namely, that its axis was the Son's generated nature.

There is a second problem inherent in the *power from power* causal model that Origen himself states. In his *Commentary on the Gospel of John*, Origen argues that the Son comes not from God but from the divine attributes: the Son is the breath of God's power, not of God Himself; he is an effluence of God's glory but not of God Himself.[74]

73. Williams, *Arius*, 134, remarks on Origen's use of Wisd. 7:25–26 with Heb. 1:3 in the context of describing Origen's doctrine(s) of the Son's production out of the essence. Williams suggests (135) that in these accounts, Origen has in mind certain Valentinian gnostic understandings of generation that he wishes to refute (or at least avoid). The judgment that Origen uses Wisd. 7:25–26 primarily as an anti-Gnostistic text is shared by Grant, "The Book of Wisdom," 471–72; and Logan, "Wisdom Christology," 128–29. I would add that Origen's anti-Gnostic account of the second Person's generation has the side effect of emphasizing the Son's generative nature.

74. This language has caused some consternation among modern scholars. Greer, *Captain*, 47, contrasts the "subordinationist" exegesis of Wisd. 7:25 in *Commentary on John* with the exegesis of Wisd. 7:25 in *On First Principles*, which he finds less subordinationist. Similarly, Williams, *Arius*, 134, contrasts the exegesis in the commentary on John with the exegesis in the commentary on Hebrews fragment. Stead, *Divine Substance*, 213, also discusses the *Commentary on John* text and finds it "strongly subordinationist." I find the *On First Principles* text less "proto-orthodox" than it is described in these scholarly accounts, and Origen's *Commentary on John* exegesis is consistent with the *caveat* I have tried to raise on the *On First Principles* material; namely, that the phrase *power from power*, if it is used only as an example of *X from X* causality, is not a statement of common nature, contrary to McFadden, "Exegesis," 42, who believes that the phrase *power from power* is a clear statement of consubstantiality.

For he is an image of the goodness and brightness, not of God, but of God's glory and of his eternal light; and he is a vapor, not of the Father, but of his power; and he is a pure emanation of God's almighty glory, and an unspotted mirror of his activity.[75]

This *Commentary on John* passage implies distinctions between God and His glory, light, and power, a distinction already hinted at in *On First Principles* 1.2:9. *On First Principles* says that Christ is said to be an effluence not of the light or the glory but of the power; *Commentary on John* says that the Son is an effluence not of God but the power of God. In *On First Principles* the difference between Power and the other attributes is important; Origen goes so far as to offer a definition of power (though not of the other titles). In *Commentary on John* what power means is not important, except to the extent that power, like wisdom, and light, is not God simply, but something else. In short, in *On First Principles,* δύναμις is understood as a feature of God's own existence; in *Commentary on John,* power is specifically distinguished from God's own existence. Indeed, in *Commentary on John* Origen uses *power* to develop another kind of argument entirely:

. . . to signify that the Word has his own individuality, that is to say, lives according to himself, we must speak also of powers, not only of power. "For thus says the Lord of the Powers" is a phrase which occurs in many places [in Scripture], certain divine spiritual beings being named powers. As, therefore, there are many powers of God, each of which has its own individual existence, so also Christ possesses substance in the beginning.[76]

In short, in *Commentary on John,* the understanding of power as external to God's own nature or existence serves as the conceptual support for the individual existence of the second Person. This is a very important point. Williams[77] gives a useful summary of Origen's concern with establishing the reality of the Son's separate existence that shows that this concern is expressed most clearly in *Against Celsus* (*Contra Celsum*) and the

75. Origen, *Commentary of the Gospel According to John, Books 13–32,* trans. Ronald Heine (Washington, D.C.: The Catholic University of America Press, 1993), 13:153, p. 100. Similar language appears in *On First Principles* 1.2.9.

76. Origen, *Commentary of the Gospel According to John, Books 1–10,* trans. Ronald Heine (Washington, D.C.: The Catholic University of America Press, 1989), 1:291, p. 94. See *Commentaire sur Saint Jean,* ed., trans., and comm. Cécile Blanc, Sources Chrétiennes, vol. 120 (Paris: Les Editions du Cerf, 1966), 1:291.

77. See Williams, *Arius,* 132.

*Commentary on John,* and not in *On First Principles.*[78] If again we look forward to the reception of Origen's language in the fourth-century controversies, we can note that whatever the inherent subordinationism might have been in formulas such as "power from power" and "power among powers," the inherent claim to a separate, real existence in such expressions was understood by Marcellus of Ancyra, for example, who rejected all such multiple powers and *X from X* language.[79]

78. Since both *On First Principles* and *Commentary on John* are early works, written in the order just given, and the *Dialogue* is late (245), but not as late as *Against Celsius* (248), it is impossible to suggest that Origen's opinion on the unity between Father and Son developed in a certain direction. It is interesting to note, however, that Origen's "weaker" statements on the unity afforded by the Son's generation "power from power" occur in a scriptural commentary, while the stronger statements are in more speculative or doctrinal works.

79. Despite Marcellus' repudiation of Origen's theology, he shares with Origen the basic assumption that statements in favor of the Son's full divinity are made at the expense of statements in favor of the Son's independent existence, and vice versa. The difference between Origen and Marcellus is that Origen preserves a positive understanding of the Son's independent existence at the expense of a doctrine of His full divinity, while Marcellus sacrifices the Son's independent existence for the sake of an unqualified statement of His full divinity.

# 4 Doctrines of Power in the Nicene and Pro-Nicene Controversies

## *Doctrines of Power in the Nicene Controversy*

ATHANASIUS' RETROSPECTIVE ACCOUNT of the proceedings at Nicaea emphasizes the debate at that Council over the exegesis and import of the title δύναμις for the second Person. Those opposed to Arius' theology believed that his doctrines were refuted by descriptions such as "the Word is of God by nature Only-Begotten, Power, Wisdom of the Father, Very God, as John says, and as Paul wrote, brightness of the Father's glory and express image of his person."[1] Athanasius' appreciation of the utility of δύναμις in trinitarian doctrine, and his apparent advocacy for the term at Nicaea, depended upon the understanding that δύναμις named a single characteristic of God and as a title referred exclusively to the Son. God had only one power, and that power was the Son alone. With such an interpretation of 1 Cor. 1:24 and the other allied scriptural references to the second Person as God's power, δύναμις would serve as a credible, scripturally-based term to describe the full union between Father and Son.[2] Eusebius and others accepted these descriptions of the second Person because they could offer a different exegesis of the supporting texts. For example, just as the second Person is said to be "of God," so is humanity said to be

1. *Letter to the Bishops of Africa* (*Ad Afros*) 5; *NPNF* 4:491.

2. While Athanasius suggests that the Arian doctrine of "two wisdoms, two powers," etc., depends upon exegesis of 1 Cor. 1:24, Hilary of Poitiers attributes a similar doctrine to Arian exegesis of texts such as Mark 10:18 and 1 Tim. 6:15. See Hilary, *On the Trinity,* 4:8.

"of God." Those with whom Athanasius was aligned understood 1 Cor. 1:24, "Christ the Power and Wisdom of God," as both describing the second Person's identity and attributing a unique relationship between the second Person and God, namely that the Son (only) was God's own power and wisdom. From such a description of the second Person, one could conclude that Christ was not a creature. However, those more sympathetic to Arius' theology, in particular Eusebius of Nicomedia and Asterius the Cappadocian, found nothing unique in these titles, since Scripture referred to God's "many powers."

Eusebius and Asterius did not share Athanasius' understanding that δύναμις was the proper name of the Son alone. Though Athanasius says that Eusebius and others offered competing exegeses of God, Image, Glory, and Power so as to claim these titles for their own theology, Athanasius treats only the counter-exegesis to Power in any detail. Against the claim that power named a unique relationship of the second Person to the first, Eusebius' side argued that Scripture spoke of God's several powers, including the infamous example of the Exodus reference to the locusts of the plagues being called "God's great power." In fragments preserved by Athanasius in *Discourse against the Arians* and *On the Councils of Ariminum and Seleucia,* Asterius speaks of two types of divine power[3] (and wisdom): the first is God's own (ἴδιος) power; the second type of power describes a class of ministers of God's will, the most important of whom is Christ, but the term also applies to lesser ministers who are subordinated to Christ. Athanasius cites to polemical effect Asterius' doctrine that the locusts and caterpillars are described as God's "powers" in the Bible. Of the two types of power Asterius recognized, there is only one of the first kind, but there are many, perhaps an unlimited number, of the second. Like Origen in the *Commentary on John,* Asterius asserts that there are many powers and that the Son is only one of them. Unlike Origen, Asterius does not offer this

3. In the first *Discourse against the Arians* (*Orationes Contra Arianos*), Athanasius elides Arius' text with Asterius': in the *Thalia,* Arius says that there are two Wisdoms and another Word in God besides the Son, and in other texts "of theirs they" teach that there are many powers (*Discourse* I, 2.5). In *Discourse* II, 18.37, Athanasius reports the same doctrine of power(s) and attributes it explicitly to Asterius. In the *Councils of Ariminum and Seleucia* (*De Synodis*), 17–18, Athanasius gives extensive quotations of this doctrine from Asterius' *Syntagmation.*

doctrine in support of the real and separate existence of the Son: ". . . there are many powers; one of which is God's own by nature and eternal; but that Christ, on the other hand, is not the true power of God; but, as others, one of the so-called powers. . . ."[4]

Arius' own writings refer to two classes or kinds of wisdoms, but not, specifically, to two classes or kinds of powers.[5] Nonetheless, Athanasius understands Arius' "two-wisdoms" doctrine as equivalent to Asterius' doctrine of "two (kinds of) powers." In *Discourse* I, Athanasius says that Arius taught that

> . . . there are two "Wisdoms," one which is proper to God and exists together with him, and [the other] the Son who has been brought into this Wisdom; only by participating in this Wisdom is the Son called Wisdom and Word. Wisdom came into existence though Wisdom, by the will of the God who is wise.[6]

In the *Thalia* Arius calls titles like Power, Wisdom, and Word ἐπίνοιαι of the second Person, by which he means impressions or roles. Ἐπίνοια names the epistemological standing or class of those "countless" qualities such as Power, Wisdom, and Word that the Son, alone of all creatures, possesses. As Arius says, "Hence He is conceived in numberless ἐπίνοιαι: Spirit, Power, Wisdom, God's Glory, Truth, Image, and Word."[7] In Athanasius' epistemology, ἐπίνοια is understood negatively, and means "fan-

4. *Discourse* I, 2.5; *NPNF* 4:309.

5. In Arius scholarship of the 1950s and early 1960s, the nature of Arius' doctrine of *wisdom from wisdom* was the object of some debate. G. Christopher Stead takes pains, in "The Platonism of Arius," *Journal of Theological Studies* 15 (1964): 16–31, to distinguish his opinion that Arius held to a "two-level" theory from Wolfson's opinion of Arius' "two-stage" Logos. In Arius' system, Stead says, "terms such as wisdom and logos [*sic*] have two meanings." These homonyms are attributed to both Father and Son, ". . . the Son's attributes are . . . parallel to the Father's; but his wisdom is a generated wisdom . . . the true and ingenerate wisdom is an inalienable attribute which belongs to the Father alone." (20). It is surprising how much like Eunomius Stead makes Arius sound, for Eunomius' own explanation of the common attribution of titles such as Light, Power, and Wisdom, etc., is precisely as Stead says: "Our response" to such titles, according to Eunomius, "is to say that the one 'light' is unbegotten and the other begotten. When spoken of the Unbegotten, does 'light' signify an entity other than that signified by 'the Unbegotten'?" *Apology* 19:8–10; *Extant Works*, 57.

6. *Discourse* I, 2, 5; Williams' translation in *Arius*, 100.

7. Arius considers all of the second Person's titles to be of one kind; namely, they are all ἐπίνοιαι. Arius probably would have acknowledged some priority of one title to another (for example, Son is preferred over Door), but he would not have acknowledged differences in the way these titles refer.

tasy," "fiction," or "something known only nominally," a sense not far from Eunomius'. As both Stead[8] and Williams[9] remark, the positive use of ἐπίνοια as a term for attributed qualities goes back to Origen. Given Arius' radical apophaticism, his use of the term is not, in itself, negative. Williams, in particular, finds a positive sense[10] to ἐπίνοια in the *Thalia;* he interprets the term in light of the passage that follows it, for there Arius says, "Understand that He is conceived to be Radiance and Light. One equal to the Son, the Superior is able to beget; but one more excellent, or superior, or greater, He is not able." But if one reads the sentences that introduce the term ἐπίνοια, it is clear that, as an attribution, ἐπίνοια is associated with the creaturely status of the Son and the derived nature of his attributes. "Hence the Son, not being (for he existed at the will of the Father), is not God and he is alien from either. Wisdom existed as Wisdom by the will of the Wise God."[11]

Both Arius and Asterius seem to have taught that titles like Wisdom, Power, Word are used in two senses.[12] In the first of these two senses, such titles refer to specific qualities or properties in God.[13] As such they are

8. G. Christopher Stead, "The *Thalia* of Arius and the Testimony of Athanasius," *Journal of Theological Studies* 29 (1978): 2052; see 36.

9. Rowan Williams, "The Logic of Arianism," *Journal of Theological Studies* 34 (1983): 56–81, see 76–77.

10. Ibid., especially, "The purpose of the ἐπίνοια language is not to stress the Son's inferiority and mutability—quite the contrary. We are being reminded that he is the most perfect image possible of the innumerable glorious divine qualities."

11. Williams may have changed his mind on the question of Arius' use of ἐπίνοια, for in *Arius,* 224 ff., he finds that Athanasius' attack on the term ἐπίνοια "has succeeded in identifying a dilemma for Arius. In so far as the work of Christ is to reveal to us a saving knowledge of the Father, it is of real importance that his being should truly show what the Father is like."

12. Éphrem Boularand's judgment is that the doctrine of two wisdoms, powers, etc., is Platonic in origin. The purpose of this doctrine is, in his opinion, to give a full description of the Son's status as creature; see *L'Hérésie d'Arius et la "foi" de Nicée,* 2 vols. (Paris: Éditions Letouzey & Ané, 1972), 1:75. Robert Gregg and Dennis Groh have little to say about this doctrine of the two wisdoms, powers, etc. They acknowledge that it is a "potentially confusing scheme" in *Early Arianism: A View of Salvation* (Philadelphia: Fortress Press, 1981), 105. They accept Bishop Alexander of Alexandria's report on this Arian teaching without qualification, except to speculate that this doctrine, too, was a part of the apparatus supporting the central Arian thesis of divine adoption.

13. Williams, "Logic," 59, returns the question of the two kinds or senses of power and wisdom to Arius' doctrine of the Son not being proper to God's substance. For Williams, Arius' purpose in denying that the Son is proper to God's being is to avoid reducing "the Son to being an impersonal quality" since this is what Arius took *proper,* ἴδιος, to mean. One feature of this early Arian theology, common to Arius and Eusebius, was a vigorous concern for the real, that is, separate, existence of the second Person. As I have already pointed out, in Origen the concern for this

eternal aspects of God's nature. In the second of the two senses, Wisdom, Power, Word are primarily (but not exclusively) titles of the Son. These titles refer primarily to the Son because of his status as perfect creature, but other creatures may properly be called by these titles insofar as they fulfill God's will. As is the case with any attribution of these titles to a creature, these titles are attributed to the Son only in a derived and equivocal sense.

### *Eusebius of Caesarea's Hierarchy of Powers*

In the works of Eusebius of Caesarea, one finds a fully developed and articulated theology of the two kinds of divine power. Eusebius distinguishes between the power of God that is unique to His own nature (and thus unique to the Father) and a second kind of power that is rather a result of God's nature and is attributed to various creatures, though primarily to the Son. This doctrine of multiple powers plays an important role in Eusebius' account of Christ's saving work.

In Book 7 of his *Preparation for the Gospel,* Eusebius offers a lengthy discussion of the scriptural account of first principles. There is first the "Being of the God of the universe, which is without beginning and uncreated, incapable of mixture and beyond all conception." After this first Being, there is "a second Being and divine Power, which subsisted as the first beginning of all originated things and was originated from the first cause, calling it Word, and Wisdom, and Power of God."[14] In this and later accounts, Eusebius emphasizes the creator status of the second Being. He says, for example,

> Next to the being of God, the Universal King, which is without beginning and unbegotten, they teach that Beginning which is begotten from no other source than the Father, being both First-born and fellow worker of the Father's will, and

---

separate existence is expressed in markedly subordinationist language (as in the *Commentary on John*). Arius, Eusebius, and Marcellus all agreed that full divinity implied imperfect distinction for the second Person.

14. *Preparation for the Gospel* 7:12:2, *La Préparation Evangélique,* Livre VII, ed. Guy Schroeder and Édouard des Places, SC, vol. 215 (Paris: Les Éditions du Cerf, 1975), 222–24; translated by E. H. Gifford in *Evangelicae Praeparationis,* three tomes in four volumes (Oxford: Oxford University Press, 1903), 3:1.346. The Wisdom title allows Eusebius to draw on Old Testament Wisdom literature, including Wisd. 7:25, a favorite for Origen, and Prov. 8:22, which was to become a favorite in anti-Nicene polemic.

perfectly likened unto Him. And this Beginning is before all originate things which followed, on which account they are wont to call it the Image of God, and Power of God, and Wisdom of God, and Word of God.[15]

In his account of scriptural first principles, Eusebius introduces the second Person as the "first principle of creation."[16] This second power is the creator or demiurge of the cosmos; indeed, the second Person is frequently identified with the demiurgic power.[17] Eusebius speaks of the ". . . One divine Power . . . for the creative Power is One, and One is the Word, Creator of the Universe, in the beginning with God. The One Creative Power of God is at the Head of [the universe]."[18] In Eusebius' teaching, the transcen-

15. *Preparation for the Gospel* VII, 15, 1–3; Schroeder and des Places, SC 215, 236–38; Gifford, 3:1.351. There is an implicit exegesis of John 1:1 in this second paragraph, in which "In the beginning" is understood not as a temporal reference but as a reference to the second Person himself who is identified with "the beginning" of creation. Eusebius' description of the mediating role(s) of the second Person suggests the influence of Philo's "two-powers" language, as when Eusebius says that ". . . all things subsist by the creative Word of God . . . [and] that God is not only the Organizer and Maker of the whole, but also the preserver, administrator, and the king, and ruler, overlooking all things with his divine power, and present with all things, arranging and administering all things in order."

16. ". . . [Having described] the God of the universe the next thing to do is to review the doctrines of the Hebrew philosophy concerning the first principle of things created. Thales of Miletus declared that the first principle of all things is water, Anaximenes the air, Heracleitus fire, Pythagoras numbers, Epicurus and Democratus corporeal atoms, Empedocles the four elements. Let us look also at the oracles of the Hebrews. Next to the Being of the God of the universe, they introduce a second Being and divine Power, which subsisted as the first beginning of all originated things and was originated from the first cause." *Preparation for the Gospel* VII, 12, 1; Gifford, 3:1.346.

17. The relatively rare use of "demiurge" in Arius has triggered an enormous amount of scholarship on the role of the concept, as well as Plato's *Timaeus,* in his theology. Arius' understanding of the role of the Son is thought to derive from Plato's doctrine of the Demiurge in the *Timaeus* because, in part, in one set of fragments Arius twice uses the word demiurge (in its verb form, δημιουργέω) of the Son. However, Arius' use of demiurge simply provides the occasion for finding the Platonic doctrine of the δημιουργός as well as the influence of the *Timaeus* generally in Arius' thought, for the assumption is strong among scholars that the doctrine of a "divine intermediary" owes to Platonism in general and the Timaean demiurge in particular. H. M. Gwatkin's reference in *Studies of Arianism,* 2d ed. (Cambridge: Deighton and Bell, 1900), 20, to Numenius' doctrine of the demiurge was but the first of many modern associations of Arius' theology with the Timaean demiurge. (The same text from Numenius is later cited by Stead to show the theological—and not cosmological—content of Arius' monad language.)

18. *Demonstration of the Gospel* 4:5, in *Die Demonstratio Evangelica,* ed. Ivar A. Heikel, *Eusebius Werke,* sechester Band, GCS (Leipzig: J. C. Hinrich, 1913), and *The Proof of the Gospel Being the Demonstratio Evangelica of Eusebius of Caesarea,* trans. W. J. Ferrar, 2 vols. (London: SPCK, 1920), 1:169. As with Arius' doctrine that the Son is "the perfect creation, but not like one among other creatures," Eusebius uses the doctrine of creation to distinguish "the second Being and divine Power" both from created things and from God. For Eusebius the Arian doctrine of the Son's

dence of the Father is complete, and the divine presence in creation is attributed to the creative, governing (second) power while God the Father acts in creation only through His Mediator whom He sends and oversees. Yet Eusebius dwells upon the unity of that Mediator: in what seems to be a response to pagan polytheism, he develops extensive arguments for the unity of the Creator. The same arguments appear in Athanasius' *Against the Pagans.*[19] Several of these arguments will reappear in Gregory of Nyssa's theology but as arguments for the unity of the Trinity;[20] in particular, the arguments from the unity of the human body despite its different organs and limbs and from the unity of the human mind despite its multiple operations.[21]

Eusebius finds support for his doctrine of the unity of the creative power, as well as his identification of the second Person with this creative power, in 1 Cor. 1:24.[22] Does the order of the cosmos reveal an origin from

---

creation out of nothing goes too far and erases the distinction between the Son and creation proper. McFadden, "Exegesis," 29, speaks of Eusebius refusing to accept that "the Son is a creature." It is precisely the doctrine of creation ἐξ οὐκ ὄντων which distinguishes the production of the cosmos from the generation of the Son (McFadden cites *Demonstration of the Gospel* 5.1.15, to this effect). Hanson, in his article, "Who Taught *ΕΞ ΟΥΚ ΟΝΤΩΝ?*" in *Arianism: Historical and Theological Reassessments,* ed. Robert C. Gregg, Patristic Monograph Series, no. 11 (Cambridge: Philadelphia Patristic Foundation, 1985), 79–83, believes that Arius taught the doctrine early on but modified his opinion under pressure from Eusebius and Asterius. Hanson also distinguishes Aetius' theology from Eunomius' on this point: Aetius seems to have taught ἐξ οὐκ ὄντων, Eunomius did not.

19. *Against the Pagans,* 39.

20. See *Demonstration of the Gospel* 4:5. I note in passing that in *Demonstration,* 4:5, Eusebius refers to the multiple and different effects of fire or the sun as cases where multiple, different effects do not prove the existence of multiple, different causes: "Fire, again, by its nature purifies gold, and melts lead: wax it dissolves, clay it hardens, wood it dries, by one burning power [δύναμις] accomplishes so many changes" (Ferrar 1:171; Heikel 157:15–18). Origen uses this same analogy, and Gregory will emphasize it (and fire) in his challenge of Eunomius' claim that a cause has only one effect.

21. In Eusebius' use of the analogy of "one soul and one power [δύναμις] of reason despite multiple operations," he concludes with the observation that "No one has yet supposed that there are more souls than one in one body." That Eusebius should be wrong about this, as he is, is puzzling. When Gregory uses the same analogy, he mentions those who do indeed believe that there are more souls than one in one body: see *On the Soul and Resurrection,* Migne, 46:49A; *NPNF* 5:439.

22. McFadden, "Exegesis," 25–26, has the same observation: ". . . particularly in [Eusebius'] apologetical treatises he has occasion to stress the existence of a single power and wisdom who created the world, and who is entrusted with its care and administration. Far better than the multiplicity of causes and powers proposed by the Pagan philosophers is the teaching of the Hebrews."

chaos and chance, Eusebius asks, or an origin from God's Word and God's Wisdom and God's Power?[23] Or again: if a ball of clay is shaped into a figure with arms and legs and many other small parts, do we understand that there must be a separate potter for each of these parts or one potter who can make many different things?[24]

> Why, then, in the case of the universe, which consists of a unity in many parts, must we suppose many creative powers, and name many gods [as the Pagans do], and not confess that which is "the power of God and the wisdom of God" in one power and in one goodness supports and gives life to all things at the same time?[25]

Here is the intersection of Eusebius' cosmology and his Christology. The absolute transcendence of God the Father means, as Eusebius makes clear, that the second Person—and not the first—is the principle of creation. Furthermore, Eusebius cannot countenance multiplicity in the first cause. The second Person's nature as "perfect image" of the first Person requires that the unity of the first is imaged in the second. Eusebius did not believe, as Arius may have believed and Eunomius certainly later believed, that the second Person has a composite nature.

Eusebius' cosmological emphasis on the uniqueness of the second power after God the Father's own transcendent power loses its clarity when he turns to the remainder of creation.[26] Eusebius' celestial hierarchy is

23. Eusebius is very struck by the fact that opposing elementals (the hot, the cold, etc.) in composites hold together without destroying each other or repelling into chaos. He regards this coexistence by the elementals as a peace imposed by the ruling Creator; indeed, he regards this peace as convincing evidence of the origin of the cosmos in a single ruling power, whose presence is still felt. Gregory is similarly impressed by the way opposite elementals coexist, and he has the same judgment about the value of this dynamic as proof of God's continuing role as Creator. Gregory will take this mediating role further, however, and apply it to specific theological doctrines. For example, in *Catechetical Orations* XVI, one effect of the Resurrection is that the Son, that is, God's Power, now holds together the disparate elements of body and soul since without "the cement of His Divine Power," these opposites could not coexist.

24. A similar use of figures made from a ball of clay appears in Gregory's *On the Soul and Resurrection,* Migne 46:77D; more accessible for the reader may be Moore and Wilson, trans., *NPNF* 5:446.

25. *Demonstration of the Gospel* 4:5; Heikel, 157:4–9; Ferrar, 1:171.

26. Eusebius' confusion at this precise point is, I take it, due to his Origenist heritage and typifies what scholars have said about the intellectual exhaustion inherent in Origen's old system being the "cause" of the Arian crisis. In Origen's system, the eternal generation of the second Person is not unique since all immaterial, rational existents are eternally generated. Eternal generation is not, as it would later be, the key indicator of the second Person's unique status. In Eusebius' system, the second Person's description as God's power is unique in only a limited fashion since

completed by his description of "the intelligent and rational powers" that "came after this Beginning" and that "pass man's nature to describe, both for multitude and for variety of form." This multitude of powers finds its "Great Captain" in the second Person. These powers are those described by Paul in lists such as that of Col. 1: 15, namely, thrones, dominions, powers, etc. This use of power occurs frequently in the literature of the era, including Gregory of Nyssa's writings, but in Eusebius' theology, this class of divine ministers and powers plays an important role in describing Christ's saving work.

Eusebius summarizes his theological hierarchy in this way:

> . . . we must think of the order in incorporeal and intelligent Beings also [in this way: first,] the unutterable and infinite power of the God of the Universe embracing all of them together; and the second place, next to the Father, being held by the power of the Divine Word. . . . And next after this second Being there is set . . . a third Being, the Holy Spirit. . . . But this Spirit, holding a third rank, supplies those beneath out of the superior powers in Himself, notwithstanding that He also receives from another.[27]

This summary refers to four classes of powers: the unutterable and infinite power of God, which is incomparable; the power of the divine word; the third holy power, the Holy Spirit; and those superior powers beneath the Spirit. The emphasis throughout Eusebius' work is always on the relationship between the first and second powers, the Father and Son (or Word) respectively, since their relationship alone is that of Original to Image: everything else is an "image of an image." The Son's function is to mediate[28] and to reveal the otherwise totally ineffable power of God the Fa-

---

all creation–at least all immaterial, rational creation–must be understood as God's power in the sense of obeying God's will and ministering to His purpose.

27. *Preparation for the Gospel,* 7:15; Gifford, 3:1, 351–52. I will return to this passage in the next chapter when I discuss Eunomius' theological hierarchy.

28. ". . . the Divine Word and Divine Wisdom and Divine Power oversees and protects the heaven and the earth likewise. . . . He is their Ruler and Head and king. . . . And He is called Sun of Righteousness, and the True Light, carrying out and cooperating in His Father's commands, wherefore He is also styled minister of the Father and Creator. . . . He alone stands midway between the unbegotten God and the things after Him begotten" (*Demonstration of the Gospel* 4:10; Heikel, 167:28–35; Ferrar, 1:184, translation slightly altered). Asterius has a similar doctrine of the function of the Word: "God [was] willing to create originate nature, [and] when He saw that it could not endure the untempered hand of the Father, and to be created by Him, [He] makes and creates first and alone one only, and calls him Son and Word (Λόγος), that, through him as a

ther, the power He alone images.[29] All the created powers, including and indeed especially the Son, are described in Eusebius' writings in ministerial or servantile language. Yet Eusebius' pleasure in populating the immaterial and intelligent realm does not blind him to the polemical need (against the Pagans) to distinguish carefully these angelic ministers from the multiple gods the Pagans postulate and worship.

Such are the doctrines received from the Hebrews, which we have preferred to the erroneous polytheism and demonism of the Greeks, knowing and duly honoring divine powers as servants and ministers of God the universal King, but confessing Him alone as God, and worshipping Him alone: for even the Only-Begotten of God and First-born of the whole world, the Beginning of all, commands us to believe His Father alone true God, and to worship only Him.[30]

Into this context of a host of ministering powers, directed by the second power, in the service of the Father, Eusebius introduces the fall of some angels and the establishment of a second line of "power." This apostate spiritual power finds its expression in demons, devils, and the host of pagan gods.[31] Arrayed against this dynasty is the "Power of our Savior," Who manifests His power in miracles, and Who passes this power on to his disciples.[32] The economy of salvation is thus the efficacy of divine power

medium all things might thereupon be brought to be" (*Discourse against Arius* II: 17:24; *NPNF* 4:361).

29. It is also the case that only for the Son is it true that His very being is an image of the Father, that the Son alone takes His being from the Father. But the character of this derivation is obviously what is at issue in the Nicene controversy, and the causality implicit in Eusebius' doctrine of the Son's unique derivation will be treated below in the discussion of the relationship of δύναμις to πρόσωπον (and οὐσία) and βουλή.

30. *Preparation for the Gospel* 7:15–18; Schroeder and des Places, SC 215:246.110; Gifford, 3:1, 355–56.

31. Eusebius' hierarchy of powers finds an echo in Gregory's *Cathechetical Orations*, where he speaks of God creating "another power" who is, as it were, the dark angel of the earth. Typically for Gregory, the advent of evil in this power is described in terms of oppositions: just as darkness comes when one closes one's eyes to the sunshine, so when the devil shut his eyes to the Good, a moral darkness was born in him, and "he knew the opposite of the good." The sense of power in these passages is that of delegated authority. This moral-political use of the term is consonant with the kind of causality Gregory is describing, for the devil is not a creative power (like a demiurge), and his opposition to God is not a contest between competing causes. The devil is a mutinous lieutenant; indeed, it is most accurate to understand the devil and the other angelic powers as, literally speaking, political creatures. His sin is of the moral-political variety, which is the only kind it ever could be.

32. Eusebius says that Jesus worked ". . . his miracles by a divine power, which also the holy writings bear witness that He had, saying that the Word of God and the highest Power of God

over apostate power. Eusebius quotes Porphyry (a human example of apostasy for Christians of the era) on the triumph of Christ's power and then adds his own comment:

. . . [Porphyry says that] "since Jesus began to be honored no one ever heard of any public assistance from the gods." For why do not rather the gods prevail over the power of Jesus? . . . [The gods] have all fled and given over all humanity into [His] power.[33]

Eusebius' emphasis on the Son's ministerial function is pervasive in his writings; such an emphasis on the Son as minister is not found again in anti-Nicene theology until Eunomius, who, like Eusebius, links the Son's ministry with His status as creator.[34] However, this emphasis by Eusebius on the intrinsic nature of the Son's ministerial function should not be understood principally in opposition to the theologies of Alexander and Athanasius and the latter's interpretation of Nicaea. Although Eusebius gave some intellectual support to Arius before Nicaea, after Nicaea he and Asterius wrote not against Alexander or Athanasius but against Marcellus of Ancyra. While today we scrutinize the Greek trinitarian literature of the 320s through to the 350s for its relationship to Arian or Athanasian ("Nicene") theology, the dominant concern at the time was not the theologies of Arius or Athanasius but the theology of Marcellus. The condemnation at Nicaea of Arius and the promulgation of the ὁμοούσιος creed shifted the focus of concern from the confrontation between Alexander of Alexandria and Arius to the debate between Marcellus, a staunch proponent of Nicaea with his own particular interpretation of its theology, and those who had been uncomfortable first with Alexander's theology and then later with οὐσία language. Both Eusebius and Asterius wrote works combatting

---

dwelt in man's shape and form, nay, even in actual flesh and body therein, and performed all the functions of human nature. And you yourself may realize the divine elements of this power, if you reflect on [Jesus' transformation of poor men into] agents carrying through a work that transcends all reason. But this surely was the manifestation of the divine will and the divine power in them. And when He had acquired His followers, He breathed into them His divine power" (*Demonstration of the Gospel* 3:7; Heikel, 140:24–141:3; Ferrar, 1:156).

33. *Preparation for the Gospel* 5.1.10; Schroeder and des Places SC 262:244; Gifford 3:1.197.

34. See, for example, *Apology* 15:12–15. "[The Only-begotten] . . . is therefore the Only-begotten God of those things which came into existence after him and through him. Since he was begotten and created by the power of the Unbegotten, he became the perfect minister of the whole creative activity and purpose of the Father" (*Extant Works*, 53). I will return to the question of this theme in Eunomius' theology.

the errors, as they perceived them, of Marcellus. Their later writings, like those that remain of Marcellus, are thus frequently apologetic and reactive in character.

Simply put, Marcellus' interpretation of Nicaea seems to have emphasized the unitative nature of God by rejecting language that supported the reality of the distinctions between the divine persons.[35] Eusebius and Asterius, on the other hand, favored language that emphasized the real distinctions among the divine Persons and so supported the real existence of the second Person. Lienhard points to formula such as "two οὐσίαι, two δυνάμεις, two πράγματα" as favorite expressions of Eusebius to express both the plurality in the Godhead and the reality of that plurality.[36] Marcellus understood this choice of language as tantamount to the Eusebians inventing a second God. In particular it was the attributed reality of that plurality that especially concerned Marcellus, for his own understanding stressed the purely economical or dispensational nature of the distinctions between the Persons. This understanding was encapsulated in Marcellus' doctrine of the temporary character of the Son's reign, which signaled the temporary character of the Son's separate existence from the Godhead. Greek creeds of the 340s and 350s, such as the Dedication creeds, regularly condemn the doctrine of an end to Christ's reign and oppose this doctrine with a positive statement of Christ's "kingdom without end".[37]

35. McFadden's delicate sense of nuance in treating Marcellus deserves some mention. McFadden makes the same points about the circumstances of the transmission of Marcellian fragments as will later be made by other scholars about Arius' fragments: ". . . first, we may expect a certain distortion of Marcellus' doctrine, especially due to the fact that the fragments of his treatise were being read out of context. Secondly, since Marcellus, Asterius and Eusebius use the same words to mean quite different things, there is a vast confusion in their debate. It is very easy for Eusebius to select passages from Marcellus whose formulations seem openly heretical, but which Marcellus used to combat the anti-Nicene heresy of Asterius" ("Exegesis" 20). Neither of McFadden's remarks is incorrect, but this sense of caution is nowhere to be found when McFadden reads Arius.

36. Joseph Lienhard, "*Contra Marcellum:* the Influence of Marcellus of Ancyra on Fourth-Century Greek Theology" (Habilitationsschrift, Albert-Ludwigs-Universität, 1986), 39–40, 87.

37. Δύναμις appears in the Dedication creeds as part of their anti-Marcellan orientation. That δύναμις would have an anti-Marcellan context (like the "kingdom without end" clauses that are the usual grounds for describing these creeds as anti-Marcellan) follows from the fact that Marcellus (in what Hanson calls the early and middle stages) denied that the title δύναμις named a separate existent, and, in particular, he refused the formula "power from power" (according to Acacius as recorded by Epiphanius, *Panarion* 72, 9). Marcellus taught that there is only one δύναμις in God, that it is of God's nature or unity, and he would have rejected any model of divine unity based on an *X from X* causality (for example, *light from light, life from life*) since these suggest

Marcellus' complaint is that his adversaries, Eusebius and Asterius, teach that there are "two essences, two things, two powers" in God. These adversaries teach "a second God, separate in essence and power from the Father." Marcellus recognizes that the attribution of two essences, two powers, means the attribution of two real and separate existents: two things, two Gods. In Marcellus' theology, God's true existence is that of a divine Monad: the reality of God's unity supersedes any division or distinctness in God. Marcellus expresses this doctrine by insisting on the singularity of any of those properties or titles that name real existence: essence, power, subsistent, even word.[38] The lack of reality or true existence in apparent real distinctions in God, such as the apparent distinction between the Father and the Son, is signaled in the temporary existence of these distinctions: the Son's existence, like that of his reign, is temporary and will come to an end. Marcellus' term for this temporary separate existence is ἐνέργεια.[39]

In both his work against Asterius and his letter to Julius of Rome, Marcellus rejects *X from X* descriptions of the Son's identity.[40] Marcellus' objection to *X from X* formula, is, in the case of a "Power from Power" formulation, that if the Son is Power from Power, then He is not really divine Power but an image of that Power. Marcellus' objection looks back to one of Origen's interpretations of "Christ, the Power of God": Christ is from the

---

a second X distinct from the first X. In one fragment Marcellus accuses his opponents of teaching two substances, two powers, two things, and he argues that if something is an image of power, it is not power. He would especially reject the use of δύναμις in an *X from X* model, since for him δύναμις serves as the ground of divine unity: there must be only one divine power, since there is only one divine nature, one divine monad. Later theologians such as the Cappadocians pick up on this sense of δύναμις one *nature*, one *power*—if the same *power*, then necessarily the same *nature*, and vice versa.

38. McFadden, "Exegesis," 22, says that for Marcellus, "Logos [*sic*], power, substance, hypostasis [*sic*] are really one and the same thing." He adds that for Marcellus "Power and Wisdom, then, are understood as divine titles, but are not applied to a distinct divine Person." Lienhard, "Influence of Marcellus," 86, makes the interesting point that Marcellus uses the words οὐσία or ὑπόστασις only when characterizing the theology of his opponents: Marcellus' own prefered term is πρόσωπον, which is used to the effect that God is only one πρόσωπον, one speaker.

39. Lienhard makes two points about Marcellus' use of ἐνέργεια which I want to emphasize. Firstly, he argues that Marcellus uses ἐνέργεια in his own doctrine, while δύναμις is a Eusebian term that Marcellus uses only as he reports or refutes Eusebian theology ("Influence of Marcellus," 87). Secondly, Lienhard argues—primarily against Zahn—that δύναμις and ἐνέργεια are not to be understood in the Aristotelian sense of potentiality and actuality (89–90).

40. See Epiphanius, *Panarion* 72.2.13.2 and 72.6.19.1.

Power of God, and so is Power, but is not the Power of God itself [αὐτός]. Marcellus' objection also takes heed of the way the Arians use theological titles: Asterius can equivocate about even the title "Son," interpreting it so that there is no sense of the generation of a nature. Moreover, Marcellus observes, when his opponents speak of the Son as Word, Wisdom, and Power, they mean a second of each of these, not the true Word, Wisdom, or Power co-extensive with divinity. In Marcellus' opinion, the multiple hypostases language of his opponents expresses metaphysically the two kinds of power (etc.) presupposed by *X from X* formulations: there is the power of the Father's hypostasis, and there is the power of the Son's hypostasis. The two kinds of power (etc.) are as different as the being of the two hypostases are different. Marcellus rejects this line of reasoning and asserts that the titles Son, Power, Wisdom, and Word are all used in reference to these aspects of true divinity, each of which is inseparable from God. Marcellus' identification of the Son with the inseparable Power (etc.) of God constitutes his argument for the full divinity of the Son and the unity of the Father and Son. Such an argument provides no support for the separate existence of the Son except through using temporal and activity language: the Son's distinction from the Father is expressed in time, in the economy of the Incarnation; the Son's individuality (over against simple divinity) lies in the Son's origin as the ἐνέργεια of the divine essence.

### *The Creeds of 340–360*

Δύναμις occurs in a number of creeds produced in the 340s and 350s. One may observe that δύναμις is not used in creeds that we would recognize as anti-Nicene (or "Arian"),[41] although δύναμις does appear in some creeds of a non-Nicene (often called "Eusebian") character. For example, the Third and Fourth Creeds of Antioch both identify the Son as God's "Word, Power and Wisdom." However, the appearance of δύναμις in the Second Creed of Antioch is of a different order than in the two creeds of Antioch just mentioned. Second Antioch says that the Son is the exact Image of the Godhead, the οὐσία, the βουλή, the δύναμις, the δόξα. Here power is part of a description of the complete divinity: essence, will, power,

41. Δύναμις does not occur, for example, in the creeds of Sirmium 357 (the "Blasphemy"), the Dated Creed, Seleucia, Rimini, and Constantinople, 360.

glory. "Power" is set between "will" and "glory," which suggests that δύναμις is being used in its political sense and that in some real way the list describes a descending order of unity or reality. Such a suspicion seems confirmed when one recognizes that the creed's formula has its precedent in Asterius' theology. He says, ". . . the exact image of his substance, and will and glory and power . . . ," although power has an even more diminished place in this sequence. What Asterius' statement and the Second Creed have in common is, first, a definition of the Son as the Image of God and second, the identification of what exactly the Son is an image of—if indeed He is "the Image of God." In the case of Asterius, to call the Son the Image of the Power is to say that the Son is a Power Himself but not the original Power of God. Still, the doctrines of Asterius' fragments 1 and 2, on the one hand, and fragment 21 and the Second Creed of Antioch, on the other, are not consistent. Neither the creed nor Asterius' fragment 21 could be taken to suggest that the Son is a second Will or a second Glory the way that, in Asterius' fragments 1 and 2, He is a second power (although Marcellus evidently took Asterius to be arguing for a second glory).[42] The difference among the doctrines of the Asterian fragments can probably be attributed to context: fragments 1 and 2 are chosen by Athanasius for their resemblance to Arius' doctrine of "two wisdoms." The fragment contained in *Against Marcellus* is part of a straightforward *X from X* formulation, the kind of trinitarian model Marcellus could not accept.

The grouping of "power" with terms like "will" and "glory" also reminds one of similar language in Eusebius of Nicomedia, who speaks of "disposition and power." Gregg and Groh have argued that such language is political-moral in origins and that "disposition and power" establishes "from the will" as an alternative etiology to "from the essence."[43] When the meaning of power is related to words like disposition, will, and glory, power is then positioned as over against the nature or essence.[44] Eusebius'

42. Epiphanius, *Panarion* 72.6.12.

43. "[In] embracing these terms and setting this phrase, [will, disposition, power] over against all essentialist language, Eusebius proclaimed the Son's likeness to his Father to be one of virtue!" (Gregg and Groh *Early Arianism*, 101).

44. Hanson, *The Search*, 565, cites related language from Gryson's *Scripta Arriana Latina* in order to support his judgment that creation "from the Father's will, not his nature" is a quintessential Homoian doctrine: "[The Father] with consciousness, power and will created, established,

own formula gives us the means for recognizing the different senses that can be attached to δύναμις: the Son is different from the Unoriginate in "nature and power," but like the Unoriginate in "disposition and power." On the one hand, when power has a sense that links it to nature, then this attribution is rejected. On the other hand, when power has a sense that links it to the will, then this attribution is accepted.

When Δύναμις (as well as Λόγος and Σοφία) appears in the creed of Sardica, it is, as one would expect, with an entirely different sense from that of Asterius, Eusebius, or the creeds of Antioch. The Son is God the Father's Word, Power, and Wisdom. Moreover, the creed continues, the Son is the Power of God and the Word of the Father, besides which there is no other. The Son is the Power that God as a being has; the Son is the Word that God as a rational being has; the Son is the Wisdom that God as a knowing being has. God has no other Δύναμις, Λόγος or Σοφία than the Son. There is no talk of "image" here and its attendant conception of a "first" and "second" power, word, or wisdom. Almost as significantly, the creed presents δύναμις as a category of God's being similar to λόγος or σοφία. Like Word or Wisdom, there is nothing external about Power. Compared to these three concepts, the kind of unity suggested by βουλή and δόξα is clearly relative, for while one could imagine that at some point God would not will (Eunomius imagined just this), one could never imagine an unreasoning, foolish, and powerless God. The theology of δύναμις in the creed of Sardica is a complete repudiation of "two-powers" theology and any understanding that δύναμις is something other than very divinity. The creed continues the logic accepted by both sides that links the number of powers in God (one or two) to the number of hypostases in God (one or two).[45]

It cannot go unremarked that, if indeed it is the case that δύναμις is found in creeds of a non-Nicene or "Eusebian" character and is as well missing from anti-Nicene or "Arian" creeds, it is also true that δύναμις is

---

generated, and made the Son before everything, according to what He, God the Father almighty, wished, determined and ordered for the Son. . . ."

45. For an account of the way in which different "counts" of hypostasis may be used to distinguish the opposing theologies of the early stages of the fourth-century trinitarian controversy, see Joseph Lienhard, "The 'Arian' Controversy: Some Categories Reconsidered," *Theological Studies* 48 (1987): 415–36.

missing from the creeds of Nicaea 325 and Constantinople 381, that is, Nicene creeds.[46] In fact, after Sardica, it is a general fact that δύναμις disappears from creeds (even while it becomes more visible in polemical works). I think this absence may be explained in large part by context. All the creeds of Antioch have an anti-Marcellan intention behind them. For example, I have already noted Marcellus' objections to the *X from X* generative language to be found in Second Antioch. I take the use of δύναμις in these creeds to be either directly anti-Marcellan (because he objected to *X from X* and two-powers type theologies) or indirectly anti-Marcellan (because such theologies and a substantial use of δύναμις are favorites of Marcellus' foes, Eusebius of Caesarea and Asterius). As the anti-Marcellan thrust of conciliar theologies falls away, so too do many of the touchstones of such theologies. Anti-Marcellan impulses are completely missing from the "Blasphemy," the Dated Creed, Seleucia, Rimini, and Constantinople, 360. Ὁμοούσιος, promoted by Nicaea, is the target. Constantinople, 360 is the highwater mark of Homoian conciliar theology; instead, one begins to see the development of a genre of anti-Nicene polemical literature (of which Eunomius' *Apology* may be considered one of the earliest specimens). "Two-powers" doctrine, with *X from X* formulas treated as traditional touchstones, appears in anti-Nicene polemics consistently from Eunomius' *Apology* to Palladius' rebuttal of Ambrose's *On the Faith* to the "Arian Sermon" and the theology of Maximinus (as expressed in the debate with Augustine). It must be granted, however, that Eunomius' attachment to any "two-powers" doctrine and *X from X* theology was, in the *Apology*, formal at best. From the perspective of his *Second Apology* (*Apologia Apologiae*), written in the late 370s and early 380s, the minor appearance of "two-powers" language in the earlier *Apology* seems to be a sign of the fact that in 360 Aetius and Eunomius had not yet come to the point where their own theology was distinguished from Homoian theology. The mature "Heterousian" theology of the *Second Apology* conceives of divine production in ways for which two-powers doctrines are irrelevant. It is possible to interpret Eunomius' theology in the *Second Apology* as a profound reinterpretation of *X from X* reasoning, but this seems an artificial insight.

46. Δύναμις is also missing from the anti-Arian creed of Antioch, 325.

If we return the credal documents of the 340s, there we encounter two opposing theologies employing δύναμις to describe the union between God (the Father) and the second Person. The creeds of Antioch continue a theology of two powers that one finds articulated earlier in the writings of Asterius; for example, a theology that, while conceptually related to the two-wisdom theology of Arius, is also a traditional derivation of δύναμις doctrines in Clement and Origen. The creed of Sardica represents a theology in which the single Power of God is identified with His Son (and vice versa). A doctrine of the Son's identity as the "Power of God" conceives of the Son's unity with God in terms of the technical sense of δύναμις: the Son is to the Father as affect is to being. What is not clear in such statements is whether the "being" is divinity or the Father (just as the same is not always clear in δύναμις-based descriptions of the Trinity). Frankly, it would seem that consistency requires that being is indeed the Father, for otherwise one is left searching for a term with which to relate the Father to divine being. If being is the Father, then He is implicitly identified with the divine essence. If anyone involved in the early fourth-century controversies felt the limitations of such a statement, it was Marcellus, who seems to have identified that divine being that has affect with the "Monad."

As noted, when the creeds from the 340s are compared to the important ones of the next decade, one notices a change. Two-powers theology disappears from anti-Nicene creeds.[47] However, "one-power" theology, by contrast, does not disappear. One-power theology, in which the Son is identified as the Power of God just as He is identified as the Word of God in "one-word" theologies, becomes an avenue for opponents of anti-Nicene theologies to explore divine unity. At this point in time sympathetic accounts of Nicaea begin to appear that associate that original theology with power language; the most obvious of these is, of course, Athanasius'. By

47. One implication of what I am saying here is that scholarly accounts that portray Homoian theology simply as the next step in the development of the Eusebean anti-Marcellan theology of the 340s are incomplete and inadequate, and to that extent, false. The theology of the 330–340s is empty without *X from X* and two-powers type theologies, in which—as Second Antioch shows us—δύναμις plays a highly visible role. In the last chapter of this monograph I present an argument against Eunomius by Gregory that turns precisely on the lack of continuity between earlier "two-powers" doctrines and Eunomius' theology.

the end of the 350s we can identify an interest in one-power theology with Nicene or pro-Nicene theologies.[48] The difference between "Nicene" and "pro-Nicene" theology can be described precisely in the shift from the "one-power (one-nature), one hypostasis" doctrine of Marcellus (and early Athanasius?) to the "one-power (one-nature), three hypostases" doctrine of Hilary and Gregory of Nyssa. As we shall see, Gregory will not accept or continue the logic that associates the number of powers with the number of hypostases: he will argue for three hypostases and one power.

### *Athanasius' Understanding of the "Power of God"*

In his writings Athanasius frequently refers to the second Person as the "Power of God"; he understands this description of the second Person to be a testimony to the unity and common nature between the first and second Persons. In *First Discourse against the Arians,* Athanasius reclaims 1 Cor. 1:24 and Rom. 1:20 by reinterpreting them as proofs for the Son's eternal existence. From created things, he says, we know of the existence of God's power, ". . . even His eternal Power and Godhead; and what the Power of God is, he teaches us elsewhere himself, Christ is the Power of God and the Wisdom of God."[49]

If we compare similar arguments by Origen and Athanasius, we may learn something of the character of Athanasius' doctrine of the divine power. Origen's argument need only be characterized here as an argument following the *like from like* form. Origen begins with the understanding that God's own power is not only eternal (since it is co-extensive with His nature or existence), it is eternally productive; from that eternal power is generated another eternal power.[50] The second power's source in the first power that is God αὐτός is a guarantee of that second power's eternal existence, ". . . since God always had both the power and the will, there was never the slightest reason or possibility that he should not always have had

48. The anti-*anti-Nicene* theology of Basil of Ancyra shows no interest in power models of unity but uses wisdom models instead.

49. *First Discourse against the Arians* 4:11; *NPNF* 4:312.

50. At *First Discourse against the Arians* 7:29; *NPNF* 4:323, Athanasius disagrees with Origen's idea that an eternal cosmos follows from an eternal power: ". . . although God always had the power to make, yet the things originated had not the power of being eternal."

this good thing that he desired. This proves that there always existed that breath of the power of God, having no beginning but God himself."[51] However, although Christ, the power of God, may be eternal in Origen's doctrine, the doctrine is still that of the existence of two powers.

Athanasius' argument, in contrast, does not follow an *X from X, power from power,* line of reasoning.[52] The potential for error in Origen's "two powers" language is very evident to Athanasius for he repeats once again and in detail Asterius' doctrine of the two classes of power, namely, God's own, and His intermediary power(s).[53] Athanasius argues instead that Power, like Son and Wisdom, is a unique title.[54]

Athanasius is especially emphatic that the description "Power of God" means that the second Person is co-eternal with God the Father, as for example, in the *Second Discourse:*

> . . . God has a Son, the Word, the Wisdom, the Power, that is, His Image and Radiance; from which it at once follows that He [the Son] is always; that He is from the Father; that He is like; that He is the eternal offspring of His [the Father's] essence.[55]

Here, the attribution of Word, Wisdom, and Power serve as proofs of the second Person's eternal existence as well as His resemblance to His source.

In Athanasius' early works,[56] however, his understanding of δύναμις is of such a traditional and general nature that the use of δύναμις does not significantly advance his case for the full and true divinity of the second Person. Although Athanasius never gives an explicit definition of δύναμις,[57]

51. *On First Principles* I, 2, 9; Butterworth, 23.

52. See "All these passages [that is, Heb. 1:3, 1 Cor. 1:24, John 1:1, etc.,] . . . signify the eternity of the Word, and that He is not foreign but proper to the Father's essence. For when did anyone ever see light with radiance? Or who dares to say that the expression can be different from the subsistence, or has a man not lost his mind if he thinks that God was ever without Reason and without Wisdom?" (*Discourse* II, 18:32; *NPNF* 4:365). And see ". . . God has a Son, the Word, the Wisdom, the Power, that is, His Image and Radiance, from which it at once follows that [the Son] is always; that He is from the Father; that He is like; that He is the eternal offspring of [the Father's] essence" (*Discourse* II, 18:34; *NPNF* 4:366).

53. Ibid., 18:34; 4:368.

54. Ibid., 18:38; 4:368.

55. Ibid., 18:34; 4:366.

56. For the purposes of this argument, *Against the Pagans* and *On the Incarnation* need only be earlier than *Discourses against the Arians,* a dating that no one disputes. Whether these two works were produced before or after Nicaea is irrelevant to my point.

57. Athanasius never approaches the clarity, or at least self-consciousness, about using *power* that one finds with Hilary, for example: "It is clear that the truth, or genuineness, of a thing is a

his understanding of what Power means in 1 Cor. 1:24 can frequently be deduced from the context of the citation, since in both *Against the Pagans* and *On the Incarnation,* implicit discussions of δύναμις frequently precede his use of 1 Cor. 1:24. For example, at *Against the Pagans* 40, Athanasius argues that the Son is the "Power of God"; both the immediate context and the previous discussion of δύναμις at *Against the Pagans* 29 give a political sense to δύναμις as a title of the second Person through 1 Cor. 1:24. Again, at *On the Incarnation* 31–32, the sense of δύναμις seems to be nothing more than ability. In *On the Incarnation* 19 and 31, where Athanasius cites 1 Cor. 1:24, as well as at *On the Incarnation* 48, where he discusses δύναμις but without the Pauline reference, the sense of δύναμις is that of a magical capacity, just as it often is for Eusebius of Caesarea.[58]

In *Against the Pagans* and *On the Incarnation,* Athanasius regularly offers lists of accumulated titles for the second Person as proof of His co-essential status with the Father. One such doxology appears at *Against the Pagans* 46:

> . . . good offspring of a good Father and true Son, he is the Power of the Father, and his Wisdom and Word, [but] not so by participation; he is Wisdom itself, Word itself, and the Father's own Power itself, Light itself, Truth itself, Righteousness itself, Virtue itself; Image, Brightness, Resemblance.[59]

There is an ambiguity in the titles of this doxology, and indeed all of these titles could have been used by Eusebius of Caesarea. Athanasius seems to have recognized the ambiguity or incompleteness of relying on the titles by themselves, for the burden of his argument is carried by the addition of αὐτός (itself) to the list of titles. This is particularly significant in the phrase, the Father's own power itself. Athanasius' argument is that God's existence includes a wisdom, word, and power (a traditional judg-

---

question of its nature and its power [*virtus*]." *On the Trinity* (*de Trinitate*) 5:3, CCL 62:153, *NPNF* 9:86. Ambrose as well offers at least a simple statement of what he understands power—*virtus*—to be: "[the Arians] attribute the original source of their being to the power [*virtus*] of God. But what is power, but the perfection of nature?" *On the Faith* (*de Fide*) 1.5.39, CSCL 78, 17:15, *NPNF* 10:206.

58. As in *Demonstration of the Gospel* 3:7, where Eusebius speaks at length of the miracles worked by the divine power, of this divine power being passed on to the Apostles, and the power of Jesus' name (against demons).

59. *Against the Pagans* 46:52–59, in *Athanasius: Contra Gentes,* trans. and comm. E. P. Meijering (Leiden: E. J. Brill, 1984), 29.

ment that no one ever disputes), and that the second Person is to be identified with the specific wisdom, word, and power included in God's own existence. This latter identification is what is disputed in the two-powers theologies of Asterius and Eusebius of Caesarea, and the two-wisdoms theology of Arius. Despite Athanasius' subtle development of title doxologies, two problems remain in his use of δύναμις in the doxologies in writings such as *Against the Pagans* and *On the Incarnation.*

*The Development in Athanasius' Theology*

The first problem is that Athanasius associates titles of the kind that can be understood as true existents in themselves—namely, Power, Wisdom, and Word—with titles that normally do not carry a connotation of separate existence—namely, Light, Truth, Righteousness, and Virtue.[60] The ontological connotations of the first set of titles are reduced to equivocation through association with a second set of titles that includes physical metaphors such as Light and as well as metaphors of value such as Righteousness. The sense of *power* remains only that of a physical or moral metaphor, a sense that in fact Athanasius uses regularly in *Against the Pagans* and *On the Incarnation.* Physical metaphors such as light continue the problems of materialism that Origen, Eusebius, and Athanasius all try to escape since they suggest a material understanding of the essence. The moral metaphor inevitably suggests the possibility of a union other than that of common nature or essence, such as an agreement of wills. Athanasius never settles upon or emphasizes δύναμις as an ontological term, that is, a term used with others like φύσις, οὐσία, etc. Instead he uses it either socially or metaphorically. There is no advance over Origen's use of the term; to a certain degree, there is even a falling back from the kind of union δύναμις describes in *On First Principles,* since Athanasius, unlike Origen, does not recognize the difference between the kind of title *power* is and the kind of title *righteous* (for example) is.

In all his writings, Athanasius shows a limited understanding of what power (especially) and wisdom mean as attributes and a limited understanding of how these attributes are associated with an existent. As a result,

60. The first kind of title I call ontological, the second kind I call doxological.

his argument for the unity between God and the power and wisdom of God (that is, the Son) is not based on what power and wisdom are conceptually but on the claim that the power and wisdom in question is God's own (exploiting the genitive form, but also using ἴδιος language as in *Against the Pagans* 46 cited above).

The second problem with Athanasius' argument is exemplified by both *Discourse* II (quoted earlier) and in *Against the Pagans* 46 (quoted just above), where he links titles such as Power, Wisdom, and Word with the mechanism or ontology of "Image and Radiance" (in *Discourse* II) and "Image, Brightness, [and] Resemblance" (in *Against the Pagans* 46). This kind of image or radiance language is offered as the grounds for identifying the different attribute-titles given to the second Person with the same attributes in God the Father. Athanasius denies that the Son is called these by participation and instead insists that the Son is to be identified with the first existence of this attribute, that is, as the attribute exists in God. But image and radiance models are Athanasius' preferred models for describing the second Person's unity with the first, and in themselves they remain open to a subordinationist "participatory" interpretation, if only because Athanasius does not ground his own Nicene interpretation of the models in a clear non-participatory explanation.

This non-participatory explanation needs to be stated in terms of God's very existence, that is, His essence, in order to prevent continuing equivocation. Athanasius' account in *On the Synods* of what drove the original Nicene Fathers to use ὁμοούσιος is as well an account of what drove him not only to understand Nicene theology fundamentally in terms of ὁμοούσιος but to need to speak primarily in terms of God's essence.[61] This kind of account does not occur, it is worth remarking, until rather late in Athanasius' career. There are partial, incomplete, expressions of an essence-based explanation in *Discourses against Arius:* one notes, for example, how

61. Athanasius says as much at the end of *On the Synods* 54, where he offers a powerful restatement of the central thesis of the work, that is, that titles such as Son, Light, and Wisdom are given not through "sharing" or "participation" but "by nature," thus leading to the conclusion that the Son is properly called "not [even] Like-in-essence, but Co-essential." And then Athanasius says, "This is why the Nicene Council was correct in writing what was correct to say, that the Son, begotten from the Father's essence, is co-essential with Him" (*NPNF* 4:479).

*Discourse* III begins with essence language immediately.[62] But a clear expression is not to be found in Athanasius' work until *On the Synods,* where he finally offers a real alternative to "participation":

The Son is not such [that is, a Son] by participation, but, while all things originated have by participation the grace of God, [the Son] is the Father's Wisdom and Word of which all things partake, it follows that He, being the deifying and enlightening power of the Father, in which all things are deified and quickened, is not alien in essence from the Father but coessential. For by partaking of Him, we partake of the Father; because the Word is the Father's own.[63]

In earlier works Athanasius had used this kind of description of the Son as God's wisdom and power to argue only for the Son's eternity; here in *On the Synods* he uses these titles to argue for coessentiality. Participation, on the other hand, is used exclusively to describe creation's relationship with the second Person. Athanasius finally uses δύναμις in association with (what I have called) an ontological term like οὐσία.[64]

Athanasius' fondness for radiance language remains nonetheless, as when he understands "The sun rose upon Him when the Form of God passed by" (Gen. 32:31) as equivalent to "The Word of the Lord came to me."[65] Yet, in all of Athanasius' exploration of radiance language, he never uses δύναμις to describe the constituents of that radiance although he knows that δύναμις is used to describe properties of fire.[66] In short, while 1 Cor. 1:24 is a favorite proof text for Athanasius throughout his career, his understanding of δύναμις remains limited in all of his writings. My own judgment is that Athanasius' influence as the source and exemplar of Nicene theology in the second half of the fourth century has been very much

62. Charles Kannengiesser has pointed out that the description of the Son's unity with the Father in *Discourse* III contains several phrases that are new to the work overall: see *Athanase d'Alexandrie: évêque et écrivain* (Paris: Beauchesne, 1983), 312–13. This new language, coupled with the kind of maturity of focus I have suggested above, indicates to Kannengiesser that Book 3 is not by Athanasius. Whether one agrees with Kannengiesser or not (and I cannot), Hanson, *The Search,* 418, is right that Kannengiesser's arguments have shown the considerable development in thought in Book 3 over Books 1 and 2. The relevance of Kannengiesser's argument for my point here is that the changes in Athanasius' use of δύναμις which I have outlined above are consistent with, indeed part of, an overall change in Athanasius' theological reflection.

63. *On the Synods* 51; *NPNF* 4:477.

64. This use of δύναμις with οὐσία occurs again in *On the Synods* 52, when Athanasius speaks of God's Power (referring to the second Person) as being "proper to the Father's essence."

65. *On the Synods* 52; *NPNF* 4:478.

66. Athanasius refers to heat as a δύναμις in *Against the Pagans* 27.

overstated by scholars. However, even if one allows as fact their speculations that Athanasius' theology was foundational for western Nicene sympathies, then on the question of "one power, one nature" Athanasius cannot have been the source or authority, since he lacks this very doctrine. Athanasius' use of "one power" theology never develops beyond the early Nicene "Christ is the 'one power' of God" understanding that indeed is characteristic of "Nicene" theology (and western anti-Arianism as expressed at Sardica). We shall see, however, that Latin polemicists for a Nicaea type trinitarian theology move beyond the Athanasian-Sardican understanding of "one power." Their understanding of "one power" is not altogether new—it was present in, for example, Tertullian and was one of two options offered by Origen. The pro-Nicene doctrine of "one power" is new to the extent that it was not a feature of the Nicene theology of the first half of the fourth century. "Pro-Nicene" theology is not simply identical to the "one power, one nature" doctrine, as though it had no other essential components, but a "one power, one nature" doctrine distinguishes the pro-Nicene theology of the second half of the fourth century from the earlier "Nicene" theology.

### *Western Pro-Nicene Theologies of God's Power*

We have already seen how Origen used 1 Cor. 1:24 together with two other δύναμις texts, Wisd. 7:25 and Heb. 1:3, to offer an account of the second Person's relationship with God the Father. These three texts are used in mutual explication, and their associated presence in later authors' works is evidence of Origen's influence. What distinguishes 1 Cor. 1:24 from the other two texts is that both Wisdom and Hebrews use δύναμις to describe divine generation or production, while the Corinthians' language describes a permanent relationship based upon the fact that God is rational. Here it helps to remember that the early Apologists' use of λόγος as a model of unity spoke of God's λόγος as His δύναμις λογική, as Daniélou pointed out some years ago.[67] However, as I have already discussed, Ori-

67. Jean Daniélou, *Message évangelique et culture hellenistique* (1961), 318–24 (*Gospel Message and Hellenistic Culture*, ed., trans., and with a postscript by John Austin Baker [Philadelphia: Westminster Press, 1973], 347–53). William McFadden has shown that Justin, Tatian, and Athanagoras did not appeal to 1 Cor. 1:24 in support of the title δύναμις for the second Person; see "Exegesis," 47.

gen's understanding of the unity described by the title δύναμις is ambivalent: in his *Dialogue with Heraclides* Origen uses "two Gods, one power" as a formula for divine unity, while in his *Commentary on the Gospel of John,* his claim that the Son is the breath of God's power, but not of God himself, separates δύναμις from φύσις.

Early theology in the West, by contrast, made almost no use of the 1 Cor. 1:24 reference to *virtus:* Irenaeus never cites 1 Cor. 1:24;[68] when Tertullian does use *virtus,* it tends to be by the authority of Luke 1:35, but overall he prefers *potestas.* McFadden and Moingt both came to this conclusion working from two very different methodologies. In his dissertation on the pre-Nicene use of 1 Cor. 1:24, McFadden reports only one clear reference by Tertullian to this text: namely, at *Against Praxeas* 19:2, where Tertullian uses 1 Cor. 1:24 to show that the Wisdom mentioned in Prov. 8 is the Son, since the Son is "the Wisdom and Power."[69] Similarly, Moingt argues that Tertullian's understanding of the Trinity as *unius potestatis* is not like that of either the Apologists or the Nicenes; although ". . . il [Tertullian] connait bien la notion révélée que le Fils est la virtus Patris, mais ne s'en sert pas pour expliquer l'unius potestatis."[70] Furthermore, when Tertullian's theology is reshaped to provide Nicene polemic, as it is in the theology of Gregory of Elvira, *virtus* and 1 Cor. 1:24 are absent. In this regard, however, Gregory's theology is unusual, for it is generally true that before Nicaea, the theological weight of power is not attached to 1 Cor. 1:24 in Latin theology, while after Nicaea, the theological weight of power is attached to 1 Cor. 1:24.

For example, Phoebadius of Agen presents a more complex reworking of Tertullian's theology for the times: as Hanson points out, Phoebadius defines substance as that which "subsists by its own intrinsic (*intra se*) power (*virtus*)" and likewise he regards *virtus* as "a synonym for *substan-*

68. In *Against the Heresies* 2:2.5, Irenaeus speaks of the instrumentality of the Son in the act of creation—the Father created through the Son—and he includes a reference to John 1:3 as an authority for this doctrine. However, according to both the index to the ANF volume and McFadden, Irenaeus never refers to John 5:19, Rom. 1:20, or 1 Cor. 1:24.

69. McFadden, "The Exegesis," 63–68, esp. 65 and 67.

70. See Joseph Moingt, *Unité et processions,* vol. 2 of *Théologie trinitaire de Tertullien,* 4 vols. (Paris: Aubier, 1966–1969), 838 n. 2. Moingt identifies two senses of the phrase *God's power:* the first, that of the single power of the Father, Moingt finds in Tertullian; the second, that the Son is this power, Moingt does not find in Tertullian (see also 838–39, including nn. 2 and 3).

*tia*".[71] This latter conclusion is peculiar. Whatever Phoebadius may have owed to Tertullian (and Hanson makes out that he owed quite a bit), he did not find this doctrine in Tertullian. There are other influences at work here, and I am inclined to second Hanson's suggestion that Marcellus may have contributed something to Latin Nicene theology in general and to Phoebadius' theology in particular.[72] Hanson's reasons for suspecting the influence of Marcellus are vague; mine, however, are only slightly less so—the immediate effect of Marcellus' theology upon Latin theology is a virtually untouched scholarly topic. Marcellus' theology may be a source for Phoebadius' because Marcellus emphasized the unity between nature and power, and in his disputes with Asterius and Eusebius, he could be seen as rehabilitating or reclaiming 1 Cor. 1:24 for the Nicenes (before, in fact, Athanasius took that task upon himself): I say "could be seen" because I agree with Lienhard's opinion that Marcellus uses power only to refute Asterius' use of the term, and his own theology initially made little use of that title.

The Nicene and pro-Nicene uses of power-based descriptions of the unity between Father and Son depend upon an understanding of what a "power" is. So much is obvious, but this fact should not, for all that, be overlooked. If "power" conceptually did not carry some sense that related it to, for example, substance, nature, or essence—if, for example, "power" is understood simply as a translation of *ἐξουσία*—then power-based arguments could not move a doctrine of divine unity of nature forward. In the pro-Nicene interpretation, "power" implies the degree and kind of unity that obtains in an existent between what an existent is and the existent as it is capable of affecting and being affected, that is, insofar as it is real or exists. This understanding of the relation of a power to a nature, for example, is justifiably called a technical sense of power. The pro-Nicene polemical use of power theology turns precisely on some degree of understanding of this technical sense of power; when a sensitivity to the technical sense is lacking, power theology carries little of polemical weight for Nicene or pro-Nicene arguments. There are enough examples of power (δύναμις) being used in Greek theologies of different varieties with the techni-

71. Hanson, *The Search,* 518.
72. Ibid., 519.

cal sense that a cumulative case can be made that Greek Christian theology shared an understanding of the "technical" sense of power, and, like other theologies, used it to describe the being of the divine. The same confidence may not arise when one turns to Latin Christian theology. Nonetheless, one of the tasks of this chapter is to demonstrate that power theology was widely appreciated in Christian theology. I do not understand this appreciation in the West to depend simply on the importing of eastern conceptual idioms.

One regular feature of western articulations of Nicene and pro-Nicene trinitarian theology is a clear sign of the invocation by the author of the "technical" sense of power (usually *virtus*). In particular one can identify three polemicists for Nicaea who make explicit what I have called the technical sense of power: Phoebadius of Agen, Hilary of Poitiers, and Ambrose of Milan. Against initial expectations perhaps, the explicit turn to the technical sense of power is not as fully developed in Ambrose as it is in Hilary, casting serious doubts upon the standing scholarly consensus that Hilary's thought is innocent of philosophical influence and support.

Phoebadius says, "There . . . signified by means of the word substance, or power, or divinity."[73] and "That power, which is in need of no external aid, is said to be substance, just as we said above, that power is whatever it owes to itself."[74] Hilary says, ". . . since power is the very reality of the nature. . . ."[75] Ambrose says, "What is power, but the perfection of nature?"[76] Phoebadius' comments are the least sophisticated, for he has trouble articulating a difference between power and substance: the two are so close conceptually they collapse into one another.[77] Hilary and Ambrose are both influential representatives of Latin pro-Nicene theology, and I will have more to say about them shortly that will put their statements in context; for the time being, however, these three statements stand as cases in

73. "*Ibi enim per substantiae uocabulum aut uirtutem aut diuinitatem significari*" (Phoebadius, *Contra Arrianos* 8.1; CCL 64.31.5).

74. "*Quae quidem uirtus, quia nullius extraneae opis indiget, dicta substantia est, ut supra diximus: quidquid illud est sibi debens*" (*Contra Arrianos*, 8.3; CCL 64.31.10–13).

75. ". . . *cum uirtus naturae res esset* . . ." (Hilary, *On the Trinity* 9:52.10–14).

76. "*Quid est enim virtus nisi perfecta natura?*" (Ambrose, *On the Faith* 1:5.39; CSCL 78.17).

77. It is Phoebadius' use of substance rather than nature that causes Hanson to see the influence of Tertullian.

which Latin apologists for Nicaea make explicit their technical understandings of power in order to make clear how the term can support their arguments. In each case *power* is shown to be the kind of word that "nature" or "substance" is; and in each case *power* is understood to be conceptually related to nature or substance. Although not philosophers, these three theologians use what is recognizably a philosophical sense of power. This common use of the philosophical sense of power provides continuity among the otherwise diverse expressions of western Nicene and pro-Nicene theologies as they appear in the latter half of the fourth century.

### *Marius Victorinus*

Victorinus wrote his major work against Arianism over the years 360–362, or about the time of the flourishing of Homoian theology and the watershed of Heterousian literature in the Greek-speaking world. His enthusiasm for the term ὁμοούσιος is breathless if compared to Basil's or Gregory of Nyssa's polemics, yet like Hilary his contemporary, as well as Ambrose and Gregory, Victorinus argues for the essential unity of the Father and Son based on an exegesis of 1 Cor. 1:24. Victorinus expresses the old ontological theology and the new psychological theology through the concept of power—which appears variously as *virtus, potentia, potestas, facultas, vis,* and the Greek δύναμις.

The uniqueness of Victorinus' understanding of 1 Cor. 1:24 deserves particular notice, for while his doctrinal conclusions are similar to Hilary's and Ambrose's, his rationale in support of the creed of Nicaea, and in particular for "ὁμοούσιος" (Victorinus prefers the Greek term), is wholly distinctive. Victorinus' exegesis of 1 Cor. 1:24 builds upon the psychological sense of both power and the Nicene term ὁμοούσιος,[78] as, for example, when he compares the Father and the Son to vision:

> But the potentia and sapientia are like seeing: the potentia of sight has seeing within it. . . . seeing is begotten by the potentia of sight and is itself its only-begotten. Seeing is therefore homoousion with the potentia of sight and the whole is one.[79]

78. The psychological context of ὁμοούσιος is already suggested by Stead, when he notes that the only pagan use of ὁμοούσια in the third and fourth centuries he could find was in the psychologies of Plotinus and Porphyry. See *Divine Substance,* 215.

79. *Against Arius* 1A; Clark, 154, modified.

We would normally translate the "*potentia* of sight which produces seeing" as the "faculty of sight." The continuity of meaning with physics becomes clear later in the text when Victorinus moves from the *potentia* of sight to the *potentia* of fire. Victorinus' argument for the ὁμοούσιον nature of either the soul or the persons of God is based on the understanding of a *like from like* causality. Fire produces heat yet remains in that heat; heat flows from fire yet remains in fire.

Traditionally this *like from like, X from X,* causality is expressed in Christian formulations such as "Light from Light," "Life from Life," "Power from Power," "Essence from Essence," "Wisdom from Wisdom," or "God from God."[80] The formula "Power from Power," like that of "Essence from Essence" or "Wisdom from Wisdom," poses special problems, however, because each of these three formulae plays upon an equivocation: in one sense of the term, the power used in "power from power" is simply another case of derivation, as if one were to say "political power from political power." But in another sense of the word "power," all *like from like* expressions are in fact examples of power or faculty relations. Victorinus' fundamental understanding of what "power" means in the expression "Power from Power" is not that it denotes just one example of an *X from X* power-physics causality, but that it denotes specifically and in a proper way the fact of *X from X* power-physics causality. In Victorinus we find:

> The Logos, the Word, is Light from Light, Spirit from Spirit, and substance from substance, insofar as one is the cause of the other, so that by power they are always together. For the shining of the light is not separated but is always in the light. . . .[81]

Victorinus goes on to imagine—in echoes of *Republic* 508–9—a fire that has no need of air for its light, and sight that has no need of light for it to see: "The wisdom and power of God," Victorinus concludes, "is that not God himself?"[82] The analogy among the late Nicenes, East and West, is consistent: for Hilary, fire is the *natura,* heat the *virtus;* for Victorinus, fire is the *substantia,* heat the *potentia;* and for Gregory of Nyssa, fire is the φύσις, heat the δύναμις.

Both the use of *power from power* as a generic formula of participation

80. *Against Arius* 1A, 32; Henry and Hadot, 280:37–42; Clark, 141. See note 18 for the full text.
81. Ibid.
82. Ibid., 1A, 40; Clark, 154–55.

like, for example, light from light, and its use as the genetic formula of what causes participation can coexist in the same author. Gregory of Nyssa is an example of an author who uses *power from power* in both (what I am calling) the generic and genetic senses. However, anti-Nicene authors such as Acacius and Eunomius (and some French Augustinians)[83] tend to understand *power from power* as just another example of *like from like* causality, of the same order as, for example, "light from light," etc. Victorinus, on the other hand, never uses the formula *power from power* as equivalent to the other examples of like from like causality; it is always prior. An example of this prior role of power is found in Victorinus' description of the derivation of power not as a process of duplication but as a process of activation:

> For just as from the Spirit comes only Spirit, and from the true only the true, and from God only God, so also from substance comes only substance. . . . Consequently, that which is born of [it, that is, substance], the image, is not by division, nor by emanation, but by radiance; not by extension, but by appearance, not so much duplicating the power as activating the power.[84]

However, Victorinus shares with the anti-Nicene exegesis of 1 Cor. 1:24 a doctrine that no Greek pro-Nicene could ever hold: namely, that there are multiple powers in God. Indeed, Victorinus' comparison of the senses of power given to God and the Son is in itself not distant from Asterius' when he says:

> The Logos is therefore Father and producer of all things . . . . But power of this kind which belongs to the Logos, the power of establishing and making another, should not be understood in the same way as the power which is the cause of all things, God.[85]

None of the Cappadocians, for example, could say such a thing, since for them *one nature–one power* is a universal axiom. Gregory's argument against Eunomius is explicitly built upon the psychological foundation that just as the mind has only one δύναμις, so too God has only one δύναμις, while the Cappadocian argument for the divinity of the Holy Spirit on the basis of His common δύναμις with the Son and Father is well known.

83. See my "De Régnon Reconsidered," *Augustinian Studies* 26:2 (1995): 51–79.

84. *Against Arius*, 3:1; Henry and Hadot, 436:16–438:33; Clark, 220–21.

85. *First Letter to Candidus* IIIB, 18; Henry and Hadot, 156:5–9; Clark, 74.

Victorinus' doctrine of a power unique to the Father (namely, the power to generate the Son) is not, strictly speaking, anti-Nicene: given Victorinus' Chaldean/Porphyrian tri-power language, such a distinction among powers makes sense, but within a doctrinal context this kind of attribution of separate powers is an example of the anachronistic character of Victorinus' religious sensibilities and language.

When Victorinus offers an analogy between the soul and God, he says that the soul was given three powers because it is an image of the "*potentia* and *sapientia* of God," which is here interpreted as a trinitarian formula: "*potentia*" refers to the Son, "*sapientia*" the Holy Spirit, and "God" the Father. Victorinus explains that *potentia* means the faculty or processional power of Life, which is also the primary sense he gives to λόγος. *Sapientia* has the expected intellectual association with knowledge but refers to the Holy Spirit. This triad that Victorinus attributes to the soul is a version of the three powers he attributes to God: namely, to be, to live, and to know. To be is that inward power of identity, while to live and to know are the two powers of the outward motion. *Power from power* is the genetic formula of what causes participation because it describes the procession of the two powers to live and to understand out of the paternal power to be. These two movements occur in God, they also occur in the soul.

Despite Victorinus' philosophical sophistication and the unique intricacies of his thought, Victorinus' theology is frequently relatively primitive, and his arguments for the identification of the Son with the creative power reveal various strands of theological thought coming together under the influence of a normative Nicene Creed. For example, more than the other pro-Nicenes, Victorinus maintains the traditional identification of the Father as the source of the Son and ultimately of the Son's creative capacity.[86]

86. See *First Letter to Candidus,* Clark, 74. Note that the title "Father" in the passage refers to the second Person. The phrase "father and creator" is taken from the *Timaeus.* Also, note the John 1:3 citation. The *Letter* is an early statement by Victorinus and may not represent his later thought. In *Against Arius* II, Victorinus gives a slightly different understanding of the relation between the first two Persons: "For God is *potentia* and the Logos is *actio,* but each one is in the other. For that which can be is power, and that which is, can be. Therefore, power itself is action, and action itself is action by power. Therefore, both the Father acts and the Son acts; and the Father is on that account Father, because power begets actions, and on that account, the Son is action because action comes from power" (Clark, 201, modified).

## *Hilary of Poitiers' Power Theology*

Hilary's argument[87] that the Son has the same power as the Father is couched in his rebuttal of an Arian teaching that identifies God (the Father) as "true God" and so distinguishes Him from the Son (who is not "true God").[88] Hilary argues that the Son is included in the determination "true God" because Scripture shows the Son to possess the same nature, power, and name as the Father.[89] According to Hilary, to determine whether two things are truly named by the same name, one compares the "nature and power [*virtus*]" of a thing:[90] If these are the same, the two existents have the same name in the same way, for ". . . natural powers are evidence of the truth [of a name]; let us see, by this test, whether He [the

87. The careful reader will notice two judgments reflected in the texts I treat here from Hilary. First, I am working from a limited number of books in *On the Trinity* (primarily books 5 and 7) so that there might be some literary or thematic unity to the passages and arguments I extract. Second, although I believe that a case can be made that Hilary regularly uses *virtus* and *potestas* as synonyms, I will not take the time to argue the case here and instead will prescind from that question by working only from passages that use *virtus* (since the Latin of 1 Cor. 1:24 uses that word).

88. The original occasion of introducing this teaching is the creed contained in Arius' *Letter to Alexander,* 2: "Our faith, from our ancestors, which we have learned also from you, is this. We know one God—alone begotten, alone everlasting, alone without beginning, alone true, alone possessing immortality, alone wise, alone good, alone master, judge of all, manager, director, immutable and unchangeable, just and good, God of Law, Prophets, and New Testament." From book 5 onward, Hilary no longer identifies his opponents as "Arian," and there are reasons for suspecting that the opponents he has in mind are of a more contemporary variety.

89. Indeed, Hilary will argue that Old Testament appearances of God are appearances of the Son. Hilary puts much emphasis on the fit between nature and name. Although his understanding is that the only source of knowledge about God is God's own self-revelation, his emphasis on name is nonetheless striking in the context of Eunomius' own emphasis on the decisive character of the name in distinguishing essences. The positive presence of an understanding of divine name in Hilary's theology suggests that Eunomius' emphasis on names should not be understood as an isolated development in late fourth-century trinitarian thought.

90. *On the Trinity* 5:3; Smulders, CCL 62, 153:15; *NPNF* 9:86. Hilary then offers the example of wheat as an illustration of nature and power: "true wheat is that which grows to a head with a beard bristling round it, which is purged from the chaff and ground to flour, compounded into a loaf, and taken for food, and renders the nature and the uses of bread. Thus natural powers are the evidence of truth. . . ." The example originates in the Hippocratic writings, where φύσις καὶ δύναμις first becomes a description of that which exists, and from which Plato, as he says, borrowed his own understanding of φύσις καὶ δύναμις. Hilary's acquaintance with this formula may have come from medical sources, as suggested by his use of wheat to illustrate the relationship of nature to power; wheat (and bread) is a favorite example of φύσις καὶ δύναμις among the Hippocratics.

Son] . . . is God."[91] The unity between the first and second Persons is discovered and articulated in terms of common nature and common power; this is Hilary's phrasing repeatedly. "[He] Who possesses both the nature and the *virtus* of God . . . had at his disposal the *virtus* of the divine nature[s] to bring into being . . ."[92] or, "that by a bodily similitude [of "the Son's hand"] you may learn the *virtus* of the one divine nature which is in both; for the nature and the *virtus* of the Father is in the Son."[93]

Hilary's use of an *X from X* model of divine production is relatively minor and is predominantly limited to the early books of *On the Trinity* (*On the Faith*).[94] This lack of emphasis on an *X from X* argument for continuity of nature is matched, as one would expect, by a shift from understanding "*virtus*" as identifying the Son specifically to "*virtus*" as identifying the source and sign of unity between Father and Son. Such a shift requires a reinterpretation of the usual exemplar of *X from X* causality, fire from fire, and this is just what we find happening in the later books of *On the Trinity.* Indeed, this shift takes place where we would expect it to, namely, in the context of countering anti-Nicene interpretations of the kind of unity shown between Father and Son.

Hilary's treatment of fire as an analogy of divine production comes as he offers a counter-exegesis to the anti-Nicene understanding of John 5:19 and John 10:30 (here, especially). This section of *On the Trinity* 7:16–29 is peppered with appearances of *power* (mostly *virtus* but also *potestas*). Hilary says, for example, that the Son can perform the same works as the Father because the power (*virtus*) and nature of God dwell in him.[95] Romans 1:4, *destinatus est Filius dei in virtute,* gives Hilary the grounds for saying that the Son is a product of God's *virtus,* a use of the term suggested

91. *On the Trinity* 5:3.15; *NPNF* 9:86.

92. Ibid. 5:4.7; CCL 62, 154; *NPNF* 9:86.

93. Ibid. 7:22.48–50; CCL 62, 286; *NPNF* 9:128. Gregory of Nyssa has a similar exegesis of "hand," though the scriptural text he works from is Ps. 77:10, "the right hand of the most High." Gregory says, ". . . by right hand we understand the Power [δύναμις] of God, which made all things, which is the Lord . . ." (*GNO* 2:143; *NPNF* 5:185). Or again at *GNO* 2:170; *NPNF* 5:194, Gregory interprets "hand" in Isa. 66:2, "My hand made all things," as meaning "the Power [δύναμις] of the Only-Begotten."

94. See *On the Trinity* 2:20.

95. Ibid., 7:17.32.

by its received philosophical sense of "causal capacity."[96] Fire is then introduced as an alternative analogy to birth: fire from fire does not diminish the first fire; fire producing fire transmits all the properties of fire without itself losing any. The presence of light, heat, combustion, and motion in the product all testify that fire has indeed transmitted its nature, for whatever is by nature fire has these properties, and whatever has these properties is by nature fire.[97]

I want to pause briefly from discussing Hilary's argument that the Father and Son have a power in common to emphasize and make explicit my judgment about Hilary's knowledge of "power" as a philosophical concept. The use of power language in association with the example of fire as a model of etiology strongly suggests the elemental background of "power" in philosophy. Hilary is cognizant of, and drawing upon, the technical sense of the concept of *power.* Evidence that Hilary's knowledge of the use of *power* as a term with a specific etiological sense is available. A persuasive example of Hilary's use of *power* in its technical etiological sense is his use of the causal sequence, nature-power-operation, a sequence one finds in Galen, Iamblichus, Julian, and, for that matter, Eunomius.[98] In *On the Trinity* 9:52, Hilary gives a definition of power that says ". . . power is the very reality of the nature, and the operation is the capability of the power. . . ." In Latin, the passage reads: "*cum virtus naturae res esset et operatio ipsa virtutis sit potestas. . . .*"[99] The advantage of citing the original language is that the reader can see immediately the elements of the sequence.[100] There is the nature, the power (that is "the very reality of the nature"), and there is the operation ("the capability of the power"). It does not strain credulity to say that here Hilary's understanding of power is articulated in as sophis-

96. Romans is cited at *On the Trinity* 7:24.42; that the Son is a product of God's power is at 28.21.

97. Ibid., 7:29.3. On the other hand, Hilary warns that his reader must not imagine that the meaning of "fire from fire" requires a second wick (see 6:12.34–35).

98. On the existence of this sequence, see my "The Background and Use of Eunomius' Causal Language," 217–36; Reynolds, "The Essence, Power and Presence of God," 351–80.

99. ". . . since power is the very reality of the nature, and the operation is the capability of the power . . ." (*On the Trinity* 9:52.10–14).

100. One might tentatively suggest that, separated from the kind of reading I am here offering, Hilary's statement makes little sense.

ticated a philosophical manner as Origen gave sign of in his own definition of power.[101] Hilary uses the sequence specifically as a resource for pro-Nicene theology: the burden of the use of "power" as a resource for pro-Nicene theology is carried precisely by the unity it names with nature, a unity (one may add) that has no, and can have no, parallel in a theology like Eunomius' (as we shall see in the next chapter).

There are other signs of "power" being used in its philosophical sense by Hilary, where the conceptual debt that "power" and production language owes to elemental etiology is there to be seen. We find statements of the unity of God's power in terms suggestive of the "biochemistry" from which this language originated. Thus Hilary says, "God, who is Life, is not a being built up of various and lifeless portions; He is *virtus,* and not compact of feeble elements. . . . [He] is the living God, the eternal *potestas* of the living Divine nature. . . ."[102] The same overtones of mixture physics can be heard in the writings of Gregory of Nyssa, as this sample shows:

> In [the] case [of the Holy Trinity] there is no mixture or conflux of qualities to think of; we comprehend a δύναμις without parts and composition. . . .[103]

Similarly in Ambrose:

> No separation, then, is to be made of the Word from God, the Father, no separation in *virtus,* no separation in wisdom, by reason of the Unity of the Divine Substance. . . . For the *dei virtus* knows no void. Nor, again, is the *virtus* of the one increased by the *virtus* of the other, for there are not two powers, but one *virtus;* nor does Godhead entertain Godhead, for there are not two Godheads, but one Godhead.[104]

We can return now to discussing Hilary's understanding that the Father and Son have a power in common. In Book V of *On the Trinity,* Hilary argues that the power (*virtus*) common to the Father and Son is creation.[105] One passage in particular can give a complete representation of Hilary's

101. In chapter three I offered that Origen's definition of power and activity at *On First Principles,* 1.2.4–9 may be indebted to Stoic sources. Hilary's debt to philosophy has been consistently understated, though in comparison with Origen, it seems that on "power" his language more probably owes to Platonic or medical sources.

102. Ibid., 7.27, 130. *Virtus:* CCL, 294.11, 14, 15. *Potestas:* 294.20.

103. *GNO* 1:95; *NPNF* 5:57.

104. *On the Faith* 4; CSEL 78, 3.36, [35]; *NPNF* 10:266.

105. *On the Trinity* 5:4.17.

doctrine of the divine creative power in the Trinity and, despite its length, deserves repeating here.

When the Law says, "And God said, Let there be a firmament," and then adds, "And God made the firmament," it introduces no other distinction than that of Person. It indicates no difference of *virtus* or nature, and makes no change of name. . . . The language of the narrator says nothing to deprive Him [the second Person] of Divine nature and *virtus;* nay rather, how precisely does it communicate His true Godhead. The *virtus* to give effect to the word of creation belongs only to that nature with Whom to speak is the same as to fulfill. . . . Thus in the Son of God we behold the true Divine nature. . . . It is not merely that He can do whatever He will, for will is always the concomitant of *virtus;* but he can do whatever is commanded of Him. . . . [So do not deny] the true nature of Him Whose name reveals His *virtus,* whose *virtus* proves His right to the name.[106]

In all the passages cited here, Hilary's arguments are pointed toward the conclusion that the power and nature of the Father and Son are the same; Hilary's theology is, in this context, a "one power (one nature), multiple hypostases" doctrine. What is noteworthy about Hilary's use of power to support a doctrine of divine unity is that the older use of power (in which Christ is identified as the Power of God) has very little continuing presence in Hilary's theology. He does occasionally identify Christ as the Power of God for the purpose of establishing the Son's unity with the Father, but such occasions are rare (occurring mostly in the early books) and never serve as pivotal arguments. At one point in book 7, for example, Hilary refers to Christ as the Word, Wisdom, and Power of God; rather than argue for the Son's unity by remarking upon the unity that Word, Wisdom, and Power have in God, Hilary interprets these titles as indications of the divine nature that is present in the Son. Indeed, in response to a theology that interpreted the title "Power of God" as identifying the Son as the "inward

106. *Ibid.* 5:5.2–35; CCL 62, 154–55; *NPNF* 9:86. Compare Hilary's language with Gregory's: ". . . the mighty Moses in the record of creation instructs us about the Divine Power, ascribing the production of each of the objects that were manifested in the creation to the words that bade them be. For 'God said,' he tells us, 'Let there be light, and there was light'. . . . For God, when creating all things that have their origin by creation, neither stood in need of any matter on which to operate, nor of instruments to aid Him in His construction: for the Power and Wisdom of God has no need of external assistance. But Christ is the Power of God and the Wisdom of God, by Whom all things were made and without Whom is no existent thing . . ." (*Refutation of the Creed; GNO* 2:340–41; *NPNF* 5:111).

force" ("*internae potestatis*") of God's being,[107] Hilary offers a substantial argument against understanding the Son as a property of God. If the Son is born (as "Son" connotes), Hilary argues, then the Son has an independent and substantial existence, and "cannot be regarded as a property," for a property "can have no independent existence."[108] Here Hilary is probably distinguishing his own power theology from Tertullian's, which was, as we have seen, predicated upon treating "property" and "product" as equivalents in the Godhead.

Hilary will use power with limited christological connotations in his description of the divine in Jesus. In these cases power is used as a virtual synonym for nature. Exegeting Philippians 2:5–7, for example, Hilary will note that the divine power is not lost in the Incarnation but that the Son takes on a power that He previously lacked, namely, humanity. Or, "power" will refer to the divine power in Jesus that performs miracles.[109] Hilary's limited use of any doctrine identifying the Son with the Power of God means that 1 Cor. 1:24 figures less decisively as an authority in his theology than it does for other pro-Nicenes, including Gregory of Nyssa. Where 1 Cor. 1:24 does figure more directly in Hilary's theology is in the disputing of the exegesis of John 5:19. Hilary establishes, via 1 Cor. 1:24, that the second Person "in very truth is God [and that] the essence of the Godhead exists in" Him and "is expressed" in the names, Wisdom and *Virtus.*[110] "He is God from God . . . indistinguishable from [the Father] in nature, and therefore inseparable. . . . This is the lesson which his title[s] . . . are meant to teach us [namely, that] Christ is the wisdom and the *virtus* of God. . . ."[111] In the conclusion of his counter-exegesis of John 5:19, Hilary returns to the unity of nature indicated by the common *virtus:* "And now that we have seen Him endowed with the *virtus* of that nature, note how this results in unity, how one nature dwells in two."[112]

107. Ibid., 7.11.19–20; CCL 62, 270; *NPNF* 9:122. Such a doctrine could be referred to Sabellius (as the venerable editor of the *NPNF* thinks), to Marcellus, or to the τόνος model of unity anathematized at the Council of Sirmium, 351.

108. Ibid., 7.11.24 ff.; CCL 62, 271; *NPNF* 9:122.

109. This use of power may owe more to the traditional sense of *virtutes* in a "great man" than to the philosophical sense of power of a nature.

110. *On the Trinity,* 7:11.1–4; CCL 62, 270; *NPNF* 9:122.

111. Ibid., 11.16–19.

112. Ibid., 7:21; CCL 62:283:29 ff.; *NPNF* 9:127, modified.

The pro-Nicene understanding of the ontological status of the Son's activities is expressed well in their counter-exegesis of John 5:19,[113] which had become a proof-text in anti-Nicene polemic no earlier than 359. Eunomius uses John 5:19 in two of his works: the *Apology*, delivered in the winter of 359–360, and the *Creed* of 383, prompting replies by Basil of Caesarea and Gregory of Nazianzus. Basil's rebuttal is in his *Against Eunomius*, written by 363; Gregory's is in his *Oration* 30, delivered around 380.[114] (I am inclined to believe that Eunomius' argument from John 5:19 represents the first anti-Nicene use of this passage.) Palladius also uses John 5:19, as, much later, does Maximinus.[115] In 366 Germinius cites John 5:19 as a reason why he cannot accept heterousian theology, as Hanson points out.[116] In the much earlier and already discussed *Against the Pagans* 46, Athanasius uses John 5:19 as evidence that the Son is indeed the power of God: for only someone who was the power of God could do the same things that God did—namely, to create. However, this early use of John 5:19 with 1 Cor. 1:24 by Athanasius argues, like similar arguments by Eusebius of Casarea, for a single creator. A consciously trinitarian application of the joint exegesis of these two scriptural texts has to wait until the Athanasian (?) *To the African Bishops* 5–7, where these two scriptural texts are used against the Heterousians (or the "Anomians") and the Council of Rimini. Didymus likewise explains John 5:19 via 1 Cor. 1:24 in his *On the Trinity* (if indeed Didymus is the author of this work).[117] Like Hilary and other pro-Nicene

113. The importance of John 5:19 for trinitarian doctrine begins with Origen who, in *On First Principles* 1.2.6, understands this scriptural passage as a description of the unity between image and original: "[The] image preserves the unity of nature and substance common to father and son. For if all things that the Father does, these also the Son does likewise, then in this very fact that the Son does all things just as the Father does, the Father's image is reproduced in the Son . . ." (Butterworth, 19, translation slightly altered).

114. Gregory of Nazianzus does not cite 1 Cor. 1:24 in refuting the Eunomian exegesis of John 5:19. Norris, in his commentary on *Oration* 30:10–11, *Faith Gives Fullness to Reason*, 169–71, correctly refers to Gregory's use of his "philological and logical skills" and his use of "dialectical exegesis" to combat Eunomius' view, for while Gregory uses illustrations drawn from Scripture, he argues from philology and logic, not from Scripture. In contrast to both Basil and his friend, Gregory of Nyssa seems unaware of any anti-Nicene connotation to John 5:19 and never treats the passage: this behavior is due, I believe, to Gregory's exclusive interest (in his *Against Eunomius*) in Eunomius' *Second Apology*, where Eunomius does not use John 5:19.

115. Michel Meslin charts the use of John 5:19 by Palladius and Maximinus in his graph of Arian scriptural references in *Les Ariens d'Occident* (Paris: Éditions du Seuil, 1967), page unnumbered.

116. Hanson, *The Search*, 594.

117. *On the Trinity*, 1:16.24; Buch I, Jurgen Honscheid, 94.

polemicists,[118] Ambrose also has an exegesis of John 5:19 in *On the Faith* that uses 1 Cor. 1:24 to support the claim that action depends upon power (or capacity), and that common power means common nature: "Now is there anything impossible to God's *virtus* and wisdom? These, observe, are names of the Son of God. . . . He is *virtus,* not as having through weakness obtained increase of strength, but being Himself *virtus*. . . ."[119]

In his *Contra Eunomium,* written perhaps three years after Hilary's return to the West, Basil of Caesarea draws on the same interpretation as that found in Hilary's work for his counter-exegesis of the contested sense of John 5:19.[120] Basil argues against Eunomius' exegesis of John 5:19 by offering an alternative interpretation: he begins by making explicit the link between Christ's actions and the power that produces these actions and so interprets John 5:19 via 1 Cor. 1:24. The similarity of action testified to in John 5:19 is thus witness to the identical power that must exist to produce the common actions. And the common power means common essence: ". . . the identity of the powers verifies the equality [of essences]. . . . For Christ, it is said [in 1 Cor. 1:24], is the power of God, which is to say that the paternal power resides entirely in him."[121] Basil then concludes (and he cites John 5:19) that this is the reason one sees the action of the Father in the Son.[122]

Furthermore, Basil reworks the description of the Word as the true Power and Image of the Father without change—ἀπαράλλακτος—in his own exegesis of John 5:19 in *On the Holy Spirit* (a description one also finds in Athanasius' *Defence of the Nicene Definition*). Again we have an example of Basil building a pro-Nicene interpretation of John 5:19 by interpreting this contested passage through the lens of 1 Cor. 1:24: ". . . if in essence [the Son] is without change, so also is He without change in power. . . . And

118. Victorinus is too far away to know of this development in Greek anti-Nicene polemic and too early to see its manifestation in polemical texts or to witness its role in Latin Homoianism.

119. *On the Faith* 4:43 [42]; Faller, CSEL 78, 171:25–32; *NPNF* 10:267.

120. Obviously this is not an influence relationship. The roughly contemporary character of these two works (both written in the early 360s) is testimony to the widespread presence of the question regarding John 5:19 felt by Nicene polemicists at the time. It seems likely that Hilary encountered the question regarding John 5:19 while in exile, but one cannot discount the possibility that other western concerns with John 5:19 are indigenous.

121. *Against Eunomius* 1:23.17–21; Sesboüé, SC 299:254.

122. Ibid., lines 22–23.

Christ is the power of God, and the wisdom of God."[123] We can further note that Gregory of Nyssa will later use the same argument—power via 1 Cor. 1:24—to interpret John 5:22.[124]

### *Ambrose and "One Power" Theology*

We can gain a sense of Ambrose's understanding of power-based trinitarian theology by examining, albeit briefly, three texts in which that theology appears. The chronology that separates *On Virginity* (*de Virginibus*), book 3, from *On the Faith* (*de Fide*), book 1, and from book 4 of that same work as well, allows us to survey the development in Ambrose's thought on the subject of power trinitarian theology, even though the first and last of these treatments are separated by about four years.[125] While the time separating the writing of book 1 from the writing of book 4 of *On the Faith* is no more than two years, the two works represent significantly different levels of polemical sensitivity on Ambrose's part. These years were decisive in Ambrose's theological life, when the direct confrontation with local Homoianism forced him to grow in doctrinal sophistication.[126]

*On Virginity* 3 begins with Ambrose recalling to his sister Marcellina the sermon she had heard from Liberius when she received her veil from him in Rome. This early work by Ambrose is usually dated to 377, while

123. *On the Holy Spirit* 8:19; *NPNF* 8:13–14. Power and Wisdom are in the lower case in the original translation.

124. The association of these two texts will be found in Origen, *On First Principles* I.2.6, who comes to the Johannine passage in a discussion dealing with the scriptural evidence for the Son as the image of God provided by Wisd. 7:25, Heb. 1:3 and 1 Cor. 1:24. Augustine refers to the Arian exegesis of John 5:19 in his *De Symbolo ad Catechumenos* 5. Like "Basil's" (that is, Evagrius') *Letter* 8.9, Augustine understands the statement that "the Son can do nothing without the Father" as a declaration of the Son's extraordinary relationship with the Father, since common activities require a common nature and only a common nature can produce common activities.

125. As with my overview of Hilary, I limit my discussion of the appearance of power doctrines in Ambrose's *On the Faith* (*de Fide*) to only two books. It seemed best to have one book from each of the two stages the work was written in (that is, before and after Palladius' reply). The reasons for treating the first book of *On the Faith* will become obvious; similarly, my choice of book 4 is not simply arbitrary, since of the last three books, it presents the most arguments based on the concept and language of power. Decisions about exactly which passages to build from were—with only one exception—based on the same criterion as for Hilary: "*virtus*" passages show the trail of traditional power-language exegesis more obviously than "*potestas*" language. The one exception to the self-imposed rule of here limiting myself to "*virtus*" passages presents a formulation that may or may not be Ambrose's own, namely, 1.1.6.8.

126. See Daniel H. Williams, *Ambrose of Milan and the End of the Nicene-Arian Conflicts* (Oxford: Claredon Press, 1995).

Liberius is thought to have died in 366. The address that Ambrose speaks of would probably have occurred after Liberius had returned from exile and after the death of Constantius when Liberius had recovered his Nicene faith. In short, *On Virginity* 3 reports theology sympathetic with Nicaea, as articulated sometime in the early 360s, and that, in 377, Ambrose thought it worth recommending. (Liberius' speech seems to be regarded by Ambrose as something like a creed at 3:4.20.)

The summary of trinitarian and christological doctrine in the "sermon" runs from sections 2 to 4 of chapter 1, book 3. First comes what I regard as a traditional declaration of "genetic" christology: Jesus was human because of his mother and divine because of his father. *X from X* reasoning is applied to explain both Christ's humanity and divinity. Ambrose's christology is lacking, however, for the ostensive humanity Mary contributes is in fact described only as "body."[127] The parallel description of the Son "resembling" His Father in power is also not as full as it might have been (being an echo of "image" theology), and it thus reinforces the sense of confusion or hesitancy a reader gains from the use of double negatives rather than straightforward assertions. The Son is "not unequal" to, "not separated in power" from, "not confused" with, the Father.[128] Yet what is being accomplished here should not be underestimated since the latter part of this formula (that is, "*non verbi extensione aut prolatione confusus, ut cum patre mixtus*") reveals the author rejecting expansion-of-the-Godhead type doctrines associated with Marcellus and Photinus.

Further positive statements follow that identify the Son as God on the basis of common traits (although the conceptual apparatus is not made explicit) through a distinctive exegesis of the prologue of John: the Word is eternal since John says "in the beginning"; the Word has power without separation since John says "the Word was with God";[129] and the Word is of unbegotten divinity since John says "And the Word was God." Old forms

127. Soon afterwards the humanity of Christ is (appropriately to the occasion) cast in terms of Christ's "brotherhood" to those who are taking the veil.

128. ". . . *non impar generantis, non potestate discretus, non verbi extensione aut prolatione confusus, ut cum patre mixtus, sed ut a patre generationis iure distinctus sit*" (*De Virginibus* 3.1.2.5–7). Here occurs the only case of *potestas* in the three sections under discussion.

129. I take this connection between power and word to depend upon Romans 1:20 ("the word of his power"), even if in a mediated fashion.

of expression for the Son's unity with the Father appear: Son, Word, Arm [of the Father], Wisdom, and Power, all titles that echo with the resonance of Scripture. In each case the Son is identified with the Father's property named by the title: He is the Son of God, the Word of God, the Power of God, etc. This is single-power theology of the (old) Nicene kind.

Single-power theology, I have argued, was developed and articulated in the fourth century by Nicenes as a counter-argument to the two-powers theology typified by Arius and Asterius. That original intention travels with the doctrine, for "Liberius'" treatment of the Trinity ends with what is recognizably a traditional anti-Arian argument: If Christ is the Power of God, how could God have ever been without His Power? Any attack on the Son as God's Power is an attack on the fact of God's Power. In this case the single-power theology is used not to refute directly any lingering two-powers theology but to argue for the Son's eternity. Eternity, godhead, and power had earlier all been made equivalent to one another (in Liberius' exegesis of John's prologue) as signs of the Son's divinity. The guarantee of the Son's eternity provided by His identity as the Power of God is a hallmark of Ambrose's use of power theology, but he was not the first to use this line of reasoning.

### *On the Faith*

*On the Faith* 1 and 2 were written by early 378 in response to the Emperor Gratian's request for a statement of Ambrose's faith. The work marks Ambrose's own unequivocal entry into the battle against the anti-Nicenes. *On Virginity* shows the first signs of Ambrose's targeting of non-Nicene theology, but there his opponents remain unnamed. That silence is given up in *On the Faith.*

Chapter one of the first book is nothing but an extended argument countering the "Arian" doctrine of divine power(s) with a Nicene doctrine. First Ambrose summarizes Arian theology as the belief in many powers ("*potestas*," as is consistently the case in chapter 1). This summary is part of a catalogue of heresies: the Jews deny that God's Son was begotten before all ages; Sabellius confuses the Father and the Son, maintaining that they are the same "person"; and Arius believes in many, diverse powers, a belief that contradicts the testimony of Scripture ("Hear, O Israel, the Lord your

God is one").[130] Thereafter Ambrose asserts in as many ways as he can accumulate that there is only one Power in God, one Power in the Trinity. For example, Ambrose says that if God is one as Scripture says, then the name and the power are One. Or, Ambrose takes John 10:30 as testimony that there is no separation between the power and nature of the Son and Father. Or, again, the commandment to baptize shows that the Trinity is one power, and this indeed is the faith we confess, Ambrose says: fullness of divinity and unity of power. The term is *potestas* rather than *virtus*, but the thought is the same as seen before. "Nature and power" describes the whole of true existence (or the identity); "unity of power" means "real unity"; "one power" means "one nature."

After the first chapter Ambrose mixes *potestas* and *virtus*. At one point (17:112), *potestas* and *virtus* seem to be used interchangeably. The first appearance of *virtus* occurs as Ambrose takes up the contested exegesis of John 5:19, and the argument flows into a reference to 1 Cor. 1:24. The introduction of 1 Cor. 1:24 (and its textual echoes in the recurring references to "Power and Wisdom") guarantees the use of *virtus* in associated arguments. John 5:19 introduces into the text variations on the term "*operationes*," and the "power" that "operations" spring from is regularly, I think, called the *virtus*. The association of these two terms reflects the link between these terms in the technical causal language found in psychology, biology, and metaphysics I have already described in this study.

The later three books of *On the Faith* show significant differences from the earlier two.[131] Book 3 has a greater sensitivity to christological issues than books 1 and 2, for example. Overall, Ambrose's characterization of his opponents is more nuanced than it was in the earlier books. It also seems more contemporary, in the sense that Ambrose is dealing with a theology whose proponents say things that Arius never said. Books 1 and 2 seem largely content to attack the theology condemned in the anathemas of Nicaea, 325, but books 3–5 contain a grappling with doctrinal positions that arise only from the late 350s onwards. For example, in 1:2.12, Ambrose pro-

130. At this point Ambrose shows no awareness of the claim Homoians had at one time on this passage, a claim Hilary had to struggle hard to overturn.

131. See Daniel H. Williams, "Polemics and Politics in Ambrose of Milan's *De Fide*," *Journal of Theological Studies* n. s. 46 (1995): 519–31.

duces John 5:19 as a proof-text without any evident awareness of its history as a support of anti-Nicene theology. However, in 4:4.38, Ambrose turns directly to the "Arian" (Homoian) exegesis of the Johannine text. Ambrose's counter-exegesis of John 5:19 proves to be the pivot in his advancing of power theology, and his argument is worth pausing over.

At 4:3.35, Ambrose asserts that neither Word nor Power nor Wisdom can be separated from God the Father because the divine substance is one. The rest of this paragraph is given over to assertions of divine unity built, it should be observed, not on the doctrine of "one substance" but on that of "one power" (*virtus*). The power of one divine person is not increased by the power of another, Ambrose argues, because there are not two powers but one; not two godheads but one.

But the "Arians" deny that the *potestas* of the Father and the Son are one, and they do this on the basis of John 5:19. If the Son can do nothing "of Himself" but only what He sees the Father doing, then the powers of the Father and of the Son (and their respective natures) differ from one another in this obvious manner: the Father can do anything "of Himself" and without following any example. But what can it possibly mean, Ambrose asks (at 4.42) that the Son can do nothing of Himself? Is it reasonable to speak of incapacity in He who is the power (and wisdom) of God? 1 Cor. 1:24 decides the issue by identifying the Son as capacity Itself. Given the scripturally-attested capacity (*virtus*) of the Son, John 5:19 must mean that whatever the Son does, He does what the Father does. The argument turns, as it regularly will, to the evidence of common operations, and the common power required to produce common operations, and then to the common substance connatural to the power.

### *Doctrines of "One Power"*

Ambrose's articulation of power theology allows us to recognize a peculiar feature of Nicene theology in the second half of the fourth century. Two doctrines of "one power" coexist, without any tendency to replace one another. The first of these two doctrines is the older "Nicene" doctrine that there is only one power in God and that Power is the Son. This doctrine treats "Power" as the same kind of title as "Word" or "Wisdom": they each name some unique aspect of God's being that exists in itself ("hypostatically") in continuing relationship (identity is not always too strong a word) with What or Who it exists "in." This doctrine alone is found in *On Virginity.* The second "one power" doctrine to be found in Ambrose's *On the Faith* (and in writings of the other Latin authors described in this chapter) is the understanding that is distinctive to what I call "pro-Nicene" theology: the "one power" is the single power of the single nature or substance of the Godhead. "Power" is the same kind of title as "eternal" or "good" or "omnipotent": whatever is this, is God. Since the Son has the same power as the Father, the Son is God as the Father is God. I offer the terms "neo-Nicene" and "pro-Nicene" as technical, if still somewhat fluid, names for two kinds of trinitarian theology based on Nicaea. To a certain extent it is appropriate to understand these two theologies as two understandings of Nicaea, and one can also understand the difference between the two to be that of sequence: pro-Nicene is later (although pro-Nicene theology does not wholly replace neo-Nicene theology). The two terms correspond approximately to the difference between Athanasius' trinitarian theology and the trinitarian theology of, for example, Gregory of Nyssa. Distinguishing features of the two forms of "Nicene" theology include: (1) neo-Nicene theology identifies the Son as the single, proper "Power" of God, while pro-Nicene theology understands the Father and Son to share the "Power" of God, and thus to share the same nature; and (2) neo-Nicene theology is not engaged in the debate over John 5:19, while pro-Nicene is.

Both of these "one-power" doctrines depend upon some prior understanding of what a "power" is, since the claim to unity with nature, substance, or existent depends upon recognizing power as something about a thing that it always has as long as it is what it is. This is the minimal understanding of what a "power" is if it is to function for asserting a kind of unity. Even this minimal understanding of what "power" means reflects the philosophical and scientific uses of the word, within which the reason for the presupposed unity between power and whatever is explained. A power is the distinctive affective capacity of any specific thing that exists. A power is the capacity of anything that exists to affect or be affected. Powers are a class of entities by virtue of which all things are able to do what they are able to do (like sight and hearing). A power is that which is related to other powers and produces effects. All these are Plato's definitions of power. Hilary says that a power is the very reality of the nature. Ambrose calls it the perfection of nature. The general Nicene understanding of "power" is that it is the intrinsic capacity of a nature to affect, insofar as that nature is what it is (as opposed to some other nature with another power) and exists. The original philosophical development of "power" functions as a necessary precondition to the polemic, even if the actual use of the technical concept proceeds from only a derivative, casual awareness of the use of "power" in technical literature (for example, philosophy, medicine, etc.). However, with the Latin pro-Nicene authors treated in this chapter, we do not have to be content with attributing only a derivative awareness of the technical sense of the concept "power" (*virtus* especially but *potestas* as well) because, as I have already pointed out, the authors themselves offer definitions of "power" that locate the meaning precisely in the technical senses of the term. Gregory will take this explicit awareness of the philosophical sense of "power" even further.

Given that both doctrines of "one divine power" presuppose the technical sense of "power," each doctrine nonetheless reflects a particular degree of dependence. The Nicene doctrine that "the Son is the one power of God" has the advantage of seeming closer to the wording of the original scriptural passages, especially the identity passage of 1 Cor. 1:24, "Christ, the Power and Wisdom of God," even if what Paul meant by "power" may not have been what fourth-century exegetes of all varieties thought he meant.[132] By contrast, the pro-Nicene doctrine that "the Son has the same one power as God (the Father)" is, it has to be admitted, somewhat further from a simple reading of the New Testament passage. This "distance" is, I would suggest, an effect of a greater sensitivity to the technical background of the concept of power (and the terms δύναμις, *virtus* or *potestas*). In short, there is a kind of interpretation of "Christ, the Power and Wisdom of God" that is more simply Scripture-based, and there is a kind of inter-

132. When New Testament scholars read 1 Cor. 1:24 in ways that implicitly or explicitly exclude a metaphysical sense to "power," they are asserting that the sense of the passage is innocent of any of the technical senses of "power," especially the cosmological sense. While there has been an explosion of awareness among New Testament scholars regarding the many connotations of "wisdom," the same is pointedly absent concerning "power"—despite the work of scholars such as Segal and Fossum.

pretation of this passage that works more or less explicitly with the philosophical tradition of use of the language. The original philosophical sense of the terminology is not wholly absent in even the first of these two kinds of interpretations, for if it were, 1 Cor. 1:24, as well as Rom. 1:20 and Heb. 1:3, would bear no existential reading whatsoever (which is the case for modern exegetes who exclude the philosophical, transcendent sense of δύναμις from these texts). However, the second doctrine, the pro-Nicene doctrine of "one power," depends more on the technical sense of "power." It goes almost without saying that the pro-Nicene doctrine of "one power" will make no sense to a reader of a pro-Nicene text who is completely ignorant of the technical sense of the term. Most of the persons discussed in this chapter, whatever their opinions of Nicaea, cannot be imagined to be ignorant of the technical sense. Those of whom one might imagine it to be so, Phoebadius and Hilary, in fact show evidence of some acquaintance with traditions of discourse about "power": Hilary, in particular, reveals evidence that he could use power in very technical senses indeed. Instead of ignorance, one can determine that some authors in the controversies either declined to accept that the concept of power applied to God's being, or failed to find it a useful theological concept. "Two-power" doctrines depend as much as Nicene "one-power" doctrine on some awareness of what "power" means. I will suggest in the next chapters that Eunomius offers an understanding of divine productivity, in fact an understanding of divine being, that excludes the kind of productivity presupposed in technical uses of power. I will also suggest that Gregory's use of power in his trinitarian theology builds upon technical senses of power.

# 5 Eunomius' Theology of the Trinity

## *Introduction*

ATHANASIUS' WRITINGS FROM THE 340s and 350s describe the continuing trinitarian controversies as the enduring legacy of Arius' theology. In Athanasius' mind, the relationship between the theology of his opponents and the theology of Arius is so strong that he believes that by refuting Arius' doctrines, he also refutes the doctrines of those who later declined the Nicene doctrine that the Father and Son are ὁμοούσιος. This same tendency to define the controversy as a crisis provoked by Arius and his sympathizers appears frequently in the West: Latin bishops as late as Ambrose and Augustine quote Arius when they wish to characterize the theology of those they oppose.

The fact that Athanasius is a "Greek" can be misleading for an understanding of the trinitarian controversies east of the Nile, especially for an understanding of the resolution of that controversy in the events leading up to the Council of Constantinople in 381. If one argues (as Athanasius argued) that those who reject ὁμοούσιος hide their "Arianism" and do not acknowledge their dependence on Arius' theology, then one is left to explain the fact that even those Greeks who oppose anti-Nicene theology only rarely, if ever, refer to Arius' writings in any substantial way. Athanasius and Latin Nicenes quote Arius to refute anti-Nicene theology; Greeks who write either against anti-Nicene theology (as the Homoiousians wrote against the Heterousians), or in favor of Nicaea (as the Cappadocians did eventually) do not refer to Arius except in rhetorical flourishes. Among these Greek polemicists, the enemy to be defeated is not Arius, but Eunomius and his less prolific mentor, Aetius. From sometime in the middle of the 350s until after Constantinople 381, their doctrine that God (the Father) and the Son have different essences (thus the label heterousian for their theology) offered the greatest conceptual challenge to any theology that even resembled the faith of Nicaea.[1]

The earliest work that we have of those few remaining from Eunomius is his *Apology,* originally delivered as a speech at Constantinople in December 359 or January 360.[2] The *Apology* is both a manifesto of Eunomius' own doctrines and an attack on Eunomius' enemies, the Homoiousians and the Homoousians. Eunomius begins his discussion of God in the *Apology* with a long and detailed argument for why God is without any prior cause, ending with the conclusion that ". . . if it has now been demonstrated that God neither existed before himself nor did anything exist before him, but that he is before all things, then what follows from this is the Unbegotten, or rather, that he is unbegotten essence."[3] This existence without any prior cause is what Eunomius means by ἀγέννητος (which I will usually translate either as ingenerate or unproduced). As he admits, ἀγέννητος had long been recognized as a characteristic of the highest being.[4] But Eunom-

1. While the Homoians were more significant in both the East and the West, Eunomius' theology eventually came to define Greek opposition to Nicaea. Although Socrates and Sozomen portray Aetius and Acacius as equals in the opposition to Nicaea, the fact remains that no one wrote treatises entitled *Against Acacius.* Those who wrote against Eunomius include: Basil of Caesarea, Apollinarius, Didymus the Blind, Theodore of Mopsuestia, Diodore of Tarsus, Theodoret of Cyrus, and Gregory of Nyssa, as well as Basil of Ancyra. Most of Gregory of Nazianzus' *Theological Orations,* and a number of sermons by John Chrysostom, are also directed against Eunomius' theology. Eunomius' name is known to Latin Nicenes such as Victorinus, Ambrose of Milan, and Augustine.

2. Unless otherwise noted, all translated passages from the *Apology* appearing in this study are from *Eunomius: the Extant Works,* ed., trans. and intro., Richard P. Vaggione (Oxford: Clarendon Press, 1987). This critical edition of the *Apology,* with Vaggione's translation, will hereafter be cited as *Extant Works.*

3. *Apology* 7:9–11, *Extant Works,* 40–41. This chapter in the *Apology* begins: "It is in accordance, therefore, both with innate knowledge and the teaching of the fathers that we have made our emphasis that God is one, and that he was brought into being neither by his own action nor by that of any other, for each of these is equally impossible" (7:1–3). Eunomius adds that whatever is first must be God, and that whatever comes into existence as a result of another is a creature (7:7–9), and concludes with the statement given (7:9–11).

4. "To some it will seem useless and superfluous to develop an argument for things that are commonly acknowledged as though they were subject to doubt." *Apology* 7:13–15, 40–41. See also *Apology* 7:1–3, quoted in the previous note.

ius reworks the traditional material to support his claim that ἀγέννητος is the essence (οὐσία) of God, and not just one divine characteristic among others; indeed, Eunomius identifies divinity with this characteristic, as when he says, ". . . God is the only true and only wise God because only he is unbegotten."[5] In his interpretation, when the tradition says that God is ingenerate, the meaning is that the essence of God is ingenerate.[6] There are no other characteristics in the essence; the essence is ingenerate, and only ingenerate.[7] Eunomius will later distinguish two classes of names for God in addition to ingenerate: first, there are those names that sound different from, but mean the same thing as ingenerate, such as "He that is," and "One, true, God."[8] Second, there are those names that are equivocal, for example, Scripture's reference to God's "eye."[9] For Eunomius every meaningful name for God is a synonym for ingenerate.

### *The Non-Generative Status of the Simple Essence*

After having established that there can be no general material or logical attributions to the divine essence,[10] Eunomius focuses his argument on the attribution of causality or productivity to the divine essence.[11] Productivity

5. *Apology* 22:1, *Extant Works,* 62–63. The phrases "only true" and "only wise" are reminiscent of the earlier stage in the debate, as is Eunomius' conclusion that these traits indicate the uniqueness of God's nature just as the term "only begotten" [*μονογενής*] indicates the uniqueness of the Son's nature.

6. One text which illustrates this conclusion is *Apology* 7:11, quoted above. A similar conclusion appears at *Apology* 8:17–18, *Extant Works,* 42–43: ". . . then 'the Unbegotten' must be unbegotten essence."

7. This is Eunomius' conclusion at *Apology* 8:14–18, *Extant Works,* 42–43.

8. *Apology* 17:1–3, *Extant Works,* 54–55.

9. *Apology* 16:9–14, *Extant Works,* 52–55.

10. The difference between material and logical (as I call them) attributions of God is not great for Eunomius. Logical attributions are discussed in general from *Apology* 10:1 to 11:17; *Extant Works,* 44–47, while material attributions were discussed earlier at *Apology* 8:14 to 9:21; *Extant Works,* 42–45.

11. Note that the apparently causal relationship given by John 14:28 is discussed in *Apology* 11 as a relation of equality. Chapter 12 begins the discussion of "the only-begotten." The reference to John 14:28 by Eunomius is interesting since it is used in a similar context in the "Blasphemy of Sirmium." The pertinent section of the Creed is "There is no question that the Father is the greater. For it can be doubtful to none that the Father is greater than the Son in honor, dignity, splendor, majesty, and in the very name of Father, the Son Himself testifying, 'He Who sent Me is greater than I.' And no one is ignorant that it is Catholic doctrine that there are two Persons of the Father and Son, and that the Father is greater and the Son subordinated to the Father . . ." (J. N. D. Kelly, *Early Christian Creeds,* 3rd ed. (New York: Longman Inc., 1972), 286.

in a material sense, such as emanation (as Eunomius sees it) or sexual reproduction, is disposed of quickly.[12] Eunomius' arguments against causality considered in terms of a logic or a metaphysics are more detailed. The question of God's productivity is central to Eunomius' and Aetius' thought, and their response represents what is distinctive of, and fundamental to, their theology.

Aetius had said earlier in his *Syntagmation* that God's essence was wholly identical to ingeneracy. With this assumption Aetius proved that any product could not be from the essence but must instead be by the authority [ἐξουσία].[13] For example, Aetius says,

> If cause is assigned to every generate thing, and the ingenerate nature is uncaused, ingeneracy does not reveal cause but indicates essence.[14]

and

> If everything originate has been originated by something else and the ingenerate substance has been originated neither by itself nor by another essence, ingeneracy must reveal essence.[15]

And finally:

> If God is not entirely ungenerated, nothing hinders him from having generated essentially. But if he is entirely ungenerated, he was not partitioned essentially in generation, but he made the generate to exist as a hypostasis by his authority [ἐξουσία].[16]

The logical form of Aetius' theology is clear: the simplicity of the Deity makes him identical in essence with ingeneracy; the notion of essential generation presupposes a compound essence; and the appropriate alternative nonessential mode of production is by authority, that is, ἐξουσία. It should also be noted in passing that both Aetius and Eunomius tended to understand essential production in material terms: the essence is "parti-

12. *Apology* 12:4–7; *Extant Works*, 48–49.

13. Propositions 5, 7, and 8 make this point. Prop. 5, for example, says: "If the Deity is ingenerate in essence, what was generated was not generated by sundering of essence, but he posited it by his ἐξουσία." Wickham, "Syntagmation," 545, translated ἐξουσία as *power,* while I prefer *authority,* thus reserving *power* for δύναμις.

14. Ibid., prop. 27, Wickham's translation, 548, slightly altered.

15. Ibid., prop. 28, Wickham's translation, 548, slightly altered.

16. "Syntagmation," Prop. 7, Wickham's translation, 545, slightly altered: I have changed *power* to *authority.*

tioned" (διαστάσει) in essential production.[17] For both Aetius and Eunomius essential production seemed necessarily to presuppose a materialist understanding of essence, which they, of course, could not accept. The Eunomian doctrine that essential production implies compoundedness in the essence depends on the two related assumptions that any existent that has multiple characteristics or traits is compounded and that what is compounded is necessarily material.[18]

Eunomius denies that any causality can be attributed to the essence. The two possible sorts of causality he considers are essential, or natural production,[19] and nonessential production.[20] Either of these immaterial causalities might be attributed to an existent, and each of these is represented by theologies in the Nicene controversy.[21] For Eunomius, the issue turns upon the question of essential causality. His argument against it is straightforward, once allowance is made for the previous conclusion that the essence is ingenerate in an exclusive way. Eunomius says that any product of the essence must have the same essence as its source;[22] this statement explains what is meant by essential or natural causality. This understanding

17. Proposition 5, quoted above, typifies this insistence in Aetius' thought. For the Greek reference, see Wickham, "Syntagmation," 541; for Eunomius, see *Apology* 9:5; *Extant Works*, 42; 15:5, 52.

18. The Heterousian emphasis on language such as ἐνέργεια and ἐξουσία predates Eunomius' *Apology*. In 358 Basil of Ancyra convened a local council to condemn doctrines that were recognizably Heterousian and to exile Aetius and Eunomius. After this council Basil and George of Laodicea wrote circular letters to present their case against the unnamed Heterousians. Both these documents provide significant reports of Heterousian theology. (George quotes fragments from a Heterousian document.)

The original Heterousian emphasis on ἐνέργεια and ἐξουσία followed from their claim that οὐσία-based language (used by both the supporters of Nicaea as well as Basil and George) was fundamentally materialistic. Any description of divine generation or the relationship between the first and second Persons in terms of οὐσία carried materialistic concepts of (re)production into the Godhead. Heterousian polemic regularly charged the opposition with implicitly attributing emanation or division to the divine essence. Most of the Heterousian reasoning seems to borrow from the earlier cosmological debates already described. However, for the Heterousians, the clearest proof of this materialism was the preference the Homoousians and Homoiousians showed for the titles "Father" and "Son."

19. For example, *Apology* 15:4–5; *Extant Works*, 50–53.

20. *Apology* 15:9–10, 16:7–9; *Extant Works*, 52–53.

21. Certainly the Homoousians and probably the Homoiousians may be understood as presuming some kind of essential production. The Homoians and the Heterousians understood production to be nonessential, that is, by the will.

22. For example, ". . . but if God is unbegotten in the sense shown by the foregoing demonstration, he could never undergo a generation which involved the sharing of his own distinctive nature with the offspring of that generation" (*Apology* 9:1–3; *Extant Works*, 42–43).

is shared by virtually everyone in the controversy, including Athanasius.[23] As an example of a product originating from an essence, I suggest that of a child, who is a natural product and who shares in the same essence—humanness—as its parents. Any nonessential product, for example, a work of art, has another essence that is not that of its producer. If one could reduce the essence of the productive source to one characteristic,[24] as Eunomius does with his understanding of God's simplicity, then any product of the essence must have this one characteristic,[25] and the lack of this characteristic indicates that the product is not from the essence. Since God's essence is ingenerate, any product of His essence must also be ingenerate.[26] But what is generated cannot have as its essence to be ungenerated; such an essence would include a contradiction.[27]

In chapters 9 and 10 of the *Apology,* Eunomius argued that since he has made it clear that the divine essence can have no essential products, then the essence can have no products at all. The divine essence cannot be considered as the source or capacity for nonessential production either, since this would introduce parts into the essence. The "capacity" to produce ac-

23. Stead, *Divine Substance,* 260–66, esp. 262.

24. This process of reducing something to one characteristic is carried on by Aristotle in *Categories,* 7a32–7b9. Wickham says of this tendency in Anomean thought: "For Aetius and Eunomius, ingeneracy is the essence of God, that is, is God" ("Syntagmation," 552).

25. Thus he says, ". . . if the one name [of the essence] is 'Unbegotten' it cannot be [also called] 'Son', and if [properly called] 'Son' it cannot be 'Unbegotten'" (*Apology* 11:13–14; *Extant Works,* 46–47).

26. Note that at *Apology* 15:5; *Extant Works,* 52–53, when Eunomius says, ". . . we have not ascribed begetting to the essence of God (it is unbegotten)," he is arguing that since God's essence is unbegotten, it cannot beget, just as (Eunomius continues) since the essence is incorruptible, it cannot be partitioned.

27. This argument, in all its forms, was worked out in detail by Aetius in his *Syntagmation.* Aetius began his treatise with the question, "Whether the ungenerate Deity can make the generate ingenerate?" (see Wickham, "Syntagmation," 541–49). The next thirty-six propositions argue that the essence of the Generate (the Son) cannot be the same as the Ingenerate. Some of the propositions were based upon the linguistic theory that names are of essences. For example, propositions 12, 13, 17, and 26. Wickham discusses this linguistic theory on pages 557–58. But the majority of the propositions were based on the simplicity of the divine essence as ἀγέννητος, where ἀγέννητος is understood to mean "without prior cause," and upon the resultant paradox involved in "producing an essence which is unproduced." (Most of the propositions may be so described, but see, in particular, prop. 9, 10, and 11.) The thought is the same as Eunomius', though the expression is more terse. Wickham, "Syntagmation," 537, says that historical sources testify to there being no significant doctrinal differences between Aetius and Eunomius. While I believe that whatever Aetius taught, Eunomius maintained, I am not as certain that all of Eunomius' doctrines are simply from Aetius.

cidents would be distinguishable from the characteristic "unbegotten" (which here Eunomius takes to mean "without prior cause"), which is the divine essence. Attribution of such a capacity to the essence would require some further logical category, such as property, quality, etc., which, in Eunomius' view, does not exist in a simple essence. In this case, if any capacity is not essential, that is, producing a product with the same essence as itself, then the capacity cannot be properly attributed to the essence at all.

### *The Character of Eunomius' Doctrine of* Ἀγέννητος

One of the striking features of Eunomius' thought is his argument that ingenerate—ἀγέννητος—is conceptually not a privation [στέρησις] because if it were a privation, then some state or condition [ἕξις] would then be prior to being unbegotten, namely, begottenness, since privation is the absence of a given property. But begottenness presupposes something prior (the begetter), so it cannot be the prior state to unbegottenness.[28] This argument has become the occasion for speculation on Eunomius' philosophical sources, speculation that began in the controversy itself and that has continued into present-day scholarship. Basil of Caesarea argued that Eunomius is influenced by the *Categories,* since there Aristotle argues that privations are secondary substances.[29] Basil's argument gives Anastos the opportunity to remark that "Basil heatedly repudiates Eunomius' reference to privation because, he says quite rightly, it is based upon Aristotle's *Categories*."[30]

The problem with Basil's (and Anastos') comments, as Mortley has pointed out, is that in fact "Aristotle does not make this claim in the *Cate-*

28. ". . . God both was and is unbegotten. He is not such, however, by way of privation [στέρησις]; for if privatives are privatives with respect to the inherent properties of something, then they are secondary to the positives. But birth has never been an inherent property of God!" (*Apology* 8:7–10; *Extant Works,* 42–43).

29. Basil quotes *Apology* 8:7–10 (given just above) in his *Against Eunomius* 1:9; after giving the passage, he says that Eunomius takes the privation language from the *Categories.* Basil replies to Eunomius' argument by saying that names with privative forms, such as ἀπτήαρτος, as well as ἀγέννητος, are privative in appearance yet when they are applied to God, they do not indicate the lack or loss of some quality but a condition beyond the possibility of such a lack. These terms are not used as privatives; they are not even used in their normal experiential sense (see Sesboüé, SC 299, 199–201). Anastos, "Basil's *Κατὰ Εὐνομίου*," 84–86, summarizes Basil's argument.

30. Raoul Mortley, *From Word to Silence,* 2 vols. (Bonn: Peter Hanstein Verlag Gmbh., 1986), 2:140, citing Anastos, 84.

*gories*."[31] Mortley shows, however, that such a connection between privation and primary and secondary substances was a feature of later commentaries (which Mortley describes as "Neo-Aristotelian") and that much of Eunomius' vocabulary resembles the vocabulary of these philosophers.[32] The fact that Eunomius' negative theology produces a seemingly positive description of God is but another feature of his theology that is common to these Neo-Aristotelian Platonists. Mortley, then, has given us a setting for Eunomius' understanding of privation that locates it within a hellenistic appropriation of Aristotle that brings him into line with the doctrines and presuppositions of Neoplatonism.

Eunomius' understanding of the fundamental nature of God's essence is to be found in the premises leading up to his conclusion that the identity of this kind of essence is signified by the term *unbegotten*. There are three such premises regarding the nature or kind of God's essence: first, ingenerateness cannot be attributed to only a part of God, since God is without parts; second and conversely, there is nothing in God that is other than ingenerate, because God is simple; finally, God is not both ingenerate and some other state of being, because God is *one*. By this argument Eunomius demonstrates that God's essence can have only one characteristic. Although the argument appears to be general in form, in fact it is quite specific: Eunomius discusses only two states of being, ingenerate and generate (unproduced and produced),[33] and his point is to deny that God can be both, and thus the Son cannot be God.[34]

31. Ibid., 2:140. Mortley's argument is that although in the *Categories* Aristotle does discuss privations and negations as well as priority and posteriority, he does not connect these two issues. Wickham, "Syntagmation," 561, had already cast some doubt on whether Basil had actually read the *Categories*.

32. Two important such examples are ἐπίνοια and στέρησις: the first is another term attributed to Aristotle but which in fact figures prominently only in his commentators (*From Word to Silence*, 2:152), while the second is a term usually reserved for mathematics (ibid., 2:131–33), contrary to E. Vandenbussche's comments at "La Part de la dialectique dans la théologie d'Eunome le technologue," *Revue d'histoire ecclésiastique*, 40 (1944–45): 47–72, 53.

33. References for Eunomius' discussion of ἀγέννητος have already been given in notes 14 of this chapter. Γεννητός is applied to the Son at *Apology* 12:2; *Extant Works*, 46, though a general comparison of unproduced to being produced (that is, unbegotten to born) is the subject of *Apology* 8:8–9:12; *Extant Works*, 42–45.

34. Chapter 12 of the *Apology* is the first of a series of chapters that argue that the names for the two Persons must be different. Chapter 12 speaks of the Son's names "offspring" and "thing

Eunomius' emphasis on ingenerateness as divinity's fundamental and distinguishing characteristic, (that is, as the term that best names the kind of existence peculiar to God) has been understood both as a mark of his doctrinal continuity with Arius and as a sign of his distance from the theologies of his anti-Nicene contemporaries. The first understanding is a feature of both Eunomius' adversaries and modern accounts of that confrontation, while the second understanding, that Eunomius' emphasis on ingenerateness distinguishes his theology from those of his fellow anti-Nicenes, is largely a feature of modern scholarship.

## Ἀγέννητος *in the Early Trinitarian Controversy*

In his *On the Synods,* Athanasius gives the reader fragments of a work by Arius.[35] These fragments begin:

> God himself is inexpressible to all beings. He alone has none equal to him or like him, none of like glory. We call him unbegotten on account of the one who by nature is begotten.

Thereafter continues a doxology of God's unique status:

> We sing his praises as without beginning because of the one who has a beginning. We worship him as eternal because of him who was born in the order of time.[36]

French scholars in the early part of this century emphasized the philosophical origins of Arius' use of the concept unbegotten, ἀγέννητος. Scholars such as de Régnon[37] and Lebreton supported their characterization of

---

made" (*Apology* 12:3–4; *Extant Works,* 48–49). Chapter 14 carries on the *reductio ad absurdum* of the titles "Son-who-was-not-begotten" and "Father-who-did-not-beget" (*Apology* 14:7–19; *Extant Works,* 50–51). Chapters 15 and 16 discuss the meaning of the creator/maker titles for either Person, and so on. All of these arguments depend on the underlying premise of Eunomius' theory of language, which is stated succinctly at *Apology* 12:7–9, *Extant Works,* 48–49: "We do not understand his essence to be one thing and the meaning of the word which designates it something else. Rather we take it that his substance is the very same as that which is signified by his name."

35. *On the Synods,* 15.

36. I use Williams' translation of this text for its clarity and accessibility; see *Arius,* 101–2. The Greek texts have been gathered together by Charles Kannengiesser in *Holy Scripture and Hellenistic Hermeneutics in Alexandrian Christology; The Arian Crisis* (Berkeley: The Graduate Theological Union and the University of California, 1982), 41–47.

37. Étude 16 of de Régnon's *Études sur la Sainte Trinité* is devoted to a treatment of ἀγέννητος as a theological title. Jules Lebreton summarized his own conclusions on the same subject in "ΑΓΕΝΝΗΤΟΣ dans la tradition philosophique et dans la littérature chrétienne du IIe siècle," *Récherches de Science Religieuse* 16 (1926): 431–43.

Arianism as philosophical Christianity by building on the common complaint of Athanasius and the Cappadocians that the anti-Nicene emphasis on the term ἀγέννητος came from pagan philosophy.[38] However, the fact that this complaint comes late in the controversy, when anti-Nicenes such as Aetius and Eunomius are building an alternative theology on ἀγέννητος and related terms,[39] suggests that the concern for this title for God is an epiphenomenon of the controversy beyond Alexandria in the 350s and not an accurate characterization of Arius' own theology.[40] It is more accurate to understand the later emphasis on the ἀγέννητος—ingenerate—in Arius' theology, as well as the argument that the term is borrowed from philoso-

38. This same argument is fully developed by Pollard in *Johannine Christology,* 188–91. Pollard accepts Athanasius' report that ἀγέννητος was primarily philosophical in origin and that it was a central doctrine in Arius' own theology. Pollard first endorses Athanasius' report on pages 104–5 of "The Origins of Arianism," *Journal of Theological Studies* 9 (1958): 103–11.

39. I mean by related terms the other α-privative titles Eunomius offers as synonyms for ἀγέννητος: ἀμερής, ἁπλοῦς, ἀσύνθετος, and ἀσύγχυτος (see his *Apology* 8:15–16). In *From Word to Silence,* Mortley has argued in detail that such terms reflect Eunomius' status as a negative theologian. (Mortley's work has not yet received the attention it deserves.) In general the question of the role of apophaticism and negative theology in anti-Nicene theology has been seriously undertreated. In *Mystical Theology* (reprint, London: James Clark and Co., Ltd., 1973), Vladimir Lossky cast the Arian controversy as a controversy between apophatic and kataphatic theologies by ignoring Arius and featuring Eunomius (as he is portrayed by Socrates and Sozomen).

40. Aetius published his *Syntagmation* in 359, and Eunomius delivered his *Apology* in the winter of 359/360. *On the Synods* was obviously written by Athanasius after the Councils of Rimini (Ariminum) and Seleucia, which were held in the summer and fall of 359; Quasten gives it a date of late 359 in *Patrology,* 3:62, while Hanson, *The Search,* 420, gives 359–361. Athanasius complains about the Arian use of Unbegotten, and faults its pagan origins, in *Defence of the Nicene Definition,* 7:28; NPNF 4:169, usually dated at 351 (for example, by Quasten, *Patrology,* 3:61), though Hanson gives 356/357 (*The Search,* 419). Quasten gives 358 as the date for *The Discourses against the Arians,* (*Patrology,* 3:27), while Hanson says 339–345 (*The Search,* 419). Kopecek believes that Aetius' *Syntagmation* was written in reply to Athanasius' *On the Synods:* see pages 216, 221, 240–42 of his *History.* The first clear reference we have to a theology that may be called anomoian or heterousian is in the letters of Basil of Ancyra and George of Laodicea; they are, of course, writing against such a theology. Both Basil and George include summaries of their opponents' doctrines, which include statements on the Son's unlikeness in essence to God and the Son's likeness to God's will that produced him. Doctrines such as these were condemned at the Council of Ancyra in 358. Scholarly judgments on the role of Aetius and Eunomius in the Council of Seleucia in 359 are still very confused, partly from a tendency to seek clear and distinct divisions in theologies and parties (between "Homoian" and "Heterousian" theologies, primarily) when there were none. A good illustration of the confusion surrounding the role of Heterousians at Seleucia is found in Hanson's account of this Council; on page 372 of *The Search,* he says, "No representative of the extreme Neo-Arians was present [at Seleucia], unless we count the slippery Eudoxius. . . .", yet on page 375, he says that Eudoxius "consorted at this council with several Neo-Arians. . . ."

phy, as a response to the theology of later anti-Nicenes, which those sympathetic to Nicaea projected back onto Arius.[41] Work by several scholars help support this conclusion.

Stead, for example, noted that Bishop Alexander of Alexandria's own creed begins with the phrase "one unbegotten Father," and that Alexander never criticized Arius for his use of ἀγέννητος.[42] Williams carried this perception further: he has argued that in the controversy in Alexandria, the emphasis on ingenerate actually begins with Alexander. Williams observes that the charge that Alexander taught two ἀγέννητα can be found in two Arian texts, the letter of Eusebius of Caesarea to Euphraton, and Eusebius of Nicomedia's letter to Paulinus.[43] Williams' conclusion is that Arius spoke for those who found the idea of two ingenerates both unintelligible and heresy. Their response was to emphasize the unique nature of God the Father.[44]

41. Kannengiesser believes that the *Thalia* of Athanasius' *On the Synods* shows the influence of a redaction by a Heterousian editor; Kannengiesser goes so far as to suggest Aetius himself; see *Holy Scripture and Hellenistic Hermeneutics,* 16. Kopecek has argued against this opinion in his response to Kannengeisser's paper (published together with that paper, 54) and properly so. But by making this suggestion of a Heterousian redactor, Kannegiesser has brought to light our difficulty in determining how much of what we understand as Arian (in the strict sense of this word) is shaped (perhaps not quite as literally as the hypothetical Heterousian redactor) by the latter era of the trinitarian controversy, that is, from 357 onwards.

42. Stead, "Platonism of Arius," 17.

43. Williams, "Logic of Arianism," 57.

44. That the Arians emphasized God's unique nature is agreed upon by all scholars, but there the consensus ends. Traditional scholarship found in this emphasis a "Jewish monotheism" in which the Son figures as a demi-god, after the fashion of intermediary powers in Philo's writings or in Pseudo-Aristotle's *On the World.* At the opposite end of the spectrum of interpretation, Gregg and Groh emphasize in *Early Arianism,* 86, that the Father's unique status was understood by Arius less as ontological than as His "unqualified sovereignty."

In his article on the "Platonism of Arius," 17, Stead remarks on the distinctive character of Arius' doxological formula of μόνον ἀγέννητον, μόνον αἴδιον, μόνον ἄναρχον, μόνον ἀληθινόν, μόνον ἀθανασίαν ἔχοντα, μόνον σοφὸν, μόνον ἀγαθὸν, μόνον δυνάστων. These terms are taken from Arius' *Letter to Alexander,* ". . . we acknowledge one God, the only unbegotten, the only eternal, the only one without cause or beginning, the only true, the only one possessed of immortality, the only wise, the only good, the only sovereign." See Williams, *Arius: Heresy and Tradition,* 247, for the English, and Kannengiesser, *Holy Scripture and Hellenistic Hermeneutics,* 42, for the Greek. This early list resembles the doxology given above: "We call him unbegotten on account of the one who by nature is begotten. We sing his praises as without beginning because of the one who has a beginning. We worship him as eternal because of him who was born in the order of time. The one without beginning established the Son . . ." (Williams, 102–3). Arius' list suggests to Stead ("Platonism of Arius," 31) the Neoplatonist Atticus since both authors "accumulate the theological predicates upon a single Creator and Father." In *Johannine Christology,* 188–92, Pollard,

In some influential modern accounts of ingenerate as a title for God in the Arian controversy, the emphasis has been on the precedent for the use of this title set by the Apologists. This emphasis has reinforced the scholarly assumption that the typical early Christian use of *ingenerate* was as a theological category or title for describing the difference in nature between the Father and the Son. Overall, contemporary scholarly opinion on the antecedent use of ἀγέννητος (γεννητός) falls into two schools. The first school consists of scholars who consider Arianism fundamentally a Christian phenomenon and who emphasize the soteriological content of Arianism; these scholars find the precedent for Arius' use of *ingenerate* in the theology of early Christian writers, such as Justin and Athenagoras (as distinct from pagan philosophical sources). The second school consists of scholars who understand Arianism as reflecting the common concerns and language of both Christianity and philosophy; these scholars find the origins of Arianism in cosmology and emphasize the use of *ingenerate* by third-century Christian writers in common with philosophical sources of the day. I have found that one consideration that neatly dramatizes the differences between these two schools is their respective evaluations of the importance of Methodius of Olympus.

Scholars such as Kopecek, Gregg and Groh, and even Hanson, offer histories of the theological use of *ingenerate* that emphasize the role of the Apologists and either minimize or ignore any influence by Methodius. For example, in his detailed discussion of the background of ἀγέννητος Kopecek gives Methodius not even one complete sentence;[45] Gregg and Groh

like Gwatkin, links this list of predicates to the use of ἀγέννετος and considers that all of these titles show the philosophical nature of Arius' conception of God. Barnard, on the other hand, sees in Arius' list the influence of the theology of Athenagoras' *Leg* 10 ("The Antecedents of Arius," 172–88, esp. 174). Friedo Ricken also finds signs of Arius' debt to previous Alexandrian theology, while adding that Arius' negative theology went beyond that of his Christian predecessors ("Nikaia als Krisis des altkirchlichen Platonisme," *Theologie und Philosophie* 44 (1969): 321–41, esp. 323–29). Kannengeisser endorses this part of Ricken's conclusion but criticizes him for his remaining emphasis on Middle Platonism and the failure to push that emphasis back into Neoplatonism (*Holy Scripture and Hellenistic Hermeneutics,* 25). The most intriguing modern treatment of the doxology is by Gregg and Groh when they show the biblical sources (primarily 1 Tim. 6:15–16) for Arius' formula (*Early Arianism,* 89–90). They do not, however, confront the point that Williams later makes: literary resemblances between this doxology and either Scripture or other creeds part company over Arius' use of ἀγέννητος (Williams, *Arius: Heresy and Tradition,* 96).

45. *Neo-Arianism,* 1:265.

do not mention him at all (or at least he does not appear in the index of *Early Arianism*); and though Hanson rehearses several problems with Gregg's and Groh's soteriological interpretation, his summary of Methodius' doctrine in one paragraph is cursory and never goes so far as to accept any significance of Methodius for the trinitarian theologies of the fourth century.[46] An entirely different evaluation of Methodius is found in the writings of Stead, who argues that Methodius was probably a direct influence on Arius for doctrines of the priority of the Father, His creation by a sovereign act of will, and the rejection of an argument from relations.[47] Likewise, Williams places great emphasis on Methodius and the third-century debates on creation as influences on fourth-century debates on the Trinity.[48]

As I have already noted, what is distinct about Eunomius' use of ingenerate is his insistence that this term describes, indeed, names, the very essence of God. The earlier attributions of ingenerate to God by Arius and Asterius never went so far as to claim that God's essence (οὐσία) was ingenerate since, especially for Arius, such a claim would offend a deeply felt, if vaguely expressed, apophaticism. Arius says that the essences of the Father and the Son are unlike each other, but he never goes so far as to identify God's essence with ingenerate.[49] However, while one never finds in

46. Hanson's treatment of Gregg and Groh appears at *The Search*, 96–98; his treatment of Methodius appears at pages 83–84. Hanson is generally keen to limit the influence of philosophy in all the stages of Arian and anti-Nicene theology.

47. See Stead, "The Platonism of Arius," 28–30.

48. Williams, *Arius*, 169. One can also note the work of Brooks Otis, who had earlier made similar arguments for the importance of Methodius in "Cappadocian Thought as a Coherent System," *Dumbarton Oaks Papers* 12 (1958): 97–124, esp. 118 n. 60. Both Otis and Williams depend greatly on the work of Lloyd Patterson (as do I), especially his "*De libero arbitrio* and Methodius' Attack on Origen," *Studia Patristica* 14 (1976): 160–66, and "Methodius, Origen, and the Arian Dispute," *Studia Patristica* 17:2 (1982): 912–23.

49. In the extant fragments of the *Syntagmation*, Asterius makes very few references to essences: fragment X (as Hanson numbers them, *The Search*, 34) says that the Son is called such because of a "birth from a father and as peculiar to his substance (οὐσία)," and fragment XI speaks of the one essence and nature of Wisdom as opposed to the many wise things. *By essence* and *by nature* and *itself* (αὐτός) all seem to have the same meaning. Later anti-Nicenes (and some modern scholars) have understood Arius' statement that "We call [God himself] unbegotten because of the one who is by nature begotten" to mean that the fundamental difference between the existence of God (the Father) and the existence of the Son is that the former is unbegotten (that is, uncaused), while the latter is begotten (that is, caused). For example, in *Commentary on the Acts of Aquileia*, Maximinus remarks approvingly on Palladius' claim that God the Father is the

the writings of Arius and his early sympathizers an identification of God's essence as ingenerate, one does find this identification in a fragment from Dionysius of Alexandria's *Against Marcellus,* preserved (exclusively) in Eusebius of Caesarea's *Preparation for the Gospel.* In that fragment Dionysius says: "For if God is the absolutely unoriginate, and if the being unoriginate is, as one might say, His very essence. . . ."[50]

This extract from Dionysius' work is included by Eusebius as part of an extended argument in the *Preparation for the Gospel* for creation *ex nihilo,* that is, against a doctrine of the coeternal or unbegotten existence of matter. Eusebius selects passages from Dionysius, Origen, Philo, and "Maximus" (actually Methodius[51]) that contain arguments for the doctrine that God is "the one sole Creator of all things, including the substance underlying bodies. . . . ,"[52] a doctrine that Eusebius regards as the great insight of the Hebrew religion (and, by appropriation, of Christianity).

All the quotations from these authors reproduced by Eusebius are concerned with demonstrating that God's existence must precede that of matter, or else God and matter are equals, and God cannot genuinely be spoken of, in the words of Origen, as "Creator, Father, Benefactor, Good Being, or anything else that is with good measure predicated of God."[53] Each author describes the state of being without prior cause as ingenerate, and the argument turns on whether both God and matter, or God alone, can be said to

---

only ingenerate and interprets Arius' confession of one true God, alone ingenerate, alone eternal as meaning that God is ingenerately eternal, ingenerately good, ingenerately immortal, and ingenerately invisible (304r, 38). Or again in the Letter of Auxentius on the creed of Ufilas, Maximinus notes that Ufilas knew that the one true God is the one ingenerate (304v, 42). See *Scolies Ariennes sur le Concile d'Aquilée,* ed. Roger Gryson, SC 267:233 and 237.

50. *Preparation for the Gospel,* 7:19, 3; Gifford, 3:1, 266. The Greek may be found in *La Préparation Evangelique, Livres VII,* trans., and comm. Guy Schroeder, ed. Édouard des Places (Paris: Les Éditions du Cerf, 1975), SC 215:266. There are other general similarities in Dionysius' and Eunomius' language: like Eunomius, Dionysius frames the question of two ἀγέννητα in terms of the unsuitability of "likeness" language and describes the existence of the Unbegotten with a series of α-privative titles that are contrasted with the existence of begotten nature. Dionysius' explicit description of God's essence as Unbegotten is a specific Christian precedent for Eunomius' doctrine, while Dionysius' use of like/unlike categories and α-privative titles illustrates how commonly used theological language of the era was applied to the particular problem of the "chronology" of creation.

51. The extract is now recognized as being from Methodius' *De libero arbitrio* as Patterson's article, "Methodius' Attack on Origen," 162, makes clear.

52. *Preparation for the Gospel* 7:18, 11; Gifford, 3:1, 361.

53. Ibid., 7:20; 363.

be ingenerate, for in these accounts, existence is divided into two kinds: ingenerate and generated. The assumption common to all these authors is that if God and matter are equally coeternal, then God is not God over matter; indeed, as the passage from Origen suggests, then God is not God. If God and matter are both ingenerate, then God's creative activity is the same as that of a human artist who works from preexistent matter to craft his products.

Eunomius offers a very similar argument in the *Apology* for his doctrine that God's essence is ingenerate or unbegotten. He says:

> Just as the maker must be in existence before the thing he brings into being, and the thing made must be later than its maker, by the same token a thing cannot exist before or after itself, nor anything else before God . . . if it has now been demonstrated that God is before all things . . . then what follows from this is that God is the Unbegotten, or rather the Unbegotten essence.[54]

As in the works that Eusebius cites, the contrast between the existence of God and the existence of things made is drawn at the level of essences. In the earlier works quoted by Eusebius, the necessity for speaking at this level of contrast is demonstrated, while in Eunomius' argument, the reference to essences appears as an assumption.[55]

One particular aspect of Eusebius' argument by proxy deserves special attention: the longest quotation he provides is one in which Methodius shifts the argument that God alone is ingenerate from a material or artistic model to a moral model. If matter is ingenerate, Methodius hypothesizes, then either evil is an essence, or it is an accident that God created.[56]

54. *Apology* 7:4–11; *Extant Works,* 40–41.

55. In chapter 8:7–18 of the *Apology,* Eunomius argues that since the attribution of Unbegotten is based upon neither στέρησις nor ἐπίνοια, God must be unbegotten essence. Mortley, *From Word to Silence,* 2:137, has shown that the language and form of this argument in chapter 8 resembles the language and form of arguments in the negative theology of contemporary Neo-Aristotelianism. Mortley is correct to locate Eunomius' theory of theological language in this philosophical tradition. However, the duplication in chapters 7 and 8 of the argument that God's essence is ingenerate shows Eunomius drawing upon two separate traditions that both argue to the same end. It may be that only the argument in chapter 7, which follows a *bona fide* Christian tradition, was offered in the original oral presentation by Eunomius of this "Apology" at the Council of Constantinople, 360, and that the technical, originally non-Christian, argument of chapter 8 was added for the publication of the *Apology* in 362/3.

56. *Preparation for the Gospel* 7:22, 31–34. Patterson, "Methodius' Attack," 163–65, and Williams, *Arius,* 168, explain the link Methodius made between the doctrines of preexistent matter and of matter as the source of evil.

Though Eunomius does not appeal to this kind of argument in his own writings,[57] the terms in which Methodius makes his argument are the same key terms Eunomius uses to argue that God's essence is ingenerate.[58] Methodius makes a distinction between names attributed to the essence and names that follow from accidents: examples of the latter include the grammarian being so named because he possesses the accident grammar, just as the rhetorician is so named because he possesses the accident rhetoric. Whenever someone is named in this way, ". . . his essence is neither the art of rhetoric, nor grammar, but receives its name from its accidents."[59] Furthermore, if something is named after accidents, then it may have opposites predicated of it.

The important distinction for Methodius is between what something is (and is called) in essence, and what it is (and is called) through accidents, or as he also speaks of them, actions (or activities, ἐνέργειαι).[60] Actions or activities come into being, Methodius says, when the agent is present, and when the agent does not exist, there is no action, since actions, unlike essences, depend upon something prior for their existence. Finally, in Methodius' account, if something is an activity and not an essence, then it is said to be a work [ἔργον][61] of that essence. With this background in

57. Patterson, "Methodius, Origen and Arius," 920, offers a vague comment on the continuing effect of Methodius' critique on the "later Arianism" of Aetius and Eunomius. My point is to offer observations on the general similarity between Methodius' and Eunomius' attention to the γεννητός and ἀγέννητος distinction and on the specific similarity in the language they both use to argue for that distinction. Otis and Patterson both refer to the influence of Methodius on Gregory's doctrine of διάστημα, while Williams covers the role of διάστημα in the early controversy. There are other Methodian influences on Gregory: the interpretation of the "coat of skins" as the passionate body, for example, or the doctrine of an exact number of preexistent souls whose birth in bodies constitutes the organic unity of mankind and sets a limit to the number of people who can or will be born. It should be noted that this last doctrine is also attributed to Eunomius by Nemesius of Emesa in *On the Nature of Man* 1:17. Nemesius says that Eunomius taught that the world was only half-full of its intended population, that fifty thousand people were being born each day, and that when the full number had been reached the world will end in the resurrection of the dead.

58. Otis seems content to assume the direct influence of Methodius on the Cappadocians and their immediate contemporaries, while ignoring intermediate examples of this concern with creation and ingenerate, for example, Eusebius. Otis thereby misses the important point that the cosmological use of ἀγέννητος and γεννητός is not simply something that sets the stage for Arius' theology; Eusebius' collection of these texts shows that the link with cosmology was still felt in Eusebius' (and Arius') day.

59. *Preparation for the Gospel* 7:22, 30; Gifford, 3:1, 371.

60. Ibid., 7:22, 25, 26, Schroeder and des Places, SC 215, p. 296.

61. Ibid., 7:22, 29, p. 296.

mind, we can return to a detailed treatment of Eunomius' theological language.

*Extra-essential Production: The Activity and Its Products*

Eunomius' term for the productive operation or activity is ἐνέργεια,[62] and for the product or work, ἔργον.[63] Eunomius repeatedly emphasizes the separate existence of the activity from the essence and characterizes the thought of an activity "connected" to the essence as "Greek."[64] In his opinion, any connection between activity and essence in Christian theology betrays the true faith through the hellenization of that faith. What Eunomius means by the separate existence of the essence and activity is made clear by the argument he offers in support of this proposition. He says that if the activity were essential, then the activity would exist whenever the essence did;[65] in the case of God, eternally. But the activity did not exist eternally, so it cannot be essential.[66] That is, if the activity is necessarily connected to the essence, then it will exist coextensively in time with the essence. But the activity is not coextensive in time and so it cannot be necessarily connected. To make this point, Eunomius refers to those pagans who believe that the world is coeternal with God and who unite the activity to the essence, a reference that echoes the cosmological arguments found in Origen, Methodius, and Eusebius.[67] But the cessation (or perhaps better, the possibility of cessation) of a creative act proves that it had a beginning and is not eternal, for "nothing could have come completely to an end which did not start from some beginning."[68]

62. In the *Apology,* ἐνέργεια is first introduced as an epistemological term (for example, *Apology* 20:8; *Extant Works,* 58), and then is used in causality, as in, for example, *Apology* 22 and 23. In the *Second Apology,* ἐνέργεια and ἔργα are used immediately in the causal sense and then used in terms of knowledge (see GNO 1:72:114 and 1:73:1015).

63. Ἔργον first appears with any significance in *Apology* 23:5 ff. But the related verb forms appear earlier: at 9:17, *Extant Works,* 44, and 11:8, 46, for example. Neither of these appearances seems to foreshadow the later use of ἔργον. However, Prop. 8(b) of the *Syntagmation* uses ἐργαμένης (Wickham, "Syntagmation," 541) in what may be a suggestion of the technical sense.

64. *Apology* 22:10; *Extant Works,* 62–63, and, apparently, 23:15–16; 64–65.

65. Ibid., 23:910; 62–65.

66. Ibid., 23:11–16; 65–66.

67. Ibid., 22:11–12; 62–63.

68. Ibid., 22:14–15; 62–63. In the *Second Apology,* Eunomius says that "As all generation is not protracted to infinity, but ceases on arrival at some end, those who admit the origination of the Son are obliged to say that He then ceased being generated, and not to look incredulously on the beginning of those things which cease being generated, and therefore also surely begin. . . . ."

Eunomius argues that the activity had a beginning for reasons that are central to his understanding of ἐνέργεια as a causal term. He argues that if the divine activity existed, it would produce works; that is, whenever activity exists it produces works, insofar as it exists.[69] The works would then be eternal as well. Christians do not believe this, and cannot, but the Pagans do and make the cosmos coeternal with God. Eunomius' assumption here has gone unnoticed in scholarly literature: the work exists co-temperaneously with the activity because the activity is understood to exist only as productive.[70] An activity cannot be unproductive at any time that it exists; if it does not produce, it does not exist. The existence of its products indicates whether the activity exists or not.[71] Eunomius says:

> We recognize that the divine essence is without beginning, simple and endless, but we also recognize that its action [ἐνέργεια] is neither without beginning nor without ending. It cannot be without beginning, for, if it were, its effects [ἔργα] would be without beginning as well. On the other hand, it cannot be without ending, since, if the effects come to an end, the action which produced them cannot be unending either.[72]

This understanding of activity is distinctive and leads us to a consideration of Eunomius' theology of divine productive capacity and his specific use of the terms δύναμις and ἐνέργεια. Eunomius does not associate ἐνέργεια with δύναμις—an activity with a power—except perhaps in a loose fashion: where one might expect δύναμις to mean faculty or capacity and ἐνέργεια the act proceeding from that faculty, his use of ἐνέργεια collapses faculty and act into one term. The alternative sense of δύναμις that Eunomius uses instead of faculty or capacity is the term's political or moral sense. Eunomius' understanding of productive capacity centers on the term ἐνέργεια rather than δύναμις, although it may be added that the use of either of these terms is governed by Eunomius' fundamental teaching: that God's productive capacity is not an essential attribute, property,

69. "[I]f the effects come to an end, the action which produced them cannot be unending either" (*Apology* 23:7–8; *Extant Works*, 62–65).

70. For example, *Apology* 23:13–15; *Extant Works*, 64–65, which is quoted in full below.

71. Thus, an eternal activity would have an eternal product, as Eunomius argues at *Apology* 23:8–15; *Extant Works*, 62–65. This is also the meaning in Eunomius' statement that "We, ourselves, however judge the action [ἐνέργεια] from its effects [ἔργα] . . ." (*Apology* 23:45; *Extant Works*, 62–63). The very existence of the activity is ascertained from the existence of the products.

72. *Apology* 23:58; *Extant Works*, 62–63.

or quality but exists only as an act of the will.[73] This insistence on the primacy of God's will resembles the Arian emphasis on the priority of God's will in all production. But Eunomius moves beyond the Arian tradition by his doctrine of the separate status of God's will. The most important indicator of the separate status of God's will is its separate existence in time from the essence. Eunomius thus concludes:

> . . . Granted the effects [ἔργα] had a start, the action [ἐνέργεια] is not without beginning, and granted the effects come to an end, the action is not without ending. There is no need, therefore, to accept the half-baked opinions of outsiders and unite the action to the essence. On the contrary, we must believe that the action which is the truest and most befitting God is his will [βουλή].[74]

For Eunomius the activity or will comes to be and passes away while the essence is eternal. It is important to note that Eunomius does not say that it is only the work, or product of the activity, that comes to be and passes away, but that the activity itself, which produces the work, is both intermittent and temporary.[75]

### *Activity as a Temporary Cause: Clement, Galen, and Origen*

If Eunomius is working with the distinction between a cause that is intermittent and temporary, on the one hand, and a cause that is constant and permanent, on the other, then he is building upon an etiology with recognizable antecedents in Hellenistic thought. Clement of Alexandria, for example, identifies a set of "Stoic" causal distinctions that seem quite similar to those one sees in Eunomius' writing. In the first kind of cause, the effect and cause are coterminus in time: while the cause is present or exists, the effect remains, but if the cause ceases for any reason, the effect likewise ceases.[76] This is fundamentally the kind of cause Eunomius attributes to God's energy, for the Son began to exist when the energy began. The Son exists as long as the energy exists, but if that energy ceases (an option Eunomius feels compelled to leave open), then the Son, the effect

73. This is suggested at *Apology* 16:5–9; *Extant Works,* 52–53, and expressed clearly at *Apology* 24:1–3; *Extant Works,* 64–65. See also 28:12–14; 74–75. The sense, though not the exact language, is in *Syntagmation,* Props. 5 and 7.

74. *Apology* 23:14–17, *Extant Works,* 64–65.

75. At ibid., 23:6–8; 62–63.

76. *Miscellanies* 8:9, 33.1. Clement calls this the "synectic" cause.

of that energy, will cease to exist. The possibility that Eunomius is in fact drawing on this idea of cause as witnessed by Clement is reinforced by the fact that Clement himself uses ἐνέργεια language when he describes this intermittent and temporary kind of cause.[77] By contrast, the second kind of cause is distinguished by the permanence of its effect, such that if the cause ceases, the effect would nonetheless continue to exist.[78] Clement uses δύναμις language when speaking of this kind of cause.[79] Clement calls this idea of cause "Stoic," which may indeed have been its origins as he knew it, but by Clement's time similar kinds of distinctions, using the same language, can be found in a variety of sources.

For example, a similar sense of activity can be noted in Galen's understanding of the causal language. Galen speaks of the stomach as an example of a single power with multiple activities, in which the existence of these activities and their works varies over a period of time.[80] The single faculty of digestion (and the single organ, the stomach) has the multiple functions of gestation, growth, and nutrition,[81] while the existence of these activities or functions, and their effects, varies over a period of time.[82] These activi-

77. Ibid., 8:9, 33, 2–3; ANF 2:567.

78. Ibid., 8:9, 33.1–32.3. Clement calls this the "procatartic" cause.

79. Δύναμις occurs at 31.3, 32.1, and 32.2.

80. *On the Natural Faculties,* trans. A. J. Brock, The Loeb Classical Library, vol. 13 (1916; reprint, London: William Heinemann Ltd., 1979), 1:6:12; 1:10:24. (This work is hereafter abbreviated as *ONF.*)

81. Galen lists three effects [ἔργα] common to all faculties in nature: formation of the different parts of the animal in the womb; the growth to full size of each part after birth; and the maintenance of each part for as long as possible once maturity has been reached (*ONF* I, V, 10, 16–17). The faculties that correspond to these effects and that produce them are: Genesis, Growth, and Nutrition (*ONF* I, V, 10, 18–19). In chapter 6, Galen speaks of genesis in several organs; the stomach is mentioned at I, VI, 13, 22–23, and I, VI, 15, 24–25. Growth is discussed in I, VII, but only in a general, illustrative way. Similarly, nutrition gets a paragraph in I, VIII, 19, 30–31. The real discussion of nutrition begins at I, X, 20, 32 ff. and continues through to the end of I, XII, 30, 49.

82. As indicated in the previous note, Galen associates each faculty with stages of development in the organism: genesis or gestation with *in utero* life; growth with the development to maturity; and nutrition with the organism's life at maturity. Each organ possesses all three faculties and may employ them simultaneously: the organs in the fetus, for example, are producing, developing, and maintaining the new parts of the body, but each part receives only the action of one faculty. As the part develops and moves from one stage to another, it receives different activities from the faculty. See *ONF* I, VII, 16, 26–27, and I, VIII, 19, 30–31, where Galen says of nutrition: "For when the matter which flows to each part of the body in the form of nutriment is being worked up into it, this activity is [that of] nutrition, and its cause [αἰτία] is the nutritive faculty [δύναμις]. Of course, the kind of activity here involved is also alteration, but not an alteration like that occurring at the stage of genesis."

ties do not coexist but replace one another, and when a specific activity ceases to exist, so do its associated effects. Galen's description of the cessation of activities and their associated effects is thus a description of synectic causality. Faculties, on the other hand, remain constant over a period of time and are not described as changing.

Nonetheless Clement's specific treatment of the notions of cause in *Miscellanies* 8:9 is important for the Eunomian controversy because the very account he gives of cause is used in a specific fashion by both sides in the controversy and not only because it forms part of the historical background of central terms. For example, Gregory of Nyssa repeats Clement's argument that a single cause can produce multiple, even opposite, effects, against Eunomius' claim that for each activity, there is one and only one product.[83] Clement's account of the types of causes also reveals the background of Origen's speculation on the Trinity. For example, Meijering points out that in *On First Principles* Origen argues that insofar as God's productive capacity exists, it must be productive.[84] Meijering's particular point is that Origen used this notion of cause as always productive insofar as it exists in his argument for the eternity of the Son and the Cosmos. Meijering paraphrases Origen's thought thus: "Since God has always been almighty there must have always been a creation, a product of his almightiness."[85] Meijering concludes that "Origen . . . postulates . . . eternal products of God's creative power."[86]

83. GNO 1:140:10–24; NPNF 5:71. The argument that a single cause can have multiple effects is not uniquely Clement's, of course; it is a commonplace of the era. Origen holds a similar opinion about the multiplicity of effects following from a single cause, as does Eusebius of Caesarea. These two authors provide early testimony to some of Gregory's favorite illustrations of multiple effects following from a single cause, in particular the example of the sun having different effects upon different objects: some things are baked by the sun, others grow, etc. I have already remarked (in chapter 3) that for Eusebius this kind of argument was used to prove monotheism against polytheism by arguing for the unicity of the first cause over against a hypothetical pagan multiplicity of first causes. Gregory transforms this traditional argument into one for the unicity of God within the three Persons. What is important to note now, however, is that as in the case of the psychological implications of Methodius' (and others') cosmological concerns about creation *ex nihilo,* Eusebius' cosmological argument for monotheism is transformed into a trinitarian argument.

84. Meijering, "Athanasius on the Father as the Origin of the Son," 89–102.

85. Ibid., 90. Crouzel makes the same point when he refers to Origen's conclusion that "There was no time when he [the second Person] did not exist" (see SC 253:48 n. 55).

86. Meijering, 99. Meijering also compares the opinions of Origen, Athanasius, and Arius on the questions of God's eternal power and the eternity of the world. On the first point, Athanasius agreed with Origen but identified this Power with the eternal Son. On the second point, Athana-

Two other points about Origen's description of the Son's production are noteworthy. First, Origen's description of the Son being produced by the Father's will is reminiscent of Clement's description of the perfect cause; namely, God's will alone is sufficient to insure the Son's existence. Second, Origen's understanding is that insofar as God's productive capacity exists, it is productive; and since God was never without this capacity, He was always productive, and thus the eternal existence of the Son is demonstrated. Eunomius, on the other hand, used ἐνέργεια to refer to a causality which ceases to be when not productive. Eunomius describes the ἐνέργεια in just such terms in his argument that the ἐνέργεια or activity is not essential. I have already cited the passage from *Apology* 23 where Eunomius says, "... if the effects [ἔργα] come to an end, the action [ἐνέργεια] which produced them cannot be unending either."[87]

Thus, the activity and product always coexist: at no time does activity exist without a product, nor does the product exist at any time without activity. Activity sustains the product's existence; it does not merely initiate it. Eunomius then argues that since the product of the activity, the Son, is not ingenerate, but rather temporary in his existence, then the activity that produced him must be temporary in its existence.[88] Moreover, that which is temporary is not essential; therefore, the activity is not essential.[89] Origen and Eunomius thus argue from a common premise to opposite conclusions: if the productive capacity and the product are understood to exist coextensively, then either the capacity and its product are temporary (Eunomius) or the capacity and its product are eternal (Origen). Neither allows, or is concerned with, the possibility that the capacity may exist without a product.

These different conclusions regarding the nature of divine production find expression in different descriptions of that productive capacity. Ori-

---

sius believed as the Arians did that the world (for Athanasius, excluding the Son) had a beginning in time, that is, was not eternal.

87. *Apology* 23:7–8; *Extant Works*, 62–63.

88. "It is therefore childish and infantile in the extreme to say that the action [ἐνέργεια] is unbegotten and unending (making it identical with the essence) when not one of it effects [ἔργα] is capable of being produced either unbegottenly or unendingly!" (*Apology* 23:8–11; *Extant Works*, 62–65).

89. *Apology* 23:15–16 and 24:2; *Extant Works*, 64–65; both have been given in the body of the text above.

gen uses δύναμις to describe the productive capacity, while Eunomius uses ἐνέργεια to describe the productive capacity. Origen uses δύναμις in particular to describe both the source that produced the Son, as well as the Son's own nature. Eunomius, on the other hand, seems to omit δύναμις from his sequence. Though Eunomius uses δύναμις apart from the sequence, as I have already noted, ἐνέργεια is his preferred term for the Son's source.[90] In Origen's theology, the Son's origin in the δύναμις of God assures the Son's coexistence with God, since God could never be without His δύναμις. Origen understood the Son's origin in the δύναμις of God to guarantee the unity of God and the Son. On the other hand, for Eunomius, the Son's origin in the activity or operation proves the temporal nature of the Son as opposed to God's eternal nature, since the Son shares a common nature with His source, the activity. As I have discussed earlier, the activity has a temporary existence, and, Eunomius emphasizes, it is not contemporaneous with the essence. This temporal description applies equally to the nature of the Son.[91]

90. I note that in *Apology* 15:13; *Extant Works*, 52, δύναμις is used of the creative capacity of the Son, and at 15:14, it refers to the instrument of creation by which God created the Son, and only the Son.

91. Gregory of Nazianzus offers a confirmation of the contemporary understanding of essence–activity. Speaking of the type of being of the Holy Spirit in *Oration* 31:6, Nazianzen says, "[a]nd if He is an activity [ἐνέργεια], clearly He must be put in operation, because he has no active power and ceases with the cessation of his production, that is the kind of thing an activity is." For the Greek, see *Grégoire de Nazianze: Discours 2731 (Discours Théologiques)*, ed. and trans. Paul Gallay and Maurice Jourjon, SC 250 (Paris: Les Editions du Cerf, 1978), 286. Norris offers an interesting analysis of this text in his commentary, *Faith Gives Fullness to Reasoning*, 281, where he emphasizes the different interpretations each party had of ἐνέργεια. Gregory understood the term to mean accident, but Norris does not say what Eunomius thought, or rather, why Eunomius' understanding excluded that meaning. Norris does say that Eunomius understood ἐνέργεια to mean will. Why not, then, an accidental will? I have been arguing precisely this: that Eunomius' understanding of ἐνέργεια is that of accidental causal faculty, or, equivalently, cause of accidents (to the essence). Norris does not pursue the causal implications of ἐνέργεια, nor does he mention the classification of causes implied in Gregory's argument. Instead he seems led to a static understanding of ἐνέργεια as simply a category of attribution by Gregory's use of accident (συμβεβηκός). Norris acknowledges the psychological implication of Nazianzen's argument when he asks (for Gregory), Could an ἐνέργεια be a subject, or be referred to as a subject? (264).

As Nazianzen goes on in his argument, it is clear that he and Eunomius have a common understanding of the lack of ontological and psychological independence of any product of an activity. For Gregory, to be an activity is to exist in a passive way and to lack the ability to have original and independent intentions and feelings. Gregory argues that if the Spirit is an activity, then "How is it then that he acts and says such and such things, and defines, and is grieved, and is angered, and has all the qualities which belong clearly to one who moves, and not to move-

### *The Nature of the Son*

When Eunomius discusses the Son's production, his purpose is to establish that since the Son is created directly by God's will,[92] His essence is prior to all other created essences and is, by virtue of its one prior cause, unique among all created essences. Eunomius describes the Son as the exclusive product of the Father,[93] and maintains that it is the Son who produces "creation," or the cosmos.[94] Though the Son is Himself a product, Eunomius is hesitant to say that He was "created," though eventually he will do so.[95] Instead, Eunomius emphasizes that the Son is not a product as the cosmos is a product.[96] Vaggione has noted the Arian background of the Eunomian formula that describes the Son as "produced," "created," or "made" (γέννημα, κτίσμα and ποίημα, respectively).[97] Such descriptions are supported by scriptural texts like Prov. 8:22, a widely used anti-Nicene proof-text. Vaggione also points out that, for Eunomius, as perhaps for Arius, these terms describe a creation that is unlike other creations, and thus a creature who, if not God, is nonetheless unlike other creatures.[98]

In the *Apology* Eunomius is similarly circumspect in describing the Son as a product [ἔργον]; indeed, he never says directly that the Son is a product. Nonetheless, Eunomius' argument for the non-eternal existence of the Son in *Apology* 23 is an argument to the effect that no product can be without a beginning. Ἔργον is another term that could be supported

---

ment?" That is, attributes are predicated of an entity, not of yet another attribute, namely, motion (*Oration* 31:6). Eunomius does not frame the existence appropriate to an activity in the negative terms that Nazianzen uses: the activity's dependence on the essence is a straightforward restatement of the accidental nature of everything that is produced when compared to the unique nature of the Essence. Nazianzen clearly understands that ἐνέργεια describes a type of existence that is neither independent nor continuous, and for this very reason, he rejects the term and the notion of divine causality it communicates.

92. *Apology* 17:10–12; *Extant Works*, 54–55.

93. Ibid. 15:14–16; 52–53; see also "The Eunomian Creed" of chapter 28:6–8; 74–75.

94. Ibid. 15:11–16; 52–53.

95. Ibid. 24:6; 64–65, where Eunomius is quoting Col. 1:15–16.

96. Ibid. 15:7–11; 52–53; this thought is elaborated on at 28:20–22; 74.

97. Richard P. Vaggione, "Οὐχ ὡς ἕν τῶν γεννημάτων: Some Aspects of the Dogmatic Formula in the Arian Controversy," *Studia Patristica* 17 (1982): 181–87, here 183.

98. Ibid., in particular: "When scripture uses begat, create, or make in a divine context it refers to an action fundamentally different from that so designated among men. . . . for the Son is not only 'the first-born of all creation', he is also 'the image of the invisible God' (Col. 1:15). . . ."

by Prov. 8:22—"The Lord created me as the beginning of His ways unto His works"—and its sense in the literature of the era is clearly one of creature. Eusebius regularly uses the term to refer to created things, as, for example, when he speaks of God, "whose products are the sun, and the whole heavens, and the cosmos"[99] or says that God "is not the heaven, nor the aether. . . ."[100] Likewise, in Eusebius' extract from Origen's *Commentary on Genesis,* Origen uses ἔργον for the product of an artist's craft and the products of God's creation.[101]

Eunomius gives a clear description of the unique status and function of the Son in chapter 15 of the *Apology:*

> . . . we assert that the Son was begotten when as yet he was not. We do not, however, include the essence of the Only-Begotten among things brought into existence out of nothing. Rather, on the basis of the will of the one who made him we establish a distinction between the Only-begotten and all other things, affording him the same pre-eminence which the maker must necessarily have of his own products.[102]

To paraphrase this material in more explicitly hierarchical language: first there is the unique and exalted nature of the Son's source, which ensures the unique status of the Son since, as Eunomius adds elsewhere,[103] produced essences differ according to the activity or will that produced them. Second, the Son's unique and direct production by God's will insures his own special and powerful (that is, demiurgic) status.[104] The Son stands to the cosmos as a maker to his artifacts.[105] There is no question of equality

99. *Demonstration of the Gospel* 4:6; Heikel, 159:18–20; Ferrar, 1:174.

100. *Preparation for the Gospel* 3:10, 11; Gifford, 3:1, 114. Two other examples can be cited. At 7:10, 3; Gifford, 3:1, 339, Eusebius says, "The sun himself, the heavens, and the world, the earth and all things upon the earth, and all that are considered products of nature serve His commandments and ordinances. . . ." At 8:18, 6; Gifford, 3:1, 360, Eusebius distinguishes between the image and likeness of God and the human body, which he calls a "work of God."

101. *Preparation for the Gospel* 7:20, 1–3; Gifford, 3:1, 363. While there is no association of δημιουργή and δύναμις in the *Timaeus,* there is a definite association of δημιουργή and ἔργον at 41A: θεοὶ θεῶν, ὧν ἐγὼ δημιουργὸς πατήρ τε ἔργον . . . ," a well-known passage because of its reference to the Creator and Father.

102. *Apology* 15:7–11; *Extant Works,* 52–53.

103. GNO 1:72:23–73:3; NPNF 5:50, slightly altered: ". . . because sameness of activity produces sameness of product [ἔργα], and difference of product indicates difference of activity." Moore and Wilson give "work" where I prefer "product" for ἔργον.

104. *Apology* 15:12–13; *Extant Works,* 52–53.

105. Ibid., 15:9–11; 52–53.

between the Son and "creation." Indeed, Eunomius concludes that the Son is ". . . the Only-Begotten God of these things which came into existence after him and through him."[106]

After Eunomius introduces the theorem of proportionate dignity described above, he begins to move from a discussion of language and the knowledge of God to a discussion of causality and the theological hierarchy.[107] In the preceding chapter of the *Apology,* Eunomius had argued that the difference between attributing "Light," or "Life," for example, to God and to the Son was that when applied to God, the titles must mean Ungenerated Light or Life, and when applied to the Son, they mean Generated Light or Life.[108] The difference between the two essences, for example, ungenerated and generated, governs the meaning of the two sets of attributes, even when the two sets sound alike or seem to be identical.[109] The introduction of the sequence, essence–activity–product, allows Eunomius to use causal language to describe the difference in meaning between the titles applied to God and those applied to the Son.[110] Thus chapter 21 of the *Apology* begins with Eunomius asserting the ridiculousness of attributing the same essence, activity, authority, or name both to God and to the Son. Eunomius ends the chapter by explaining the different meaning of common titles in terms of the causal sequence. He says:

> For we confess that the Lord Jesus is himself Only-Begotten God, immortal and deathless, wise, good; but we say too that the Father is the cause of his actual existence and of all that he is, for the Father, being unbegotten, has no cause of his essential goodness.[111]

106. Ibid., 15:13–14; 52–53.

107. The theorem is introduced in *Apology* 20:14–15; *Extant Works,* 6061; chapter 21 contains terms such as ἐπίσημος (21:1) and διακρίνω (21:15) that continue the discussion of the means and objects of knowledge. There is also an apparently non-causal use of οὐσία and ἐνέργεια (21:2). On the other hand, chapter 21 ends with Eunomius' conclusion that the prior epistemological arguments have brought him to a conclusion regarding causality (*Apology* 21:15–20; *Extant Works,* 60–62). Finally, chapter 22 begins a discussion that clearly treats οὐσία and ἐνέργεια as causal terms (22:11; 62) and treats the problem at hand as a misunderstanding of causality, that is, the suggestion of a pagan-like doctrine of a unity between the οὐσία and the ἐνέργεια. Chapter 23 continues the causal line of thought with a detailed discussion of the relationship between cause and effect. Neither Eunomius' theory of language nor his description of the ways of knowledge figures in the remainder of the *Apology.*

108. *Apology* 19:8–10; *Extant Works,* 56–57.

109. Ibid., 19:16–19; 58–59.

110. Ibid., 21:1–4; 60–61.

111. Ibid., 21:15–19; 60–63.

This sequence of uncaused and caused is treated by Eunomius as a theological hierarchy, which is now described by the terms previously used to describe the kinds of knowledge, namely, essence, activity and product, etc. With these terms Eunomius can organize the complex causal relationship within the divine life into a suitable hierarchy.

The causal hierarchy of essence–activity–product is also evident in Eunomius' description of the Holy Spirit in the *Apology.*[112] Eunomius says that the Holy Spirit is a product of the Son's activity, who acts under the authority of God. Thus, since the Holy Spirit is third in both "dignity and order" (ἀξία καὶ τάξις),[113] he is third in "nature" (φύσις), for the order of their creation is the order of their natures.[114]

The reference to the Holy Spirit also serves to show that the initial use of essence, activity, and product to describe the relationship of God to the Only-Begotten is generalized to describe all causal relationships. The relationship of essence to activity, and activity to work is repeated in the productive activity of the works that were generated by the first activity. Thus, the sequence "essence, activity, and product," which describes the relationship of God, His will, and its product, the Son, also describes the relationship of the Son, his creative ability, and its product(s). The first occurrence of the causal sequence remains the fundamental one, since only in that divine hierarchy of God (essence), will (activity), and Son (product) is the essence (God) wholly uncaused. In every other occasion the productive essence is itself the product of the activity in a prior causal sequence. For example, the Son is, from one point of view, the unique product of the first activity, but from another point of view, He is an essence with his own activity and resultant products.[115]

In the *Apology* Eunomius gives a summary of attributions that are used to distinguish God from the Son.[116] These attributions, namely, essence, activity, authority, and name, establish the unique identity of an existent

112. Ibid., 20:15–17; 60–63; 25:4–10; 66–67; 25:22–25; 68–69; and 28:14–16; 74–75.

113. *Apology* 25:22–23, *Extant Works*, 66–67.

114. Ibid., 25:4–5; 66–67.

115. Ibid., 20:15–19; 60–61.

116. Ibid., 21:1–3; 60–61: "Hence, if they [the Homoiousians] think it not ridiculous to ascribe the same qualities equally to both of them [that is, God and the Son]—essence, say, or action, authority, or name (thereby doing away with the differences between the names and their objects). . . ."

and place the existent in a hierarchical order (τάξις).[117] Eunomius gives this list of attributions just after he has argued that true methods of knowledge reveal that God and the Son are not the same (or similar) in essence.[118] He ends this argument with a reference to a third criterion for distinguishing the two Persons: someone who creates by his own authority must be different from someone who creates by the authority of another.[119] Eunomius introduces this criterion in the context of how God is truly known, but the criterion actually suggests the question of causality: how is God's mode of production different from the Son's mode of production? From this point the argument in the *Apology* is focused on causality, and the list of attributions given at *Apology* 21:2 offers an introduction to the terms in which that causality will be described.[120] Eunomius' argument will turn upon establishing that there are different relationships of unity, or different degrees of unity, that may exist between an entity and each of these identifying attributions. In particular, the unity of the existent and the essence is one of identity, while the union between the existent (which is essence) and activity is only one of an association by will or command (βουλή or ἐξουσία).

Eunomius establishes his understanding of essence by his prior arguments on the unity and simplicity of God's essence. He does not distinguish the essence from the existent in any explicit way; his arguments are directed at establishing the absolute simplicity of the essence. Thus, the degree of unity between the existent and the essence is high, for the existent is identified with the essence.[121] Essence is Eunomius' preferred, if not ex-

117. Ibid., 18:13–16; 56–57: "These people [the Homoiousians], if they really did have any concern for the truth, ought rather to have acknowledged that since the names are different, the essences are different as well (at any rate, that is the only way they could have kept the proper order [τάξις]. . . )."

118. See ibid., 20:510; 58–59.

119. Ibid., 20:19–21; 60–61.

120. Thus Eunomius concludes chapter 21 with a statement about causality and describes this statement as a conclusion derived from his arguments about true knowledge: "For we confess that the Lord Jesus is himself 'only-begotten God', immortal and deathless, wise, good. But we say too that the Father is the cause of his actual existence and of all he is, for the Father, being unbegotten, has no cause of his essence or goodness. This is the understanding to which the preceding arguments have brought us" (*Apology* 21:15–20; *Extant Works,* 60–63).

121. Eunomius does not say that "the existent is the essence"; he simply never speaks of the existent itself in any other terms but the essence. This identification of existent with essence is typified by *Apology* 7:11; *Extant Works,* 40–41, where, after excluding any existent prior to God,

clusive, term for individual existent. Much of Eunomius' argument against multiple qualities in God, for example, depends upon an identification of existent with essence, as will be discussed in detail.[122] On the other hand, Eunomius carefully distinguishes the activity from the essence, and he seems to understand that the relationship between the existent (that is, essence) and activity is merely one of exclusive association. Eunomius argues in detail to establish that the essence is distinct from the activity:

> . . . we do not consider it unhazardous to have to unite the activity to the essence. . . . There is no need, therefore . . . to unite the activity to the essence. On the contrary, we must believe that the activity which is the truest and most befitting of God is his will, and that his will is sufficient to bring into existence and to redeem all things. . . . Accordingly, if this argument has demonstrated that God's will is an activity, and that this activity is not essence but that the Only-Begotten exists by virtue of the will of the Father. . . .[123]

The distinction between essence and activity, and the latter's equation with the will, serves two purposes in Eunomius' system: it preserves the nonproductive state of the essence; and it preserves the non-willful state of the essence. Both production and will are not characteristics of the essence; both production and will are characteristics of the activity. With such an understanding of divine causality, Eunomius is able to deny that the Son shares, or is similar to, God's essence[124] and to assert instead that the Son is similar to the activity.[125] These two doctrines are the subjects of the rest of chapter 24.

In Eunomius' system, each essence has an activity that is associated with it uniquely.[126] In the case of the Unbegotten Essence, at least, this

---

Eunomius concludes ". . . what follows from this is the Unbegotten, or rather, that He [God] is unbegotten essence." A similar argument, with a similar conclusion identifying God with the unbegotten essence occurs at *Apology* 8:14–18; 42–43. Vaggione explains this tendency in Eunomius' thought thus: ". . . in the absence of matter, the individuality of an entity and its essence must be identical" ("Dogmatic Formula," 185).

122. An example of this sort of argument is *Apology* 8:14–18; *Extant Works,* 42–43.

123. *Apology* 23:5–24:2; *Extant Works,* 62–65.

124. Eunomius specifically denies that the Son is either ὁμοούσιος or ὁμοιούσιος at *Apology* 26:23; *Extant Works,* 70–71. He denies that the Son is the image of the essence at *Apology* 24:8–10; 64–65.

125. "The word image, then, would refer the similarity back, not to the essence of God, but to the action [ἐνέργεια] . . ." (*Apology* 24:10–12; *Extant Works,* 64–65).

126. This unique association is stated in terms of epistemology at *Apology* 20:79; 64–65 and 24:12; 64–65. A clear statement of this doctrine in terms of causality can be found at GNO 1:72:8–9, 15–18; NPNF 5:50.

association is not one of nature, that is, common essence, but rather one of will. The association of the activity and the will is a matter of choice and not of necessity.[127] Eunomius' identification of God's activity with His will means that the activity and the will are the same existent, and that will (choice) best describes the origins and nature of both God's activity and that activity's product, and that it describes as well the type of unity that exists between the activity and the essence. In short, the activity, and its products, are chosen, or willed to be.

### *The Natural Unity of Essence and Name*

The last term in the list of attributions that serve, in Eunomius' system, to distinguish existents from each other and to place them in their proper order in the hierarchy is that of names. The question of the degree of unity between the essence and names is important because in both the *Apology* and the *Second Apology*, Eunomius supports his case that God is exclusively ingenerate—ἀγέννητος—with a theory of language. That is, the description of God as essentially uncaused (and thus uncausing as well) depends to a large part on the particular theory of language that Eunomius uses to support his hierarchical theology. In chapter 18 of the *Apology*, Eunomius says that names themselves signify the essence.[128] Names are understood to be given by God and not simply produced by convention.[129] In the *Second Apology* names are included in the productive hierarchy:[130] there is a name for (the product of) every activity.[131] In both works Eunomius' argument depends on his prior theological assumptions, and he develops these assump-

127. *Apology* 23:5–6; *Extant Works,* 62.

128. Ibid. 18:18–20; 56–57.

129. Cf. *Apology* 8:1–6; *Extant Works,* 40–43. "When we say 'Unbegotten,' then, we do not imagine that we ought to honor God only in name, in conformity with human invention; rather, in conformity with reality, we ought to repay him the debt which above all others is most due God: the acknowledgement that he is what he is. Expressions based on invention have their existence in name and utterance only. . . ." In book 2 of the *Second Apology*, for example, at GNO 1.315:31–316:3, Eunomius says the titles for God that Basil offers are by human invention, while at GNO 1.345:12–16, Eunomius speaks of those names made by God.

130. "[T]here must of course be included in this account the activities that follow each essence, and the names germane to these activities" (GNO 1:72:7–10; NPNF 5:50). As Bernard Barmann comments, "Above all, it is to be noted that the ὀνόματα are listed among the ontological principles . . ." ("The Cappadocian Triumph over Arianism" [Ph.D. diss., Stanford University, 1966], 138).

131. GNO 1:72:8–10. The most extensive statement by Eunomius of his theory of language is in book 2 of his *Second Apology;* it is scattered from 272:13 to 348:7 in GNO 1.

tions in a distinctive fashion. Eunomius assumes that Unbegotten (ἀγέννητος) is the name for God *par excellence*, and he assumes that God exists as an essence in the radically simple way described above.[132] If both these assumptions hold, then Unbegotten must name the essence. There is nothing else in God for the term to name. Thus in Eunomius' system, "Names designate essences, and different names designate different essences."[133] This apparently epistemological postulate has a precise theological point in the controversy.[134] Unbegotten must mean Unbegotten essence, and Begotten must mean Begotten essence.[135] The mere attribution of different

132. Previous scholars have cited both Stoic and Christian writings (principally Clement and Origen) as sources for Eunomius' theory of language, but the immediate precedent for Eunomius' theory in the writings of Eusebius has not been mentioned. Eusebius maintains, at *Preparation for the Gospel* 11:6, 1–8, that the Hebrews, like the Greeks, had a philosophy of logic. He demonstrates this by showing that the doctrines of the *Cratylus* (as he understands them) are found in the Pentateuch, especially in Genesis. (In the *Second Apology,* Eunomius casts his theory of names as an exegesis of Genesis.) Interestingly, Eusebius finds in the *Cratylus* the doctrine that "names were given to things by nature and not conventionally," a doctrine that he endorses (see *Preparation for the Gospel* 11:6, 9). However, Eusebius does not go farther and say that these natural names reveal essences, though he does include etymological speculation about the resemblance between a name and what it names typical of the *Cratylus.* An interest in etymologies, it should be said, does not necessarily indicate an essence-based epistemology; in the *Cratylus* etymologies are referred to δυνάμεις not οὐσία, and Eunomius' thought never shows any interest in etymologies.

133. *Apology* 18:13–14; *Extant Works,* 56–57.

134. In his apologetics Asterius begins with the disputed verbal evidence of the Son's commonality with the Father, that is, their shared titles found in Scripture and tradition, and offers what is fundamentally a causal explanation for the fact of these common titles: the Son is called Power because he is a *Power from the Power.* Kinzig has argued that there is an implicit but "elaborate theory of language" in Asterius' theology of two powers, etc., that distinguishes "between the intrinsic or innate and the derivative attributes of a person or thing. Attributes of a person or thing may either originate from his or its essence . . . or else may be secondary ascriptions to the person or the thing . . . and hence do not designate its essence" (*In Search of Asterius,* 128). This is a linguistic statement and application by Kinzig of a participation model. In Eunomius' theory of language the distinction is between true ascriptions that refer to the essence and false ascriptions that do not: there are no primary versus secondary ascriptions since, to use Kinzig's distinctions, all attributes originate from the essence. Eunomius' theory of language thus reflects his rejection of any essence-based participation causality.

135. *Apology* 19:9–10; *Extant Works,* 56–57. Eunomius distinguishes between univocal and equivocal names for God. Those names that depend on the notion of unbegotten, such as eternal, are univocal names for God. These names can be attributed only to God and are all synonymous with Unbegotten (see *Apology* 19:16–18; *Extant Works,* 58–59). Those that do not require the notion of unbegotten, such as good, are equivocal names. These names can be applied both to God and to the Son but do not imply that the essence is shared. For Eunomius only univocal names are true names because only univocal names refer to the essence.

The theory that univocal names refer to the essence is central to Eunomius' arguments in the *Apology* and *Second Apology* that God alone is unbegotten, and only unbegotten. One of Euno-

names testifies to the differences in essences and reveals the nonsense of the argument by the Homoiousians, who say that the two essences are alike.[136]

In Eunomius' account, the fact that the Scriptures sometimes refer to God and the Son by the same names—Light, Life, Power—does not indicate any common essence between the two.[137] Each of these names is to be understood in terms of the essences to which it refers. For example, Light applied to God means Unbegotten Light. Light applied to the Son means Begotten Light.[138] It is the essences that determine the content of these additional attributions, and so there can be nothing in common between "Unbegotten Light" and "Begotten Light" since there is nothing in common between Unbegotten and Begotten.[139]

> Our response, then, to such a person is to say that the one 'light' is unbegotten and the other begotten. . . . Just as the unbegotten differs from the begotten, so 'the light' must differ from 'the light', and 'the life' from 'the life', and 'the power' from 'the power', for the same rule and method applies for the resolution of all such problems. If, then, every word used to signify the essence of the Father is equivalent in force of meaning to 'the Unbegotten' because the Father is without parts and uncomposed, by the same token that same word used of the Only-Begotten is equivalent to 'offspring.'[140]

This interpretation of the common attribution of titles such as life, light,

---

mius' clearest statements on the relationship between name and named, and in particular that the name and nature of God is the simple unbegotten, is at GNO 1:368:6–18; NPNF 5:299: "The Life that is the same, and thoroughly single, must have one and the same outward expression for it, even though in mere names, and manner, and order it may seem to vary. For true expressions derive their precision from the subject realities they indicate; different expressions are applied to different realities, the same to the same; and so one or other of these two things must of necessity be held; either that the reality indicated is quite different (if the expressions are), or else that the indicating expressions are not different." His teaching that God can be known essentially cannot be separated from his understanding of the nature of language. The importance of this theory of language for Heterousian theology predates Eunomius: Aetius uses arguments based on the same theory in his *Syntagmation*, as Wickham, "Syntagmation," 560, notes. Propositions 16, 19, 20, 26, and 36 all presuppose this theory of language. Eunomius, Basil and Gregory all regard their theories of language and of knowledge as central to their theologies, and each side in the controversy assumes this centrality in its opponents. This centrality explains the argument over names and "ἐπίνοιαι" from the *Apology* to Basil's *Against Eunomius* to the *Second Apology* to Gregory's *Against Eunomius*.

136. *Apology* 18:12; *Extant Works*, 56–57.

137. Ibid., 19:8–16; 56–59.

138. Ibid.

139. Ibid., 19:13–16; 58–59.

140. Ibid., 19:8–19; 57–59.

and power seems to presuppose the language of two powers, etc., while at the same time implying that expressions of an *X from X* type do not describe continuity of nature.[141] Indeed, Eunomius' argument that these common titles name different essences is a rejection of any participation of the Son's nature in God's nature.[142] Eunomius implicitly accepts the language of two powers, etc., but does so in a way that eliminates the Eusebian sense of this language, namely, as a statement of "the great chain of being" that runs from God to the Son and onto creation.[143] When Eunomius fi-

141. Eunomius' use of δύναμις here, together with a Syriac fragment attributed to Eunomius where he cites 1 Cor. 1:24, has led Vaggione to consider this mention of δύναμις a reference to 1 Cor. 1:24 (see *Extant Works,* 56, apparatus, and 174). Vaggione covers this opinion with the proviso that "... there is no ... entirely certain use of 1 Cor. 1:24" (174) in the works of Eunomius, but this does not stop him from finding at least three references by Eunomius to 1 Cor. 1:24. I see no convincing reason to take this step.

142. In *From Word to Silence,* Mortley emphasizes the link in Eunomius' apophaticism to that Greek philosophy built on the skeptical aspect of Greek thought, such as the "Socratic method" dramatized by Plato in his early dialogues or the *reductio ad absurdum* that is typical of his late dialogues. For generations after Plato, Platonic philosophy was identical with the skepticism and programmatic anti-dogmatism of Arcesilaus and Carneades. This heritage is often forgotten in the face of the more positive, more dogmatic, Platonism revived by Antiochus of Ascalon (130–68 B.C.E.) and usually associated with the "Middle" and "Neoplatonic" periods. Mortley suggests that this anti-ontological habit of thought plays an important part in the origins of dogmatic "transcendental" Platonism. For example, the rise of "transcendental" Platonism is associated with an exegesis of the *Parmenides,* as E. R. Dodds showed long ago in his "The *Parmenides* of Plato and the Origin of the Neoplatonic 'One'," *Classical Quarterly* 12 (1928): 129–42. Dodds argued that one can trace the rise of school Platonic transcendentalism to a tradition of exegesis on Plato's *Parmenides,* in which concepts such as the "One" are progessively hypothesized. But the process of thought that is thus hypostasized as emanation and hierarchy remains the mirror image of abstraction and stripping away (see Mortley, *From Word to Silence,* 1:132–35.) The effect upon Platonism is the development of two separate technical languages of ontological negation and privation. The difference between negation and privation is of central importance for the Eunomian controversy, since—Mortley argues—Eunomius' theology follows in detail the technical negative theology of his day though it has been understood as a radically positive theology using privative language.

143. There is a similarity between Eunomius' rejection of continuity of existence running from God to Son to the cosmos and Arius' rejection, as Williams describes it, of "the language of participation in or imitation of the divine οὐσία" (*Arius,* 233). Williams believes that Arius' Christian theology was engaged in dismantling the analogical ladder between the absolute transcendent and all that follows. Rowan Williams had already argued in "Quest of the Historical *Thalia,*" in *Arianism: Historical and Theological Reassessments,* ed. Robert C. Gregg (Cambridge: Philadelphia Patristic Foundation, 1985), 1–36, that Arius had to modify his own radical apophatic theology in his encounter with the more kataphatic Lucianist theology of Eusebius of Caesarea and Asterius. In his subsequent book on Arius, Williams once again emphasizes the apophatic nature of Arius' theology and links this apophaticism to Neoplatonism (though not specifically as evidence of influence: see *Arius,* 224–28). Indeed, Mortley's more recent *From Word to Silence* suggests that what was "philosophical" about Eunomius' theology was its apophaticism, that is to say, his radical

nally turns to describing the Son as an "Image," as he does in chapter 24 of the *Apology*, he pointedly rejects any likeness between the Son and God's essence; rather, the likeness is between the Son and the activity of God that produced Him. The Son is the image of God's creative power—Eunomius uses δύναμις—because He makes manifest all the effects of that power; that is, He manifests all of creation. As Eunomius says:

> . . . What person who knew the Only-begotten himself and then perceived all the things made through him [John 1:3] would not acknowledge that in him he had seen the power [δύναμις] of the Father?[144]

## *The Demiurgic Power*

Eunomius' earliest discussion of the notion of productive capacity is in chapters 15 and 16 of the *Apology*. Eunomius begins chapter 15 by eliminating inappropriate notions of divine productivity and then speaks of the unique nature of the Son.[145] Eunomius uses δύναμις to name productive capacities in God and in the Son: the Son has the "demiurgic" power through which God creates,[146] for the Son alone was created, and created directly, by the power of God.[147] Δύναμις is first used in the phrase δημιουργικῆς δυνάμεως as applied to the Son,[148] to explain His creative

negative theology. I agree with Williams that the apophatic impulse of Arius' theology has been underemphasized, but he needs to say more about how exactly Arius' apophaticism differs from that of Eusebius. I believe that Williams understates Eusebius' own apophatic religion precisely because Eusebius does not require a radical division in being between God and Son: Eusebius' apophaticism is not the same as Arius' or Eunomius'. When Gregg and Groh say that in "Arian" doctrine there is no *analogia entis* between the Father and the Son (*Early Arianism*, 98), they are correct for the two specific authors they cite: Arius and Eusebius of Nicomedia, but not for Eusebius of Caesarea.

144. *Apology* 24:14–15, *Extant Works*, 65.

145. Eunomius summarizes the types of production that his previous arguments have eliminated, namely, begetting, partition, and the addition of form to a formless substrata or matter (*Apology* 15:5–7; *Extant Works*, 52–53). There for the first time in the *Apology*, Eunomius suggests the will [γνώμη] as the productive source of the Son: "[O]n the basis of the will of the one who made him [that is, the Son]" (*Apology* 15:9–10; *Extant Works*, 52–53). However, Eunomius does not immediately follow up the reference to the will; he does say that the Son's origin is unique, or rather, that the Son is the unique product of this originating source (*Apology* 15:9–11; *Extant Works*, 52–53). Later, of course, Eunomius will make it clear that this originating source is God's will or activity (see *Apology* 24:1–4; *Extant Works*, 65–64).

146. Ibid., 15:13; 52–53.

147. Ibid., 15:14; 52–53.

148. Ibid., 15:13; 52–53.

role and capacity: all things are made through Him, for the creative capacity was begotten in Him.[149] Δύναμις is next used to describe the Son's unique source,[150] which qualifies Him to be the "perfect minister of the creative activity and intention of the Father."[151] In each occurrence, δύναμις is used of the demiurgic capacity, which is Eunomius' term for the creative capacity. It is the notion of the demiurge—δημιουργός—whether expressed as noun, adjective, or verb, that is the central notion for Eunomius in this description of divine productivity.[152] The reason why δύναμις is used here at all is that "demiurgic power" was a Christian stock phrase, where the two words are used together idiomatically as one term. Eunomius uses, indeed emphasizes, δύναμις in this context because the doctrine of the Son acting as creator through the reception of a delegated power is a traditional way of subordinating the Son to God (the Father).

The same association of δύναμις with δημιουργός is found, for example, in the theology of Eusebius of Caesarea. A typical example of this association occurs in *Demonstration of the Gospel:*

> There is one general identical divine power, governing the whole universe, creative of the heavens and of the stars, the living things in the earth and air and sea, the elements generally and individually, and all kinds of natural things. . . .[153]

The purpose of this and other similar statements by Eusebius is to show that there is only one power that created the cosmos, and not many.[154] For example, in the *Preparation for the Gospel,* Eusebius contrasts the pagan account of the origin of the world by many gods that have no love for humanity with the Christian account of the origin of the world by Jesus, "our Savior," who is "Maker of the whole Cosmos" and "the one sole divine

149. "For we acknowledge, in conformity with the blessed John, that 'all things were made through him,' since the creative power was begotten coexistentially in him from above . . ." (*Apology* 15:11–13; *Extant Works,* 52–53).

150. Ibid., 15:14; 52–53.

151. *Apology* 15:15–16, *Extant Works,* 52–53, which continues, "Since he alone was begotten and created by the power of the Unbegotten, he became the perfect minister of the whole creative activity and purpose of the Father."

152. *Apology* 16:16; *Extant Works,* 52–53.

153. *Demonstration of the Gospel* 4:5; Ferrar, 1:170.

154. For example, *Preparation for the Gospel* 3:13, 57.

power pervading and ordering all things".[155] The term for the creative force remains δύναμις.[156]

Eusebius believes the language of a demiurgic power to be Platonic in nature. One proof of this belief is his quotation from Atticus on Plato's claim that the world is "the noblest work" of a Maker "invested . . . with a power by which he made the world which did not exist. . . ."[157] By contrast, Aristotle (Atticus says) did not leave any power in God to do good. (This is clearly an episode in the "providence" debate.)[158] Furthermore, Eusebius interprets the *Republic* 509 B passage in terms of creation:

> Herein Plato says most distinctly that the intellectual essences receive 'the good', meaning of course from God, not merely the property of being known, but also their existence and essence. . . . So far he [Plato] does not regard the ideas as coessential, nor yet suppose that they are unbegotten, because they have received their existence and their essence from Him who is not an essence, but far transcends essence in dignity and power, whom alone the Hebrew oracles with good reason proclaim as God, as being the cause of all things.[159]

The implications of this text for trinitarian doctrine appear in the proof that ideas are neither coessential with God nor unbegotten "because they have received their existence and their essence from Him who is not an

155. Ibid., 3:6, 6. The same argument occurs at 7:15, 5.

156. This description of δημιουργεῖν as a function of δύναμις may be contrasted with Origen's description of δημιουργεῖν as a function of σοφία. When Origen offers his exegesis of John 1:1, "In the beginning. . . ." he understands this phrase to mean that the Word is the maker of the material universe: it was the Word who said, for example, "Let there be light" as recorded in Genesis. This role as Demiurge falls to the Word insofar as he is the Wisdom of God; Origen does not use Power to describe the Word as Demiurge. See *Commentary on John* I, 19:109–11, Blanc, SC 120:119.

157. *Preparation for the Gospel* 15:6, 7; Gifford, 3:2, 863.

158. What we have from Eusebius of the immediate context of Atticus' comment makes it very interesting for the subject of the trinitarian controversy. Eusebius provides the fragment from Atticus to illustrate how most Platonists believe that God is the Maker and Creator of the universe while the Aristotelians do not. Atticus is concerned with resolving the tension between the claim that there is a Creator who is good (that is, providential) and the criticism that if matter is not ingenerate (because it was created), then it must eventually dissolve, and therefore there is no providence because the world ends badly (because it ends). The assumptions that Atticus disputes—that everything that is imperishable is so because it is uncreated, that everything that has a beginning must end—are found in Eunomius' *Apology,* stated explicitly, as descriptions of the nature of the Son.

159. *Preparation for the Gospel* 11:21, 5–6; Gifford, 3:2, 586.

essence." The Son, too, is neither coessential with God nor unbegotten for the same reasons.

However, the association of δύναμις and δημιουργός found in the writings of Eunomius and Eusebius is not a feature exclusive to anti-Nicene theology: Athanasius, for example, uses the same language in *On the Incarnation,* where he speaks of the Demiurge's "power [δύναμις] over the universe."[160] Furthermore, the common description of the demiurgic capacity as a δύναμις does not remove this language as a focus of debate: in his *Councils of Rimini and Seleucia,* Athanasius disputes Asterius' doctrine that there is one Power that generates the Son and the world and that this Power is not the Son.[161]

However, while both sides acknowledge the Son as "Demiurge," each side draws a different conclusion from the title. For Eusebius and what became anti-Nicene theology, the Son's status as Demiurge restates His intermediate, and not fully divine, nature. The capacity to create is a power that properly belongs to God the Father but has been delegated by God to the Son to use as His obedient minister and servant (language that Eunomius favors as well). Eusebius says:

> So long, then, as he [the Son] is with the Father, and steers the Providence of the Universe with Divine Power [δύναμις], the Divine Word and Wisdom and Power [δύναμις] oversees and protects the heaven itself and the earth likewise. . . . He is their Ruler and Head and King. . . . And he is called Sun of Righteousness, and the True Light, carrying out and cooperating in his Father's commands, wherefore he is also styled minister of the Father and Creator. . . . He alone in his ordained rank knows how to serve God, and stands midway between the unbegotten God and the things after him begotten. . . .[162]

A clear example of the opposing understanding of the Son as Demiurge is offered by Basil of Ancyra, who pointedly rejects the kind of description of the Son as Demiurge found in the writings of Eusebius and Eunomius. Basil's criticism is that no matter how exaltedly one portrays the Son, if He is not uncreated, he is still classed among the created.

160. *On the Incarnation* 53, NPNF 4:65.

161. Asterius interprets Rom. 1:20 as describing God's power in creation and distinguishing that power from the Son (and placing Him on the side of creation).

162. *Demonstration of the Gospel* 4:10; Heikel, 167:25–35; Ferrar, 1:184.

For whether . . . [someone] speaks of Him [the Son] . . . as excelling in his function as the first to come to be, or whether as abiding in the creation of other things, he will still not exclude him from the concept of things made. . . . But as made, he will be the first of things made and an instrument for the Maker by means of which the Creator fashions everything.[163]

Basil argues that the anti-Nicene way of speaking of the Son as "first of all creation," or "the instrument of creation," contradicts the concept of Sonship: if the title "Son" is given truly, then the talk of an intermediary status is nonsense (much less the suggestion that He is "made"). If one takes "Son" seriously as a title, Basil says, any doctrine of an intermediate status is excluded; if one does not take the title seriously (by which Basil means univocally), no quantity of honorific titles such as "first of creation" can hide what is, for Basil, nothing more than Arianism.[164]

The Cappadocians' argument that the demiurgic power of the Son reveals His natural unity with God the Father turns upon the understanding that any creative power must be united to the essence. They stress the natural unity of divine essence and divine creative power, implicitly denying that creation is a capacity that can be delegated away and exist apart from the essence. Their argument may be summarized as "Where there is power, there is the essence." The Cappadocians sometimes take this natural unity between essence and power to mean that the Son is the creative Power of

163. *Panarion* 73, 4.1–68; Amidon, 295.

164. Basil goes on to argue against an interpretation of "Son" as an equivocal title that can be attributed equally to the only begotten and humans (5.1, 1–3). While scholars have discussed the apparent anti-Heterousian thrust of Basil's letter (as, for example, Hanson, *The Search*, 355), few have remarked upon the resemblance between the doctrines Basil opposes and those of Asterius and Eusebius from a generation earlier. The idea that the Son is the "first of things made" and an instrument by which the creator makes everything appears in fragment 3 of Asterius, "Christ is the first of things which have come into existence," while fragment 8 describes the Son as a mediator through which "the rest of creation could be created." The equivocal interpretation of doxological titles, which Basil is so concerned to refute, is found in many of Asterius' fragments, perhaps most clearly in fragment 10, where he says that "he is called Son for the sake of those who are made sons" and fragment 16, where he says that all the titles given by Scripture to Christ are also given to us. (Athanasius gives Asterius as the early spokesman for the equivocal exegesis of doxological titles, as I have already noted in chapter 3.) Finally, Basil's lengthy defense of *X from X* causality generally and the *Wisdom from Wisdom* formula in particular recalls Asterius' claim that the titles Word, Power, Wisdom, and Son are all given to the second Person only for the sake of extending these titles to redeemed humanity, and that because the Only Begotten is none of these properties as they exist in God's nature (see fragment 1), he has these titles only as he manifests the properties "through the products of his ministerial activity."

God and that the Son's unity with God the Father is that of power to essence, while at other times they argue that if the Son shares in the power, He must share in the essence. It is this last argument that is remembered as classically "Cappadocian"; I shall discuss both these arguments in detail in chapter 6.

Unlike Basil of Ancyra, the Cappadocian reply to Eunomius emphasizes the epistemological or revelatory function of creation. Basil of Caesarea's rebuttal of Eunomius' doctrine of the creative power establishes the basic themes his brother Gregory will later take and emphasize. In one important passage, Basil of Caesarea argues that if, as Eunomius claims, the essence and the power do not coincide, then the products of that power can tell us nothing about the essence that produced them through its power.[165] First, it should be noted that Eunomius does not in fact explicitly speak of a power that is separate from the essence, though Basil's conclusion to this effect is a correct one: Eunomius does teach a separation between the essence and its productive capacity. Second, Basil's argument assumes that there is a fundamental analogy between the Producer and the products:[166] Mortley has shown how far Eunomius is from this assumption, and I have described Eunomius as following Arius in his rejection of the "analogical ladder."

Gregory's rebuttal of Eunomius' understanding of the Son as demiurgic power is related to the contrast I have already drawn between Eunomius' doctrine of ὄνομα as σημεῖον of God and Gregory's doctrine of δύναμις as σημεῖον. The links, indeed, the ontological continuity, between the divine nature and its power, on the one hand, and between Power and its products, on the other hand, are important to Gregory because he believes that the artifacts of creation, rather than language, provide the best indicator of God's nature. He remarks, in a passage clearly indebted to Rom. 1:20: "His eternal Power and Godhead are understood, being clearly seen through the creation of the world. . . .[167]

Furthermore, the knowledge that there is no action in a creature that moves on its own accord but that everything "depends on a power who is

165. *Against Eunomius* 2, 32:18–35; Sesboüé, SC 299:134–35.
166. Ibid., 32:8–9; 132–33.
167. GNO 2:290:17, NPNF 5:272.

inscrutable and sublime" is an understanding ". . . not given in articulate speech but by the things which are seen, and it instills into our minds the knowledge of divine power more than if speech proclaimed it with a voice."[168]

*The Son as Demiurge*

In chapter 16 of the *Apology,* Eunomius treats the nature of the creative or demiurgic capacity. He says that if one argues that God is a father as a human is a father, that is, in a corporeal way, then one must also say that God is a creator, or demiurge, in a corporeal way, requiring a preexistent matter to which God presumably adds form.[169] But, as Eunomius points out, neither is an appropriate understanding of demiurgic activity in God, for God creates by His authority [ἐξουσία] alone: ἐξουσία μόνη δημιουργεῖν.[170] The sense of authority, as used here, is that of the sovereign authority of the will, or, as I call it, the political–moral sense. If one assumes that δύναμις is used as a term independent of the idiomatic expression, it then seems to be synonymous with ἐξουσία, since Eunomius uses either term to name the immaterial source or nature of God's productive capacity. Moreover, if power [δύναμις] is understood to be used in this political sense as synonymous with authority [ἐξουσία] then Eunomius' description of the Son as perfect minister (ὑπουργός)[171] due to his creation by God's power rests clearly on a political–moral model throughout. Thus, the direct and unique creation of the Son by the authority of God makes Him the perfect minister.

Eunomius' interpretation of the divine activities performed by the Son is that their performance testifies to the Son's perfect obedience as a servant or minister to God (the Father). The Son's role as creator, in particular, shows the perfect agreement between the Son's will and God's will,[172] while

168. Ibid. The coolness Gregory reflects towards speech is foreshadowed by Macrina's comments in *On the Soul and Resurrection:* Macrina cautions Gregory against dialectic because it is a power (δύναμις) that can be used for good or evil, the same intrinsic moral ambiguity attributed to the passions.

169. That is, at *Apology* 15:13, 15:15b, 16:34, 16:6, and 16:8; all at *Extant Works,* 52–53.

170. *Apology* 16:8, *Extant Works,* 52–53.

171. Ibid., 15:15; 52–53.

172. It should be remembered that Eunomius understood "God's will" to be equivalent to "the Father."

at the same time indicating the difference in their natures, for the Son creates only in obedience to God and only by virtue of the capacity to create that God has delegated to Him. "He who creates by His own power is entirely different from him who does so at the Father's command. . . ."[173]

This conclusion in the *Apology* is supported by an appeal to John 5:19—for He "who does so [that is, creates] at the Father's command and acknowledges that he can do nothing of his own accord. . . ."[174] The same scriptural text is appealed to later in the *Apology:* "For we confess that only the Son was begotten of the Father and that he is subject to him both in essence and in will (indeed he has admitted that he 'lives because of the Father and that he can do nothing of his own accord'). . . ."[175] The Son's very identity and existence are expressed in terms of this action in obedience. ". . . [W]hat the Son is everlastingly is what he is also rightly called: offspring, obedient Son, most perfect Minister of the maintenance and preservation of all existing things. . . ."[176]

In these texts Eunomius gives his interpretation of what the activities traditionally attributed to the Son mean, namely, that the Son's actions correspond to God's intentions. Implicit in this understanding is not only an assumption about the difference in kind of action between God and the Son but assumptions about the specific kinds of action that are particular to God. God does not create, He commands creation (He commands into being a creature to carry out the command to create); God does not maintain and preserve all things but commands that all things be maintained and preserved, and so on.[177]

In the *Second Apology* Eunomius repeats the understanding that the Son's demiurge power was delegated to Him by God.[178] He says that the Son ". . . was entrusted (ἐπιτέτραπται) by the Father with the construction of things visible and invisible . . . for the power has been allotted to him

173. *Apology* 20:20–21; *Extant Works,* 60–61.
174. Ibid., 20:21; 60–61.
175. Ibid., 26:21–23; 70–71.
176. Ibid., 27:2–5; 70–71.
177. Although this idea of God's role strongly resembles the politicized cosmology found in *On the Cosmos,* where the unique glory of God is shown in the mediated character of His action, Eunomius' immediate source for such an understanding of God's role is the Genesis account of creation. Gregory's quotations from the *Second Apology* in *Against Eunomius* II make it clear that Eunomius looked to Genesis to support his understanding of God and of language.
178. GNO 2:282–83; NPNF 5:237–38.

for the production of things made. . . ."[179] Once again, the relationship between the Father and the Son, and in particular the Son's reception of a productive capacity or role, is described in moral or political terms. In this case, the terms are ἐπιτρέπω and ἀποκληρόω.[180] Eunomius intends these terms to anchor the description of the Son's creative power in its source, which is the disposition of the Father, by emphasizing that the Son acts only in obedience to the Father and with the ability given to Him by the Father for the allotted task. This specific use of δύναμις, rather than the other senses of the term described in my earlier chapters, fits well Eunomius' understanding of the Son as ontologically other than, and inferior to, God (the Father).

### *Power and Moral Union*

When Gregory of Nyssa produces the quotation from the *Second Apology*—that the Son "was entrusted by the Father with the construction of things . . ."—for comment in his *Against Eunomius,* he emphasizes the moral or political aspect of Eunomius' language. For Gregory, the term ἐπιτρέπω means that the creative capacity of the Son depends upon an ἐξουσία or authority,[181] without which the Son lacks both the courage and the power to create.[182] Gregory returns to the term "ἐξουσία" three times in one paragraph,[183] first linking it to δύναμις,[184] then to ἔργα,[185] (at the same time linking δύναμις to ἔργα as well), and finally linking ἐξουσία to ἀρχή and κυριότητος.[186] For Gregory, Eunomius' use of political language

179. Ibid., 282:5–10; 237.

180. Ἐπιτρέπω is at GNO 2:282:5; ἀποκληρόω is at GNO 2:282:8.

181. Gregory argues to this effect immediately after he presents the fragment quoted above, that is, GNO 2:282:13–283:26.

182. GNO 2:282:24–25.

183. Gregory's comments are "Accordingly the term 'entrusted' suggests that his office and power in creation came to Him [that is, the Son] as something adventitious, in the sense that before He was entrusted with that commission He had neither the will [or courage] nor the power to act, but when he received authority [ἐξουσία] to execute the works [ἔργα] and power [δύναμις] sufficient for the works [ἔργα], then He became the artificer [or δημιουργός] of things that are, the power [δύναμις] allocated to Him from on high being, as Eunomius says, sufficient for the purpose" (GNO 2.282:22–29; NPNF 5:237).

184. Ἐξουσία and δύναμις appear at GNO 2.282:23–24 and 25.

185. Ἐξουσία and ἔργα (with δύναμις) are at GNO 2.282:25–26.

186. Ἐξουσία, ἀρχή and κυριότητος appear at GNO 2.283:7. It will be remembered that κυριωτάτης occurs in the first theological fragment of the *Second Apology:* "The statement of our

to describe the transmission of demiurgic power is inappropriate, or more accurately, incommensurate with the kind of power that is transmitted.[187] In Gregory's opinion, the power of creation is beyond any expression by political–moral language, and such language seems to him arbitrary and belittling. Given Gregory's judgment on the fullness of the Son's divinity, this opinion on Eunomius' use of political–moral language to describe the Father–Son relationship comes as no surprise.

However, Gregory's reading that Eunomius uses δύναμις to mean ἐξουσία, and that the acquisition of this δύναμις by the Son is political–moral in nature, is not simply tendentious. Political language of this sort occurs repeatedly in the *Second Apology* and other Eunomian works.[188] For example, earlier in the *Second Apology,* Eunomius said that God creates without constraint or need, according to His own authority, and that His own will as power is sufficient for all that is made.[189] Eunomius goes on to say that God's will determines the goodness and the time of creation.[190] Eunomius emphasizes rhetorically, through repetition, the primacy of God's will in creation: "God . . . begets and creates according to . . . His will. . . . All good is according to His will . . . for it is a weakness to make what one does not will.[191]

In this section of the *Second Apology,* Eunomius says that "God has dominion over his own power. . . ."[192] For Gregory, Eunomius' phrase κράτει δυνάμεος suggests Philo's phrase δυνάμεος αὐτεζουσίω.[193] In Gregory's opinion, if God has dominion over His power, then God is not

---

doctrines consists of the Highest [ἀνωτάτη] and Absolute [κυριωτάτη] Being [οὐσία]. . . ." GNO 1.72:1, Hall, 57 (slightly altered), NPNF 5:50.

187. See GNO 2:283:7–26; NPNF 5:237, for this line of reasoning by Gregory. Typical of Gregory's thought in this long paragraph is his comment: ". . . [Eunomius says of the Son] that to Him that is above all rule, and authority, and dominion, there has been allotted, as though He were put in some hollow spaces, power [δύναμις] from on high."

188. For example, in chapter 28:14–16, 74–75: ". . . [God made the Holy Spirit through His Son] creating him by his own authority and commandment." See also *Apology* 17:12; *Extant Works,* 54–55; and the *Creed,* 1:810, 150–51.

189. GNO 2.216:3–13, and 217:17–19; NPNF 5:211–12.

190. Ibid., 216:18–21; 5:211.

191. Ibid., 216:7, 10, 12; 5:211.

192. Ibid., 217:17–19; 5:212.

193. The GNO sees here a reference to Philo's *Allegorical Interpretations* 3.73, but David Runia, *Philo in Early Christian Literature,* 246, doubts that Gregory's attribution can be "substantiated from the Philonic corpus that we still possess." See F. H. Coulson and G. H. Whitaker, trans., *Work of Philo,* The Loeb Classical Library (1930; rpt. London: William Heinemann Ltd., 1979), 1:348–49.

one with that power.[194] But Eunomius does not seem to mean this in his passage. He intends, instead, to emphasize the priority of God's free choice in any act of production or creation. But Gregory is not far wrong in his interpretation, for Eunomius does believe that the creative capacity is separate from God's essence, which is truly God.[195] It is, in fact, this separation that insures God's freedom from necessity or need, according to Eunomius.[196] Gregory's reading of Eunomius is burdened heavily by sarcasm and hyperbole, but Gregory understands accurately that Eunomius' preferred model for God's productive capacity is a political–moral one. Eunomius does not hide, or even deny, this preference and indeed insists on it with great force and clarity when he says that God's activity is His will.[197]

Clearly Eunomius is never as explicit in his assertion that God's power is His authority as he is in his assertion that God's activity is His will, but he returns to the first formulation regularly. The doctrine that God's power is His authority is as descriptive of Eunomius' causality as is the doctrine that God's activity is His will. Both these doctrines serve to separate the productive capacity from God's essence by providing an alternative "seat" of production. Understood in this perspective, activity and power are virtually (but not quite entirely) synonymous, as seems to be case, for example, in the Eunomian Creed of *Apology*, chapter 28: "God creating the Spirit by his own authority and commandment, but by means of the action and power [ἐνέργεια καὶ δύναμις] of the Son."[198] However, since ἐνέργεια and δύναμις can have very different meanings from each other, as has already been discussed, one of the two terms must provide the governing sense. For Eunomius the dominant term is clearly ἐνέργεια, insofar as it suggests will. The relationship between the terms is based on their respective meanings: as activity is to will, so power is to authority, or, reversing the middle terms, as activity is to power, so will is to authority.

This Eunomian emphasis on a political–moral understanding of divine unity is responsible for Gregory of Nazianzus' discussing the question of

194. GNO 2.218:8–219:17; NPNF 5:212. Gregory says, for example, "Is He [God] something else than His own power, and Lord of a power that is something else than Himself?" (GNO 2.218:8–10; NPNF 5:212).

195. *Apology* 23:15–17; *Extant Works*, 64.

196. Ibid., 20:20–21; 60–61.

197. Ibid., 24:1–2; 64–65.

198. Ibid., 28:16, 26; 74–75.

God's titles according to "His Authority . . . and His Providence"[199] immediately after he discusses the special names of the essence in his reply to Eunomian theology. In *Oration* 30, Gregory of Nazianzus turns from rebutting Eunomian scriptural exegesis to offering his own positive interpretation of the titles of the Son.[200] He begins with the fundamental statement that "God cannot be named," which is pointedly the opposite of Eunomian doctrine.[201] According to this Gregory, theological titles refer to God's attributes and not to His essence.[202] There may be a certain likeness, or partial truthfulness to a title, but no more. The first kind of title that Gregory discusses is made up of those "special names of His essence," as, for example, "He Who Is" and "God."[203] The second kind of title that Gregory of Nazianzus discusses is that of God's authority and government.[204] Examples of such titles would be "King of Glory (δόξα)" or "King of Powers" (δύναμις).[205]

Unlike Eunomius, Gregory of Nazianzus does not understand these political–moral titles as descriptions of the source of unity between God and the Son. Instead, he explicitly contrasts these titles with the "proper names," of the Trinity, namely, Father, Son, and Holy Spirit.[206] This last set of names indicates the source of unity within the divine hierarchy. For example, regarding the second Person Gregory says, "I take the view that he is called 'Son' because he is not simply identical with the Father, but stems from him."[207]

From this point Gregory moves on to discuss the many titles of the Son,[208] including those such as Wisdom, Power, and Light which Eunomius discussed in the *Apology*.[209] However, Gregory diminishes the importance

199. *Oration* 30:19; Gallay and Jourjon, SC vol. 250, 264, 128B1–2.

200. Gregory's counter-exegesis to the ten scriptural texts the Eunomians use to support their theology fills *Oration* 30:2–15.

201. *Oration* 30:17; Norris, 273.

202. Ibid., 273–74.

203. Ibid., 30:18; 274–75.

204. Ibid., 30:19; 274. This section begins, "God's other titles fall into two distinct groups. The first belongs to his authority, the second to his providential ordering of the world. . . ."

205. See *Oration* 30:19; Gallay and Jourjon, SC vol. 250, 264, 128B1–8.

206. Ibid., 30:19; 266, 128C20–21.

207. *Oration* 30:20; Norris, 275.

208. Ibid., "Wisdom" occurs at page 268, 129A5; "Power" at 129B 17; "Light" at 129B30, and "Life" at 270 129C33.

209. *Apology* 19:3–16; *Extant Works*, 56–59.

of the earlier political–moral language and moves on to find the Son's full divinity expressed in titles such as "Wisdom," "Power," "Image," "Light," and "Life."[210] Eunomius, on the other hand, has understood the aforementioned titles as equivocal attributions, which do not testify to the Son's full divinity,[211] and he emphasizes political–moral language as a better description of the unity in the divine hierarchy. This use of the political–moral sense of δύναμις suits Eunomius' theology of a minimal degree of unity between God and the productive capacity, since this sense assumes unity with the essence. Thus, when δύναμις can have a political–moral sense, Eunomius will use it, and, conversely, when he uses δύναμις it tends to have a political–moral sense. Eunomius' use of δύναμις limits the term to the sense of either "might," "authority," "activity," or to the role of equivocal attribute in a doxological list of titles.

### *Conclusion*

Eunomius' theology combines an emphasis on the complete ontological transcendence of God with an emphasis on the accessibility of the means or instruments of human salvation. The first emphasis translates into doctrines of God's uniqueness, a difference between His existence and the existence of everything else, and the incommensurateness of these two kinds of being. The second emphasis translates into doctrines of the creation of the world by an agent who is himself created and of the existence of sure means of knowing the ontologically transcendent God, specifically, through names and through the effects of God's activities. This knowledge provides the basis for an account of the relationship between God (the Father) and His first servant, His "Son."

Although Eunomius' theology has been portrayed as outside the sensibilities of mainstream fourth-century Christian thought, much of Eunomius' language is borrowed from his predecessors and undoubtedly was recognized as such by his contemporaries. Eunomius' primary description of God is that of a being that by nature neither is produced nor produces. His primary description of the Son is as a being that is produced and produces. The Son's relationship with God is determined by His unique status

210. *Oration* 30:20.
211. *Apology* 19:12–16; *Extant Works*, 58–59.

as the single effect of God's activity and as the obedient instrument or servant of that activity (a description with its own cosmological connotations, as I will show in chapter 6). The Son's relationship with the cosmos is described in terms of His role as creator; the Son can fulfill this role because He receives from God the power (δύναμις) to create.

# 6 The Pro-Nicene Doctrine of Divine Productivity

## *Introduction*

FOR A SIGNIFICANT AND INFLUENTIAL SEGMENT of patristic scholarship, the Eunomian controversy has been understood as a defining episode in the development of a distinctly Christian sense of divine transcendence. Von Balthasar, Daniélou, and Lossky all describe the debate between Eunomius and the Cappadocians as a debate over whether, to what degree, and how, God is knowable by the human mind.[1] In this scholarly tradition the question of divine transcendence is considered a part of Gregory's "mystical" theology and so is separated from his trinitarian, that is, "doctrinal" theology.[2] However, authors such as Heine[3] and Canévet[4] have proposed alternative interpretations of Gregory's "mystical" writings such as *Life of Moses* and his *Commentary on the Canticle of Canticles* which place these works within a polemical context.[5]

1. Von Balthasar, *Présence et Pensée: Essai sur la philosophie religieuse de Grégoire de Nysse;* Daniélou, *Platonisme et théologie mystique: doctrine spirituelle de Grégoire de Nysse;* and Lossky, *Essai sur la théologie mystique de l'église d'orient.* Von Balthasar and Daniélou focus on Gregory of Nyssa.

2. The clearest example of this division can be found in Lossky's *Essai sur la théologie mystique.* In this work, Lossky refers to Eunomius in his chapter on gnosiology and not at all in his chapter on the Trinity; according to Lossky, the fundamental drama of the Eunomian controversy is not the equal divinity but the integrity of apophatic theology.

3. See Heine, *Perfection in the Virtuous Life.*

4. See Canévet, *Grégoire de Nysse et l'herméneutique biblique.*

5. The most recent statements of the scholarly understanding of the Eunomian controversy as a debate over divine transcendence may be found in Mortley's *From Word to Silence* 2:128–59, and Wiles's "Eunomius: Hair-splitting Dialectian or Defender of the Accessibility of Salvation?" I have

The older, still influential, description of the Eunomian controversy has provided the conceptual umbrella for many important accounts of Gregory's theology, as well as providing the commonly-accepted criteria for determining what are the fundamental features of Gregory's theology, namely, the presence of certain recurring themes. For example, it was von Balthasar who first emphasized Gregory's use of διάστημα as a fundamental feature of the latter's understanding of God.[6] Thereafter the role of διάστημα in Gregory's theology became a dominant theme in mainstream scholarship. The common scholarly emphasis on the concept of infinity in Gregory's theology has a similar history.[7] This thematic approach has occasionally been criticized for its lack of an historical sense; an example of this kind of problem is the treatment of Eunomius, who appears in the three French-language accounts virtually as a doctrinal double of Origen, so that Gregory's conceptual opponent is not Eunomius but Origen *redivivus.*[8] Yet the dominant form of Gregorian scholarship remains thematic.

In most mainstream accounts of Gregory's theology of divine transcendence, the subject of this transcendence is usually found to be the divine essence or nature. It is the divine essence that is spoken of as transcendent.

---

already summarized Mortley's work. Wiles's account of Eunomius' theology may be understood as a recent expression of his overall concern with the relationship between doctrine and philosophical language. Yet the virtue of Wiles's account is that it links Eunomius' and Gregory's "gnosiologies" with their respective trinitarian theologies. In his 1968 paper, "The Doctrine of Christ in the Patristic Age," *Working Papers,* 38–49, Wiles refers positively to the fact that the early Church Fathers neither allowed the mysteries of the faith to remain puzzles that could not be critically evaluated nor turned them into philosophical puzzles that could be solved by the application of rational intellect alone (see page 38). These are the alternatives he thinks are being dramatized in the Eunomian controversy, except that Wiles believes that the Cappadocians have not been recognized for indeed allowing the mysteries of the faith to remain puzzles that could not be critically evaluated, while Eunomius has been improperly charged with turning doctrine into philosophical puzzles that could be solved by the application of rational intellect (see "Eunomius: Hair-splitting Dialectian," 164).

6. See Otis for this observation in "Cappadocian Thought as a Coherent System," 109 n. 35: "It was, so far as I know, Balthasar who first realized the great significance of the Cappadocian use of the term διάστασις or διάστημα."

7. In addition to the Otis article mentioned above, see his "Gregory of Nyssa and the Cappadocian Conception of Time," *Studia Patristica* 15 (1976): 327–57; David Balàs, "Eternity and Time in Gregory of Nyssa's *Contra Eunomium,*" in *Gregor von Nyssa und die Philosophie,* 128–53; and Ekkehard Mühlenberg, *Die Unendlichkert Göttes bei Gregor von Nyssa: Gregors Kritik am Gottesbegriff der Klassischen Metaphysik,* Forschungen zur Kirchen und Dogmen Geschichte 16 (Göttingen: 1966).

8. For Daniélou, see *Platonisme et théologie mystique,* 7–8; for von Balthasar, see *Présence et pensée,* xvii; and for Lossky, see *Essai sur la théologie mystique,* 30–31.

This judgment follows in part from the presumption of a simple symmetrical opposition between Eunomius' and Gregory's theology of God: since Eunomius taught that God's essence (οὐσία) was knowable, then Gregory taught that God's essence was not knowable. Another factor contributing to this scholarly emphasis on οὐσία is the need to present Gregory as a fully-fledged member of the ὁμοούσια club. There has been, earlier in this century, a tendency among some scholars to confine the turmoil in trinitarian theology to events surrounding Nicaea and thus to imagine that the first Council of Nicaea solved the problem of "Arianism." Such accounts overemphasize the continuity between the theology of Nicaea (that is, ὁμοούσιος, whatever it meant) and Cappadocian theology. Moreover, earlier in this century Gregory's reputation as a paradigm of orthodox trinitarian theology had been impugned through the influence of Harnack, who had characterized Gregory as a semi-Arian appearing in the guise of a Nicene.[9] Countering Harnack also meant emphasizing the continuity between Nicaea and Gregory's theology. Finally, this hermeneutical emphasis on οὐσία was undoubtedly also supported by then contemporary modern philosophical scholarship, especially the reconstructed Aristotelianism used explicitly by French Catholic scholars[10] and implicitly by Neo-Palamite scholars.[11]

9. This is Harnack's characterization of the theology and creed normally associated with the Council of Constantinople, 381. Harnack thought of Gregory as providing the conceptual means of co-opting, and betraying, Nicaea I. See *History of Dogma,* 3:4, 86–87. Though Harnack's judgment of Gregory no longer has any significant influence, it is clear that his opinion of Gregory, when tied to the charge that Gregory was a "Hellenizer," figured significantly in the minds of those writing on this subject in France circa World War II, for von Balthasar, Daniélou, and Lossky were all concerned to show that Gregory was not a Hellenizer.

10. The obvious example that prompts this remark is the Thomistic scholarship that reached its climax in, for example, Etienne Gilson's *Being and Some Philosophers,* 2d ed. (Toronto: Pontifical Institute of Medieval Studies, 1952). However, more significant is the patristic scholarship following from Théodore de Régnon, who was the author not only of the massive *Études sur la Sainte Trinité* but also of *La Métaphysique des Causes d'après saint Thomas et Albert le Grand,* 2d ed. (Paris: Victor Retaux, 1906). I know of no exploration of de Régnon's debt to Thomism for his paradigm that the trinitarian theology of the East began with the multiplicity of persons and the trinitarian theology of the West began with the unity of nature, although the running argument among French Augustinians/Thomists (for example, Paissac, Malet, Guillou) over whether or not this paradigm is true suggests that Thomists do in fact have something at stake in a paradigm which now seems obvious to most scholars and which, in any case, no longer shows signs of its Thomistic origins.

11. See my "De Régnon Reconsidered," *Augustinian Studies* 26 (1995), 51–79.

*Two Doctrines of Divine Transcendence*

In the Eunomian controversy two different understandings, in fact, two different theological traditions, of divine transcendence do indeed face each other. Since the controversy is over the relationship between the first and second Persons, the issue of divine transcendence is expressed in terms of divine productivity. For Eunomius the transcendence of God requires that He cannot be understood to generate a product that has the same kind of existence He has, since that kind of existence is to be uncaused or unproduced, and any product will necessarily (that is, by definition) be caused. The uniqueness of God's kind of existence means that any productivity must exist outside His nature.

One of the ways in which Gregory uses power as a title of the divine nature (rather than as a title of the Son) is in the phrase "transcendent power," δύναμις ὑπερκειμένη; indeed, I have found "transcendent" is used more often of the δύναμις than of the φύσις or οὐσία, and it is Gregory's understanding of the divine power as transcendent that I will treat in this chapter. Gregory also speaks of the δύναμις as ὑπερκείμενόν τε καὶ ὑπερέξον (transcending and surpassing"),[12] language which is reminiscent of the *Republic* (ἀλλ᾽ ἔτι ἐπέκεινα τῆς οὐσίας . . . καὶ δυνάμει ὑπερέχοντος), and is representative of some School Platonic traditions of transcendence. Gregory applies this language to the divine power, it should be emphasized, and not simply to the divine essence or nature.

For Gregory the transcendence of God includes the capacity to produce; indeed, Gregory's conception of this capacity as a δύναμις means not only that this capacity exists as a natural capacity in God, but because this capacity is the δύναμις of the divine nature, God's kind of existence is the kind that (re)produces. The distinction among Persons means that the inherent productivity of the divine nature has two different expressions or appropriations. The first Person is productive (that is, is God) by generating the Second; the second Person is productive (that is, is God) by creating. Yet Gregory's fundamental insight, and his argument against Eunomius, remains clear: the divine nature, insofar as it is the divine nature, is

12. *GNO* 2.139:10, *NPNF* 5:184.

productive.[13] The unity between the divine δύναμις and divine φύσις is such that Gregory is led to speak of the transcendent δύναμις more than the transcendent φύσις, with the result that the title "divine δύναμις" replaces "divine φύσις" in Gregory's writings. (Alternately, one may set Gregory's writings in a sequence according to their use of "divine power" as the preferred title for God.)[14]

### *The Unity of the Divine Nature and Power*

Eunomius' initial statement of belief in the *Second Apology* is fundamentally an attempt to describe a causality that is not "natural" to God. In the *Apology* Eunomius appealed to a political or moral relationship to explain the productivity that is the cause of both the Son's existence and His delegated creative capacity. The political–moral language is no longer predominant in the *Second Apology,* though Gregory still finds it in Eunomius' doctrines. Eunomius undoubtedly thought that he had sufficiently described an "extra-natural" causality to account for the relationship between God and "the Son," yet it is precisely the recognition that Eunomius has cast his trinitarian theology as a causality that provides Gregory with the lever to overturn Eunomius' reasoning.

Gregory first uses power language when he responds to Eunomius' description of the activities that produced the Son and Holy Spirit as "bounded by their works." Gregory offers his own exegesis of "activity," "works," and "bounded by."

> He [Eunomius] uses the name works for the Son and the Spirit, activities for the powers [δυνάμεις] effective of them by which they were produced. . . . The expression "bounded by" indicates the equal status of the being that was produced with the power which constituted it, or not so much the power as the activity of the power, as he himself calls it. . . .[15]

13. If Meijering, *God Being History,* 97, is correct, a similar though less developed form of this argument appears in Athanasius' thought. Meijering argues from Athanasius' insistence that without the Son the Father is ἄσοφος and ἄλογος to Athanasius' belief that "the Father's divine perfection consists in the fact that He is the Father of the Son."

14. As Gregory's theology matures his use of the phrases "divine power" and "transcendent power" increases. The phrases appear relatively rarely in *On the Making of Man* but regularly in *Life of Moses,* suggesting that the former work was written before Gregory had fully developed his own response to Eunomius and that the latter is a late work and not an early one. The chronology that I suggest is in fact the commonly held chronology.

15. *GNO* 1:98:7–11; Hall, 70–71, translation slightly altered.

Though Gregory here introduces *power* to explain *activity* (the activity is a power by which they are produced), his point must be that Eunomius does not mean that the Son's origin is a power. This is the point condensed in Gregory's phrase "as he himself calls it." Gregory notes that Eunomius contrasts the product not with power but with the activity of power. *Power,* that is, δύναμις, does not occur in the Eunomian fragment as Gregory has quoted it, and nothing in the text (apparent ellipsis, etc.,) or in secondary sources suggest that Gregory has omitted Eunomius' own use of *power.* Gregory's reading of Eunomius' use of activity is to understand it in relation to the concept of power. Gregory recognizes the causal language Eunomius employs, recognizes where Eunomius has omitted an important etiological concept, and supplies that concept, for it is basic to his own trinitarian theology and understanding of divine existence.

In his account of Eunomius' theology in *Against Eunomius* 1, Gregory offers his understanding of the three possible relations that can occur between the divine nature (considered in itself) and divine causality (that is, the divine considered as a cause or source). The first possibility, that it is a power in the conventional sense, is excluded when Eunomius "names it" an activity and not a power. Gregory will later contrast the union of a power with its existent, which he calls συμφυής,[16] with the unity between a willed action and the originating will,[17] by which he means the difference between natural effects and artificial products (for example, the heat of fire versus a man building a house). Another way Gregory draws out these two types of causes is when he speaks of the communication of heat and cold to iron, and the inherently temporary and transitory nature of these communicated properties, as opposed to the permanence of heat in fire or cold in ice.[18]

In *On the Making of Man* Gregory uses a similar distinction when he treats the question of why humans are born without the natural capabilities they need to survive: for example, fur to stay warm, fast legs to run away from predators, and sharp claws to rip meat. He refers to these natural capacities as δυνάμεις, and contrasts them with the artificial capabili-

16. *GNO* 1.147:18.
17. *GNO* 1:147:15–18; *NPNF* 5:73.
18. *NPNF* 5:61.

ties humans provide for themselves.[19] In *Against Eunomius* Gregory uses this sense of natural production to characterize his own doctrine of the origins of the Son in the Father, while the sense of artificial production is used to characterize Eunomius' doctrine of the Son's origin.

The second possible causal relation is what Gregory initially suggests Eunomius has postulated: a power-like source that is without a power's unity with its existent. "An essential Power, self-subsisting, which works its will by spontaneous impulse."[20] Gregory's immediate interest in such a source is that it must be considered as a mediating entity between God and the Son, where the Son is not second after the first essence but third after the subsisting source. Gregory recognizes in the language of a self-subsisting essential Power the description of a separate person because he uses similar language to give a positive description of the nature of the Son's existence. In *Against Eunomius* 3:4 he says, "[W]e understand that Power of God, which made all things, which is the Lord, not in the sense of depending upon Him as a part upon a whole, but as indeed being from him, and yet contemplated in individual existence."[21] A similar description can be found in *The Catechetical Oration:* "[T]he Word of God has been shown . . . to be a *power* essentially and *substantially existing*."[22] In short, Eunomius' description of the separate existence of the divine activity sounds to Gregory like the kind of description he himself could offer of the real existence of the Son (insofar as He is identified with the power).

The theological problems with attributing the Son's origin to a subsisting intermediary power must have been obvious to all sides, for even if Gregory is here hinting at Philonic influences on Eunomius, he passes quickly to his next criticism: Eunomius is suggesting a source that lacks

19. *On the Making of Man* 44 141AB; see also NPNF 5:392. I take this to be a general reference to the Prometheus myth recounted in the *Protagoras* (which I discussed in chapter 2).

20. *GNO* 1:99:8.

21. *GNO* 2:143:6–10; *NPNF* 5:185.

22. "Τὸ γὰρ εἶναι λόγον θεοῦ καὶ πνεῦμα θεοῦ, οὐσιωδῶς, ὑφεστώσας δυνάμεις . . ." *Catechetical Orations* 4:1, ed. and trans. Louis Méridier, *Discours catechétique* (Paris: Librairie Alphonse Picard et Fils, 1908), 20; *NPNF* 5:478. In Eunomius' *Creed* of 383, he describes the Son as a subsisting power, δύναμις ὑφεστῶσα (*Extant Works,* 153:6), language which shows that Eunomius responded to Gregory's earlier criticism of his theology by appropriating some of Gregory's own terminology (for example, the italicized phrase from *Catechetical Orations*).

real existence, that is, a power that is ἀνύπαρκτο[23] and ἀνυπόστατον.[24] This is the third possible relation between the causal source and the divine nature. Gregory will alternate between condemning Eunomius for holding a doctrine of the second relation and for holding the third; this third possible causal relation, however, most fits Gregory's overall argument in book 1 that Eunomius has introduced opposition into the divine life.

For if God's activity has no real existence (that is, is anhypostatic) . . . then surely the product will be perceived by nature to be of the same kind as the nature of that which constituted the work. . . . That which is produced from and is contained by an unreality can itself be conceived as nothing else but a nonentity. It is against nature for opposites to be bounded by opposites.[25]

However, in *Against Eunomius* 3, Gregory's criticism of Eunomius' description of God's relationship to His creative power emphasizes the separate existence Eunomius seems to attribute to this power. In this later book Gregory calls Eunomius' statement that God has dominion over his own power nothing more than an appropriation of a phrase from Philo.[26] Gregory's criticism is that Eunomius, like Philo, teaches that the δύναμις exists outside God's nature and is subservient to God's will.[27] These two doctrines are in fact equivalent, for if something is outside the divine nature, it is necessarily subservient to God's will, and only what is outside God's nature is subservient to that nature: God's nature is not subservient to itself. Indeed, the obvious fact that something cannot be subservient to itself is Gregory's point of departure in criticizing Eunomius for teaching a separate δύναμις. Gregory argued that if "God has dominion over his own power," as Eunomius says, then God is not one with that power: "Is He [God] something else than His own power, and Lord of a power that is something else than Himself?"[28]

23. *GNO* 1.100:4

24. Ibid., 1:100:6.

25. Ibid., 1:100:24–101:6; Hall, 72. The passage continues, "Water is not bounded by fire nor light by darkness nor what is by what is not." I have altered one sentence of Hall's translation in favor of Moore's and Wilson's, where the sense seemed clearer in the older translation.

26. *GNO* 2:217, 17–19; *NPNF* 5:212.

27. Cf. Jean Daniélou on Gregory and Philo in *L'Etre et la temps chez Grégoire de Nysse* (Leiden: E. J. Brill, 1970), 86–87.

28. *GNO* 2:218, 8–10; *NPNF* 5:212.

This remark by Gregory is just the first round in an entire volley of criticisms directed at Eunomius' understanding of δύναμις:

God, he says, has dominion over His own *power.* Tell me, what is He? Over what has He dominion? Is He something else than His own *Power,* and Lord of a *power* that is something else than Himself? Then *power* is overcome by the absence of *power* [that is, we are back to the kind of oppositions refuted in book 1]. For that which is something else than *power* is surely not *power,* and then He is forced to have dominion over *power* just in so far as He is not *power.* Or again, God, being *power,* has another *power* in Himself, and has dominion over the one by the other. . . .[29]

The veritable explosion of references to δύναμις in Gregory's reply to Eunomius' statement that God has dominion over His own power suggests that there is something in this claim that would seem to Gregory quite radical in its implications. One clue to what might be so extreme in Eunomius' statement lies in Gregory's attempt to interpret Eunomius' doctrine as a kind of two-powers theology, as when he says that if Eunomius is right, then God, being power, has another power in Himself. Though this is a crude restatement of two-powers theology, it suggests how Gregory understood the passage from Eunomius and what about it provoked such a defense of the divine δύναμις.

Eunomius' phrase for what God has dominion over is ἰδία δύναμις.[30] This phrase has a history in two-powers theology. According to Asterius, Christ is the second power of God, who is "visible through the products [ἔργα] of his ministerial activity."[31] This much at least sounds Eunomian, including the ministerial reference. However, Asterius' phrase for the First Power, God as Power, is ἰδία δύναμις. For Eunomius the ἰδία δύναμις is the subject of God's dominion, that is, is not God. Even Asterius would have been scandalized by this phrasing! Again it is clear just how completely Eunomius has eliminated δύναμις from his understanding of God's

29. Ibid. 2:218:6–13; 5:212. I have emphasized each appearance of *power* in the text that is a translation of δύναμις. Gregory ends his attack with a kind of "third man" argument against the idea that God has dominion over His power. How can God have dominion except through power? Does this power have dominion over the first power through the aid of yet another power?

30. GNO 2:218:7.

31. Hanson, *The Search,* 33.

being and productivity, and, as a minor point, how far he was from the Eusebian-Asterian two-powers theology.

### *The Philonic Delegation of Power*

Gregory recognizes in Eunomius' complete separation of the creative capacity from God's nature something from Philo. At some level in his own theology, Philo did not separate causality from God's own nature. In *Allegorical Interpretations* 1.3 (to be discussed in the next chapter) Philo describes true action as the property of God alone. Yet this understanding did not prevent his finding God's causality enacted through the activity of mediating powers. It may have been the property of God to act, but Philo nearly always describes this action in terms of the δυνάμεις.

> . . . the central place is held by the Father of the Universe, Who in the sacred scriptures is called He Who Is as His proper name, while on either side of Him are the senior powers, those nearest to Him, the creative and the kingly. The title of the former is God, since it made and ordered the All; the title of the latter is Lord, since it is the fundamental right of the maker to rule and control what he has brought into being.[32]

and

> For when out of that confused matter God produced all things, He did not do so with His own handiwork, since His nature, happy and blessed as it was, forbade that He should touch the limitless chaotic matter. Instead He made full use of the incorporeal powers. . . .[33]

and

> [There is] the creative Power called God, because through this [power] the Father who is its begetter and contriver made the universe, so that "I am thy God" is equivalent to "I am the Maker and Artificer."[34]

The separation of power from God is what seems to Gregory to be Philonic in Eunomius' theology. In Gregory's remarks Philo figures as the mask for any doctrine that describes God's δύναμις as separate from the nature and possessing an intermediate and independent existence, which is definitely

32. *On Abraham* 24:122; Coulson, Loeb 6:63, slightly altered.
33. *Special Laws* 1:329; Coulson, Loeb 7:291, slightly altered.
34. *On the Change of Names* 29; Coulson, Loeb 5:158, slightly altered.

how Gregory understands Eunomius' doctrines. Whether or not Eunomius hypostasized the productive capacity, as Gregory charged, it is clear that Eunomius limited the use of δύναμις either to describing the intermediate status of the Son as the creating minister of God or to describing the intermediate status of the cause of the Son Himself.[35] Given the character of Gregory's comments, there is no point in troubling over whether he is being fair to Philo, who is referred to only as an important example of the understanding of δύναμις Gregory wishes to refute.[36] However, there is no denying that Gregory recognized a genuine tradition in Hellenistic thought, namely, one that removes causality from the highest being and considers it a lower or secondary form of being.[37] Two influential examples from this tradition will substantiate the existence of the doctrine of delegating production and providence to intermediate causes as well as illustrating the contours of the reasoning.[38]

The first example of this philosophical tradition is the Pseudo Aristotelian *On the Cosmos:*

> Some of the ancients were led to say that all the things of the world were full of gods . . . but in saying this they used terms suitable to the power of God but not to his essence. For God is indeed the preserver of all things and the creator of everything in the cosmos . . . but he does not take upon himself the toil of the creature . . . but uses an indefatigable power, by means of which he controls even things that seem a great way off. God has his home in the highest and first place, and is called supreme for this reason. . . .[39]

35. "The Neo-Arians were always exceedingly concerned to avoid any suggestion that God had intimate contact with the bodily world; Eunomius went so far as to say the Son 'actively carried out the things which belong to love of humanity' but God 'remained inactive with respect to such grace'" (Kopecek, *Neo-Arianism,* 159).

36. The Philonic reference also allows Gregory the opportunity to reduce Eunomius' theology to a form of Judaism, by now a conventional Nicene and pro-Nicene polemical device.

37. See, e.g., *On the Cosmos* 6; Furley, Loeb 385:19–25.

38. C. K. Mathias has recently identified the same tradition in a slightly different way on page 63 of "Parallel Structures in the Metaphysics of Iamblichus and Ibn Gabirol," in *Neoplatonism and Jewish Thought,* ed. Lenn E. Goodman (Albany: State University of New York Press, 1992), 61–76. Mathias singles out Hellenistic philosophers who taught "a 'self-generating' second principle that creates itself out of the quiescent first principle." Among those who held this position Mathias includes the author of "*De Mundo,* Numenius, the *Codex Bruciacianus,* the Peratae, and the *Chaldean Oracles.*" Mathias is noncommittal about placing Philo wholly in this tradition, as am I.

39. *On The Cosmos* 6; Furley, Loeb, 385:17 ff. The word "supreme" is ἀνωτάτω, later a favorite of Eunomius.

One feature of this kind of causality is clear in this work, namely, the understanding that the unity between the highest Being and causality is best described as a "political" (for example, royal) union. The prominence of this political language in *On the Cosmos* leads one to recognize the same, if less prominent, use of political language by Philo; even those scholars who insist that, for Philo, the powers are existentially one with God and only seem separate and multiple to creation, also remark upon the significant role given by Philo to political descriptions of the powers, for example, "King" and "Lord." It is precisely this kind of political language that appears in Eunomius' *Apology* and, in the fragment appearing in *Against Eunomius* 3:7, prompts Gregory's strong rebuttal.

### *Numenius' "Lazy" One*

Another important example of a doctrine of separating the productive capacity from the First Being can be found in the teachings of Numenius,[40] a name often mentioned in scholarship as typifying the general philosophical climate of Alexandria in Arius' day[41] and, indeed, as the source for Arius' use of "dyad" and "demiurge."[42] Numenius taught a triad of Gods that included the First God, also known as the Good, the One, or the Father; and the Second God, known principally as the Demiurge.[43] The First God is described as unmoving, at rest, overseeing, and other such terms, all to suggest the complete transcendence of the First God. In contrast, the Second God, the Demiurge, gets his hands dirty with primordial matter and is like the sharecropper who works in the fields while the landowner remains inactive but reaps the rewards from a distance. The First God,

40. Numenius' extant writings can be found in the Édouard des Places edition, *Numenius Fragments* (Paris: Societé d'Edition 'Les Belles Lettres', 1973). Des Places directs the reader to Festugière's commentary on the fragments in his *La révélation,* 4:123–32. The contemporary reader is better served by first reading John Dillon's treatment of Numenius in *The Middle Platonists* (Ithaca: Cornell University Press, 1977), 361–79; Dillon also considers Numenius' influence on early trinitarian theology in his article, "Logos and Trinity," 1–13.

41. Williams, *Arius,* 223.

42. Stead, "Platonism of Arius," 19–22. Dillon thinks that Origen found his distinction between "the good" and "good" in Numenius ("Logos and Trinity" 7).

43. The Third God, whose exact identity is a matter of confusion in scholarship for he shares the creative activity of the Second God yet is somehow identified with the product of that activity, is irrelevant to our discussion.

according to Numenius, is the "creator" only because he is said to be the cause of the Demiurge.[44] Numenius calls the First God the Good, in imitation of *Republic* 509 B, but the sense of spontaneous fruitfulness found in *Republic* 508 B is entirely missing.[45]

Numenius, like Philo, remarks that God is identified with the creator, though Numenius means to suggest by this remark the inadequacy of the commonly held conception of God: the true God is beyond creating, is inactive and self-perfect. Judgments that *"I am your God" is equivalent to "I am the Maker and Artificer,"*[46] which one finds not only in Philo but also in Numenius and the *Chaldean Oracles,*[47] are very important to note, for there is a double meaning contained in them that reveals clearly the two alternative understandings of transcendent causality. *"I am your God" is equivalent to "I am the Maker and Artificer"* can summarize the understanding that what is worshipped is only the Demiurge, who is intrinsically a second class God, while there is a non-acting Transcendent Being behind (or above) this Demiurge who is of a more exalted rank. This understanding is clearly that of Numenius, of the author of *On the Cosmos,*[48] and of many others, not the least of whom is Eunomius. On the other hand, a statement such as *"I am your God" is equivalent to "I am the Maker and Artificer"* can be an affirmation of the productive capacity of the First Being

44. This and the previous two sentences represent a free, but faithful, summary of pertinent doctrines from Numenius' fragments 11, 12, and 13.

45. Under different circumstances, the two understandings of the relationship between the Highest Transcendent and the first productive causality could be written as a history of the exegesis of *Republic* 509 B, for Numenius understands that text to describe a motionless, inactive "First God," while Plotinus, representing the other understanding of the first cause, understands *Republic* 509 B as testimony to the inevitable over-flowing of the One.

46. *On the Change of Names* 29; Coulson, Loeb 5:158, slightly altered. See above, note 36.

47. Numenius, fragment 17D, says, "Since Plato knew that among men the demiurge is the only divinity known, whereas the Primal Intellect . . . is completely unknown . . . [and so Plato said] 'O men, that Intellect which you imagine to be supreme is not so, but there is another Intellect prior to this one which is older and more divine.'" The *Oracles,* fragment 6, say, "All things the Father brings to completion, and handed them over to the Second intellect, whom all you race of men call the First." Dillon brings these two sources together to show the similarity between their doctrines and to explore the possibility that one influenced the other (*The Middle Platonists,* 363). Unlike Numenius and the *Oracles,* Philo never suggests that there is something facetious about the identification.

48. Festugière remarks on the similarity between the doctrine found in *On the Cosmos* and that of Numenius in *La Révélation* 4:128.

or of the creative capacity of divinity itself: to create is indeed a Godly ability. This latter understanding is Plotinus' and Gregory's.[49]

### *Gregory's Doctrine of Transcendent Power*

The traditional understanding of δύναμις allows for two kinds of connotations of the term. Δύναμις may mean the specific capacity to affect that any existent has insofar as it exists and insofar as it is what it is. This δύναμις is usually understood as that capacity or feature that is most distinctive or characteristic of the existent. Δύναμις may also mean any of the several capacities to affect that a specific existent has because it is what it is. Both of these meanings assume that the δύναμις is included in the nature of an existent. An example of the first sense of δύναμις that I have mentioned often is the heat of fire; on the other hand, dryness, ever-moving, consuming of fuel, etc., are all examples of the second sense of δύναμις when used of fire.[50]

When Gregory uses connatural power in this second sense, he frequently includes δύναμις among the several capacities to affect that he lists; in this case, δύναμις means the ability to affect (as opposed to a non-active, passive, kind of existent) or power in its non-technical sense (that is, physical or political power).[51] God's primary δύναμις, however, is the capacity

49. The reader will again notice that I have not included Philo's name in either of the two competing lists. An earlier generation of scholars—notably Goodenough and Wolfson—spoke with great certainty on the root monotheism of Philo's theology and on the purely functional character of the powers for his theology. More recently, Alan F. Segal argues that Philo "unabashedly calls the logos a 'second God'" (*Two Powers in Heaven* [Leiden: E. J. Brill, 1977], 164–65). David Winston, *Logos and Mystical Theology in Philo of Alexandria* (Cincinnati: Hebrew Union Press, 1985), 13–15, has similar judgments on the overall conceptual dominance of Greek philosophy in Philo's thought.

Philo's use of δυνάμεις, the powers, is so obvious that one can be misled by simply comparing his understanding of the term to that of other authors. His understanding of the powers probably depends more on Jewish exegetical developments than one might otherwise expect, given the rich history of the term elsewhere. But the concept that carries the real freight of a disassociated causality in Philo's theology is the Logos, for it is the mediating entity that provides the buffer between God and creation, and not the powers (as it is in *On the Cosmos*), and not the Demiurge, as it is for Numenius.

50. I refer the reader back to chapter 1 for my discussion of primary versus secondary attribution of δυναμ[ε]ις to an existent.

51. A good example of this shift from the first sense of δύναμις to the second sense occurs at *GNO* 1:95:113, where Gregory moves from using δύναμις as that which in God is "without parts or composition" to naming δύναμις as one among several "good things piously attributed" to God.

to produce or create, and it is this capacity that is the distinguishing characteristic of the divine nature.[52] This judgment by Gregory has, of course, a definite polemical edge to it, since Eunomius and non-Nicenes like Eusebius of Caesarea said that the Son creates through the power that God (the Father) delegates to Him. However, if the power to create is in fact a power,[53] then it is connatural to God, and, as part of His nature, creating can no more be delegated than an eye can delegate seeing or fire delegate burning. Wherever one finds the power of producing, one must also find God, just as wherever one finds seeing or burning, one must also find an eye or fire.

Gregory's doctrine of transcendent productivity stands in stark contrast to both the anti-Nicene and some School Platonic doctrines of mediated causality. He is clear that the Power that brings the cosmos into existence is fully transcendent. Gregory says, for example:

> [T]here is no question that the universe is bordered by the Power [δύναμις] of the Creator and lies within creation's limits. But the Power [δύναμις] that creates beings, which by itself bounds the nature of originated things, has itself nothing to contain it. . . .[54]

52. In one place Gregory calls this δύναμις Providence and specifically compares it to heat in fire and cold in ice (see *GNO* 1:154:25–155:15). That Providence includes creation and beneficent lordship over those created things may be seen in the Atticus passage I quote below. See also cosmological use of *power* in his *Hexameron.*

53. While the capacity to create was sometimes spoken of simply as δημιουργεῖν, it was commonly described as a δύναμις. Indeed, as I have already noted, the description of the capacity to create as a power is an innovation of Platonism in the Hellenic era. In the *Timaeus* Plato did not speak of the Demiurge as a δύναμις, but his Middle Platonic readers saw that identification and emphasized it. Atticus provides a good example of this interpretation of the Demiurge: "But according to our hearing, whereas Plato claims for the world that it is the noblest work made by the noblest of Creators, and invests the Maker of all with a power [δύναμις] by which He made the world which did not previously exist . . ." (*Preparation for the Gospel* 15:6; Gifford 3:2, 863; des Places, SC 338:266:18).

54. *GNO* 1.135:15–19, Hall, 89, Hall's translation slightly altered. The word "bounds" is a translation of συμπεριγραφή, a term which appears in Eunomius' summary of his beliefs, and also appears in Gregory's statement that "Things are naturally circumscribed (συμπεριγραφή) only by what is opposite to them," which in fact is the understanding Gregory gives the term here. (As I have already noted, περιγραφή appears in Origen's *Commentary on the Gospel of John,* where it is used to name an independently subsistent existent.) Gregory's use of the term here indicates his revision of Eunomius' formulas. This kind of correcting of Eunomius' doctrines is more pronounced in the next passage I quote. In all these quotations I have corrected Hall's punctuation, for although he regularly capitalizes "divine" terms like Creator or Nature, he fails to do the same with Power.

This understanding is shortly restated by Gregory in an even more pointedly anti-Eunomian form:

It is before all beginning, it provides no tokens of its own nature, but is known only in being incomprehensible. This is in fact its most characteristic mark, that its nature is superior to every concept by which it might be recognized. . . . For every thought that applies to the uncreated Power [δύναμις] is '"high"' and is the first principle, and demands the name most authentic.[55]

In this passage Gregory takes Eunomius' own language for describing the transcendent Essence or Being (οὐσία) and applies it to the divine power as a description of the kind of existence appropriate to the Power. High [ἀνωτάτω] and most authentic [κυριωτάτη] are Eunomius' terms for the First Essence: "the highest and most authentic being."[56] Gregory's point is simple: the transcendence and priority Eunomius found in (and limited to) the uniquely divine essence of God the Father is in fact properly attributed to the power common to the three Persons. To refute Eunomius, Gregory attributes the transcendent language associated with the unique essence to the common power. I emphasize that Gregory appropriates and applies this transcendent language to the δύναμις, and not simply to the φύσις. In a polemic one expects disputed language to be reclaimed: what is noteworthy is that Gregory reclaims it for the Power.

Gregory offers these descriptions of the transcendence of the Power in the course of distinguishing between the kinds of existence of the Uncreated and the created: the sequence or interval that characterizes created

55. *GNO* 1:137:13–19; Hall, 90.

56. *GNO* 1.72:1–2, Hall, 57. Another borrowing from 72:1–2 is at 137:18, πᾶν γὰρ τὸ νοούμενον ἐπὶ τῆς ἀκτίστου δυνάμεως ἄνω ἐστὶ καὶ ἀρχή ἐστι καὶ τὸν τοῦ κυριωτάτου λόγον ἐπέχει which echoes Eunomius' language at 72:12, νοουμένης κατὰ τὴν ἰδίαν ἀξίαν (ἀνωτάτω appears at 72:1). In a passage from 136:24–25, he speaks of the power as ὑψηλὴ καὶ μακαρία, "high and blessed", which also suggests that Gregory is re-working Eunomius' own language. With one minor exception (at *GNO* 2.270:1), ὑψηλός appears with great regularity in both *Apologies* as Eunomius' standard word for a blessed author who is about to be quoted, as, for example, "so says the blessed" Apostle John or Paul. It has no theological significance. The single occasion of ὑψηλός (at *GNO* 2.236:17) is in a list of terms describing the Father's unique and transcendent status: the Father (that is, the οὐσία God, and not simply the ἐνέργεια "the Father") is absolute virtue, life, light unapproachable, and all that is ὑψηλός in word or thought. Gregory is probably paraphrasing Eunomius' thought at *GNO* 1.136:27, while 137:18 is a concerted attempt explicitly to rework Eunomius' own categories of transcendence and claim them for the divine power.

existence is not to be found in Uncreated existence, for created existence is finite, while uncreated existence is infinite.[57]

For that Power [δύναμις] which is without interval, without quantity, without circumscription, having in itself all the ages and all the creation that has taken place in them, and overpassing on all points, by virtue of the infinity of its own nature, the unmeasured extent of the ages, either has no mark which indicates its nature, or has one of an entirely different sort, and not that which creation has.[58]

Or again from *Against Eunomius* 1:

These experiences are proper to the things in creation, [that is,] their life being divided between memory and expectation in accordance with temporal division. But to that high and blessed Power, to which all things are always equally instantaneously present, both what is past and what is awaited are seen to be firmly held by the Power which embraces all.[59]

The appearance of Power in these descriptions of the Transcendent is distinctive. Gregory has not taken the course of separating the divine power from the transcendent existence. Moreover, in each of these passages, Gregory refers to the transcendent power, not, as one might expect, to the transcendent nature. It is not simply the case that Gregory considers power and nature so united that he can freely substitute one term for the other: Gregory uses *power* in preference to *nature.*

57. In his "L'aspect cosmologique de la philosophie d'Eunome pour la réprise de l'Hexaemeron basilien par Grégoire de Nysse," in *El "Contra Eunomium I" en la Produccion Literaria de Gregorio de Nisa,* ed. L. Mateo-Seco and J. Bastero, 203–16, Michel Esbroeck examined this section of *Against Eunomius* 1 in detail and interprets parts of Gregory's argument as evidence that the Eunomian controversy in general and the Cappadocian contribution to that controversy in particular was a debate in cosmology. According to Esbroeck, *Against Eunomius* 1 should be understood as another commentary on Genesis, similar to the explicitly cosmological commentaries produced by Basil and Gregory in the mid and late 370s. The three passages Esbroeck singles out are: Gregory's discussion at *GNO* 1:124:6–15 of the creation of the stars and the heavens; the reference to Gen. 1:6 ff. at *GNO* 1:129:20–28; and at *GNO* 1:136:8–13, the reference to the study of the Demiurge. (This last passage appears among the transcendent Power texts I have been citing.) Esbroeck is right to recover the cosmological context of the trinitarian controversy; I have tried to show, however, that this context extends throughout the trinitarian debate, and so, contrary to the opinion of Esbroeck, there is nothing peculiarly cosmological about the Cappadocian contribution. But in his details Esbroeck has it right.

58. *GNO* 2:210:11–17; *NPNF* 5:209.

59. *GNO* 1:136:22–27, 89–90; *NPNF* 5:69.

*Power and God's Being*

Gregory's preference for δύναμις as the title for the divine is consistent both with the fundamental character of his understanding of the kind of existence the divine has and with his understanding of the character of human knowledge. God's is the kind of being that acts, and activity is the kind of knowledge we know best. There is a happy coincidence between these two facts, so that however unique and unlike anything else God may be, God is recognizable as a Being that acts, and insofar as God acts, we can form meaningful concepts about Him. The traditional description of existence as a sequence of causes stops at the δύναμις. This kind of epistemology first appears in the Hippocratic writings and is systematized by Galen, as I have described earlier. A similar account of a nature can be found in Julian's *Hymn to King Helios,* where he describes Helios by giving an account of his powers, activities, and works, while he leaves knowledge of the essence to be deduced from what is known from the powers. Gregory uses the title *divine power*—θεία δύναμις—as his preferred title for God because δύναμις is as far back in the descriptive sequence ἔργα—ἐνέργεια—δύναμις—οὐσία as he can meaningfully speak.[60]

It is important to remember that in this causal sequence the further back in the sequence one goes, the greater the correspondence between the causality and the nature. For example, the knowledge of some living thing provided by its products or effects is not as great as the knowledge provided by its activities, which is still less than the knowledge of the nature obtained through knowledge of the powers. The knowledge of human nature gained in archeology begins with artifacts, but more is learned of human nature through a knowledge of the activities that produced and required these artifacts. Even more would be learned through knowledge of the faculties that felt these requirements and developed the means of production.

Gregory relies on the different levels of knowledge available at each stage of the causal sequence to distinguish the kinds of knowledge provided of God: doxological titles, such as Lord, Physician, Shepherd, Bread, etc.,

60. For an account of the systematization of the descriptive sequence ἔργα—ἐνέργεια—δύναμις—οὐσία in the writings of Galen and for its appearance in Julian's *Hymn to King Helios,* see my "The Background and Use of Eunomius' Causal Language," 217–36.

refer to God's activities, but metaphysical titles,[61] such as immortal, invisible, wise God, refer to God's transcendent power; these latter terms are "employed and understood absolutely."[62] There are other, more significant demonstrations of Gregory's understanding of God's existence in terms of His capacity to act. In *Catechetical Orations* Gregory has an extended argument to prove that God's Word has the Power to do what He wills (which is to create). The alternative to this conclusion is very familiar to any reader of *Against Eunomius:*

> [I]t is absolutely necessary to admit that the Power of that Word is as great as the purpose, lest mixture, or concurrence, of contradictions be found in an existence that is incomposite, as would be the case if, in the same purpose, we were to detect both impotence and power, if, that is, there were power to do one thing, but no power to do something else.[63]

To prove his case Gregory establishes an analogy: just as we have speech, breath, and power, God has speech, breath, and power.[64] The first and second of these terms in the analogy obviously correspond to the second and third Persons. What is interesting is that the third term does not correspond to a person (say, to the Father), but to the reality of the previous terms. *Power* is no longer a title for a divine Person but a description of the reality of what the Person is. Human speech and breath are ineffective and insubstantial: they lack power. But God's speech and breath are different: they have power. They each exist as "an essential power,"[65] and as Power there is not just existence but productivity. God's Word, unlike our own, is

> . . . a power essentially and substantially existing, willing all good, and being possessed of strength to execute all its will; and, of a world that is good, this power appetitive and creative of good is the cause. . . . [T]he subsistence of the whole world has been made to depend on the power of the Word. . . .[66]

Gregory adds that all titles of the second Person —that is, Word, Power, Wisdom, God—are equal and acceptable insofar as they express the "eter-

61. Doxological and metaphysical are my own terms, first offered in chapter 3 to distinguish between the two kinds of titles Gregory uses here.

62. *GNO* 2:365:9–10; *NPNF* 5:119.

63. *Catechetical Orations* 1:7–8; Méredier, 12; *NPNF* 5:476

64. Ibid., 2:2–3 and 4:3–4; 16–18 and 22; 5:477–78.

65. Ibid., 2:3; 18; 5:477.

66. Ibid., 5:3; 24; *NPNF* 5:478.

nal power which is creative of all things."[67] I note in passing that this argument from *Catechetical Orations* is a forceful reworking of Origen's reasoning expressed in *On First Principles* 1:2.9. The obvious major difference between Origen's and Gregory's accounts is that for Origen, both δύναμις and πνεῦμα refer to the second Person, while Gregory has made the language into a full trinitarian formula.[68] Origen and Gregory have in common the concern that the power is equal to the will (and vice versa). Yet Origen and Gregory bring this common concern to different theological problems: for Origen, the good thing that God (that is, the Father) has both the will and the power to do is to generate the Son; for Gregory, the good thing that the Son has both the will and the power to do is to create the cosmos. However, both accounts share the understanding that power indicates independent existence. For Origen if something is "another power," it is therefore another existent; for Gregory the presence of power is proof of independent existence.[69] Gregory has attached a traditional Origenist debate over will and power to the contemporary debate over the Son's own creative capacity.[70]

67. Ibid., 5:3; 24; 5:478.

68. When Victorinus offers an analogy between the Soul and God, he says that the soul was given three powers because it is an image of the "*Potentia* and *Sapientia* of God," which is here interpreted as a trinitarian formula: *Potentia* refers to the Son; *Sapientia*, the Holy Spirit and God the Father. Victorinus explains that *Potentia* means the faculty or processional power Life, which is also the primary sense he gives to Word (Λόγος). *Sapientia* has the expected intellectual association with knowledge but refers to the Holy Spirit (see *Against Arius* 1B). (On the other hand, Victorinus is anything but consistent: see *Against Arius* 3.) This triad which Victorinus attributes to the soul is a version of the three powers he attributes to God; namely, to be, to live, and to know. To be is that inward power of identity, while to live and to know are the two powers of the outward motion. Power from power is a formula for what causes participation because it describes the procession of the two powers to live and to understand out of the paternal power to be. These two movements occur both in God and in the soul.

69. A similar understanding of power can be found in Victorinus' *Against Arius* 4: ". . . powers are the things considered as 'being' by their own force, so that they seem to be and to have all that which their existence, by the mature procession of acts, will bring them to have in their operation: but things are called acts when in realizing their natural development, they beget and make appear externally what they are potentially" (Clark 270).

70. In this passage Gregory reworks Origen's and Asterius' two-powers theology. In *On First Principles* 1:1:2.9, Origen says that Christ is a "power from a power" rather than simply saying that Christ is God's own power. (Origen offers this judgment citing 1 Cor. 1:24.) In Gregory's doctrine, power has none of the derivative sense found with Origen. Gregory speaks of God's Word, God's Breath, God's Power. One interesting parallel with Gregory's doctrine is Victorinus. Gregory uses power to describe the reality of the second and third Persons, so that both the Word and the Spirit are each said to exist in fullness (that is, they subsist as independent beings) according to the

A second example of Gregory's understanding of God's existence in terms of His causal capacity may be found in *Life of Moses.* In that work, when Gregory uses the adjective divine—θεία—it usually modifies the term δύναμις, so that θεία δύναμις is his usual term for divinity. In tome 1, there are eleven occasions of θεία modifying δύναμις,[71] only once does it modify φύσις,[72] and on five occasions θεῖα appears in the substantive.[73] The exact same pattern does not hold in tome 2, though the appearance of θεία δύναμις still dominates all uses of θεία. The use of θεία δύναμις in tome 1 fits the theology: the subject of tome 1 is the allegorical interpretation of the events in Moses' life, while the subject of tome 2 is a "contemplation" on Moses' life. In short, Gregory's interest in God as cause leads him to speak of God primarily as θεία δύναμις.

### *The Power Beyond Being*

Gregory's description of the divine power as "transcendent" appears in a wide variety of his writings: *On the Soul and Resurrection,*[74] *On the Premature Death of Infants,*[75] and *Catechetical Orations,*[76] as well as the four books against Eunomius' writings. For *transcendent,* Gregory uses, in order of frequency, ὑπερεκούση, ὑπερκειμένη, or, much less typically, ὑψηλός. The phrase δύναμις ὑπερέχοντος has a significant history, for it appears in *Republic* 509 B.[77] What is striking about Gregory's use of *power* is that

---

fullness of power. Victorinus uses power similarly in his account of the generation in unity of the Godhead. Yet Gregory's use of power does not show the distinctive Porphyrian/Chaldean concept of "one power into three" so prominent in Victorinus' thought. Gregory's use of power depends upon the commonplace, less specialized, understanding that whatever exists has power, an understanding expressed and promulgated in Plato's *Sophist.*

71. In Daniélou's text of *La Vie de Moïse,* 3rd edition, SC, vol. 1 ter (Paris: Les Éditions du Cerf, 1968), see: 17:6, p. 56; 30:1, 68; 31:8–9, 70; 38:9, 76; 42:2, 78; 44:10–11, 82; 49:3, 86; 60:5, 92; 66:3, 96; 71:4–5, 100; 74:10, 102.

72. Ibid., 47:3–4, 84.

73. Ibid., 5:9, 40; 7:2, 7:5, 7:7, 50; 47:7, 84.

74. See, for example, *On the Making of Man* M46, 92C, *NPNF* 5:449.

75. *GNO* 3:2, 77:20, and 78:25; *NPNF* 5:375.

76. See, for example, Méridier, 114:5.

77. The reference to δύναμις ὑπερέχοντος occurs at Shorey, *Republic,* Loeb, 1067. The appearance of δύναμις here suggests the interpretative question to the modern reader: when does textual similarity constitute an implicit reference? If scholars find textual echoes of *Republic* 509 B in a passage, the similarity usually centers on a description of οὐσία: a reference to 509 B is one that speaks of transcending essence. In scholarly practice, an approximate appearance of the phrase ἐπέκεινα τῆς οὐσίας (or ὑπερκειμένα τῆς οὐσίας) is considered to be a reference to 509 B. There

he understands the transcendence of the power to be a guarantee or proof that the transcendent is in itself a productive power. Gregory's interpretation, *via Republic* 509 B, of the productive transcendent power has no precedent or authority in Origen or Eusebius. As Widdicombe has recently shown, Origen uses Plato's text as a means of advancing his own theological description of the Son or Λόγος as the Revelation of the Father.[78] The revelatory function of the Son is described using an implied like from like (as I have called it, an *X from X*) causality, as in this passage from the *Commentary on the Gospel of John:*

And he who beholds Wisdom, which God created before the ages for his works, ascends from knowing Wisdom to Wisdom's Father. . . . First one apprehends the truth, so that one may come to behold the essence, or the power and nature beyond the essence.[79]

Eusebius also interprets *Republic* 509 B as referring to the Father:

Herein Plato says most distinctly that the intellectual essences receive "the good," meaning of course from God, not merely the property of being known, but also their existence and essence; and that "the good" is "not an essence, but far transcends essence in dignity and power." So far he does not regard the ideas as coessential, nor yet suppose that they are unbegotten, because they have received their existence and their essence from Him who is not an essence, but far transcends essence in dignity and power, whom alone the Hebrew oracles with good reason proclaim as God, as being the cause of all things.[80]

---

is no reason why a classical or Hellenistic writer would see this aspect of 509 B as the most interesting and noteworthy feature of the Platonic text. Applying the same standards as one usually finds used for οὐσία, every time Gregory uses δυνάμεως ὑπερκειμένης he refers to 509 B.

78. Peter Widdicombe has argued that in Origen's theology, *Republic* 509 B "acts as a handmaiden to his emphasis on the unique revelatory function of the Son" (*The Fatherhood of God from Origen to Athanasius* [Oxford: Claredon Press, 1994], 37–38, 43). He also suggests that Origen may have thought "Paul's 'eternal power' and 'divinity' [from Rom. 1:20] to be equivalent to Plato's 'dignity and power'" (37–38).

79. *Commentary on the Gospel of John,* 19.6.36–37; FOTC vol. 89, p. 176. Widdicombe concludes that Origen "is not embarking on a precise analysis of how to express transcendence in relation to being; rather, he is using the language of his philosophical contemporaries to support his theological assertion of God's exalted nature, and thus to establish that man is incapable of coming to a knowledge of God except through the Logos" (ibid., 38). My concern is that Widdicombe's account is conceived as an investigation of the relationship between "Scripture" and "Platonic cosmology" and as such operates with too firm a sense of the competing motives between them.

80. *Preparation for the Gospel* 9:2, 6; Favrelle, and des Places, SC:292.154–56; Gifford, 3:2.586. Note the comment that "the Hebrew oracles with good reason proclaim [Him] as God, as being the cause of all things."

The Origen-like relating of the Father to the Son is found in Eusebius' rare use of "transcendent power," for while Gregory refers the transcendent power to the divine nature (or to the Son), Eusebius, like Origen, refers it to the Father alone.[81] Gregory's intellectual precedent and authority for his understanding—*via Republic* 509 B— inherent power of the Transcendent is Plotinus.[82] The resemblance between these two authors in thought and language can be recognized in Plotinus' *Ennead* 5:4.1:

> If the First is perfect, the most perfect of all, and the primal power, it must be the most powerful of all beings and the other powers must imitate it as far as they are able. Now when anything else comes to perfection we see that it produces, and does not endure to remain by itself, but makes something else. . . . as fire warms, snow cools, and drugs act on something else in a way corresponding to their own nature—all imitating the First Principle as far as they are able by tending to ever-lastingness and generosity. How then could the most perfect, the first Good, remain in itself as if it grudged to give of itself, or was impotent, when it is the productive power of all things?[83]

### *Plotinus: The Good Power*

Plotinus' description of the procession of the Intellect from the One as an "over-flowing" of the One is well known and much commented upon. Plotinus is the most articulate and forceful spokesman for the idea that the power of production exists in the First Principle because of what it is. Power belongs to the First Principle and is not a characteristic of an intermediate being, and it is not something that can be delegated away. The productive capacity found in lower causes (the Intellect, the Soul) is a result of the power of the One "running down" with being to the lower hypostases. In the passage from *Ennead* 5:4.1 that I just quoted, Plotinus describes the relationship between fire and heat, snow and cold, etc., as imitations of the first generation by the One. (A metaphysical version, if

81. ". . . [the Son was begotten from the Father] *by the Father's transcendent and inconceivable Will and Power*" (*The Demonstration of the Gospel* 4:3; Heikel, 154:20–21; Ferrar, 1:168, emphasis added).

82. For a typical Plotinian interpretation of *Republic* 509 B, see "[Plato calls the One] the Good and that which is beyond Intellect and 'beyond being'" (*Ennead* V 1:8:7–9; Armstrong, Loeb, 5:41). See also, "[The First Principle] . . . is a great power, the greatest indeed of all, and arrives at being and substance: for that Principle is 'beyond being'. That is the productive power of all things . . ." (ibid., V 4, 2; 5:149).

83. Armstrong, Loeb 5:143.

you will, of "We love because He first loved us.") The most important statement of Plotinus' doctrine of the One's productivity is given in *Ennead* 5:1.6.[84] The specific language of 5:1.6 bears directly on the subject at hand:

[The activity of the One is] a radiation from it while it remains unchanged, like the bright light of the sun which, so to speak, runs round it, springing from it continually while it remains unchanged. All things which exist, as long as they remain in being, necessarily produce from their own substances, in dependence on their present power, a surrounding reality directed to what is outside them, a kind of image of the archetypes from which it was produced: fire produces the heat which comes from it; snow does not only keep its cold inside itself. Perfumed things show this particularly.[85]

Much of this passage will seem familiar to any reader of Gregory. Perhaps the most suggestive sign of influence is Plotinus' and Gregory's combination of fire and heat and snow and cold with the example of fragrance, for in neither Origen nor Eusebius are all these similes brought together conceptually or textually. Plotinus seems likely to have influenced Eusebius' choice of fragrance to describe the product (the Word) as an image of its source (God). But the general sense of Plotinus' passage is better reflected in Gregory's theology: the kind of being God is means that God will produce.[86]

84. There are several reasons why this text is worth noting. The presence of *Ennead* V 1 in Cappadocian writings is so ubiquitous that to a large degree if one speaks of Plotinian influence on the Cappadocians, one means the influence of *Ennead* V 1. *Ennead* V 1 seems to have been known by all the Cappadocians; indeed, *Ennead* V 1 is one of the few works of Plotinus that we can be certain that Gregory knew. Furthermore, portions of this *Ennead* are quoted by Eusebius and are known to Cyril of Alexandria, suggesting that *Ennead* V 1 was one of the first texts by Plotinus to have any influence on Christian thought. See Rist, "Basil's 'Neoplatonism,'" 162–64, 192–93, 209 and 215; and also Dehnhard's commentary on *De Spiritu* in *Das Problem der Abhangigkeit des Basilius von Plotin,* Patristiche Texte und Studien, Band 3 (Berlin: Walter de Gruyter & Co., 1964). Meijering, *God Being History,* 105, thinks that Gregory of Nazianzus' reference in *Oration* 29.2 to the doctrine of "over-flowing" is to *Ennead* V 2, 7–9. Norris, *Faith Gives Fullness,* 44, follows Gallay, SC 250:181, in finding the doctrine of "over-flowing" in *Ennead* V 1, 6. Gregory is more likely to be referring to *Ennead* III 8, 10.

85. *Ennead* V 1, 6:28–37; Armstrong, Loeb 5:31.

86. Meijering argues that Origen and Athanasius shared a "dislike [of] the idea of an inactive God in splendid isolation" (*God Being History,* 99). This common feeling led Origen to postulate an eternal creation and Athanasius an eternal begetting (while denying the eternity of the world). Origen, Meijering says, "stresses the eternity of the Son as God's creative Power." Of Athanasius, Meijering says, "as the eternal Father of the eternal Son, who is His creative Power, the one God was never lonely, inactive and in splendid isolation . . ." (100). What Meijering misses is that the

Conceptually what Plotinus and Gregory have in common is their insistence that the First Principle is known to be the kind of Being that produces. Both Plotinus[87] and Gregory draw conclusions about the First Cause from what each produces: the One produces Mind and, through it, Soul; God generates the Son, and through Him, creates the cosmos. Eusebius had already spoken of the Son as the image of God because of the way He was generated (that is, as an odor from perfume). Gregory is less inclined to think of the Son as transparent to the Father than to regard the fact of the Son's existence as an indicator of the kind of existence the Father lives: a life-giving kind of existence.[88] Similarly, the cosmos indicates that the Son lives the same kind of existence as the Father, since creation is proof of the life-giving existence of the Son. Thus a recurring name for the Son is Life-giving Power.[89] Gregory makes the same kind of argument for the Holy Spirit: "[T]he absence of divergence between the being of the Son and that of the Spirit is indicated by the identity of power [δύναμις] to give existence."[90]

As I have already mentioned, both Plotinus and Gregory conceive of this productivity as an expression of the Good, a doctrine Plotinus can offer with the apparent support of *Republic* 509 B. Gregory, no less than Plotinus, characterizes this productivity as following from God's goodness. Goodness and power are recurring virtues in the lists Gregory regularly

---

eternal delegation of creative power is still delegation: a doctrine that solves the problem of God's "splendid isolation" does not necessarily solve the problem of God's inactivity vis à vis creation. What is Meijering claiming for Origen that could not be claimed as well for Philo? Furthermore, there is nothing in Meijering's description of the Athanasian solution to the doctrinal problem of God's loneliness that could not be attributed to Eusebius or even to Eunomius.

87. See Rist, "There is some kind of 'necessary' connection between the two [that is, fire and heat], and it is that 'necessary' connection which we must bear in mind when we think of the importance and significance of this particular metaphor. Heat emanates from fire because fire is what it is.... [Thus the procession of the Intellect from the One presents the question:] What is the One that it emanates *Nous* and Being?" (*Plotinus: The Road to Reality,* 69).

88. Hanson quotes with approval Holl's summary of Gregory's trinitarian theology: "Holl finely says of him [that is, Gregory] that for him God was a life-imparting power existing in three forms" (*The Search,* 730). Hanson's remark is another example of how the concept of power is used *en passant.*

89. For references to the Son as "Life-giving" Power (a favorite title of Gregory's), see in *GNO* 1:120:16, 230:20; in *GNO* 2, see: 21:3, 32:2, 126:7, 132:23, 214:19, 243:21, 302:14.

90. *GNO* 1:142:27; Hall, 93.

provides as criteria of common being, in particular as criteria of common divinity.[91] The best indication of the importance of power and goodness as criteria or signs of divine being is the summary of his faith Gregory offers in *On the Holy Trinity:* "[W]e confess three Persons . . . there is one goodness, and one power, and one Godhead."[92] "[We] speak of the goodness as one, and of the power, and the Godhead, and all such attributes in the singular."[93] Similarly in *Catechetical Oration* Gregory refers to the Word as the Power that wills all good and is creative of all good as its cause. This goodness motivates the Son's creative activity.[94]

The difference between Plotinus' and Gregory's description of the generative power as the Good is that Plotinus makes explicit appeals to *Republic* 508 B–509 B for his identification of the First Productive Power with the Good, while Gregory uses language that suggests the authority of 509 B without clearly invoking the text. For example, in *On the Soul and Resurrection* Gregory says that the "real Good" possesses a nature "that surpasses every idea that we can form of the Good and transcends all other power. . . ."[95]

What the Cappadocians reject in Plotinus' account of procession from the One is the sense of the real inferiority of the Intellect compared to the One and the inevitability of generation.[96] Eunomius already had savaged

91. Gregory says, for example, "[Eunomius brings] the concept of size into the debate" to argue that one Person "is superior or inferior in goodness, power, wisdom and whatever else is piously attributed to the divine" (*GNO* 1:95:9–11; Hall, 69). Gregory's reply is that there "is no lack of wisdom or power or any other good thing in one to whom goodness is not something acquired . . ." (*GNO* 1:95:12–15; Hall, 69). Or again, "[there is] no greater or lesser. . . . of power, glory wisdom, kindness or any other good one can think of . . ." (GNO 1:126:11–16; Hall, 89). And finally Gregory lists the signs of divinity as "deity itself, wisdom and power and being good, [being] judge, just, mighty, patient . . ." (*GNO* 1:161:24–25; Hall, 103). The list of virtues goes on, though the repeated suggestion of 1 Cor. 1:24, power and wisdom, is clear.

92. *GNO* 3:1 5:18 ff., *NPNF* 5:326–327.

93. Ibid., 3:1 6:10 ff.; 5:327.

94. *Catechetical Orations* 5:2; Méredier, 25; *NPNF* 5:478.

95. M 46, 92C; *NPNF* 5:449.

96. Meijering says that "[Gregory of Nazianzus'] objection to Plotinus' doctrine of the generation is that it implies that this generation is an act against the will of the One" (*God Being History,* 105). Elsewhere Meijering notes that the Plotinian procession involves subordination since what is caused is inferior to the cause. He implies that the Cappadocians were not as sensitive to the inherent subordinationism of Plotinian language as Athanasius would have been because the Cappadocians acknowledge a kind of priority to the Father as cause (see pages 94 and 108–9). One weakness of Meijering's analysis is that he treats the question of the freedom of God's will as

homoiousian and homoousian theology for removing God's freedom. The Cappadocians were sensitive to this criticism and were undoubtedly careful not to present the Eunomians with anything to support this attack. The consistent Cappadocian rejection of Plotinian "inevitable process" language is in part an honest expression of their distance from Plotinus. But I suspect that such rejections are also partially motivated by an attempt to dissociate their theology from Plotinus before the Eunomians could, with some effect, associate Plotinian-like concepts with orthodox theology. In the *Apology* Eunomius accused those who taught the eternal generation of the Son of teaching the eternity of the world.[97] The argument for God's freedom was always the strong point of anti-Nicene theology, while the open flank of anything even resembling Nicene theology was the question of God's will in the generation of the Son.[98] Gregory's idea of divine productivity is indeed heavily indebted to the kind of productivity described in *Ennead* 5:1.6, but its Christian appropriation requires a correct appreciation of God's will.

### *Two Activities in One Power*

Gregory's own account of the Son's generation brings him to ask what "generation" means.[99] He finds that there are four senses attached to the term: first, the generation by art of something worked in matter for the sake of an imagined end-product; second, nature's generation of continu-

---

though it were not an issue under intense polemical pressure, not simply historically (that is, from Origen and Arius) but, more acutely, from contemporary anti-Nicenes like Eunomius. While he acknowledges Arius' theology as an alternative that Athanasius is opposed to, the issue of God's will is described primarily as an issue in a debate between Origen and Athanasius, or among Plotinus, Athanasius, and Gregory of Nazianzus. It is not clear from Meijering's comments what would be different in Athanasius' theology if Arius had never been born—except that Athanasius would not have had to misrepresent Origen.

97. *Apology* 22:10–12; *Extant Works*, 63.

98. The virtue of Gregg's and Groh's book, *Early Arianism*, is that it highlights the importance of the freedom of God's will for Arian and Eusebian theology. Aside from Meijering's discussion of the doctrines of God's will held by Origen, Athanasius, and Gregory of Nazianzus already referred to, one can also see Stead's "The Freedom of the Will and the Arian Controversy," 245–57. Stead is primarily concerned with the issue of the Son's free will in Arian and Athanasian doctrine, but pages 253 ff. treat God's free will.

99. Generation is γέννησις. This paragraph and what follows immediately summarizes Gregory's thought at *GNO* 2:195:2–2197:5; *NPNF* 5:204. Hanson gives a helpful account of this aspect of Gregory's thought (*The Search*, 728–29).

ous life, such as the life generated and preserved in a species despite the death of individuals of that species; third, generation by efflux found in the relationship between the sun and its ray(s), a lamp and its light, or an ointment and its scent; and finally, generation by an immaterial that results in material products, as when a thought "generates" a word. After Gregory provides this list of the different possible senses of generation, he makes the point that, as with terms like "hand," "eye," or "foot," when generation is used of God, it must be stripped of its material implications. When the material connotations are removed, Gregory accepts that three of the four different senses of generation are implied in the different titles of the second Person. For example, "Son" refers to the second kind of generation listed above; "Brightness of Glory" and "Breath of God" refer to the third kind of generation; and "Word" refers to the fourth.

However, it is Gregory's explanation of how "generation" is used of God that should be noted. Words like "fingers," "hand," and "arm" signify God's operative power but only when the corporeal sense of these terms is taken away. So too, when the Holy Spirit reveals God's

> . . . formative power, it [the Holy Spirit] calls that particular activity by the name of "generation" because the word which expresses the Divine Power must descend to our lowliness. . . .[100]

Gregory then assimilates the four kinds of generation into two kinds of activities by the divine power: generation truly called and creation. These are both activities of the divine power and nature, but each activity is the specific property of a particular Person of the Trinity: the Father generates the Son, and the Son creates the cosmos.

When generation is used of the divine power, its meaning is related to three of the four senses of generation just described. The one sense of generation that is not connoted in the phrase "divine generation" is the first sense that Gregory gives, namely, that of art. Gregory attaches this sense of generation as art exclusively and entirely to the act of creation. Yet the interesting feature of Gregory's reasoning is that because creation is recognized as a *bona fide* sense of generation and because creation is a generation by the same power that generates the Son, Gregory feels able to

100. *GNO* 2:198:79; *NPNF* 5:205.

clarify the kind of act divine generation is by examining the kind of act creation is. In other words, because creation and generation are activities of the same power, there are common features to both activities. Gregory uses this line of reasoning at least twice.[101] One occasion is in *Against Eunomius* 3:6, where he says:

> . . . just as the word which tells us in reference to God of the generation of the creation . . . declare[d] that its material substance, its place, its time, and the like, had their existence in the power [δύναμις] of His will, so here too in speaking of the Son, it leaves out of sight . . . all things which human natures sees in earthly generation. . . .[102]

This comparison of the two activities in the same Power is not an isolated occasion in Gregory's thought, for the same comparison occurs in another tome of book 3:

> . . . if they agree that the one activity [of creation] is exercised by the Divine Power [δύναμις] without passion, let them not quarrel about the other: for if He creates without labor or matter, He surely also begets without labor or flux.[103]

These two passages show clearly the extent to which Gregory's trinitarian formulations are shaped by the polemical context. Both the evident concern to describe a generation free of passion and the description of that generation in positive terms related to (but not identical to) creation are responses to Eunomius' theology. The strength of Gregory's argument in

101. The idea that the concept of creation should be used to correct ambiguities in the concept of generation (for example, passion) is a distinctive feature of Basil of Ancyra's theology. Basil's argument is that the suggestion of passion or materialism in the terms "Father" and "Son" can be corrected by applying to generation the impassibility implicit in the relationship between Creator and created (see Epiphanius' *Panarion* 73.3.1–4.2; Holl, 271–72). With this argument Basil can offer a correct understanding of the kind of relationship named by the titles "Father" and "Son." These are the titles that Basil wants to defend as the primary descriptions of the relationship between the first and second Persons.

Gregory's willingness to relate generation to creation as two activities of a single power thus owes something to Basil, though I must emphasize that this debt to Basil is another example of the polemical origins of Gregory's theology. Basil developed the conceptual association between generation and creation to purify the concept of divine generation and so save it as a *bona fide* divine activity. Gregory's comparison of the two activities is offered for the exact same reason: to remove passion from generation. Gregory then builds upon Basil's original argument, however, by making the relationship between generation and creation analogous to the relationship between the Father and the Son.

102. *GNO* 2:198:21–27; *NPNF* 5:205.

103. Ibid., 2:73:9–12; 5:159.

these passages depends in large part on the way in which he has managed to use his own positive doctrine of creation (and the anti-Nicene emphasis on creation) as a defense against the problem of passion. The Power that creates without passion also generates without passion, for creating and generating are activities of the same power.[104]

Both Gregory and Eunomius share the judgment that the kind of unity that exists between the activities of generating and creating exists between the agents of these activities, so Gregory's task is to argue that the activities are united in a common nature. The two pivotal steps in this argument are, first, the attribution of generating and creating to the same power, and second, the understanding of power in its full "metaphysical" or "ontological" sense. Eunomian theology clearly separated the subject of these two activities, not so much by associating specific activities with specific persons—Gregory does that too—but by keeping the relationship between the acting persons and their activities as a moral kind exclusively. For Gregory the relationship between the activities of generating and creating (and thus between the persons who generate and create) is a natural one because they are activities in a power.[105] Gregory goes into some detail establishing his understanding of what the unity is between nature and power; and his understanding is recognizably based upon authoritative traditions of use.[106]

104. This argument is a peculiar expression of the "communication of idioms," though obviously not between persons, but between activities. If creating is a passionless activity, and creating and generating are activities of the same power, then generating is a passionless act because both activities have the same source. The idea that all the activities of a single power would share a certain passionlessness follows from the kind of reasoning evident in *On the Soul and Resurrection* and *On the Making of Man.*

105. Meijering remarks that Gregory of Nazianzus differs from Athanasius "who emphatically denies that God's will to create can be likened to God's will to generate" (*God Being History,* 107). Gregory comfortably moves from God's will in generating to God's will in creating, something Athanasius could never do. Gregory of Nyssa is also comfortable with the notion of there being some similarities between generating and creating.

106. Some scholars have described Nicene theology precisely in terms of its rejection of Origen's "logical link between the generation of the Son and the existence of the world." George Florovsky, for example, offers this very description of Athanasius' thought in "The Concept of Creation in Saint Athanasius," *Studia Patristica* 6:4 (1962): 36–57, (esp. 39). As I have tried to show, developmental language more accurately describes the relationship between Origen's theology and late fourth-century trinitarian theology. In this case, Gregory both depends on and develops the traditional association of generation and creation to his advantage. The "link" between generation and creation may no longer be "logical," but it is revelatory of the divine nature.

## *Eunomius and the Power of Names*

Gregory finds two particular notions joined together in Eunomius' reasoning. The first is the idea that God's productive capacity, both as Father and Creator, is separate from God's essence or nature.[107] The second idea is that real knowledge of God is provided through language. For Gregory the second point follows upon the first since the separation of the productive capacity from the nature means that the products of this capacity (whether conceived as generated or created) cannot be understood as true signs of the nature. If the productive capacity is separate from the nature, then any products cannot be indicative of the nature but only indicative of that extra-natural capacity to produce. Despite his talk of "products indicating the dignities of the activities which produced them," Eunomius fundamentally rejects the idea that a product provides knowledge of its producer.

This negation follows from Eunomius' rejection (or rather, his qualification into irrelevance) of the doctrine that the Son is the image of God.[108] The Son, according to Eunomius, is not the image of God, for that would mean that He was the image of, that is, similar to, the essence or nature of God. The Son is rather the image of (and thus is similar to) the activity

107. In the pagan debate, the distinction between Father and Creator (a phrase that originates with *Timaeus* 28 C) was used to separate the Father—the First Principle—from the messy task of dealing with (or being morally responsible for) primary matter and evil. Making order out of chaos was the task of the Creator that the Father produced. In Christianity a distinction between Father and Creator may be one of several kinds. Eunomius distinguished between the Father (or rather, God) and the Creator (the Son) because, as with the pagans, the Father produced only the Creator, and the Creator produces the cosmos. Eunomius differs from the pagans in his adamant denial of any preexistent matter; creation is definitely from nothing. But from another point of view, the distinction between Father and Creator is lost since the kind of activity that characterizes each Person is the same: creation. Eunomius does not recognize the difference between the two, since all divine production is creation. The Father creates the Son, the Son creates the cosmos. See Maurice Wiles's handy summary of the debate over the phrase "Father and Creator" in "The Philosophy in Christianity," in *The Philosophy in Christianity*, ed. George Vesey, 44–45.

108. Eunomius offers a carefully worded doctrine of the Son as image in the *Apology*. When the *Apology* was given in its original oral form at the Council of Constantinople 360, Eunomius' theology still resembled the then triumphant Homoian theology in several points. I take Eunomius' tortured version of an Image theology to be his attempt to find common ground with the Homoians who owed a debt to Eusebius of Caesarea. In the *Second Apology*, Eunomius abandons the attempt to speak of the Son as the Image of God.

that produced Him, and, as such, can reveal something about that activity but can reveal nothing more. The peculiar union in Eunomius' theology of the denial of a power of production in the divine nature and an emphasis on the revelatory function of names causes Gregory's rebuttal to stress God's connatural power to produce and the revelatory function of the products of this power, not only in the case of the generated Son but also in the case of the created cosmos. We learn more about God from looking at the universe that God's power created, Gregory says, than from any words.

For Eunomius, a name signifies the essence completely and exhaustively: "We do not understand his essence to be one thing and the meaning of the word which designates it to be something else. Rather, we take it that his substance is the very same as that which is signified by his name. . . ."[109] Eunomius' claim that the name signifies the essence can usefully be contrasted with Gregory's understanding that the δύναμις signifies the essence (or, as Gregory prefers, the nature). For Gregory, God's nature is communicated by His powers or properties; Gregory diminishes the importance of our knowledge of God *via* words, for he contrasts this knowledge with the knowledge we gain through God's properties and the effects of these properties. For Eunomius, God's properties reduce to a single trait, unbegotten, and there is nothing in creation that can communicate the unproduced since there is nothing in creation that is unproduced. Only true names communicate essences—and the fact that this communication does not proceed by analogy or participation must be emphasized. Yet this communication is complete, for there is nothing in the essence that is not communicated by the name.

This point is made clear by comparing Eunomius' understanding of activity to that of name. For Eunomius, nothing that is properly attributable to the essence can be attributed to the activity. But, the opposite seems to be the case regarding the name: nothing that is properly attributable to the essence is excluded from the name, once allowance is made for the different kinds of existence that essences and names have. Yet the name and the essence are not identical, and the name does not exist in any quasi-

109. *Apology* 12:7–10; *Extant Works*, 48–49. See also his *Second Apology, GNO* 1:399:23–25; *NPNF* 5:310.

hypostatic sense, as might be the case with Philo.[110] But although the name is not identical with the essence, the degree of unity between the two is high. The high degree of unity between essence and name, as opposed to the low degree of unity between essence and activity, may be suggested by an observation: One can imagine in Eunomius' system that God (an essence) could have been, and indeed was, without His activity, but it is not clear that Eunomius' system allows that God could have been, or ever was, without His name.

A similar degree of unity with the essence applies to God's authority as well: God could never have been without His authority, for it is a result of His Uncaused Essence. For example, Eunomius equates being free of external authority with having no prior cause when he refers to God as that "essence which transcends all authority and is wholly incapable of undergoing generation. . . ."[111] In effect the authority and name are coeternal with the essence, but the eternal coexistence of these two with the essence does not pose a theological problem for Eunomius since he makes no ontological claims for the authority and the name, while he does make ontological claims for the activity. Gregory and Eunomius agree that the accuracy of a sign or revelation depends on its relationship with what is revealed. Names are trustworthy for Eunomius because God Himself makes them and uses them. Names have no such origin for Gregory.

### *Language's Dualism*

I have already referred to Gregory's concern over the inherent ambiguity of language. The first warning of this problematic ambiguity appears in *On the Soul and Resurrection*, when Macrina says that the danger of dialectic is that it can be used for good or evil, which is the same kind of problem the dialogue describes in the passions.[112] A more thorough account of the inherent ambiguity of language is found in *Against Eunomius* 1, where Gregory says that each word contains an implicit reference to its contrary. Language contains these contrary references because it mirrors the existence of the contrary elements in the created world. Just as each object,

110. According to H. A. Wolfson, *Philo*, 2:135–37.
111. *Apology* 20:10–12; *Extant Works*, 58–61.
112. M 46 42C.

each quality, "contains" its opposite, so too each noun, each adjective, "refers to" its opposite. The presence of this implicit contrary reference in language accounts for the inappropriateness of using words to describe God since God's existence contains no opposition. There is a clear sense in Gregory's thought that the cosmos has an important role as an indicator or sign of God. Despite the analogous presence of "opposition" in both material creation and language, Gregory is emphatic about the ability of creation to reveal something of its Creator, while he has no confidence that language can do the same. If both creation and language "refer" ambiguously, why does Gregory regard creation as a positive indicator of God's existence? There are several answers.

The first such reason is that Eunomius' theology demonstrates with a clear and present danger the limitations of language. Gregory's response to this danger in *Against Eunomius* builds upon what I take to have been a traditional "pious" suspicion of sophists and dialecticians (expressed with some finesse by Macrina in *On the Soul and Resurrection*).[113] This suspicion reacts to the claims that are made for the objectivity of language—indeed, the claim of objectivity that language itself may seem to invoke.[114] Creation, by contrast, makes no such claims and invokes no sense of autonomy: for Gregory, creation cries out the hand of its Creator.[115] The specter of paganism and panentheism that troubled Eusebius (at least formally) is dead

113. Ibid.

114. The extensive search conducted by scholars such as Daniélou, Wickham, Rist, Mortley, and Wiles for precedents for Eunomius' "natural" theory of language makes one conclusion clear: there were Christians before Eunomius who offered theories of language that resembled his, even if none were identical to it. Clement and Origen (and Origen's student, Eusebius), in particular, speak of this theory of language. Macrina's and Gregory's cautious approach to speech may reflect the influence of someone like Methodius (that is, an intelligent anti-Origenist) whose influence appears elsewhere in Gregory's thinking.

115. At one point in *Against Eunomius* 2, Gregory imagines the revelatory content of the heavens as a speech: when you humans gaze on we stars and planets you see that everything depends upon an unknowable and sublime Power. This statement, Gregory says, "is not given in articulate speech, but by the things which are seen, and it instills in our minds the knowledge of divine power [δύναμις] more than if speech proclaimed it with a voice" (see *GNO* 1:290:29–291:11; *NPNF* 5:272–73). The same account of the cosmos is expressed, without obvious polemical context, in Gregory's *Eleventh Homily* in the *Commentary on the Song of Songs.* "The soul sees the heavenly beauty. . . . The earth is sustained by God who embraces it. He changes the functions of the stars above. He sustains the great variety of living beings. . . . All these manifest God's power" (*Song of Songs,* trans. Cassimir McCambley [Brookline: Hellenic College Press, 1987], 207).

for Gregory; he shows no concern for the dangers of idolatry or panentheism (or even atheism).[116]

Another reason why Gregory understands the cosmos as an important indicator or sign of God's nature follows from Gregory's epistemology. While Gregory is regularly described by scholars as a "Platonist,"[117] in fact he contrasts the inherent certainty of sense knowledge with the inherent uncertainty of abstract knowledge (or in Gregory's terms, knowledge of sensibles versus knowledge of intelligibles). Sense knowledge is clear and certain; knowledge by intellect alone is neither.[118] This positive evaluation of the world of sensibles leads Gregory to see creation as a trustworthy sign of its Creator; indeed, one striking feature of Gregory's theology is the confidence with which he believes that the evidence of creation bears out his theology.[119] This confidence depends on Gregory's theological shift

116. Eusebius writes as though polytheism and pantheism are still real threats; Gregory no longer shares this concern. Eusebius casts his doctrines in the form of a polemic against this kind of paganism, while Gregory casts his arguments as a polemic against Manichaeism (which he finds implicit in Eunomius' theology). Whether Eusebius actually understood his task as a refutation of paganism or simply found it convenient to use polytheism/pantheism as a rhetorical type of his opponents, and whether Gregory actually understood Eunomius' theology as Manichaeism under a different guise or simply found it convenient to describe Eunomius' theology in this way, the two characterizations of respective opponents are noteworthy. Eusebius' battle with polytheism/pantheism establishes him as someone who is trying to cleanse creation of its association with divinity, while Gregory's battle with "Manichaeism" establishes him as someone who is not going to consider creation sullied or evil (since this is part of what "Manichaeism" means).

117. By "Platonist" is meant that Gregory believes in an intelligible realm of transcendent Ideas. Charles McGrath, for example, finds Gregory's Platonism in his division of the created world into "sensible and intelligible": ". . . a more clear and succinct indication of the extent to which Gregory's metaphysical approach is influenced by Plato would be hard to find" ("Gregory of Nyssa's Doctrine on the Knowledge of God" [Ph.D. diss., Fordham University, 1964], 38). However, see below: for Gregory intelligibles have a limited epistemological role—not true for a Platonist.

118. In *Against Eunomius* 2, Gregory recognizes two kinds of objects of knowledge, the sensible and the intelligible. Sensible phenomena provide objects of knowledge that are available for all to know and can be known with certainty. By contrast, human faculties of knowledge are not always equal to the task of knowing intelligible phenomena, for frequently thoughts fail to comprehend and language fails to communicate. Gregory seems to believe that language about sensibles is intrinsically more accurate than speech about intelligibles. Speech about sensibles never stands in for the object since the object is directly available and is always connected by direct knowledge of the object. Speech about intelligibles lacks a clear and consistent paradigm against which it can be tested (see *GNO* 1:393:14 ff.).

119. The close association Gregory makes between "to be God" and "to be Creator" also appears in Gregory of Nazianzus' *Oration* 28, written against the Eunomians at virtually the same time as Gregory of Nyssa wrote his *Against Eunomius.* The description of God's nature in *Oration* 28 dwells at length on God's role as creator and the evidence the cosmos gives of God as creator. See, for example, *Oration* 28:5 and 6, and 28:22–31. As I remarked above, however, the role of

from the one Creator reasoning to the one God reasoning I have outlined, but in Gregory's case this shift is supported by his definite sense of the veracity and the virtue of material creation.[120]

*A Pro-Nicene Cosmology*

Gregory believes that the size and intricacy of the cosmos indicates the character of the Power that created it; namely, that the creative Power is capable beyond our imagination, yet it is one or unified. This cosmological piety is not unique to Gregory or even to Christians, but it is nonetheless interesting that Gregory not only accepts this appreciation of the revelatory content of creation, he emphasizes it. The most important Christian precedent in this emphasis is Eusebius of Caesarea, for Gregory regularly takes arguments advanced by Eusebius to prove the unity of the Creator and uses them instead to prove the unity of the Godhead. This is an important point.[121] By using Eusebius' arguments, Gregory keeps his own theological language familiar or traditional, and he can build upon the detailed arguments established by Eusebius and, in some cases, Origen. More importantly, Gregory meets anti-Nicene theology in its own emphasis: the Son's role as creator. Indeed, what becomes more and more clear is that Gregory's theology, and pro-Nicene apologetic generally, used the cosmological

cosmology in the theologies of the two Gregories differs from its role in Basil's theology: God's creative activity does not have the polemical significance for Basil that it has for the two Gregories.

120. Another example of Gregory's "realism," if I may call it that, is his argument against Eunomius' theory of a God-given natural language. Basil had advanced a theory of ἐπίνοια, which Gregory certainly does not abandon, but Gregory's own addition to the case against a natural language is his own: many (if not all) of the languages known to Gregory can claim ancient origins, and they all have different words for different objects. Eunomius' theory flies in the face of the evidence of these—all equally authoritative—examples of the diversity of the action of the human intellect. Gregory is not prepared to reject the testimony of human history, and in Gregory's opinion, Eunomius' theory requires precisely this rejection of the evidence of history. Another passage from Gregory exemplifies his linguistic "realism." In book 2, Gregory speaks of how God's love for humanity is evident in God's use of language, and ". . . so the divine power [δύναμις] . . . though exalted far above our nature and inaccessible to all approach, like a tender mother who joins in inarticulate utterances of her baby, gives to our human nature what it is capable of receiving. . . ." Gregory goes on to compare God's relationship to human speech to a shepherd's use of clucking and whistling to guide his flock (*GNO* 1:348:16–349:26; *NPNF* 5:292).

121. Undoubtedly Gregory is indebted to his brother for specific cosmological doctrines as well as for Basil's example in turning to cosmological material, such as the *Hexaemeron*. Yet Basil's interest in cosmology and God's role as Creator does not include a sense of the trinitarian and polemical implications of these topics.

role of God as a means of gaining insight into God's own life; that is, a movement from what many modern theologians would call the economic to the immanent. This movement is possible precisely because of the unity of nature and power.

Like Eusebius, Gregory finds in creation evidence not only of the scope of God's creative capacity but evidence of God's continuing presence for or to creation. This latter evidence of God's presence is the more important for Eusebius as a Christian because God's presence in and for creation is the special, indeed, the defining, role of the second Person. Creation reveals the Mind that brought it into existence and that maintains it in order and indeed in existence:

> [The] gospel teaches us not to stand in awe of the visible parts of the cosmos . . . but to marvel only at the mind which in all these [parts] exists unseen, and which creates both the whole and each several part; and to regard as God one sole Divine Power [δύναμις] pervading and ordering all things, being in its nature incorporeal and intelligent.[122]

I have already discussed how this line of reasoning leads Eusebius to argue for the unity (or rather, the uniqueness) of the Creator from an analogy with the unity of the mind that rules over the multiple faculties and parts of the body. What should be noted additionally is that Eusebius' argument makes positive use of creation as an indicator of the character of God: from creation we know that God is one (not many); we know that He is all-pervasive but apart, mind not matter; and that He is concerned for his creatures because He remains present, through His Λόγος, to order and to preserve created existence. This is what mankind can learn from creation once the Gospel has removed the error of polytheism and pantheism.[123] There is nothing in this summary that Gregory could not agree to, except, of course, to query what kind of oneness is this that Eusebius is so emphatic about. Both Gregory and Eusebius are content to derive this description of God from creation, though Gregory is, in *Against Eunomius* at least, more positive about the cosmos itself than Eusebius was.

122. *Preparation for the Gospel* 3:6, 5–6; Gifford, 3:1, 105; des Places, SC 228:178. Earlier I quoted a similar passage from Eusebius at *Preparation for the Gospel* 7:11.

123. I say "the error of polytheism and pantheism" rather than "the errors" because Eusebius treats the two fundamentally as manifestation of the same kind of religion.

However, in one important point Gregory disagrees with Eusebius. Gregory understands the divine productive power that is the cause of creation to exist in the divine nature as a power exists in a nature. Therefore creation can be a sign of God because creation is the product of a power that exists in God's nature. Language, by contrast, is not a product of this power and therefore lacks this authentication. Eusebius cannot quite bring himself to follow the concept *power*—or the term δύναμις—to this kind of conclusion. The unity between divine nature and productive power that Gregory describes surpasses Eusebius' theology. Their difference on this point is due precisely to their different understanding of the status of the second Person.

The case can easily be made that Gregory's precedent and authority for associating Power, Wisdom, and Goodness with God's creative function lies in Scripture and Christian exegesis. What about pagan sources? I have argued the Platonic background of power and goodness, but the constellation of "Power," "Wisdom," and "Goodness" to describe divine nature seems in itself to reflect Gregory's exegetical synthesis of a Christian source for "Power and Wisdom" (1 Cor. 1:24) and a pagan source for the link between "Power" and "Goodness" (for example, *Republic* 509B).[124] But now the context of cosmology, with its questions of teleology and revelation, can lead us to other possible sources.

In at least two of his works, Galen (whose influence we have already discerned) makes strong arguments for the existence of a creator (that is, a Demiurge) based on arguments from design. In *On the Use of Parts,* Galen offers a substantial and heartfelt rebuttal to those who doubt the goodness of the world and the divine intention that shaped it. The same argument appears in *On the Common Doctrines of Hippocrates and Plato.* For example, in *On the Common Doctrines,* Galen remarks that while it is useless (from an empirical point of view) to argue over whether the cosmos is eternal or not, what is clear is the existence of divine providence in the cosmos.[125]

What is striking about these two arguments from design for divine providence is the presence of the linked language of power, wisdom, and

124. Rom. 1:20 would allow Gregory to associate Power with creation (even if via Origen), thus paralleling Plato's use of power in the context of creation in the *Republic* passage.

125. *On the Common Doctrines* 7:12–13; de Lacy, 589.

goodness. According to *On the Use of Parts,* when one understands the cosmos properly, one knows the "power, wisdom, and goodness" of its maker. Goodness is seen in the "best possible ordering" of the cosmos and the sharing of benefits. Wisdom is required for God to know "how everything should best be ordered." Power is required "to have accomplished his will in all things."[126] In *On the Common Doctrines,* Galen finds that the beauty of the universe, its order and design, and even "the fashioning of our bodies" reveal the power and wisdom of a good and benevolent God.[127]

Obviously Galen's understanding of divine power, wisdom, and goodness does not hypostasize these qualities: they remain as attributes (in the normal sense) of the Demiurge. Galen is interested in arguing not for God's transcendence, but rather for God's providence.[128] But the terms are linked in the understanding that there are these three particular attributes of God and that these three are decisive in accounts of divine providence and creation. In Galen's philosophy, the recognition of divine power, wisdom, and goodness is the ultimate theological judgment: nothing more can be said about God; this recognition is Galen's "true hymn of praise to our creator."[129]

The likelihood that Gregory knew Galen's writings is strong. The fact that Galen's theological use of "power, wisdom, and goodness" appears in at least two different kinds of works indicates the importance of this language for Galen. The appearance in different genres of *power* and *wisdom* increases the probability that Gregory would have encountered the terminology, although one can comfortably say that both the moral analysis of *On the Common Doctrines* and the physiology of *On the Use of Parts* would have interested Gregory. But I am content at this point to note the pagan use of the same language that figured in Gregory's theology. When Gregory spoke of divine power and wisdom (and goodness) in the context of creation, he was using honored scriptural language, doctrinally developed by

126. *On the Use of Parts* 3 [1.174], 189.

127. *On the Common Doctrines* 9:3; de Lacy, 599.

128. In general Galen represents a branch of Middle Platonism that has no interest in transcendental speculations beyond the fact of there being a good Maker: Galen has no doctrines of triadology or transcendent generations. He shows no signs of multiplying transcendent existents such as Numenius, *Chaldean Oracles,* and Neoplatonism generally exhibit.

129. *On the Use of Parts* 3 [1.174], 189.

authorities of the faith. Yet such language would also have carried philosophical authority, and the cosmological connotations would have supported Gregory's reading of divine power in terms of creation and providence.

### *Conclusion*

The opposition that scholars of various perspectives have drawn between cosmological or soteriological and dogmatic or mystical theology cannot be attributed to Gregory's theology without fundamentally misrepresenting his thought. The operative distinction for Gregory is between a God who remains aloof from the cosmos and delegates both creation and superintendence to another person, or a God whose defining trait is to be fruitful and to multiply, as it were. The transcendent character of God does not mean that God stands apart from the cosmos but that the origin of existence remains clearly and unequivocally with God and that trustworthy human knowledge of God is to be found in that most characteristic realm of human knowledge and activity, because God is first and foremost a God who acts. The paradigmatically divine capacity is production. The generation of the Son by the Father is an activity of this divine power; the creation of the cosmos by the Son is an activity of this divine power. These two activities distinguish the first two Persons of the Trinity, for it is the Father who generates the Son, and it is the Son who creates the cosmos. However implicit in Gregory's theology may be the distinction between *in se* and *ad extra* activities, or the understanding that all divine activities are actions by all divine persons in common, these thoughts are not expressed or used by Gregory for his defense of the Son's full divinity in *Against Eunomius.*

# 7 Gregory of Nyssa on the Unity of Nature and Power

## *Introduction*

ONE TENET THAT ALL SIDES in the trinitarian controversy could agree upon was that the second Person was to be worshipped as the Creator. Beyond the simple and unadorned piety of this sentiment, common ground vanished, for each side had its own understanding of how and why the Son was the Creator. Eunomius' doctrine of the Creator has already been described: the Son is the first creature, who receives from God the delegated power to create. The Son is therefore the "Only-Begotten of those things which came into existence after him and through him."[1] The Son's creative activity does not prove His true divinity but reveals His obedience to God, for "he became the perfect minister of the whole creative activity and purpose of the Father."[2] The fact that the Son creates in obedience, rather than by his own power and authority, establishes again the Son's derivative status, for "he who creates by his own authority is entirely different from him who does so at the Father's command and acknowledges that he can do nothing of his own accord."[3]

With this last statement Eunomius touches upon another common tenet: whatever the Son did He did in some kind of positive union with

1. *Apology* 15:13–14; *Extant Works*, 53.

2. Ibid., 15:15–16; 53.

3. Ibid., 21:20–21; 61. This passage leads into a reference to John 5:19: the Son "acknowledges that he can do nothing of his own accord. . . ."

God the Father. Eunomius thinks that this positive union was a moral union: the Son obeyed the Father's commands. This perfect obedience made them "one," even though the Son was a creature. Basil of Ancyra's response to this Heterousian doctrine is to show that the creationist texts that Eunomius favors could be countered with generationist texts, such as John 5:19. Basil opposed an apparently creationist text like "I was beside him" (Prov. 8:30) with the John 5:19 text that whatever the Son sees the Father doing He does likewise.[4] Basil's argument shows that the Son had "everything according to essence and absolutely as does the Father."[5] The Son's actions are a continuation of the Son's imaging of the Father, and as such are proofs of the Son's complete likeness to the Father. The limit of Basil's reasoning is, of course, that the Son's nature was not "the same" as the Person He is "like."[6] The Son creates because the Father creates, but perhaps not as (that is, in the same way) the Father creates.

Gregory's argument in *Against Eunomius* is that common capacities indicate common nature. Though this understanding is widely recognized as the "Cappadocian insight," the reasoning behind this doctrine has not been explored. In some cases, for example, common capacity would not indicate common nature (as Gregory understood common nature). Many things run, but this does not indicate a common nature among all of them. Gregory's argument depends upon determining that there are some capacities that, wherever they occur, must occur through the presence of a nature. In *Against Eunomius* Gregory prefers physical examples of common capacities and common natures. Seeing, for example, always indicates a seeing nature. Although this kind of example is true to Gregory's initial insight in *On the Making of Man* that God is like a unity of powers in one mind, the full strength of Gregory's argument is more typically expressed using analogies between God's nature and power and the nature and power of elementals.[7]

4. *Panarion* 73.8.4; Amidion, 299.

5. *Panarion* 73.8.7.

6. Ibid., 73.8.8.

7. Gregory's emphasis on physical processes such as heat from fire suggests a parallel with Athanasius. G. Christopher Stead, "The Freedom of the Will and the Arian Controversy," in *Platonismus und Christentum,* ed. Horst-Dieter Blume and Friedhelm Mann (Münster: Aschendorffsche Verlafbuchhandlung, 1983), 256, argues that Athanasius' emphasis on "physical processes,

Gregory's argument is basically that some things can only be done by the divine nature; this fact makes Gregory very interested in how a nature "does" something. Gregory turns to a "faculty" kind of causality to establish that there are some capacities that always indicate a specific nature. The kind of capacity or property that exists in a necessary or connatural union with the Divine Nature is the δύναμις.[8] The power or connatural property is also said by Gregory to be συμφυής or φυσικέν ἰδιότητα.[9] One of the most important of these is to create. The capacity to create is a power, and whoever has the power to create has a divine nature. This choice for the certain indicator of divine nature has its problems, which Gregory resolves in his argument that creation is the kind of power that cannot be possessed equivocally. Eunomius may talk about God delegating

---

like the emission of light" as "a better analogy for God's self-expression than rational intentions" is an unfortunate ("bizarre") result of his judgment that nature is opposed to free will as a source of action. Athanasius not only opposes these two concepts but devalues action by the will. A more sympathetic reading of this doctrine of Athanasius' can be found in Meijering's *God Being History,* 107. Meijering makes the point that although Athanasius had a negative judgment on the role of free will in divine generation, Gregory of Nazianzus had a very positive one that allowed him to say that generation is willed by God (rather than being simply an act of nature). Gregory of Nyssa is less interested than his friend is in emphasizing the role of God's will in generating, though his sense of the positive importance of free will for God and humanity is no less keen than his friend Gregory's. Nyssa's argument from the unity of the divine nature leads him generally to emphasize analogies to "physical processes." However, Gregory's exploration of divine generation also leads him to offer the analogy of "fire with a will," an idea that suggests that the division between nature and will may not be as firm as expected.

8. These three terms refer to the same kind of relationship between an existent insofar as it is a unity (that is, the nature) and an existent insofar as it is exists in multiplicity. While this existence in multiplicity means composition in the existent itself for material things, this existence in multiplicity does not require composition in the existent itself in the case of immaterial or transcendent existents because for transcendentals this existence in multiplicity is an existence as a cause. Plato makes use of this very distinction in *Republic* 508 B–509 B. The idea of a single cause that has multiple effects is used precisely to recognize the existence in multiplicity of transcendentals without at the same time compromising their unity.

9. The following examples will illustrate the similarity of the senses Gregory attached to each word. Δύναμις: "And what of the sun? Is it not . . . by the same *power* [δύναμις] that it warms everything?" *GNO* 1:140:17–18; Hall, 92, *NPNF* 5:71. Συμφυής: "Heat is a *natural property* of fire, luminosity to the sunbeam. . . ." *GNO* 1:147:17–18; Hall, 95, *NPNF* 5:73. Φυσικὴ ἰδιότητα: ". . . as in the case of the sun and its beam . . . or of scents and ointments and the quality they emit; for these, while they remain in themselves without diminution, have at the same time, each concurrently with itself, the *natural property* they emit: as the sun its beam, the lamp its brightness, the scents the perfume . . . ." *GNO* 2:196:12–18, *NPNF* 5:204. I will translate δύναμις consistently as power, and συμφυής or φυσικὴ ἰδιότητα, or the idea which embraces all these terms, as natural or connatural property, but there is no single translation for συμφυής that suits all contexts.

the act of creation, but for Gregory such a capability can no more be delegated than an eye can delegate seeing to an ear. In this chapter I describe Gregory's argument in *Against Eunomius* that common power indicates common nature.

*The Context of Gregory's Argument*

Eunomius defined divinity as unbegottenness, a nature that could only be attributed to God ("the Unbegotten"). Gregory's polemical strategy is to emphasize properties that are attributed to the kind of existence divinity is in general, or the nature of divinity, regardless of Person. This kind of argument had some force against Eunomius, for although he described divine nature *per se* as unbegottenness, he nonetheless frequently treats this identity as one of opposition. The concepts and the Persons of Unbegotten and Begotten are opposed to each other in the sense of naming mutually exclusive natures. Since Eunomius made divinity and non-divinity identical to specific Persons—the Unbegotten and the Begotten—Gregory's response is to focus on indicators of the divine nature apart from the Persons. As I have already remarked, Gregory establishes that some capacities or properties exist in that kind of union with the divine nature such that they are certain indicators of the existence of the nature. It is only after Gregory has done this that he then turns to the individual activities manifested in specific divine Persons.

The polemical context of Gregory's writing means that his trinitarian theology cannot start from the divinity of the individual Persons because Eunomius has begun by identifying divinity with one Person (God) and one Personal relation (unbegottenness). Gregory starts with the divine nature and turns to the individual Persons only when he has clear conceptual support to establish their common nature. This is not quite the dynamic usually attributed to Gregory's (or Cappadocian or "Greek") trinitarian the ology, but it is the only description that makes sense of the polemical con text. To begin his arguments with the individual Persons would trap Gregory in Eunomius' polemical strategy of defining divinity by relation (or the lack of relation). Gregory's first task is to demolish Eunomius' particular doctrine of divine relations, a doctrine he understands, with some justice but also habitually, as a doctrine of relations of opposition.

Gregory's argument that the Father and Son (and Spirit) have the same power is given as a response to Eunomius' claim, in his *Second Apology,* that the order or sequence (τάξις) among the Father, Son, and Holy Spirit indicates their individual rank, and that associated with each rank is a relative degree of simplicity. By this claim Eunomius provides an ontological explanation for the subordination of the Son to God the Father: the causal sequence of Father, Son, and Spirit indicates kinds of being. The dependence of the Son upon the Father, and the dependence of the Spirit upon the Son, means that the being of the Son is less *authentic* (κυριώτατος) and less *simple* (ἁπλόος) (these two terms seem to be roughly synonymous for Eunomius) than the being of God the Father, just as the being of the Spirit is both less real and less simple than that of the Son.

Gregory's reply is that there is neither "more" nor "less" to being and that sequence cannot determine the degree of being. He rejects the notion that being, considered as a subject, can be more or less: "I have never yet heard [of] a case where of two things, both of which are agreed to exist, as long as they both exist, one exists more than the other. Each of these alike exists, while it exists and because it exists."[10] Similarly, Gregory rejects the notion that sequence determines rank: "We have never before heard this philosophy, which reduces the second and the third item referred to in a sequence to the position of subordinate and subject, which is what Eunomius wants to do. . . . For he makes it a rule that the sequential order is an indication of a difference between the natures. . . . [But we say that] numerical order does not bring about diversity of the natures. . . ."[11]

These issues of opposed or contrary relationships in the Trinity as well as the question of "more or less" divinity come together in Gregory's response to Eunomius, a response that draws upon similar arguments already established in traditional authorities.

### *Basil, Methodius, and the Argument from Contraries*

When Gregory says to Eunomius that there are no degrees of being, no more or less of it, he depends on an earlier argument by Basil in his own

10. *GNO* 1:80:13–17; Hall, 61; *NPNF* 5:52.
11. Ibid. 1:85:2–14; 64; 5:54.

*Against Eunomius.* There Basil refutes a passage in Eunomius' *Apology* that contains the claim that titles given to both God and the Son are to be understood as referring to different kinds of essences. Eunomius says:

> . . . just as the unbegotten differs from the begotten, so "the light" must differ from "the light," and "the life" from "the life," and "the power" from "the power". . . . [E]very word used to signify the essence of the Father is equivalent in force of meaning to "the Unbegotten" because the Father is *without parts and uncomposed,* by the same token that same word used of the Only-begotten is equivalent to "offspring."[12]

As we shall see, this is an important argument by Eunomius since it constitutes his re-interpretation of the influential "two-powers" and "power from power" formula used by Origen, Eusebius, and Asterius to describe the unity between God and the Son.

Basil's rebuttal of this passage turns upon finding a doctrine of opposition between "unbegotten" and "begotten," "light" and "light," etc., in Eunomius' thought. Basil says that Eunomius has set up unbegotten and begotten as contraries,[13] and that the result of Eunomius' reasoning is that he sets an opposition between light and light, life and life, power and power, and all other such titles given to both the Father and the Son.[14] But what does it mean, Basil asks, to oppose light to light? The opposite of light is darkness, not another kind of light; the opposite of life is death, not another kind of life; the opposite of power is inability, not another kind of power.[15] Indeed, every light, insofar as it is a light, is as much a light as another. Lights may be large or small, dim or bright, near or far, but they are all lights.[16] If Eunomius opposes one light with another then he must mean

12. *Apology* 19:12–19; *Extant Works,* 58–59. Eunomius' argument for the different meanings of common titles forms the content of all of chapter 19. I will return directly to the description of the Father as without parts and uncomposed, which is why I have emphasized it in this quotation.

13. *Against Eunomius* 2:26, 13–18; Sesboüé, SC 305:108–9.

14. Ibid., 2:26, 21–37; 305:110–11.

15. Ibid., 2:27, 26–28; 305:114–15.

16. Ibid., 2:28, 10–15; 305:118–19. Basil's argument to this effect depends not only on a line of reasoning commonly available to the modern reader—that is, that there is a category called "light" that admits of qualifications–but also on a line of reasoning less available: there is light, pure and simple, and all such simple lights are the same. In this latter form of reasoning, differences between lights are explained as the result of physical modifications to the simple lights, such as physical impediments to the shining (earth gets in the way), so that "a bright light" is understood as a purer collection of simple lights than "a dim light."

that the second light is not light at all but the opposite of light. But the opposite of light is darkness.[17]

Furthermore, how can the Son, who is called this "light," which Eunomius opposes to true Light, be generated by God in any way since nothing can produce its own contrary?[18] Darkness cannot be produced by light, just as cold cannot be produced by hot, and water cannot be produced by fire.[19] This is the same line of reasoning that Basil offers in his second *Homily on the Hexaemeron,* where he denounces those who claim that evil has its origin from God: ". . . the contrary cannot proceed from its contrary. Life does not engender death; darkness is not the origin of light; sickness is not the maker of health. . . . in a genesis, each proceeds from its like, and not from its contrary."[20]

The association that Basil makes between contraries and traditional questions about a link between the aetiologies of evil and of matter is an important indication that the original use of such contraries language is to be found in the cosmological debates of the late third and early fourth centuries. The apparently cosmological character of Basil's argument supports my account of Eunomius' own theology. Indeed, the best example of the role of contraries language in earlier Christian cosmological debates is the same text I found to be a precedent for Eunomius' description of ingenerate or unproduced, ἀγέννητος: Methodius' *De libero arbitrio.*[21] The

17. *Against Eunomius* 2:26, 9–11; Sesboüé, SC 305:108–9. The argument from "no opposites" may be part of established anti-Homoian or anti-Eunomian polemic, if Hilary of Poitiers can be used as evidence of what was current in 360 in rhetoric against those two theologies. At *On the Trinity* 5:14, writing against the line in Arius' creed that only God is "true God," Hilary argues from the example of fire, that if fire is not "true fire," it is not fire at all. Similarly, if one deprives water of its wetness, it is not "false water"; rather, it is not water at all. (Note that Hilary's examples of what a thing must have to be what it is are exactly what Gregory would call the power.)

18. *Against Eunomius* 2:28, 17–20; Sesboüé, SC 305:118–19.

19. To complete his argument that the Son is true Light, true Life, and true Power, Basil turns to Scripture. In John 1:9, the Spirit speaks of Jesus as "the true Light." The Lord himself says, "I am the Life" at John 14:16, and Paul says that "Christ is the Power of God . . ." at 1 Cor. 1:24. See *Against Eunomius* 2:27, 10–25; Sesboüé, SC 305:112–15.

20. *Homilies on the Hexaemeron* 2:4; *NPNF* 8:61.

21. Eusebius provides a long quotation from Methodius' *De libero arbitrio* linking the cosmological use of ingenerate with a moral model: if matter is ingenerate, then either evil is an essence, or it is an accident that God created (see *Preparation for the Gospel* 7:22). As I showed earlier, the terms in which Methodius makes his argument are the same key terms Eunomius uses to argue that God's essence is ingenerate. These key terms include those that describe God as without parts and uncomposed, a description that appears in the passage from *Apology* 19, quoted above. Meth-

problem addressed in that text is the question of whether evil or matter is ingenerate. Methodius shows that matter is not co-eternal with God by proving that there cannot be a multiplicity of unbegotten simple opposites co-existing eternally with God.[22] This proof turns upon his demonstration that

> . . . nothing is contrary to itself; because it is the nature of contraries to be contrary to others. As for example white is not contrary to itself, but is said to be the contrary of black; and light is shown in like manner not to be contrary to itself, but appears in that relation to darkness. . . .[23]

What Methodius shows, through this admittedly arcane kind of argument, is that anything that is composed of contraries cannot be said to truly exist, which in this context means to exist eternally. Anything that is composed has constitutive parts that are destructive of each other. For Methodius, something composed (that is, of a mixed nature) cannot be eternal. While this may not initially seem like an argument that can have trinitarian overtones, it will—in the service of Basil and his brother Gregory.

The similarity between Methodius' and Basil's arguments lies precisely in this: that nothing is opposite to itself. Both agree that any specific kind of being is excluded only by its opposite. Neither of these statements is original to Methodius, but he is an important precedent for the theological application of this "mixture physics." Methodius uses "nothing is opposite to itself" to show that anything that is composed of contraries cannot truly exist. Basil first uses this truism to show that two natures that are contraries are mutually exclusive. More importantly, he shows that *only* two natures that are contraries can be mutually exclusive. If Eunomius wants to exclude any similarity between the natures of God and the Son, then he must acknowledge that he is setting these two in opposition: only contraries are mutually exclusive.[24]

---

odius' work contains arguments for the doctrine that God is "the one sole Creator of all things, including the substance underlying bodies . . ." *Preparation for the Gospel* 7:18; Gifford, 3:1, 361.

22. "For if God was uncreate [ἀγέννητος], as well as the simple elements out of which matter was composed, the uncreate will not be two only" *Preparation for the Gospel* 7:22, 59; Schroeder, SC 215:310; Gifford, 3:1, 375.

23. Ibid., 7:22, 64; 215:312; Gifford, 3:1, 376.

24. In the *Apology* Eunomius does not actually use opposites or contraries language, so Basil's reading of the text was, at the time, a matter of supposition. However, Basil understood Eunomius'

In the background of Basil's debate are the questions of how many eternals there can be and what an existent must be in order to be eternal. These same questions are the subject of Methodius' earlier work. Basil, following Methodius (and Gregory, following them both), finds the categories of opposition useful for this debate. Gregory follows Basil in interpreting Eunomius' theology of degrees of being as a theology of opposition. (This helps explain Gregory's repeated and emphatic descriptions of Eunomius' theology as implicit Manichaeism.) Gregory goes beyond Basil and Methodius by using contraries language, indeed, the physics of the contraries, as a means for describing the unity between Father and Son, and not simply as a means for critiquing (frequently through *reductio ad absurdum*) inappropriate doctrines.[25]

Just reading a little of Gregory gives a sense of how important the language of "opposition" is for him. In his early writings Gregory regularly uses the category of "opposition" to describe both physical and psychological relations. In *On Virginity* Gregory remarks positively upon medical philosophy's doctrine of opposite elementals and powers, and the relationships that hold among them.[26] Gregory uses these oppositions in his opening argu-

---

theology either better than Eunomius did or better than Eunomius was willing to say (in 360), for in the *Second Apology*, Eunomius uses exactly the kind of argument Basil supplied. Eunomius says, "If, as will be admitted, the divergence of the names which are significant of properties marks the divergence of the things, it is surely necessary to allow that with the divergence of the names significant of essence is also marked the divergence of the essences. . . . For we note by divergent names the different essences, fire and water, air and earth, cold and heat, white and black, triangle and circle. Why need we mention the intelligible essences, in enumerating which the Apostle marks, by difference of names, the divergence of essence?"(*GNO* 2:174:13–175:2; *NPNF* 5:196). Note that the examples Eunomius offers are all opposites: fire and water, air and earth, cold and heat, etc. Gregory's reply to this passage picks up exactly on the proportion Eunomius is suggesting between fire:water and unbegotten:begotten—"But if he [Eunomius] asserts the difference of essence to exist between the 'generate' and the 'ungenerate' as it does between fire and water, and is of opinion that the names, like those which he has mentioned in his examples, are in the same mutual relation as 'fire' and 'water', the horrid character of his blasphemy [will be revealed] . . ." (*GNO* 2:176:16–21; *NPNF* 5:196–97).

25. Gregory's development of Basil can be seen in the conclusion of Basil's critique of Eunomius discussed above. After Basil has shown that Eunomius' doctrine of two kinds of light, life and power implies two opposed natures he offers his own interpretation of such titles given to both the Father and the Son (see *Against Eunomius* 2:27, 34–39; Sesboüé, SC 305:114–15). This interpretation is surprisingly Origenist: the Son is called by the titles Light, Life, and Power because He is perfectly derived from these absolute properties in God. In short, Basil gives a traditional two-powers, *power from power* kind of theology.

26. See *On Virginity* 22.

ment in *On the Making of Man*,[27] where he defines created existence in terms of the double operations (or activities, ἐνέργειαι) of rest and motion which hold that existence together. Each object of creation consists of a mixture of the properties of rest and motion; divine nature, on the other hand, is distinguished from created nature by the lack of any presence of opposites.

This contrast between created and uncreated existence appears again in *Against Eunomius*. Gregory regularly describes created existence as consisting of a mixture of opposites; indeed, for Gregory, each individual created thing implicitly refers to its opposite.[28] Uncreated existence, that is, the existence of the Trinity, is that of a power [δύναμις] without parts or composition, sharing wisdom, power, and all other goods not only with equal access, but to the same degree.[29] No one Person has greater access to, or is more identified with, these attributes, for they belong to each Person of the Trinity as "rooted in their nature." This phrase means that the Person is "identical with the attribute rather than possessing it."[30] Gregory characterizes Eunomius' description of the Son's generation as that of an opposite produced by its opposite, a criticism drawn from the approach of Methodius and Basil.[31] Gregory's argument in Book 1 of *Against Eunomius* is that Eunomius' own description of divine simplicity is inadequate because it results in a theology of divine oppositions.[32] Eunomius' description of

27. *On the Making of Man* 44:128C–29D. As already noted, the *GNO* edition for this work is not yet available.

28. "It is high time we observed the difference between elements, and how *everything in the world that contributes to the constitution of the universe points towards what is contrary to its nature.* Some things are light and tend upwards, others are heavy and press downward. Some things stand still, others are constantly moving . . ." (*GNO* 1:143:27–144:5; Hall, 93, emphasis added). I will return to this passage.

29. *GNO* 1:95; *NPNF* 5:57. Compare *GNO* 1:126; *NPNF* 5:66.

30. Gregory uses similar language in *Against Eunomius* 3:9, where he limits the proper attribution of a property and title to those who possesses the property by nature. This argument is directed against Eunomius' understanding of the equivocal attribution of a title. As described above, Eunomius allows that good, light, power, etc., can be attributed to both God (the Father) and the Son because they are attributed equivocally: each title means something different in each case. Gregory rejects the use of equivocal doxologies: "If the Father alone is good, having goodness not as a thing acquired, but in His nature, and if the Son, as heresy will have it, does not share in the nature of the Father, then he who does not share the good essence of the Father is of course at the same time excluded also from . . . the title of good" (*GNO* 2:266:59; *NPNF* 5:230).

31. Ibid., 1:100:24 ff.; *NPNF* 5:59.

32. Depending on the specific sentence structure, Gregory uses either ἀντιτίθημι or ἐναντίος. Methodius typically expresses (being) opposite or contrary by using a form of the verb

divine simplicity must therefore be wrong, since, as Gregory emphasizes, there can be no opposition in the divine being.

*Gregory's Critique of Eunomius' Theology*

Gregory's claim never to have heard before of Eunomius' idea that sequence indicates rank and degrees of being has a certain disingenuousness about it. That sequence indicates rank, particularly in a causal sequence, is not a doctrine peculiar to Eunomius. Likewise, the associated idea that the further removed an effect is from its cause the more composed (or less simple) its existence is, is not something Eunomius invented. Mortley has argued that the presence of these ideas in Eunomius' theology indicates the substantial influence of a form of Neoplatonism (the "Neo-Aristotelians") upon his theology.[33] I have already suggested that much of Eunomius' hierarchical language can be found in prior Christian cosmological treatises (for example, works by Methodius or Eusebius of Caesarea), and one looks first to those Christian authors for precedents to Eunomius' theology. But if those Christian precedents exist, then Gregory cannot legitimately claim never to have heard such arguments before. The true purpose of Gregory's not recognizing Eunomius' grounds for a theological hierarchy is to shift the argument into his own preferred terms. We start to see Gregory's argument developing. However, there is still the question of the "more or less" of divine being.

Gregory proposes his own alternative criteria for describing the relationship between Father and Son (and Spirit). He rejects Eunomius' de-

ἀντιτίθημι/ἀντίκειμαι, while Eusebius will use ἐναντίος. Basil's statement that an opposite cannot come from an opposite uses ἐναντίος: . . . διὰ τὸ μηδὲν τῶν ἐναντίων παρὰ τοῦ ἐναντίου γίγνεσθαι (*Homilies on the Hexaemeron* 2:4; Giet, *Homelies*, SC 26 bis, 158:9–10, although his language at page 176:7 shows that Basil was comfortable with both terms). Gregory uses ἐναντίος more frequently than ἀντιτίθημι, although the latter term appears regularly, especially when Gregory refers to the doctrines of the Manichaeism. I have no evidence of Gregory preferring one term over another for some kind of philosophical reason, and I regard ἀντιτίθημι and ἐναντίος as functional synonyms (given the grammatical needs of the sentence).

33. *From Word to Silence* 2:185. Mortley has also argued that Eunomius was engaged in a philosophical argument with contemporary pagan Neoplatonists and that Gregory's confessed ignorance of these ideas indicates that Gregory was less acquainted with the philosophy of the day than was Eunomius, and thus that Gregory failed to recognize the technical character of Eunomius' arguments. I am inclined not to take Gregory's claims of ignorance as entirely honest. (Mortley discusses Gregory's claim never to have heard of the ideas on which Eunomius depends in 2: 172–73.)

scription, which is based upon order and sequence, and instead he produces a description based upon connatural power or property. Gregory's argument is that because the divine Persons share a common δύναμις or συμφυή, they also share a common φύσις or οὐσία.[34] This is the line of argument that is basic to Gregory's reasoning in *Against Eunomius*. In Book 1 of that work Gregory proceeds by finding faults in the rationale of Eunomius' sequence theology, while (not unexpectedly) building up the case for his common power theology. The broad strokes of Gregory's argument may be seen in one of his first comments on the summary of Eunomius' faith he quotes from the *Second Apology*. Gregory says:

> . . . *height of being* does not indicate superiority either in power [δύναμις] or in goodness or in anything of that kind. For surely everyone knows, except those who presume to superior wisdom, that the hypostasis of the Only Begotten and that of the Holy Spirit are indefectably perfect in goodness and power [δύναμις] and all such things. For all good things, as long as they do not admit their opposite, have no limit to their goodness, since they are naturally circumscribed only by what is opposite to them . . . [for example,] power stops when weakness takes hold, life is limited by death, light's boundary is darkness, and all in all individual good things cease when they meet their opposites.[35]

While this passage does not give Gregory's argument in its most developed form, the direction of his argument is established. Topological precedence of any sort (high, low; first, last) does not cause a difference in kinds of being. Whatever the sequence of the divine Persons, they all (but specifically the second and third Persons) have no limit to their virtues, for example, goodness and power, for virtues are limited only by their opposites. Surely, Gregory will ask rhetorically, Eunomius is not suggesting that there is something opposite to virtue in the Son and Spirit?[36] Gregory continues at some length, showing that indeed Eunomius' theology reduces to

34. The better known division in *Against Eunomius* (*GNO* 1:105:19–106) is presented by Gregory as a way to distinguish different kinds of being, and is thus the direct analogue to Eunomius' topological set of distinctions: this division of being by Gregory even has a vaguely topological arrangement to it. Gregory shows that the Son and Spirit are indeed uncreated by offering the distinctions I have been describing.

35. *GNO* 1:77:1–77:13; Hall, 60. I have emphasized the phrase "height of being," which is Gregory's play upon Eunomius' description of the first essence.

36. This criticism has some bite to it since Eusebius of Caesarea was emphatic that the Son, as an Image of God, was "unmixed with anything opposite" to Himself (see *The Demonstration of the Gospel* 5:1). Another echo of Eusebius follows shortly in Gregory's argument.

exactly this: God (the Father), who is all virtue, has produced the opposite, for only the presence of the opposite of virtue could limit that product, that is, keep the product of God (that is, the Son) from being unlimited in virtue, and thus being God.

### *The Contrast between Property and Rank*

Many of the details of Gregory's argument in this passage appear regularly throughout *Against Eunomius:* his contrast of sequence with connatural powers or properties; the specific properties he offers as indicating common nature; and his trinitarian use of the same kind of opposition language to be found in the earlier cosmological concerns of Methodius and Eusebius. A good understanding of these three aspects of Gregory's argument is essential for understanding the substance of his argument against Eunomius' theology overall. I have already spoken of the origins of Gregory's opposition language, and I will discuss the lists of specific properties Gregory believes indicate common nature at the end of this chapter.

Gregory's argument contrasting Eunomius' doctrine of sequence with his own doctrine of connatural powers is his primary argument against Eunomius' theology. Gregory makes an implicit contrast between Eunomius' false topological criteria for (kinds of) being and his own true criteria for being. Position, rank, or sequence do not determine differences in being, but a difference in goodness, power, or "anything of that kind" or "all such things" does determine differences in being. One feature of these two sets of criteria to notice is that Eunomius' criteria are directed towards finding differences in being (in particular between God and the Son), while Gregory's criteria are directed towards finding common being (again, between God the Father and the Son in particular).

It is important to understand the dissimilarity between these two sets of criteria. Gregory is not saying that all being is exactly the same; rather, he is saying that there are differences in being, but that Eunomius' description of these differences is wrong. There is no more or less of being, nor is there top or bottom. According to Gregory, *differences in being are determined first, by the presence (or absence) of certain powers or properties, and second, by the way in which these powers or properties are united in the existent.*

Gregory's polemical purpose, namely, finding signs of common being between the Father and Son, is shown in the way in which he applies these two criteria to God's being. In the first case, that of the presence (or absence) of certain powers or properties, Gregory goes to some length to show that the Father, Son, and Spirit have the same goodness and power, etc.[37] In the second case, namely, the question of how these powers or properties are united in the existent, Gregory's basic argument is that the Trinity is a simple Power, which shares all goods with equal access and to the same degree, that is to say, by nature.[38] The polemical edge of Gregory's reasoning is further revealed by the fact that he deals with the question of the Father, Son, and Spirit having the same power or property regularly and explicitly, while the question of God's simple being is usually handled indirectly, through discussions of the role of contraries. Gregory's primary polemical emphasis is on the argument for the common nature between God the Father and the Son as demonstrated in the common power(s) found between the two.

I have already referred to Gregory's claim never to have heard of the doctrine that sequential order indicates diversity of nature. Gregory follows this statement with examples of an alternate kind of association, examples that suggest an alternate interpretation of sequence or order. The examples Gregory gives are the association of fire with combustion, and fragrance with odor.[39] The example of fragrance with odor, taken from Wisd. 7:25, is a favorite analogy with Origen and Eusebius, yet it is instructive to notice how Gregory's use of this example differs from theirs.[40]

Both Origen and Eusebius use the concept of fragrance as a means of describing a form of generation of the Son from the Father that maintains an appropriate kind of unity between the two.[41] The notion that the Son

37. I have found that one can predict that any reference by Gregory to Eunomius' doctrine of the gradation in divine being indicated by sequence will be followed by δύναμις language and a counter-argument by Gregory for the unity of divine predicates.

38. *GNO* 1:95; *NPNF* 5:57. Compare *GNO* 1:126; *NPNF* 5:66.

39. *GNO* 1:87:12–13; Hall, 65.

40. Fragrance means the smell of something, while odor means the specific substance that has or produces the fragrance. In this terminology, musk oil is an odor, musk is a fragrance.

41. In his article, "The Trouble with Fragrance," *Phronesis* 35 (1990): 290–302, John Ellis gives a summary of the late Neoplatonic analysis of fragrance in commentaries on Aristotle's *Categories.* (The earliest author Ellis considers is Ammonius, c. 435/445–c. 517/526.) However, in these com-

is generated analogously to a fragrance from an odor is, for both these theologians, part of their understanding of the Son as an image of God. Eusebius says this well: "Thus also would the image of God be a kind of living image of the living God . . . but not such an image as we connote by the term, which differs in its essential substance and its species, but one which is . . . like in its own essence to the Father, and so is seen to be the liveliest fragrance of the Father. . . ."[42] Gregory, by contrast, uses fragrance to illustrate the unity between a substance and its causal capacity, and not to illustrate the unity between Father and Son.[43] His use of fragrance in this way is a good indication of how he is shifting the burden of his argument away from describing the unity of the Father and the Son directly.[44]

### *Two Arguments for Connatural Unity*

There are three occasions in Book 1 where Gregory contrasts most succinctly the argument from sequence with the argument from power. The first begins with a lengthy quotation from Eunomius to the effect that "necessity requires that the [divine] beings must be considered to be greater and less, and that some occupy the first rank . . . while others are pushed down to second place because of their inferiority of nature and worth."[45] Gregory's reply brings together all the threads of his argument, and for that reason is worth quoting at length:

> But with the divine nature, because all perfection in respect of goodness appears together in the designation as divine, it is not possible for our mind to discover

mentaries, fragrance is considered as an example of an accident inhering in a substance. This is a very different understanding of fragrance from that of Plotinus, Origen, Eusebius, and Gregory. Ellis, 300–301, remarks on the different understandings of fragrance to be found in Plotinus and later Neoplatonists who claimed Plotinus as an authority.

42. *The Demonstration of the Gospel* 5:1; Heikel, 213; Ferrar, 1:234.

43. The example of the unity between a fragrance and its (originating) substance appeals to Gregory, for in *On the Making of Man,* M 44:153c he uses the unity between honey and the smell of honey first as an analogy for the unity of the soul, as an analogy for the unity of the mind, and then as analogy for the unity of God.

44. However, in his *Refutation of the Creed of Eunomius* (written in 383 or early 384), where Gregory offers a more traditional account of Christ as the Power of God, he gives the conventional Origenist exegesis of the fragrance passage and interprets it as an image of the mode of generation of the Son (see *GNO* 2:351:17–25).

45. *GNO* 1:121:5–11; Hall, 82.

the manner or priority of honour. Where no greater or lesser possession is conceived of power [δύναμις], glory, wisdom, kindness, or any other good one can think of, but every good thing the Son has belongs to the Father, and everything the Father has is seen in the Son, by what shift shall we show the greater share of honour in the Father? If our mind were to go to kingly power and worth, the Son is a king. . . . If our soul dwells on the magnificence of creation, "all things came to be through him." . . . And if anyone thinks wisdom is to be honoured, "Christ is the power of God and the wisdom of God.[46]

This is one of Gregory's most powerful statements of his own doctrine. The effectiveness of the passage is due in large part to Gregory linking his theology with scriptural passages: the flow is from John 5:19 to John 1:3 to 1 Cor. 1:24.[47] These are three central proof-texts for pro-Nicene apologetics; the exegetical association of these texts in Nicene polemic is found consistently in a number of Greek and Latin apologists prior to Gregory. With arguments similar to those found in other pro-Nicene apologists, Gregory uses these scriptural texts to support his point that the criteria that distinguish divine being are shared by the Father with the Son.

Gregory's argument contrasting Eunomius' theology of sequence with his theology of connatural power is further developed when he begins to fill out, by illustration, his idea of a unity evidenced in identical power(s). Again Gregory is refuting a specific text by Eunomius,[48] and again he reduces Eunomius' argument to what he understands to be its core: "Is he [Eunomius] saying that the Father's being is *alone authentic and highest,*

46. Ibid., 1:126:11–25; 84. In his "Eunomius: Hair-splitting Dialectician or Defender of the Accessibility of Salvation?" Wiles argues that statements by Gregory, such as "it is not possible for our mind to discover the manner or priority of honour," show that Eunomius was resisting an attempt by the Cappadocians to "mystify" theology. Richard P. Vaggione made the same argument in his dissertation, "Aspects of Faith in the Eunomian Controversy" (Ph.D. diss, Oxford University, 1976), 137. Both these arguments were made before Mortley's description of Eunomius as a technical negative theologian.

47. Gregory begins the section by citing John 5:23 as well, which I did not include in my quotation.

48. The fragment Gregory produces from Eunomius' *Second Apology* is: "Since these are such, and in their relation to each other preserve the bond invariable, those who conduct their investigation in accordance with the inherent order of things, and do not insist on mixing and confusing everything, will surely be right, should any dispute arise from the beings, to base their belief about what is being demonstrated and the resolution of disputed points on the primary activities peculiar to the beings, and to resolve doubt about the activities with reference to the beings" (*GNO* 1:145:10–20; Hall, 94). This passage represents Eunomius' restatement of his οὐσία/ἐνέργεια distinction.

the next as a consequence quite inauthentic and the third less authentic still?"[49] Gregory's point here is that Eunomius is being inconsistent: either there is a natural bond among the three Persons, which Eunomius has declined to acknowledge or address, or their relationship is, as he prefers to say, only one of order. What Eunomius is calling the "inherent order" is in fact, Gregory adds, the distinction of hypostasis.[50]

Yet Eunomius' argument in the fragment cited at this point by Gregory does describe his idea of the kind of bond that holds between the three Persons; namely, the relationship between artisan and artifact, or more specifically, the relationship (discussed earlier) among the producer, the act of production, and the product, or in the Greek, the οὐσία, ἐνέργεια and ἔργα. Although Gregory acknowledges Eunomius' ἐνέργεια-based model, and the support for a sequence theology to be found in the ἐνέργεια causality Eunomius describes, he takes this occasion to offer his connatural power theology as an alternate causality.

> Heat is a natural property [or συμφυή] of fire, luminosity to the sunbeam, fluidity to water, gravity to stone, and one could mention many other similar instances. But if someone builds a house, or seeks office, or starts trading, or undertakes anything else that is achieved by forethought and preparation, one cannot in that case say any inherent order applies to what is done by them. The order comes about from the particular actions done to suit what the planner determines and what promotes the business at hand. . . . [Therefore, does Eunomius think that] the God of the universe manufactured this order for the Son and the Holy Spirit, and made the transcendence of the beings to be such that one is inferior to the other?[51]

49. *GNO* 1:146:4–10; Hall, 94. The phrase *alone authentic and highest,* which Hall italicizes, is a phrase from the beginning of the summary of Eunomius' theology. If one compares Gregory's "core summary" of Eunomius' doctrine with the fragment being quoted, the basic presupposition is there in Eunomius' theology as Gregory says, but it is also clear that Gregory has not yet met Eunomius' ἐνέργεια-based causality. (In his *Oration* 31:14, Gregory of Nazianzus reports a similar Eunomian doctrine of "degrees of being.")

50. *GNO* 1:147:9; Hall, 95.

51. Ibid., 1:147:17–148:9; 95. Remembering my prediction that references to sequence are followed by references to connatural powers: Gregory uses δύναμις four times in this section, aside from the passage just quoted: Does Eunomius think that God's δύναμις is shown by God producing diminished products (*GNO* 1:148:13)? Does anyone ever think that a great δύναμις is observed in diminished products (Ibid., 1:148:14)? Why call God highest and most authentic if his δύναμις is so diminished (Ibid., 1:148:18)? Eunomius' argument that the product matches the ἐνέργεια that produced him (Ibid., 1:150:11) assumes that a gimlet reveals all the δύναμις of the tinker.

In short, Gregory argues that there is no necessary sequence or relationship among artificial products, but only among natural products.[52] If Eunomius does not describe the Son (and Holy Spirit) as the products of God's nature, then he must give up his claim to find an order among them that is anything but the expression of God's will. (And if the expression of God's will, then Eunomius must explain why God produced in this way, that is, generating limited existents.)[53]

Between this rejection of Eunomius' sequence theology and the third noteworthy development of his connatural power theology, Gregory returns to the example of fire mentioned in the above passage. Fire is his preferred analogy to illustrate the union between nature and power, and Gregory uses fire as an analogy to the unity in divine production in all three books of *Against Eunomius*.[54] Gregory's use of fire to exemplify his case for the unity between a nature and its power makes clear the kind of unity he imagines to hold between the divine nature and its power(s). To understand Gregory's fire argument, it is helpful to return to the kind of Eunomian argument which prompted the example of fire in the first place.

52. Gregory's claim that there are no necessary relationships among artificial products is clearly true if one considers the relation between such products (for example, in the positioning of two bookshelves in a room, or two houses on a knoll), rather than the making of a given product (for example, in the making of a bookshelf). Gregory evidently does not consider aesthetics a matter of necessary relationships, rather of judgement calls.

53. While I do not agree with the substance of Wiles' description of Eunomius' theology in "Eunomius: Hair-splitting Dialectician or Defender of the Accessibility of Salvation?" he is correct on this point: Eunomius would not have expected this criticism by Gregory because he thought the different natures of God and the Son to be a matter of piety. Gregory can ask that Eunomius explain why God (the Father) would have generated a Son so limited in nature. But Eunomius cannot imagine that God would do otherwise since all the rules of thought guarantee God's uniqueness, and, as he exclaims in the *Apology*, no one is so impious as to imagine that the Son is equal to God! Yet Gregory accurately pinpoints the weakness in Eunomius' reasoning: by taking Eunomius' and Aetius' constant recourse to the sovereignty of God's ἐνέργεια, βουλή, or ἐξουσία literally Gregory insists upon their characterization of the generative act by God as an act of will entirely under God's control. Therefore God decided the nature of his products. The constant refrain in Aetius' and Eunomius' writings that the being of the product of divine generation could not be otherwise (than not ingenerate) reflects the Heterousian attempt to defend their doctrine of God's sovereign will from precisely the kind of criticism Gregory is making. Their defense is that God did not produce a full and equal divinity because another full and equal divinity cannot be produced.

54. Fire is also used by Hilary and Victorinus to illustrate the unity between nature and power and to support their argument that if the Father and Son have the same power they must also have the same nature. For Hilary, see *On the Trinity* 7:29; Smulders, CCL 62:296.3. For Victorinus, see *Against Arius* 1A.32; Henry and Hadot, 280.37–42, and 1A.40.

*Natural Unity and Causality Displayed by Fire*

In the fragments leading up to Gregory's distinction between two kinds of products (for example, heat and houses), Eunomius bases the difference in rank among the products (that is, the Son, the Holy Spirit, angels, the cosmos, etc.,) upon the production of each ἔργον by a separate activity: the rank among products reflects the difference in the rank of their originating activity. Each activity produces one product. (The cosmos would count as one product, for reasons adduced in Eusebius' cosmological polemics.) The dignity and rank of a product is determined by the dignity and rank of its originating activity.[55]

Eunomius' claim that each activity produces one product (one ἔργον per ἐνέργεια) is an odd one, and Gregory exploits it. Gregory replies that the same activity clearly does not always have the same effect: fire's activity, heat, has different results, for it softens bronze, hardens mud, melts wax, and destroys flesh. Similarly, the "Sun's power of warming" has different effects as well, which vary "according to the power of that receiving the effect." Gregory also refers to the single activity of drinking milk, where the transforming power of nature, digestion, distributes the parts of milk. Gregory has several discussions in *On the Making of Man* of a single cause producing multiple effects; multiple effects from a single cause figures significantly in his argument that the mind is one power. Likewise, the axiom that a single cause has multiple effects is central to important arguments in Origen's and Eusebius' theologies, a fact that neither Eunomius nor Gregory would have missed noticing.[56]

55. Eunomius here takes the maxim "first means best" quite literally since it is unimaginable to him that the best ἐνέργεια would produce second (or third!). The Son is the mediator of creation, the delegated source of every other ἐνέργεια (and thus ἔργον), and as such must be product of the first activity. Kopecek has a good discussion of Eunomius' association of ἐνέργεια and ἔργον in his *Neo-Arianism,* 2:451–54.

56. Both Origen's and Eusebius' examples of a single cause with multiple effects are heat- or fire-oriented. Origen says, "So, too, if the sun were to utter a voice and say, I melt things and dry them up, when being melted and dried up are opposites, he would not be speaking false in regard to the point in question, since by the one [μία ἐνέργεια] heat wax is melted and mud dried" (*On First Principles* 3:1.11). Origen uses a different kind of example earlier when he says that God has mercy on one person and hardens (the heart of) another person through a single operation [μία ἐνέργεια] at *On First Principles* 3:1.10.

Eusebius of Caesarea refers to the multiple effects of fire explicitly as a theological analogy:

Two points should be made clear regarding Eunomius' emphasis on the single effect of God's single activity. First, this follows from Eunomius' conception of God's simplicity. A simple cause has a single effect, a composite cause has multiple effects. Iamblichus says, "Each composite entity is composed of a multiplicity of essences and powers. . . ."[57]—a commonplace observation whose value is that it captures this judgement in the very language presently under study. Given the kind of causality that Iamblichus assumes, Eunomius would have hesitated to attribute multiple effects to a simple existent that he identified with an essence. The standard examples of a single cause with multiple effects are all of existents understood to be composite and not simple.

Yet by applying this causality so literally, Eunomius ignores the transformation of this causality accomplished by Plato in *Republic* 509 B (and elsewhere). By Eunomius' time the "transcendentalizing" of power physics is not only complete but traditional. Yet Eunomius consistently tends to suspect such a causality of implicit materialism. Eunomius claims, for example, that production by an essence must be materialistic, either as emanation, division, or sexual reproduction.[58] The only kind of causality that Eunomius accepts as guaranteed to be immaterial is what I have called the political–moral. This brings us to the second point.

Eunomius' understanding of activity as an agent with a single effect may be properly understood by remembering his doctrine in the *Apology* of the equivalence of the activity with the will, the equivalence of the ἐνέργεια with βουλή (and related terms). An activity has such a precisely determined effect because it is the expression of God's will, and God can will as determinately as He wants. In the *Second Apology* Eunomius drops any mention of God will,[59] but he assimilates the idea of God's complete con-

---

"Fire, again, by its nature purifies gold, and melts lead: wax it dissolves, clay it hardens, wood it dries, by one burning force [δύναμις] accomplishes so many changes. And thus, too, the heavenly Word of God, the Creator of sun and heaven and of the whole Cosmos, present in all things with effective power [δύναμις], and reaching through all things, showers light on sun and moon and stars from Its own eternal force. . . ." *Demonstration of Gospel* 4:5; Ferrar, 1:171.

57. *In Timaeum*, book 3, fragment 48:19–20; Dillon, *Iamblichi Chalcidensis*, 152–53.

58. See *Apology* 15.

59. The will (βουλή) figures prominently in the *Apology*, and not in the *Second Apology*, because in the late 350s Eunomius' theology was not separate, in its essentials, from Homoian theology. The *Apology* is best understood as a statement of the common ground between Anomoian

trol over His own activity into new hierarchical language. (The importance of this doctrine of God's control to Eunomius' theology is why he feels so keenly the danger of any hint of passion in the Godhead.) The control that was previously expressed in the language of the will (βουλή) is now expressed in the language of περιγράφω and παραμετρέω, that is, the language of circumscription and measuring. It is God's precise control over His activity that is described in Eunomius' statement that "the activities are defined at the same time as their works, and the works match the activities of those who effected them. . . ."[60] This kind of description of such a precise cause baffles (or irritates) Gregory, who alternately interprets Eunomius' ideas in terms of power or in terms of will:

> The expression "bounded by" indicates the equal status of the being that was produced with the power which constituted it,—or not so much the power as the activity of the power . . . so that what is produced should not be the work of the whole part of the agent, but such that an activity formed by part of the whole power had been set in motion. . . .[61]

> What then is this activity which accompanies the God of the universe [and which produces the Son] . . . ? A kind of quasi-substantial power, which subsists by itself and apparently operates by voluntary motion.[62]

Gregory believes that he has shown by his examples of fire and the sun that the one-to-one correspondence between ἐνέργεια and ἔργον cannot be true, but he does not deny that there is a continuity of nature in the causal chain. He argues, instead, that there is a correspondence between the power and the being. The continuity that Eunomius thought to find in the relation between activity and product Gregory locates in the relation between power and being. Gregory says that the activity does not reveal the nature of itself or its origin,[63] but he will accept that activity makes known (in the sense of indicating the fact of the existence of) the originating being.[64] Powers, on the other hand, reveal the nature. Gregory's under-

---

and Homoian theologies, but by the late 370s Eunomius' theology has developed beyond anything Homoian theology could countenance.

60. *GNO* 1:97:25–98:15; Hall, 70.

61. Ibid., 1:98:7–98:15; 71. In each case power is δύναμις and activity is ἐνέργεια.

62. Ibid., 1:98:8; 71 (slightly altered).

63. Ibid., 1:150:24; 97.

64. Ibid., 1:150:25 ff.; 97.

standing of the relationship between nature and power is that the latter is the expression of the distinctive characteristic(s) of the former.[65] Since both the Father and Son manifest the same power, they must share the same nature, for the same power(s) belong to the same natures. Contrariwise, different natures cannot be observed in "equal and similar effects."[66]

The best examples of the relationship between a nature and its power (φύσις and δύναμις), where the power "makes known" the nature, are fire and heat, and ice and cold. Gregory twice compares fire and its power heat, as well as ice and its power cold, to the divine nature and its powers.[67] Gregory argues that just as the power heat is a certain indicator of fire, so too the power providence, which both the Father and the Son possess, is a certain indicator of a common nature. In each case the power is the basis for our recognition of the identity of nature, since identical powers mean identical nature: ". . . surely the same relation which prevails between the outward characteristics which each manifests, must also prevail between the subjects. If the characteristics are opposed, surely what they reveal must also be reckoned opposites; if they are the same, what they reveal will not be different."[68]

65. Ibid., 1:154:25–155:15; 99.

66. Cf. Ibid., 1:155:6 and 10; 9.

67. The use of fire and burning or heat and snow and cold to describe the Transcendent Being may be seen as a convention in the School Platonism of the era since these images are used by Philo and Plotinus to the same effect. These similes play a special role in Plotinus' account of emanation because they derive from *Phaedo* 103 B–D, as John M. Rist, *Plotinus: The Road to Reality* (Cambridge: Cambridge University Press, 1967), 69, points out. I will return to the use of these similes by Philo and Plotinus later in the chapter.

68. *GNO* 1:154:25–155:15; 99. The same argument is used by Gregory in his *Refutation of the Creed of Eunomius* but in evidence for the divinity of the Spirit. "For if his work is that named, He has assuredly the same power and nature [δύναμις καὶ φύσις] as Him Who works it, and in such a one difference of kind from Deity can have no place. For just as, if anything should perform the functions of fire, shining and warming in precisely the same way, it is itself certainly fire, so if the Spirit does the works of the Father, He must assuredly be acknowledged to be of the same nature with Him" (*GNO* 2:402:15–19; *NPNF* 5:132). The analogies of fire and heat and ice and cold appear again in Gregory's *On the Holy Trinity*, written within a few years after the books of *Against Eunomius*. What is distinctive about Gregory's use of this analogy in *On the Holy Trinity* is that in this text Gregory refers to heat and cold as ἐνέργεια, and not δυνάμεις. This difference in terminology cannot be passed over lightly since Gregory's arguments in *On the Holy Trinity* and *On "Not Three Gods"* that the Father, Son, and Holy Spirit have all activities in common has been interpreted as Gregory's fundamental insight into trinitarian theology. A careful study of these two texts will reveal the limitations of this interpretation: Gregory uses the language of common ἐνέργεια in arguments involving the Spirit's divinity.

Gregory uses heat and fire later again, as well as cold and ice, to illustrate how powers and natures are inseparably related, such that the presence of the former invariably indicates the presence of the latter.[69] Again Gregory argues that each being has its distinguishing characteristics: the distinguishing characteristic of fire is heat, that of ice is cold.[70] Gregory makes explicit the understanding that the power manifests the underlying nature: "In each . . . subject some inherent characteristics are observed, by which the identity of the underlying nature is recognized. . . ."[71] These

69. *GNO* 1:176:110; Hall, 110. For Rist, *Plotinus*, 68–69, Plotinus' reference in *Ennead* 5:1.6 to the relationship of heat to fire provides a helpful illustration of the kind of necessity inherent in emanation. In the same way that "fire would hardly be what it is without giving off heat," so too the One would not be what it is without the second hypostasis proceeding from it. When Gregory uses the relationship of the power heat to the nature fire as an analogy of the relationship between divine power and divine nature, he depends upon this sense of the necessary link between power and nature to indicate the kind of unity that exists between the two. Thus, it is necessarily the case that when one encounters heat, one encounters fire, and it is necessarily the case that when one encounters Providence, one encounters God, because of the necessary relationship between powers and natures. Gregory is not at this point arguing, however, for the necessity of the existence of the respective powers given the existence of the respective natures. The argument for the necessary existence of God's power, given the existence of the divine nature, comes later in *Against Eunomius*, when Gregory describes the Son as the power of God and when he speaks of distinguishing power of the divine nature as the power to produce. A comparison of the appearance of δύναμις in Plotinus' argument with its appearance in Gregory's makes clear that while δύναμις appears in the Plotinus text almost incidentally, for the concept carries none of the argument, Gregory makes the reference to δύναμις fundamental to his argument because he is interested in the kind of existence described by δύναμις.

70. In his *Allegorical Interpretation* 1:3, Philo calls burning an ἴδιον of fire (as chilling is an ἴδιον of snow). He means by this term something that is both unique and distinctive to some specific thing: to burn is unique and distinct to fire and distinguishes it from everything else. The sense of ἴδιον for Philo is roughly the same as δύναμις for Gregory. Both authors use the relationship between fire and heat or burning to illustrate the kind of relationship they wish to attribute to God and a capacity to act. Both authors, however, cannot simply identify ἴδιον with δύναμις: Philo cannot because of the immediate influences on his understanding of δύναμις; Gregory cannot because of the immediate influences on his understanding of ἴδιον. The same Jewish liturgical identification of δύναμις with δόξα which supported Philo's frequent identification of these two would also have prevented him from using δύναμις to name what heat is of fire, that is, from equating δύναμις with ἴδιον. Similarly, Gregory cannot identify δύναμις with ἴδιον because of the recent development of the latter concept by Basil in his *Against Eunomius* 2:28. Basil uses ἴδιον to explain how each Person in the Trinity is distinguished: the first Person is distinguished by the ἴδιον of being ungenerated or of being Father (these two are not identical), the second Person by the ἴδιον of being generated, and so forth. Basil has set ἴδιον as a means of explaining in what way the Persons are distinct; in Book 1 of his *Against Eunomius*, Gregory is explaining in what way the Persons are shown to be united.

71. See, for example, Gregory's use of these terms at *GNO* 1:174:28–175:13; Hall, 109, which culminates in Gregory's statement that "Where things are different, the characteristics must surely

inherent characteristics, the powers, serve as marks or signs of the underlying nature or essence.[72] Since powers are in fact inseparable from the natures, if one denies the attribution of a particular power to an existent, one necessarily denies the possibility of the associated essence as well. Similarly, if one denies the attribution of a certain nature, then one necessarily denies as well the attribution of the powers unique to that essence.[73]

Fire's causality also provides Gregory with an example of the kind of unity that he means to refute and deny, namely, that the Son is divine because he participates in the Godhead. Again Gregory determines the unity of natures through an examination of powers or properties. In Gregory's understanding, the Son and Spirit manifest the same powers and activities because they possess the same nature, the three bonfires all give heat and light because they are all fire. According to Gregory, Eunomius' doctrine of participation amounts to the same kind of unity that exists between a piece of iron held in a forge and the heat in this iron: the iron is hot, but only temporarily.[74] The unity between iron and heat is not con-

---

be and reckoned [*sic*] different, and those which the same in terms of being, will manifestly be identified by the same marks."

72. *GNO* 1:175:10–14; Hall, 110. See also Gregory's *Hexameron,* M44:101B.

73. Again see *GNO* 1:174:28–175:13; Hall, 110. At *GNO* 1:176:11–16; Hall, 110, Gregory describes this inseparability of nature and power in terms of time. For Gregory, the essence can never be without its power(s), and powers exist for the same duration as their natures. There is no separation in existence or in time between the nature and its power(s). Gregory's argument for the temporal co-existence of nature and power is, of course, pointed against Eunomius' causality which emphasizes the lack of contemporaneous existence of divine essence and cause. In Eunomius' system, the causal capacity (the activity) is temporary because it is not essential, that is, because it is neither identical with the essence nor does it have any necessary relationship with the essence. Gregory's argument for the lack of temporal interval between the divine nature and power is part of his argument for the lack of interval, διάστημα, in the divine life, which others—Balthasar, Balàs, Otis—have treated, and which I need not develop further except to emphasize that Gregory's denial of a διάστημα in the divine life is a part of his attack upon Eunomius' sequencing or ranking of the Son and Spirit through an ἐνέργεια-based causality in which there is a διάστημα between the οὐσία (or φύσις) and its causal powers or properties.

74. This is a very important example for Gregory to use, for it originally appears in Origen's *On First Principles* 2:6:6 as an analogy describing the virtuous nature of Christ's human soul. According to Origen, while Christ's soul is not good by nature and therefore could theoretically choose good or evil, His soul embraces the good so thoroughly that a falling away is virtually impossible. Origen then offers this analogy: a piece of iron placed in fire will take on the fire, so long as the iron remains in the fire, and could never become (or receive) cold, even though in principle iron is susceptible to both the hot and the cold. In the same way, Christ's soul becomes and is good, and could never become evil.

In *On the Holy Spirit* 16:38, Basil uses the presence of fire in iron to make the same kind of natural, for it is not in the nature of iron to be hot, but only to receive heat (to become hot). The sign of the difference between the way heat or light subsists in fire versus the way heat or light subsists in iron is the fact that iron can be either hot or cold, but fire cannot be cold. Here again contraries figure in Gregory's reasoning, and again Gregory finds moral dualism in the suggestion that there are divine products that are susceptible to contrary attributions. If the Son and Spirit are good by participation and not by nature, then they are receptive to evil just as the hot iron is receptive to cold.[75]

Gregory discusses the relationship of powers to nature in a different context when he offers his own theory of names in Book 2 of *Against Eunomius;* here names are said to refer to the nature and the power of individual things.[76] In creation's compounded or complex state of existence, the nature is the real unity of a thing, while powers are the multiple components and qualities of that compounded thing. Again Gregory turns to fire as an illustration: fire is one thing in its nature, but it possesses the multiple powers of shining, burning, drying, heating, etc.[77] Speech reflects both lev-

---

point as Gregory: unlike the Holy Spirit, the angels are not holy by nature, but holiness is received by them and exists in them, just as fire is received by iron. Basil's use of this analogy is an implicit criticism of Origen, while Gregory's use of the analogy of iron in fire as an example of the wrong understanding of why the Son manifests the same power(s) as the Father is a definite rejection of Origen's reasoning on this point. More importantly, Gregory provides evidence that the Nicenes rejected the idea of using the language of moral unity that described the unity present in the Incarnation to describe the unity present in the Godhead. Gregory's argument also suggests that in fact Origen's theology of the pre-existent soul of Christ may have played a role in Eunomius' trinitarian theology.

75. "[T]o suppose that the nature of each of them [Son and Spirit] is necessarily defectible, equally receptive of opposites and lying on the boundary between good and its opposite, is utterly profane. One who says this will be arguing that it is one thing in its own proper definition and becomes something else by participation in good and evil. Thus with iron, it happens that, if it associates for a long time with fire, it takes on the quality of heat while remaining iron, but if it gets into snow or ice, it changes its quality towards the prevailing influence, taking the cold of the snow into its own intimate parts" (*GNO* 1:110:5–14; Hall, 76).

76. *GNO* 1:305:23–24; *NPNF* 5:278.

77. Gregory's theory that names refer to the powers that any single existent possesses resembles the discussion of names in the *Cratylus* as much as Eunomius' theory does. In the *Cratylus* 400 B–420 A, Plato writes that names refer to the δυνάμεις of an object. At 417 B4, for example, Plato speaks of a name that indicates the δύναμις, as he does again at 420 A2. The most important example of names reflecting δυνάμεις is the case of the gods, as when Plato mentions the δυνάμεις of Poseidon at 402, and of Apollo at 404 E–405 E, already discussed in chapter 2. This practice of finding the etymologies of divine names in divine δυνάμεις remained popular in the Hellenistic era.

els of existence—as unity, as multiplicity—by providing a name for the unified nature (that is, "fire") and by providing names for the components of fire (that is, "hot", "bright", etc.). Gregory emphasizes that "bright" does not name the unity that is named by "fire."

In this argument Gregory obviously has in mind Eunomius' identification of "Unbegotten" with "God," though his eventual point in this exegesis of Gen. 1 is to emphasize the way in which component names implicitly refer to their opposite. "Dry land," for example, not only gives "dry" as a power of "land," it distinguishes dry land from its opposite, wet water. When Genesis records that "God called the light day," the reader understands the opposition between light and dark.[78] In Gregory's account names implicitly mirror the opposition that exists in creation, and carry that opposition in their nature;[79] when names are used of the non-created, God, they project into that realm of existence oppositions that are characteristic of created being but not of uncreated being. Eunomius' error is to carry the opposition between Unbegotten and Begotten (as created names) over into the divine existents themselves. Divine nature does not share in this kind of existence where there is a distinction between what an existent is insofar as it is a single thing and what an existent is insofar as it is a unity of components. Human reason both shares this unity/component, nature/power kind of existence and is limited to the knowledge of this kind of

78. Gregory's brother Basil remarks upon this same semantic relationship between *dry* and *land* in *Homilies on the Hexaemeron,* as John F. Callahan describes in "Greek Philosophy and Cappadocian Cosmology," *Dumbarton Oaks Papers* 12 (1952): 30–57, esp. 45–46. Callahan recognizes Basil's assumption of a class of "peculiar characteristics" that "offers the nature of the thing." He also recognizes that this conception of "peculiar characteristics" is related to elemental physics: each elemental "has received a particular quality that distinguishes it from the others and permits us to recognize it for what it is. Water has for its especial quality cold; air, [has] moisture; and fire, [has] heat." Where Callahan slips is in his premature discovery of Aristotle as Basil's source for the association of a conception of peculiar characteristics with the idea of elementals (see his page 45, especially note 66). Callahan never recognizes this physics-based theory of peculiar characteristics for what it is, *power* physics.

79. I have already referred to Gregory's belief that things in themselves implicitly refer to their opposites, but the passage is worth repeating: "It is high time we observed the difference between elements, and how everything in the world that contributes to the constitution of the universe points towards what is contrary to its nature" (*GNO* 1:143:27–144:2; Hall, 93; *NPNF* 5:72). Names do not suggest their opposite as a result of being names, but as created "things," they suggest their opposite because all created things suggest their opposite. This judgment of Gregory's brings him close to the mixture physics of the Hippocratics and Anaxagoras since the reason why created things suggest their opposite is because all created things contain their opposite.

existence, but divine reason is not. "What need, then, in His case, of parts of speech when His own wisdom and power embraces and holds the nature of all things distinct and unconfused?"[80] By their nature, then, names are for the use of created reason only.[81]

The distinction between the compounded state of human existence and the simple state of divine existence occurs again when Gregory distinguishes the state of human will from the state of divine will. There is no interval between the nature and the will in God while there is an interval between human nature and will. To describe the simple state of will and nature in God, Gregory offers a tentative illustration: what if, he hypothesizes, we attribute the power of choice to a flame?[82]

It would be clear [then] that the flame will at once upon its existence will that its radiance should shine forth from itself, and when it wills it will not be impotent since its natural power [δύναμις] at once fulfills its will.[83]

The choice of fire for a hypothetical example of a simple unity of nature with will is interesting for several reasons. While fire with a will may seem an unusual possibility to modern sensibilities, Gregory is himself familiar with a psychological theory that describes fire as similar to intelligence.[84]

80. *GNO* 1:309:25; *NPNF* 5:279.

81. Though God's existence is simple in a way created existence is not, when Gregory refers to the title(s) of God, he consistently prefers multiple titles over a single one. This preference seems contrary to Gregory's insistence on the unity of God's existence since God's simplicity might seem best reflected in a single term. Clearly Gregory is led to emphasize the virtues of a multiplicity of names for God by the example of Eunomius' emphasis on a single title. Yet the most important reason for setting a description of God in multiple titles follows from Gregory's understanding of the fundamental character of created existence. Gregory's reasoning is that since created existence is composed of opposites and since our intelligence functions through the use of oppositions, God's presence in the world, either in his actions or in our knowledge of Him, will necessarily be experienced in a multiplicity. Basil also justifies his theory of ἐπίνοια by this argument. If the reader keeps in mind the perspective from which title(s) are given to God, then Gregory's shifts from attributing a single power to God to attributing multiple powers (or properties) will be less confusing. This conceptual shift back and forth between the perspective of a single nature and a single power, and a single nature and multiple powers, is supported by traditional power physics.

82. *GNO* 2:192:18.

83. *GNO* 2:192:22; *NPNF* 5:202. Gregory has already spoken of the generation of the Son using the language of the ray streaming from the Sun, "whose cause is indeed the Sun, but whose existence is co-extensive with the Sun . . . who indeed is a second Sun" (*GNO* 1:180:20 ff.; Hall, 112).

84. Another authority for using fire in this way is the Bible, since Gregory recognizes fire as a scripturally-based metaphor for God, as in Mal. 3:2,3, where "the divine power, acting like fire . . ." (see *Catechetical Oration* 24). The identification of fire with intelligence is further illustrated in Philo's allegorical exegesis of Gen. 22:7b in *On Flight and Finding* 24:132–34, where the fire of

In *On the Making of Man* Gregory refers to those who locate mind in the heart because intelligence is similar to fire, for "fire and the understanding are alike in perpetual motion."[85] Fire and heat have no role in Gregory's own psychology, but they do figure in his physiology: heat is one of the three elements found in all organisms. The immediate source of heat is the heart (and lungs) through the respiratory-circulatory system.[86]

In terms of Hellenistic theology, however, Gregory's use of fire does not lack precedent. The *Chaldean Oracles* use fire to speak of productive activity within the transcendent hierarchy: for example, "For the First Transcendent Fire does not enclose its own Power in matter by means of works, but by means of Intellect" and "For after he thought his works, the self-generated Paternal Intellect sowed the bonds of Love, heavy with fire, into all things."[87] As has already been described (and as is obvious from these

---

"Behold the fire!" is interpreted as "Behold the mind, breath all warm and on fire . . ." (Coulson and Whittaker, Loeb 5:81). Rist, *Plotinus,* 68, suggests that Plotinus uses heat from fire to illustrate the emanation of Νοῦς because of the Stoic description of the ἡγεμονικόν as a kind of emanation from the sun.

The Christian authority for Gregory's theological application of fire is Origen and *On First Principles* 2:7:3, where he gathers together the scriptural references to God as fire to support his etymology of the word "soul" (ψυχή) from "getting cold" (ψύχεσθαι). "As therefore God is fire and the angels a flame of fire and the saints are all fervent in spirit, so on the contrary those who have fallen away from the love of God must undoubtedly be said to have cooled in their affection for him and to have become cold" (Butterworth, 123). Origen's scriptural references in support of describing God as fire include Deut. 4:24 and 9:3, Jer. 5:14, and Heb. 1:7. In both his *Homilies on the Hexameron* 6:3 and *On the Holy Spirit* 16:38, Basil speaks at length on the importance of fire, including a familiar reference to the relationship between iron and the fire that sometimes inhabits it. Callahan suggests a Stoic influence in Basil's discourse "on the important role that is played by fire in the universe" ("Cappadocian Cosmology," 47). Gregory of Nazianzus provides another example of the presumed relationship between God and fire when he speaks of those "bright students of Greek etymology" who derive the word "God" "from words meaning 'to run' or 'to burn'—the idea being continuous movement and consuming of evil qualities hence, certainly God is called a 'consuming fire' [at Deut. 4:24, one of Origen's "fire" texts]" (*Theological Oration* 30.18; Norris et al., *Faith Gives Fullness,* 274).

85. *NPNF* 5:397; *On the Making of Man* 157c. In *Against Eunomius* 2, Gregory again refers to perpetual motion as a δύναμις of fire; see *GNO* 1:260:21; *NPNF* 5:261.

86. *On the Making of Man* 20–21; *NPNF* 5:425.

87. Majercik, *Chaldean Oracles,* no. 5, 50–51, and no. 39, 62–63. John Dillon has suggested that the *Chaldean Oracles* influenced Gregory of Nazianzus' trinitarian theology, which makes similarities between language in the *Oracles* and in our Gregory's writings suggestive of an influence relationship (but only suggestive). See Dillon's "Logos and Trinity: Patterns of Platonist Influence on Early Christianity," in *The Philosophy in Christianity,* ed. Godfrey Vesey (Cambridge: Cambridge University Press, 1989), 1–14.

quotations), the theology of the *Oracles* brings together ideas of transcendent Power, divine generation, and, somewhat distinctively, fire (for unlike the Stoics, fire is here not immanent). Gregory says, "Fire with a will"; the *Oracles* say, "Fire with an Intellect."[88]

*Marks of Being*

The last contrast of Gregory's theology of connatural union with Eunomius' theology of ranked beings that I will treat is found in his rebuttal of Eunomius' statement that the mode of generation is indicated by the natural rank of the one who generates.[89] Gregory's comments on this fragment from the *Second Apology* provide a good illustration of the contrast between his and Eunomius' idea of rank, and how Gregory applies his account of connatural powers, developed in the discussion of elementals (for example, fire), to explain theological titles.[90]

When Eunomius says that "the mode of generation is indicated by the natural rank of the one who generates," he means to distinguish between the kind of generation that produced the Son and the kind of generation that produced the Spirit or the cosmos. The natural analogue to this distinction in Arius' theology is the doctrine that the Son is made but not as all else was made. In Eunomius' theology, the generation of the Son by the Father must be a different kind of production than the generation of the Spirit or cosmos by the Son, because God's rank is greater ("higher") than the Son's. To be created by God is not the same as to be created by the Son, for each act of creation produces a different kind of creature. This principle is invoked in the *Apology* to explain the Son's mediating role and to justify His status as a divinity to the cosmos. The product of God's own creative

88. An interesting question that remains to be explored is whether Gregory's use of fire in the context of divine generation can be used to shed some light on the *Chaldean Oracles'* incomplete and confusing understanding of the character of the unity among the existents in the transcendent triad. If the effect of Gregory's use of fire in an analogy of divine productivity is to emphasize the unity of nature between generator and generated, is the effect the same for the *Oracles'* use of fire?

89. The word here translated as rank is ἀξία, which I have earlier translated as dignity.

90. Gregory's comparison of the power heat and the nature of fire to the power providence and the nature of God occurs at *GNO* 1:155:1–156:4; the rebuttal of Eunomius' claim that the mode of generation is indicated by the natural rank of the one who generates begins at 160:3; so the one argument follows the other relatively closely.

act receives a delegated creative capacity, by which the Spirit and all the cosmos are made. In the *Apology*, this reasoning supports the doctrine of the divine role (though not the divine nature) of the second Person. In the *Second Apology*, however, this reasoning supports a doctrine of rigid divisions among kinds of being, not only between uncaused and caused, but among kinds of causes of being.

Gregory sees in this doctrine from the *Second Apology* another restatement of Eunomius' understanding that the being of God (the Father) is alone authentic and highest, because the sole indication of God's "natural rank" is that He is ingenerate. To this single indicator, Gregory contrasts his own "indicators of rank":

In our teaching, the indicators in God of connatural rank are deity itself, wisdom and power, and being good, [being] judge, just, mighty, patient, true, creator, sovereign, invisible and unending. . . .[91]

Each of these indicators of connatural rank[92] is to be found in both the Father and the Son; indeed, Gregory chooses these indicators from scriptural titles given to the Son.[93] But Gregory's point in providing the list is to contrast Eunomius' single indicator (ἀγέννητος), which applies only to God (the Father), with a list of indicators that apply to divine nature without intrinsic reference to persons. From this kind of list he can draw the conclusions that, first, such indicators refer to both Persons, and, second, both Persons are shown to share the same nature.

. . . if each of the expressions [in his list] is recognized as having a specific meaning appropriate to the concept of God, then clearly the honourable rank connatural in God corresponds to the list of names, and thereby the being follows logically, if indeed the connatural rank indicates the underlying realities. But since the indicators of connatural rank appear the same in each of them, the identity of being of the entities [that is, the Father and the Son] to which those ranks are attributed is

91. *GNO* 1:161:23–24; Hall, 103.

92. Variations on *indicate* are offered as translations of the forms of δείκνυμι that Gregory uses. I am not satisfied with either Hall's or Wilson and Moore's translations of this argument and passage from Gregory, and I have used theirs (primarily Hall's) only as the foundation for my own. The sense of Hall's is basically right, but the importance of Gregory's contrast of συμφυής with Eunomius' φυσική is not there. I know of no suitable consistent translation for all the appearances of συμφυής.

93. As he admits at *GNO* 1:161:25; Hall, 103.

plainly recognized. If one difference of title is reckoned enough to indicate distinctness of being, how much more will the identity of so many titles argue for community of nature![94]

Once again Gregory returns to the argument that the unity of the divine nature of the Father and Son is shown by their possession of common connatural properties. Indeed, Gregory's rebuttal may fairly be characterized as pivoting upon his refusal to speak of φυσικὴ ἀξία at all. This is Eunomius' phrase, and Gregory's alternative is important: συμφυὴς ἀξία. Συμφυής has appeared in Gregory's discussion before; for example, "Heat is a natural property [or συμφυής] of fire, luminosity to the sunbeam, fluidity to water, gravity to stone, and one could mention many other similar instances."[95] By using συμφυής Gregory holds his discussion of indicators to the realm of God's natural properties, for this is the realm that we can know, and to which names of God can refer. The contrast between Eunomius' understanding of indicators and Gregory's may be summarized in this way: Eunomius understands the indicator to be identical with the divine essence, while Gregory understands the indicator precisely not to be identical with the divine essence.

In the last two sections of this chapter, I want to discuss two apparent exceptions to my thesis that Gregory's argument for the unity of the Trinity is built upon a technical use of the concept *power,* and that argument is "If the same power, then the same nature." The first of these exceptions arises directly from Gregory's writings: the use of power as a distinctly Christological title, in which the Son (or the Son's divinity) is identified as God's Power. The second apparent exception to my thesis arises out of previous scholarship on "Cappadocian" trinitarian theology, and may fairly well be described as the dominant scholarly judgement on that theology: the distinctive and fundamental concept for the Cappadocian argument for the unity of the Trinity is "operations" (or activities), as it appears in the argument, "Common operations indicate common natures." I have used the phrase "apparent exceptions" to describe these two points to suggest already my reply: both of these "exceptions" are special case applications in which the general, over-arching argument of "one nature, one power" remains in force.

94. *GNO* 1:163:2–14; Hall, 103–4.

95. Ibid., 1:147:17–20; 95.

*Christ, the Power of God*

In his later writings against Eunomius, Gregory uses power (still δύναμις) in other arguments for the second Person's unity with the First. These arguments all have in common the identification of the second Person with God's power, unlike the argument in Book 1 (an argument that returns in *On the Holy Trinity*) where Gregory very carefully speaks of power as the power of the divine nature that is common to all the Persons. The description of the second Person as the Power of God is typical of Nicene theologies from an earlier stage in the fourth-century trinitarian controversies; for example, Athanasius describes the Son as the Power of God. Like Athanasius, Gregory identifies the Son with the Power of God primarily to demonstrate the eternity of the Son rather than to provide an understanding of how the second Person is related to the First, that is, as a power is united with a nature.

For in saying that the Lord "once was not," you will not merely assert the non-existence of Power, but you will be saying that the Power of God, Who is the Father of the Power, "was not."[96]

and

He who says, then, that "He was not before His generation" absolutely proclaims this,—that when He "was not" there was no truth, no life, no light, no power . . . no other of those pre-eminent qualities which are conceived of Him. . . . If, then, the Only-Begotten God, as Eunomius says, "was not before His generation," and Christ is "the Power of God and the Wisdom of God," [1 Cor. 1:24] and the "express image" and the "brightness," [Heb. 1:3] neither surely did the Father exist, Whose Power and Wisdom and express image and the brightness the Son is. . . .[97]

Both Athanasius and Gregory found the identification of the Son with the Power of God an effective way to refute the doctrines that the second Person was created and that common titles attributed to God (the Father) and the Son are given equivocally. Athanasius found these two doctrines in

96. *GNO* 2:81:13–15; *NPNF* 5:144.

97. Ibid., 2:204:6–12; 5:207. Gregory offers the same argument in his *Refutation of the Creed*. "For if the Son, as the Scripture says, is the Power of God, and Wisdom . . . and the like, then before the Son existed, according to the view of these heretics, these things also had no existence at all. And if these things had no existence they must certainly conceive the bosom of the Father to have been devoid of such excellences" (*GNO* 2:316:6 ff.; *NPNF* 5:102).

Arius' and Asterius' theologies, respectively (although Athanasius did not distinguish between their two theologies).

Given the widespread use of the argument that *since Christ is the Power of God, He is eternal, or otherwise, God was once without His power,* the theological sophistication of the argument is difficult to analyze. How much does demonstrating the eternity of the Son accomplish as an indicator of His nature? The idea that any existent that is eternal cannot be created depends upon a prior understanding that to be caused is to have a beginning. Eunomius understands this quite clearly and in fact depends upon it for his argument that the Son both has a beginning and will have an end. Yet a strict Origenist position would not make any such assumption about an opposition between being caused and being eternal. The Origenist position also would not allow that a text like 1 Cor. 1:24 identifies Christ with God's own Power and would find the argument, "If the Son is not eternal, then God was without His Power," nonsense.

The effectiveness of the argument that the identification of the Son with God's Power means that the Son is eternal or else once God was without His Power depends upon a growing perception of the weakness in Origen's thought. For example, the strength of Origen's thought in the theology of Eusebius allows him to shake off an argument like Athanasius' (for Eusebius considers 1 Cor. 1:24 an important text for his theology). But, on the other hand, Eunomius' understanding that to be caused is to have a beginning shows an important way in which Eunomius' theology was distinctly un-Origenist. An argument for Christ's divinity from His eternity would score against any anti-Nicene theology that shared Eunomius' understanding that nothing that is caused can be eternal. Gregory has good reason to use this kind of argument, but he also has reason to try to develop it further, which indeed he does.

In *Against Eunomius* 3:4, Gregory argues that anything done by the Son is also done by God the Father, because the Son is the Power of God, and it is by His Power that God (the Father) acts. This argument is a more straightforward interpretation of the kind of identification found in 1 Cor. 1:24 of the second Person with God's power. Calling the Son the Power of God automatically provides Gregory with a doctrine of unity as long as Gregory is willing to identify the Son with the single power of God and thus avoid the ambiguities of earlier "two-powers" theologies. Like the argument that common powers mean common natures, this argument by Gregory demonstrates the unity of nature from the unity of an existent or nature with its power. It also emphasizes the specific power of creating (and the cosmos as the product of that power) as being particularly indicative of divine nature.

Whether you look at the world as a whole, or at the parts of the world which make up that complete whole, all these are works [ἔργα] of the Father, in that they are works [ἔργα] of His Power. . . for the activity [ἐνέργεια] of the Power [δύναμις] bears relation to Him Whose Power [δύναμις] it is. Thus, since the Son is the Power [δύναμις] of the Father, all these works [ἔργα] of the Son are works [ἔργα] of the Father.[98]

There are many things to be said about this passage. First, it provides one of the clearest examples of Gregory's use of the causal sequence δύναμις—ἐνέργεια—ἔργα. The power's activities produce works. In this passage Gregory uses the same causal sequence as Eunomius usually does, but with the significant addition of power. In fact, the presence of power in the sequence is not a new category that Gregory adds, but he restores the usual sequence. Gregory's understanding of the relationships between δύναμις, ἐνέργεια and ἔργα is indeed wholly conventional. The non-"Aristotelian" understanding of the relationship between δύναμις and ἐνέργεια, for example, is evident. Even Gregory's apparent lack of interest in including φύσις or οὐσία in the sequence (since neither of these terms appear in the argument) mirrors the way both Galen and Julian used the sequence (though there is more to be said about this lack of φύσις or οὐσία).[99] The relationship between the power and the activity is the same one that appears later in *On "Not Three Gods"* and *On the Holy Trinity:* ". . . we perceive the varied activity [ἐνέργεια] of the power [δύναμις]. . . ."[100] and we judge from the activity the power to which it belongs.[101]

98. *GNO* 2:147:8–12; *NPNF* 5:187. At 147:1 Gregory quotes 1 Cor. 1:24 to suggest the identification of the Son with God's Power. Moore and Wilson, the translators of the *NPNF* volume, do not include this citation in their translation.

99. While both of these authors acknowledge the priority of the φύσις or οὐσία, in practical terms they begin their accounts with δυνάμεις.

100. *GNO* 3:1a 44:7–8; *NPNF* 5:333.

101. Ibid., 44:19–21; 5:333.

The second noteworthy aspect of the passage from Book 3:4 quoted above is that by speaking of the Son as the "Power of God," Gregory implicitly treats the Person of the Father as the existent or nature that has a power. The Son is the power of God the Father, not of God the nature (as it were). If Gregory's earlier exegesis of 1 Cor. 1:24 in *Against Eunomius*, Book 1—that the Father and Son share the same Power—seemed abstract or seemed to deny the literal sense of the scriptural text, this more obvious exegesis may seem not just more subordinationist but more ambiguous. However, the context of Gregory's statement gives some insight into the precise nature of the claim he is making for the formula "the Son is the Power of God the Father." This argument by Gregory occurs in an explicitly Christological context, in response to anti-Nicene criticism that if Christ is truly divine, and Christ suffers (for example, on the Cross), then the divine nature must have suffered, including—and this is what is wholly unacceptable to the anti-Nicenes—the divine nature of the Father. Again the problem is expressed in terms of passion: if the Son is divine, and suffered the "passion" of the Cross, then divinity (including God the Father) suffered passion. The fear that a fully divine Son suffered and died implies passion in the Godhead recurs within the different generations of non-Nicene and anti-Nicene theology.

Gregory's response to this criticism is to argue that nothing can truly be said to be a passion that does not lead to sin. Whatever the Son suffered was not passion since these sufferings did not (as everyone agrees) lead Him to sin. Such acts of nature that do not lead to sin Gregory calls natural works—ἔργα! Gregory's defense of these acts of nature is a restatement of the same kind of argument he made in *On the Soul and Resurrection*. Feelings are to be judged according to their use; any feeling that follows the will of God and does not lead to sin either is a passion only in some equivocal sense, or one must admit that there are some passions that are good. And indeed, Gregory finishes his argument that the works of the Son are the works of the Father because the Son is the Power of the Father by which the Father acts by declaring that the Son acts "by the authority of His will."[102] Thus, the argument that the works of the activities of the Power of

102. *GNO* 2:147:15. *Authority* translates ἐξουσία.

God not only establishes the Son's full divinity, it also establishes God the Father's role in the economy of the Incarnation, for He does these works—which are not passions—through the activities of His own power.[103]

Gregory later offers a slightly different version of his argument identifying the second Person with the Power of God that also suggests the psychological content of δύναμις. In his *Refutation of the Creed* of 383, Gregory again identifies the second Person with God's power. Once again there is the implicit sequence of δύναμις-ἐνέργεια-ἔργα, and once again the power is understood primarily as the power that creates.

For at one and the same time did He [God the Father] will that that which ought to be should be, and His Power [δύναμις], that produced all things that are, kept pace with His will, turning His will into actions [ἔργα]. For thus the mighty Moses in the record of creation instructs us about the Divine Power [θεῖα δύναμις]. . . . For God, when creating all things that have their origin by creation, neither stood in need of any matter on which to operate, nor of instruments to aid Him in His construction: for the Power and Wisdom of God has no need of any external assistance. But Christ is 'the Power of God and the Wisdom of God'. . . . [Therefore] His will alone suffices to effect the subsistence of existing things (for His will is power [δύναμις]). . . .[104]

Although Gregory's polemical identification of the second Person with the Power of God may seem quite distinct from his primary argument that the Father and the Son share the same power (and thus the same nature), the two doctrines have several features in common. For example, both polemical uses of power work from the understanding that the presence of the power is co-extensive with the presence of the nature.[105] For the study

103. Gregory emphasizes the act of creation in this argument because the Son's role as Creator reveals Him to be divine (as the previous chapter showed) and because the act of creating is admitted by all sides to be a passionless act (unlike generation). From the time of Basil of Ancyra, anti-Eunomian polemic used the passionlessness of this act as a paradigm for God's activities.

104. *GNO* 2:340:23–341:11; *NPNF* 5:111. The reference to 1 Cor. 1:24 is obvious. Just two sentences later (at 341:13) Gregory makes the same argument citing Hebrews 1:3b—what need of instrument or matter does "the Word of His Power" have for creating?

105. An understanding evident in Origen's argument in his *Dialogue with Heraclides.* Victorinus is the only polemicist that I know of who explicitly relates ὁμοούσιος to a one-power trinitarian theology. (I suspect that the rarity of this connection is due to the relative importance of ὁμοούσιος for westerners compared to the Cappadocian tendency to use μία φύσις type formulations—at least in their polemical works.) Victorinus offers the relationship between seeing and the faculty of sight precisely as an example of ὁμοούσιος to illustrate the trinitarian sense of the

at hand, the most important aspect of Gregory's identification of Christ with "the Power of God" may be that it draws attention to the traditional, scripturally-based, Christological associations of power. The traditional association of power with the second Person gives the title authority as a basis for arguing for the divinity of the Son if Gregory can convince his readers that the sense of power as a traditional title for Christ is (what I have been calling) the ontological sense. And indeed, most of Gregory's polemical references to power in *Against Eunomius* are directed at normalizing the interpretation of the power as an ontological term, as I have shown in this chapter.

Gregory's own interest in the title *power* extends beyond the traditional Christological associations: as I first noted in the Introduction, in *On the Trinity* Gregory summarizes his faith with the formula: "We confess three Persons . . . there is one goodness, and one power [δύναμις], and one Godhead."[106] The sense of *power* here is clearly similar to Origen's in *Dialogue with Heraclides,* rather than like the Athanasian identification of the Son with Power. And yet later in *On the Trinity* (as in *On "Not Three Gods"*), when Gregory turns to arguing for the divinity of the Spirit, the recurring term is *activity,* ἐνέργεια, and not *power,* δύναμις. Indeed, in specific arguments for the Holy Spirit that parallel earlier arguments for the Son, *activity* appears in the former where *power* appeared in the latter.[107] This difference in Gregory's reasoning should be understood as the result of the pneumatological associations of *activity* given authority in Basil's treatise *On the Holy Spirit.*

term. After citing 1 Cor. 1:24, Victorinus says: ". . . the power and wisdom of God are like vision: the power of vision has vision within it. This vision is externalized when the power of vision is in action; then vision is begotten by the power of vision and is itself its only begotten, for nothing else is begotten by it. And vision encompasses the power of vision, not only within, when it is in potentiality, but above all, outside, when it is in action; so vision encompasses the power of vision. Vision is therefore ὁμοούσιον [consubstantial (*sic*)] with the power of vision, and the whole is one . . ." (*Against Arius* 1A; Clark, 154–55).

106. *GNO* 3:1a 5:18 ff.; *NPNF* 5:326–27.

107. The clearest case of this substitution is in the argument from fire: in *Against Eunomius,* Gregory says that a δύναμις of fire indicates the presence of fire; in the two later short works, Gregory says that an ἐνέργεια of fire indicates the presence of fire. The two statements are not contradictions since, as I have shown, Gregory considers an ἐνέργεια to be the activity of a δύναμις.

*Activity-Based Argument for the Divinity of the Holy Spirit*

Dating many of Gregory's writings is a notoriously difficult task, but even when the exact date of origin is not certain, it is still possible to know the chronological sequence of texts; that is, the relative order specific works were probably written in. Gregory's short works on the Trinity were almost certainly written after the first two (and perhaps all three) books of *Against Eunomius.* This is an important fact to keep in mind when one reads the short treatises, in order to be sensitive to the doctrinal context in which they were written. In *Against Eunomius* Gregory developed an argument for the unity of nature between Father and Son based upon the common power that he has shown the two to share. This argument from power enables him to utilize etiological language that has the sanction of Scripture and the authority of traditional theology, and which is given content by philosophy and medicine. In short, Gregory has a good argument. When Gregory turns to arguing in a way that includes, or focuses upon, the full divinity of the Holy Spirit, the general form of his previous argument against Eunomius remains: the common actions performed by the Father, Son, and Holy Spirit are proof of their common nature. What changes is the term in the etiological chain that he emphasizes by associating it with the divine Person.

Given the modern popularity of *On the Holy Trinity* and *On "Not Three Gods,"* it may seem incredible to note that there are no scholarly historical or contextual studies of the theology of either of these texts. It is common to cite these texts in evidence of a description of Gregory's theology, as Quasten does; it is common to cite these texts as illustrations of Gregory's theology, as Bettenson does; and it is common to cite these texts to characterize Gregory's theology, as virtually all systematicians do. However, a glance at the *Bibliographie zu Gregor von Nyssa*[108] will show that scholars have not commonly asked the question: how do we read these texts in their specific historical context? Indeed, the question, what is the specific historical context of *On the Holy Trinity* and *On "Not Three Gods"*? seems not to have been raised seriously. With that in mind, I turn now to the

108. Altenberger and Mann, *Bibliographie zu Gregor von Nyssa: Editionen, Übersetzungen, Literatur* (Leiden: E. J. Brill, 1988).

texts themselves, read in comparison with Gregory's other trinitarian works, with the trinitarian works of his brother Basil, and the trinitarian works of Gregory of Nazianzus.

*On the Trinity* says that it was written in defense of the doctrine that there are "three Persons, one Goodness, one Power, and one Godhead." There are people, Gregory says, who accuse him of teaching that "the goodness is one, and [the same] of the power, and [the same] of the Godhead, and [of] all such attributes in the singular." The general charge against Gregory and his followers is that "we do not employ in the plural any of the names which belong to God. . . ." Gregory's reply to these criticisms is to acknowledge that they indeed accurately describe his beliefs. Gregory then proceeds to explain why those attributes ascribed to God are employed (by him) only in the singular.

Gregory's attention to the singleness of the power and other terms for the divinity needs to be recognized. Gregory's doctrine was that there is one power equally present in each of the three Persons; any Person Who lacks the power of the Godhead is separate in nature from divinity.[109] Gregory can then argue that since the power of the Spirit is included in the power of the Father and Son,[110] the Spirit is divine. Gregory of Nazianzus uses a similar formula in his argument for the divinity of the Spirit. For example, he ends *Oration* 31, his *Oration On the Holy Spirit,* "To the best of my powers I will persuade all men to worship Father, Son, and Holy Spirit as the single Godhead and power. . . ."[111]

While in *On the Trinity* Gregory speaks of the one-ness of the divine Power he tends to speak of the diversity of the divine operations. Nonetheless, however many operations there are,[112] they are all performed equally and in unison by the three Persons, and because each Person performs the same activities, the activity of the Godhead is "one" (thereby demonstrating the unity of divine nature). The argument by Gregory that if it can be shown that each Person performs the same activities and the activity of the Godhead is one, then the divine nature is one is also found in *On "Not*

109. *GNO* 3a 7:4.

110. Ibid., 3a 7:22–24.

111. Norris, *Faith Gives Fullness,* 299. For Gregory's use of the formula "essence and power" in this *Oration,* see 31.16, 287, and Norris' comments on page 200.

112. Basil describes the number of operations as infinite in his *On the Spirit* 19:49.

*Three Gods*".[113] In this work Gregory says that from the different "operations of the Power above us," we develop titles for each of God's different operations, but each operation belongs to the ". . . Power [that] extends throughout the three Persons."[114] Stated thus, the operations-based argument can be seen as a variation of the power/nature syllogism I just gave. Like that power/nature syllogism the operations/nature argument depends on a technical philosophical understanding of the relationship between operations and nature, an understanding that in Gregory's time was in fact related to technical philosophical understanding of the relationship between power and nature. For the purposes of this chapter, it is enough to note that there is an intrinsic conceptual connection between a power/nature argument and an operations/nature argument that Gregory can and does exploit. The leap from power and nature language to operations and nature language is not a great one for Gregory; indeed, it is a conventional one.

As a general characterization, we can say that when Gregory's argument in *On the Holy Trinity* and *On "Not Three Gods"* is compared to his argument in *Against Eunomius,* we see that there is a shift from an argument for the unity of nature based on the single Power common to the Persons to an argument for the unity of nature based on multiple operations common to the Persons. The pivotal images of the arguments show a corresponding change as well: Gregory's shifts from the analogy of fire's power of heat in *Against Eunomius* to the analogy of fire's activity of heat in *On the Holy Trinity* and *On "Not Three Gods"*. These changes, in particular, the activity language, indicate that *On the Holy Trinity* and *On "Not Three Gods"* are polemically-motivated statements of the unity of the Trinity written primarily to defend (or establish) the full divinity of the Spirit. I make this judgement based on two observations. First, there is an association of ἐνέργεια language with Spirit theology in Basil's writings, especially in Spirit polemics in Basil's *Against Eunomius.* Secondly, there is evidence from Gregory of Nazianzus that in the early 380s ἐνέργεια language was particularly associated with the question of the Spirit's identity. I turn

113. In both *On the Trinity* and *On "Not Three Gods"*, as in *Against Eunomius,* Gregory refers to what is one in the Godhead equally as either nature or power.

114. *GNO* 3a 44:7–21; *NPNF* 5:333.

first to Basil's use of ἐνέργεια in his polemics for the Holy Spirit in his *Against Eunomius.*

Basil's argument in *Against Eunomius* for the Spirit's divinity is built upon the two scriptural texts, 1 Cor. 12:4–6 and 12:11, both of which are ἐνέργεια texts.[115]

Διαιρέσεις δὲ χαρισμάτων εἰσίν, τὸ δὲ αὐτὸ Πνεῦμα· καὶ διαιρέσεις διακονιῶν εἰσιν, καὶ ὁ αὐτὸς Κύριος· καὶ διαιρέσεις *ἐνεργημάτων* εἰσίν, ὁ δὲ αὐτὸς θεὸς ὁ *ἐνεργῶν* τὰ πάντα ἐν πᾶσιν.

and

. . . πάντα δὲ ταῦτα *ἐνεργεῖ* τὸ ἓν καὶ τὸ αὐτὸ Πνεῦμα, διαιροῦν ἰδίᾳ ἑκάστῳ καθὼς βούλεται.

Basil uses these texts, singly or together, in his two major treatments of the Spirit, in *On the Holy Spirit*[116] and in Book 3 of his *Against Eunomius.*[117] Indeed, Basil's only references to these two texts in *Against Eunomius* are in Book 3 of that work, the book devoted to arguing for the divinity of the Spirit. Gregory does not cite 1 Cor. 12:4–6 in *On "Not Three Gods",* although he does cite 1 Cor. 12:11.[118] However, Gregory's use of 1 Cor. 12:11 in *On the Faith* makes clear the polemical association of the text, and the concept of ἐνέργεια, with the Spirit.[119] In that work the scriptural passage served as a bridge between Gregory's account of what, exactly, the Spirit does and his argument that the attributes applied to the Father and Son are also to be applied to the Spirit.

Similarly, Gregory twice refers to 1 Cor. 12:4–6 in the sections of his *Refutation of Eunomius' Creed* of 383 where he argues for the divinity of the

115. The modern reader may not see this passage as a "Spirit" text since ἐνέργεια is in fact used of God (the Father), but for Basil the passage speaks of "the Spirit . . . the Lord . . . and God" in terms of a functional equality in a passage using ἐνέργεια. That is enough for him. See Michael A. G. Haykin, *The Spirit of God: The Exegesis of 1 and 2 Corinthians in the Pneumatomachian Controversy of the Fourth Century* (Leiden: E. J. Brill, 1994), 149–52, for his discussion of 1 Cor. 12: 4–6 and 12:11 in Basil's *Against Eunomius.* Haykin does not identify ἐνέργεια specifically in terms of its pneumatological connotations. The pneumatological connotations of 1 Cor. 12:4–6 and 12:11 are already there in Athanasius, as Haykin points out at pages 67–97, especially pages 94 ff.

116. *On the Spirit* 16:37.

117. Sesboüé, SC 305:168:32 and 40.

118. *GNO* 3a 51:10; *NPNF* 5:335. Haykin discusses Gregory's use of 1 and 2 Cor. as a resource for pneumatology in *The Spirit of God,* 185–201.

119. *GNO* 3a 66:11.

Spirit.[120] Neither of these two passages offers a strong argument for the Spirit's divinity, but they do show that Gregory recognized 1 Cor. 12:4–6 as a proof-text in support of the Spirit's divinity. Yet overall the *Refutation of the Creed* shows that Gregory has already begun to apply his "one power means one nature" reasoning to the Spirit.[121] One example of this argument leads Gregory to introduce the fire/heat analogy and so is worth repeating here.

After Gregory has quoted Eunomius to the effect that the Spirit accomplishes every activity, he then asks what activity it is that Eunomius refers to when he says that the Spirit accomplishes every activity. If, Gregory remarks, the Spirit accomplishes the same activity as the Father and the Son, then he "must assuredly [have] the same power and nature" [δύναμις καὶ φύσις] they have.

> For just as, if anything should perform the functions of fire, shining and warming in precisely the same way, it is itself certainly fire, so if the Spirit does the works of the Father, He must certainly be acknowledged to be the same nature with Him. . . . Accordingly, from the identity of activities it results assuredly that the Spirit is not alien from the nature of the Father and the Son.[122]

The association of the Spirit with divine activity (ἐνέργεια) is clear in this passage. The argument that the unity of the natures is demonstrated in the unity of the powers is adverted to at the beginning of the passage, but when Gregory turns specifically to the Spirit, he singles out Eunomius' reference to the Spirit and activities and takes these as an opportunity to restate his argument, so that common activities are now the signs of a common nature. However, the concept of the activity cannot, in itself, identify the kind of causal relationship between an existent and the effects that existent has, so that a specific effect necessarily signals a specific nature. I return to the illustration I offered in the Introduction: both a bicycle and a horse perform the same activity of transportation, but they have com-

120. *GNO* 2:317:7 and *GNO* 2:330:7.

121. An initial appearance of this argument can be found at *GNO* 2:331:12–20, which begins with a reference to Heb. 1:3 as a δύναμις text. Stronger statements, specifically addressed to the divinity of the Spirit, occur towards the end of the book. See, for example, ". . . in the Father, the Son, and the Holy Spirit there is one power, and goodness, and essence . . ." (*GNO* 2:399:13 ff.; *NPNF* 5:131), as well as "For if there does reside in the Father and Son a life-giving power, it is ascribed also to the Holy Spirit . . ." (*GNO* 2:400:1 ff.; *NPNF* 5:131).

122. *GNO* 2:402:11–26; *NPNF* 5:132, translation slightly altered.

pletely different natures. Only when an activity is understood as *the activity produced by the power of an existent* is the class of activities specified in such a way that an activity is the expression of a nature. Eunomius understood this fact of the terminology: his account of divine causality treats *activity* as a fundamental term; but for Eunomius, as I have shown, there is no thought of this being the activity of a power. From Gregory's perspective, Eunomius pointedly declines to understand God's activities as the activities of a power, which is why Eunomius can maintain that God's activities neither communicate nor reveal his nature. Gregory uses ἐνέργεια to describe the common act that the Trinity do, but both the sense of the terms themselves (*activity—power*) and a careful reading of Gregory's argument lead us to understand that in the logic of his trinitarian theology, *activity presupposes power.*

My second reason for saying that the ἐνέργεια language of *On the Holy Trinity* and *On "Not Three Gods"* is an indication that these texts are polemics written to establish the full divinity of the Spirit is the evidence from Gregory of Nazianzus that in the early 380s ἐνέργεια language was particularly associated with the question of the Spirit's identity. *Oration 31* suggests that an emphasis on ἐνέργεια language was a feature of the controversy in the 380s over the divinity of the Holy Spirit, for Gregory's most specific and extensive treatment of ἐνέργεια appears in his *Oration on the Holy Spirit* and not in his *Orations* on God or the Son. From Gregory of Nazianzus' attention to denying that the Spirit is an ἐνέργεια it seems that Eunomian doctrine was that the Spirit is an ἐνέργεια of the Son just as the Father is an ἐνέργεια of God.[123] This specific doctrine is never stated exactly in this form in either of Eunomius' *Apologies,* so this doctrine, if my hypothesis is correct, developed late in Eunomian theology, perhaps never to appear in written form and indeed may not be from Eunomius himself.

Gregory of Nazianzus' *Oration 31* also suggests a reason why his young friend Gregory would emphasize that the Spirit's activities are the same as the Father's and the Son's. According to *Oration 31,* critics found the Spirit

123. In both the *Apology* and the *Second Apology,* Eunomius had used ἐνέργεια to describe the activity of an essence; and in both works he suggested that the "Father" that produced Son is properly understood as an activity, ἐνέργεια, of God and not as the essence that is God.

to be a "strange" God, whose identity and salvific work were unknown: we would say that His role in the economy lacked a historical referent. By contrast, the work of the Father and the Son was clear. Gregory of Nyssa's solution to the problem of the Spirit's anonymity is to attribute all activities equally to all three Persons, even those activities traditionally associated with just one Person. This is the last form of Gregory of Nyssa's trinitarian theology, and it is important not to project this doctrine back onto the earlier stage of his writings.

Finally, the validity of interpreting Gregory's ἐνέργεια language in terms of his polemic in defense of the Holy Spirit may be seen in a significant passage from his *Third Homily on the Lord's Prayer.* This passage (M 44, 1147D–1161A.) is an important one, since it figures significantly in de Régnon's assertion that the generalized expression of Cappadocian trinitarian theology is found in the ἐνέργεια-φύσις language of this text. Gregory's argument will make more sense if we understand the use of δύναμις and ἐνέργεια in light of the points I have already made about Gregory's theology of "one power, one nature."

Gregory's concern in this work is without a doubt pneumatological, as the reference to the "Spirit-haters" makes clear. Gregory's argument is this: it is the power and activity of the Holy Spirit to cleanse us from sin (a scripturally-based description, even if from a variant text.) Elsewhere in Scripture the same activity is ascribed to Christ. Thus Christ and the Spirit have the same ἔργον, product. But if the two have the same activity, then they must have the same power, for an activity follows from a power. But whatever has the same activity and power must have the same nature. Just as the appearance of the properties illuminating and burning must indicate the same nature, fire, so too must common activity indicate the same nature of the Son and Spirit.

Illuminating and burning are not powers of fire—they are activities, so we have a slightly different argument than we had in earlier polemical pieces. We can recognize the appearance of the sequence φύσις-δύναμις-ἐνέργεια-ἔργον, yet the argument from causality is carried on further down the "chain" of causality. Gregory uses the sequence as an ascending ladder in order to discover greater and greater degrees of unity between the Son and Spirit: same product [ἔργα], same activity [ἐνέργεια], same power [δύναμις], same nature [φύσις]. Although in *Against Eunomius*, Gregory's arguments for the common nature of the Father and Son turned almost entirely on the relationship between the power and the nature, this terminology is, evidently, no longer sufficient for arguing for the common nature of the Son and Spirit. In the *Third Homily on the Lord's Prayer*, Gregory does not begin with evidence of common power between the Son and Spirit (much less common power between the Spirit and the Father). He begins by discovering commonality at the level of activity. This discovery is revealed by the presence of identical work, ἔργον. Whatever produces the same work must be the same energy. Once Gregory has the same activity, he can deduce to the same power since, as Gregory says explicitly, activity follows from power, and, as Gregory does not say explicitly, the same activity must indicate the same power (which produced them). Finally, the unity of power and activity shows the same nature. I can summarize the significance of all this with two observations. First, Gregory's argument from common ἐνέργεια to common φύσις is explicitly dependent on the relationship of activity to power. Second, the argument is framed entirely in terms of Son and Spirit; once Gregory shows common nature between Son and Spirit, his point is evidently made. Stronger trinitarian language (in the form of the passage excluded by Holl) develops Gregory's reasoning and strengthens its orthodox character.

Gregory's emphasis on power language in his anti-Eunomian works depends on a Scripture-based tradition that uses power to describe the relationship between God (the Father) and the second Person. Power is emphasized by Gregory in his anti-Eunomian works because of the polemical context broadly considered: the divine Person in question in these writings is primarily the Son. The scriptural tradition of *power* as a divine title offers less support in arguing for the divinity of the Spirit since the predominant interpretation of power texts had been to understand them as referring to the Son.[124] I have already pointed out the signs that remain in *On the Holy Trinity* and *On "Not Three Gods"* of the Christological connotation of power scriptural texts; what changes in these two texts is both

124. In *On "Not Three Gods"*, Gregory reinterprets 1 Cor. 1:24 as a full-fledged trinitarian text; similarly, in *On the Holy Trinity* Gregory reinterprets Rom. 1:20 as a reference to the one Godhead (see *GNO* 3a 7:3).

the new-found emphasis that Gregory puts on activity, as well as the details of the argument that he makes with activity.

The activity language of *On the Holy Trinity* and *On "Not Three Gods"* was no less polemically informed since in these texts it is the divinity of the Spirit that is at issue. De Régnon's judgement that the ἐνέργεια-based argument in *On the Holy Trinity* and *On "Not Three Gods"* is normative for Gregory's trinitarian theology is wrong. Gregory's argument that the identity of the nature is shown in the identity of activities in *On the Holy Trinity* and *On "Not Three Gods"*, as in the earlier *Refutation of the Creed*, represented a shift in the polemical context from the question of the divinity of the Son to the question of the divinity of the Spirit, and the formula, "common activities mean one nature," is no more fundamental than the formula, "one power means one nature." Indeed, of the two expressions, the power formula is earlier applied to Gregory's arguments for each Person of the Trinity while the activity language is used almost exclusively in defense of the Holy Spirit. It is the strong scripturally-based, Christological connotation of *power* that, in a polemical context, deters any application to the Spirit; scripturally-based associations of activity similarly recommend that term for an account of the divinity of the Spirit.

### *Conclusion*

In *Against Eunomius* Gregory's primary argument for the common nature of the Father and the Son is based on a received understanding of the kind of unity that exists between a *nature* and a *power*. Gregory argues that if the Father and Son manifest the same δύναμις then they must also share the same φύσις. Gregory supports this argument through analogies with physical examples of the unity between a δύναμις and a φύσις: the most important of these examples is the relationship of heat to fire. Gregory's theology never surrenders this analogy, although, it is true, he does not always describe heat as the δύναμις of fire.

Gregory understands power as the capacity to act that is distinctive to a specific existent and that manifests the nature of that existent. He frequently uses power in a cosmological context: not only does he understand power primarily through its application in mixture physics, but he recognizes that the mixed powers exist in opposition to other specific powers.

Gregory acknowledges that the understanding that *powers exist in opposition to the contraries* is medical in origin. A more specific theological application of the concept of contraries appeared in Methodius' arguments for God's priority over matter. Gregory's brother Basil gave these arguments a trinitarian application in his own *Against Eunomius.*

Gregory's argument that common power indicates common nature is typical of pro-Nicene polemic in both Greek and Latin writers. What is distinct to Gregory's version of this argument in *Against Eunomius* 1 is the consistent emphasis he gives to this power-based argument. Another power-based argument for the Son's divine nature that Gregory offers is to identify the Son with God's power. Just as with the argument from common powers, this argument depends on the philosophically-supported understanding that a power exists in connatural union with a nature.

Gregory understands a formula like *one nature because one power* to be a suitable and credible statement of the unity among the Persons, but he also recognizes that the same exegetical tradition that gives power authority in a polemic also tends to limit the use of the title to cases involving the second Person. Power is an important trinitarian term in Gregory's polemical theology largely because of its traditional Christological associations. On the other hand, there is nothing intrinsically more "trinitarian" about the concept of activity; like power, it has a traditional exegetical association with one Person (in this case, the Spirit). If ἐνέργεια has been read by modern scholars with the understanding that it has a broad and equal application to the Trinity, this is because a supplemental metaphysics has supplied a context that relates ἐνέργεια to the common φύσις. Modern scholarly readings of ἐνέργεια as a general trinitarian title, with equal application in demonstrating the divinity of all three Persons, depend upon the Aristotelian metaphysics of Scholasticism. The falling away of δύναμις as a general trinitarian term depends, I imagine, on the truncated influence of its supporting metaphysics.

Twentieth-century accounts of Cappadocian trinitarian theology typically feature *On the Holy Trinity* and *On "Not Three Gods"* as central statements of their trinitarian theology. Although scholars have known for some time that *On the Holy Trinity* was written by Gregory of Nyssa and not by his brother Basil, the question of authorship has not diminished the appeal these two works have had for describing either Cappadocian trinitarian theology or just Gregory's trinitarian theology. It is only recently, namely, in R. P. C. Hanson's account of Gregory's trinitarian theology in *The Search for the Christian Doctrine of God,* that the ultimate expression of Gregory's trinitarian theology is found elsewhere than in *On the Holy Trinity* and *On "Not Three Gods"*. Hanson was right to use *Against Eunomius* rather than these two other works, but his choice was motivated by his subject, namely, the fourth-century controversy over "the Christian doctrine of God." The scholarly consensus has been that neither *On the Holy Trinity* nor *On "Not Three Gods"* are works of controversy (that is, polemical texts), and so Hanson would not have found them *apropos.* My argument here has been that both *On the Holy Trinity* and *On "Not Three Gods"* are indeed polemical texts; nonetheless, I do not disagree with Hanson's choice. *Against Eunomius* does indeed give a more fundamental statement of Gregory's reasoning, and, appearances and scholarly conventions to the contrary, *On the Holy Trinity* and *On "Not Three Gods"* are texts with a more limited trinitarian application than *Against Eunomius.*

# Bibliography

## *Primary Sources*

### GREGORY OF NYSSA

*Original Language Editions*

Bellini, Enzo, ed. and trans. *Antirheticus Adversus Apollinarium.* In *Su Cristo: Il Grande Dibattito nel Quarto Secolo.* Milan: Jaca Books, 1977, 339–483.

Daniélou, Jean, ed., trans., and comm. *La vie de Moïse.* 3d ed., revised and corrected. Sources Chrétiennes, vol. 1 ter. Paris: Les Éditions du Cerf, 1968.

Downing, J. Kenneth, Jacobus A. McDonough, and Hadwiga Horner, eds. *Opera Dogmatica Minora. Gregorii Nysseni Opera.* Vol. 3, pars 2. Leiden: E. J. Brill, 1987.

Jaeger, Werner, ed. *Contra Eunomium Libri. Gregorii Nysseni Opera.* Vols. 1 and 2. Leiden: E. J. Brill, 1960.

Méridier, Louis, ed. and trans. *Discours Catechétique.* Paris: Librairie Alphonse Picard et Fils, 1908.

Migne, J., ed. *De Anima et Resurrectione.* Patrologia Graeca, vol. 46.

———. *De Hominis Opificio.* Patrologia Graeca vol. 44.

Mueller, Fridericus, ed. *Antirheticus Adversus Apollinarium. Opera Dogmatica Minora.* Vol. 3, pars 1, *Gregorii Nysseni Opera.* Leiden: E. J. Brill,. 1958.

Musurillo, Herbertus, ed. *Gregorii Nysseni De Vita Moysis. Gregorii Nysseni Opera.* Vol. 7, pars 1. Leiden: E. J. Brill, 1964.

Pasquali, Georgius, ed. *Gregorii Nysseni Epistulae. Gregorii Nysseni Opera.* Vol. 8, pars 2. Leiden: E. J. Brill, 1959.

*English Translations*

Callahan, Virginia Woods, trans. *St. Gregory of Nyssa Ascetical Works.* Fathers of the Church, vol. 58. Washington, D.C.: Catholic University of America Press, 1967.

Hall, Stuart G., trans. "Contra Eunomium I." In *El Contra Eunomium I,* edited by Lucas F. Mateo-Seco and J. Bastero. Pamplona: Ediciones Universidad de Navarra, S. A. 1988.

———. *Discourse on the Holy Pascha* (*In Sanctum Pascha*). In *The Easter Sermons of Gregory of Nyssa,* edited by Andreas Spiras and Christopher Klock. Patristic Monograph Series, no. 9. Cambridge: Philadelphia Patristic Foundation, 1981.

Malherbe, Abraham J., and Everett Ferguson, trans. *Gregory of Nyssa: The Life of Moses.* New York: Paulist Press, 1978.

McCambley, Casimir, trans. *Commentary on the Song of Songs.* Brookline: Hellenic College Press, 1987.

Moore, William, and H. A. Wilson, trans. and intro. *Selected Writings and Letters of Gregory, Bishop of Nyssa.* The Nicene and Post Nicene Fathers, Second Series, vol. 5. Reprint, Grand Rapids: Eerdmans, 1976.

Musurillo, Herbert, ed. and trans. *From Glory to Glory: Texts from Gregory of Nyssa's Mystical Writings.* Crestwood: St. Vladimir's Seminary Press, 1979.

ALEXANDER OF APHRODISIAS

Bruns, Ivo, ed. *De Anima Liber cum Mantissa.* Supplentum Aristotelicum, vol. 2, pars 1. Berlin: George Reimer, 1887.

Fotinis, Athanasios P., trans. *The De Anima of Alexander of Aphrodisias: A Translation and Commentary.* Washington, D.C.: Catholic University of America Press, 1979.

Todd, Robert B., trans. and comm. *On Blending and Growth.* In *Alexander of Aphrodisias: On Stoic Physics (de Mixtione).* Leiden: E. J. Brill, 1976.

AMBROSE OF MILAN

Faller, O., ed. *De Fide ad Gratianum.* Corpus Scriptorum Ecclesiasticorum Latinorum, vol. 78. 1962.

Schaff, Phillip, and Henry Wace, trans. *St. Ambrose: Select Works and Letters.* The Nicene and Post Nicene Fathers, Second Series, vol. 10. Reprint, Grand Rapids: Eerdmans, 1976.

ARISTOTLE

Apostle, Hippocrates P., trans. *Metaphysics.* 1966. Reprint, Bloomington: Indiana University Press, 1973.

Cooke, H. P., ed. and trans. *The Categories* and *On Interpretation.* The Loeb Classical Library. 1938. Reprint, Cambridge: Harvard University Press, 1967.

Hett, W. S., ed. and trans. *On the Soul.* The Loeb Classical Library. 1936. Reprint, Cambridge: Harvard University Press, 1964.

Peck, A. L., ed. and trans. *Parts of Animals.* The Loeb Classical Library. Cambridge: Harvard University Press, 1937.

ARISTOTLE (PSEUDO)

Furley, D. J., ed. and trans. *On the Cosmos.* The Loeb Classical Library. 1955. Reprint, Cambridge: Harvard University Press, 1978.

ATHANASIUS

Meijering, E. P., intro., trans., and comm. *Athanasius: Contra Gentes.* Leiden: E. J. Brill, 1984.

Schaff, Phillip, and Henry Wace, trans. *St. Athanasius: Select Works and Letters.* The Nicene and Post Nicene Fathers, Second Series, vol. 4. Reprint, Grand Rapids, Mich.: Eerdmans, 1976.

Thompson, Robert W., ed. and trans. Contra Gentes *and* De Incarnatione. Oxford: Clarendon Press, 1971.

ATTICUS

des Places, Édouard, ed. and trans. *Atticus Fragments.* Paris: Société d'Éditions, 1977.

BASIL OF CAESAREA AND PSEUDO-BASIL

Courtonne, Yves, ed., trans., and comm. *Saint Basilé Lettres.* 3 vols. Paris: Société d'Éditions "Les Belles Lettres," 1957, 1961, 1966.

Dehnhard, Hans, ed. *De Spiritu.* In *Das Problem der Abhangigkeit des Basilius von Plotin.* Patristiche Texte und Studien, Band 3. Berlin: Walter de Gruyter & Co. 1964.

Giet, Stanislas, ed. and trans. *Homélies sur l'Hexaëméron.* Sources Chrétiennes, vol. 26 bis. Paris: Les Éditions du Cerf, 1968.

Pruche, Benoit, ed. and trans. *Sur le Saint-Esprit.* Sources Chrétiennes, vol. 17 bis. Paris: Les Éditions du Cerf, 1968.

Sesboüé, Bernard, Georges-Matthieu de Durand, and Louis Doutreleau, ed., trans., and comm. *Contre Eunome.* Sources Chrétiennes, vols. 299 and 305. Paris: Les Éditions du Cerf, 1982 and 1983.

CHALDEAN ORACLES

Majercik, Ruth, ed., trans., and comm. *The Chaldean Oracles.* Leiden: E. J. Brill, 1989.

des Places, Édouard, ed. and trans. *Oracles Chaldaïques.* Paris: Société d'Éditions, 1971.

CICERO

Rackham, Horace, ed., and trans. *De Natura Deorum.* The Loeb Classical Library. New York: Putnam and Sons, 1933.

CLEMENT OF ALEXANDRIA

Coxe, A. C., ed. and trans. *The Stromata. Fathers of the Second Century,* The Ante-Nicene Fathers, vol. 2. Reprint, Grand Rapids: Eerdmans, 1979.

Stählin, Otto, ed. *Stromata.* Die Griechischen Christlichen Schriftsteller. 3 Vols. Leipzig: J. C. Hinrich's, 1909.

CYRIL OF ALEXANDRIA

de Durand, Georges Matthieu, ed., trans., and comm. *Dialogues sur la Trinité.* 3 Tomes. Sources Chrétiennes, vols. 237, 246. Paris: Les Éditions du Cerf, 1977, 1978.

DIDYMUS THE BLIND

Honscheid, Jurgen, ed. and trans. *De trinitate.* 2 vols. Meisenheim am Glan: Verlag Anton Hain, 1975.

EPIPHANIUS

Amidon, Philip R., trans. *The* Panarion *of St. Epiphanius, Bishop of Salamis: Selected Passages.* Oxford: Oxford University Press, 1990.

Holl, Karl, ed. *Epiphanius (Ancoratus und Panarion).* Zweiter Band and Dritter Band. Die Griechischen Christlichen Schriftsteller. Leipzig: J. C. Hinrich's, 1922 and 1933.

EUNOMIUS

Doutreleau, Louis, ed., trans., and comm. *Eunome Apologia.* Sources Chrétiennes, vol. 305. Paris: Les Éditions du Cerf, 1983.

Vaggione, Richard P., ed., trans., and intro. *Eunomius: The Extant Works.* Oxford: Clarendon Press, 1987.

EUSEBIUS OF CAESAREA

Bardy, Gustav, ed. and trans. *Histoire ecclésiastique.* Sources Chrétiennes, vols. 31, 41, 55, 73. Paris: Les Éditions du Cerf, 1952–1960.

Favrelle, Geneviève, trans. and comm., and Édouard des Places, ed. *La preparation evangelique,* Livres XI. Sources Chrétiennes, vol. 292. Paris: Les Éditions du Cerf, 1982.

Ferrar, W. J., trans. *The Proof of the Gospel Being the Demonstration Evangelica of Eusebius of Caesarea.* 2 vols. London: SPCK, 1920.

Gifford, E. H., ed. and trans. *Evangelicae Praeparationis.* Three tomes in four volumes. Oxford: Oxford University Press, 1903.

Heikel, Ivar A., ed. *Eusebius Werke.* Sechester Band. In *Die Demonstratio Evangelica.* Die Griechischen Christlichen Schriftsteller. Leipzig: J. C. Hinrich, 1913.

Klosterman, Erich, ed. *Eusebius Werke.* Vierter Band. *Gegen Marcell, Über die Kirchliche Theologie, Die Fragmente Marcells.* Die Griechischen Christlichen Schriftsteller. Berlin: Akademie-Verlag, 1972.

Mras, Karl, ed. *Eusebius Werke.* Achter Band. *Die Preaparatio Evangelica.* 2 vols. Die Griechischen Christlichen Schriftsteller. Berlin: Akademie-Verlag, 1954 and 1956.

des Places, Édouard, ed. and trans. *La préparation evangélique. Livres II–III.* Sources Chrétiennes, vol. 228. Paris: Les Éditions du Cerf, 1976.

———, ed., comm., and trans. *La préparation evangélique. Livres V, 18–36,–VI.* Sources Chrétiennes, vol. 266. Paris: Les Éditions du Cerf, 1980.

Schroeder, Guy, trans. and comm. Édouard des Places, ed. *La préparation evangélique. Livres VII.* Sources Chrétiennes, vol. 215. Paris: Les Éditions du Cerf, 1975.

Williamson, G. A., trans. *The History of the Church.* 1965. Reprint, Baltimore: Penguin Books, 1967.

GALEN

Brock, A. J., ed. and trans. *On the Natural Faculties.* The Loeb Classical Library, 1916. Reprint, Cambridge: Harvard University Press, 1978.

Furley, D. J., and J. S. Wilkie, ed., trans., and comm. *On Respiration and Arteries.* Princeton: Princeton University Press, 1984.

de Lacy, Phillip, ed., trans., and comm. *On the Doctrines of Hippocrates and Plato.* 3 tomes. In *Corpus Medicorum Graecorum,* vols. 4, 1, 2. Berlin: Akademie-Verlag, 1978, 1980, 1984.

May, Margaret Tallmudge, ed., trans., and comm. *Galen: On the Usefulness of the Parts of the Body.* 2 vols. Ithaca: Cornell University Press, 1968.

Van der Elst, R. *Traité des passions de l'âme et de ses erreurs par Galien.* Paris: Librairie Charles Delagrave, 1914.

Walzer, R., and M. Frede, trans. *Three Treatises on the Nature of Science.* Indianapolis: Hackett, 1985.

GREGORY OF NAZIANZUS

Brown, C. G., and J. E. Swallow, trans. *Select Orations of St. Gregory Nazianzen.* A Select Library of Nicene and Post-Nicene Fathers, Second Series, vol. 7. 1893. Reprint, Grand Rapids: Eerdmans, 1978.

Gallay, Paul, and Maurice Jourjon, ed., comm., and trans. *Grégoire de Nazianze: Discours 27–31 (Discours Théologiques).* Sources Chrétiennes, vol. 250. Paris: Les Éditions du Cerf, 1978.

Norris, Frederick W., comm. Lionel Wickham and Frederick Williams, trans. *Faith Gives Fullness to Reasoning: The Five Theological Orations of Gregory of Nazianzen.* Leiden: E. J. Brill, 1991.

HILARY OF POITIERS

Rocher, André, ed. and trans. *Contre Constance.* Sources Chrétiennes, vol. 334. Paris: Les Éditions du Cerf, 1987.

Smulders, P., ed. *De Trinitate.* Corpus Christianorum, Series Latina, vol. 62, 62A. 1979, 1980.

Watson, E. W., and L. Pullan, trans. *On the Councils.* In *Select Works of Hilary of Poitiers,* A Select Library of Nicene and Post-Nicene Fathers, Second Series, vol. 9. Reprint, Grand Rapids; Eerdmanns, 1979.

HIPPOCRATIC CORPUS

Jones, W. H. S., ed. and trans. *Collected Writings of Hippocrates.* 4 vols. The Loeb Classical Library. 1923. Reprint, Cambridge: Harvard University Press, 1972.

HIPPOLYTUS

Butterworth, Robert, S. J., trans. *Hippolytus of Rome: Contra Noetum.* London: Heythrop Monographs, 1977.

IAMBLICHUS

Dillon, John M., ed., trans., and comm. *Iamblichi Chalcidensis in Platonis Dialogos Commentariorum Fragmenta.* Leiden: E. J. Brill, 1973.

Festugière, A. J., trans and comm. *Traite de l'amé.* In *La révélation d' Hermès Trismégiste,* vol. 3. 1953. Reprint, Paris: Société d'Éditions Les Belles Lettres, 1983.

JULIAN THE EMPEROR

Wright, W. C., ed. and trans. *Oration IV: Hymn to King Helios.* Vol. 1. *The Works of the Emperor Julian.* 4 vols. The Loeb Classical Library, 1913. Reprint, Cambridge: Harvard University Press,

MARIUS VICTORINUS

Clark, Mary T., trans. *Marius Victorinus: Theological Treatises on the Trinity.* The Fathers of the Church, vol. 69. Washington, D.C.: Catholic University of America Press, 1981.

Henry, Paul, ed. Pierre Hadot, trans. and comm. *Traiteé théologiques sur la Trinité.* Sources Chrétiennes, vol. 68. Paris: Les Éditions du Cerf, 1960.

MAXIMINUS

Gryson, Roger, ed. *Scolies Ariennes sur le Concile d'Aquilée.* Sources Chrétiennes, vol.267. Paris: Les Éditions du Cerf, 1980.

NAG HAMMADI LIBRARY

Dirkse, Peter A., James Brashler, and Douglas M. Parrott, eds. and trans. "The Discourse on the Eighth and the Ninth VI,6: 52,I–63.32." In vol. 11, *Nag Hammadi Studies,* edited by Douglas M. Parrott. Leiden:E. J. Brill, 1979.

Wisse, Frederik, and Francis Williams, eds. and trans. "The Concept of Our Great Power." In vol. 11, *Nag Hammadi Studies,* edited by Douglas M. Parrott. Leiden: E. J. Brill, 1979.

NEMESIUS OF EMESA

Telfer, William, ed. *On the Nature of Man.* In *Cyril of Jerusalem and Nemesius of Emesa.* The Library of Christian Classics, vol. 4. Philadelphia: The Westminster Press, 1965.

NUMENIUS

des Places, Édouard, ed. and trans. *Numenius Fragments.* Paris: Société d'Éditions, 1973.

ORIGEN

Blanc, Cecile, ed., trans., and comm. *Origène: Commentaire sur Saint Jean.* Sources Chrétiennes, vols. 120, 157, 222. Paris: Les Éditions du Cerf, 1966, 1970, 1975.

Butterworth, G. W., trans. *On First Principles.* New York: Harper Torchbooks, 1966.

Crouzel, H., and M. Simonetti, ed., trans., and comm. *Traité des Principes Tome I* (Livres I et II). Sources Chrétiennes, vols. 252–53. Paris: Les Éditions du Cerf, 1978.

Doutreleau, Louis, ed., trans., and comm. *Origène: Homelies sur la Génèse.* Sources Chrétiennes, vol. 7 bis. Paris: Les Éditions du Cerf, 1976.

Heine, Ronald, trans. *Origen: Commentary on the Gospel according to John Books 1–10.* Washington, D.C.: Catholic University of America Press, 1989.

———. *Origen: Homilies on Genesis and Exodus.* Washington, D.C.: Catholic University of America Press, 1986.

Scherer, Jean, intro., ed., and comm. *Entretien D'Origèn avec Heraclidè.* Sources Chrétiennes, vol. 67. Paris: Les Éditions du Cerf, 1960.

PHILO

Coulson, F. H., and G. H. Whittaker, eds., trans., and comm. *Philo in Ten Volumes.* The Loeb Classical Library. 1929. Reprint, London: William Heinemann Ltd., 1979.

PHILOSTORGIUS

Walford, Edward, trans. *Ecclesiastical History.* In *Epitome of the* Ecclesiastical History of Philostorgius *Compiled by Photius.* London: Henry G. Bohn, 1855.

PLATO

Bury, R. G., ed. and trans. *Timaeus Critias Cleitophon Menexenus Epistles. Plato with an English Translation.* The Loeb Classical Library, vol. 7. Cambridge: Harvard University Press, 1929.

Fowler, Harold N., ed. and trans. *Cratylus Greater Hippias Lesser Hippias Parmenides. Plato in Twelve Volumes.* The Loeb Classical Library, vol. 4. Cambridge: Harvard University Press, 1920.

———. *The Statesman and Philebus. Plato with an English Translation.* The Loeb Classical Library. Cambridge: Harvard University Press, 1912.

Hamilton, Edith, and Huntington Cairns, eds. *The Collected Dialogues of Plato.* 4th ed. New York: Pantheon Books, 1966.

Lamb, W. R. M., ed. and trans. *Laches Protagoras Meno Euthydemus. Plato in Twelve Volumes.* The Loeb Classical Library, vol. 2. Cambridge: Harvard University Press, 1917.

Shorey, Paul, ed. and trans. *Plato: The Republic.* 2 vols. The Loeb Classical Library. Cambridge: Harvard University Press, 1906.

PLOTINUS

Armstrong, A. H., ed. and trans. *The Enneads.* 7 vols. The Loeb Classical Library. Cambridge: Harvard University Press, 1966–1988.

POSIDONIUS

Edelstein, L., and I. G. Kidd, ed. and comm. *The Fragments.* 3 vols. Cambridge: University Press, 1972, 1988.

PROCLUS

Dodds, E. R., ed., trans., and comm. *Elements of Theology.* 2d ed. Oxford: Clarendon Press, 1963.

Morrow, G. R., and J. M. Dillon, trans. J. M. Dillon, comm. *Commentary on Plato's Parmenides.* Princeton: Princeton University Press, 1987.

SOCRATES

*Scholastici Ecclesiastica Historia.* Edited by R. Hussey. 3 Tomes, Oxford, 1853.

Zenos, A. C., trans. *Church History.* A Select Library of Nicene and Post-Nicene Fathers. Second Series, vol. 2. Reprint, Grand Rapids: Eerdmans, 1979.

SOZOMEN

Festugière, A. J., trans. G. Sabbah, comm. *Histoire écclesiastique Livres I et II.* Sources Chrétiennes, vol. 306, Paris: Les Éditions du Cerf, 1983.

Hussey, R., ed. *Ecclesiastica Historia.* 3 Tomes, Oxford, 1860.

Zenos, A. C., trans. *The Ecclesiastical History.* A Select Library of Nicene and Post-Nicene Fathers, Second Series, vol. 2. Reprint. Grand Rapids, Mich.: Eerdmans, 1979.

ASSORTED AUTHORS IN COLLECTION

Long, A. A., and D. N. Sedley, eds., trans., and comm. *The Hellenistic Philosophers.* 2 vols. Cambridge: Cambridge University Press, 1987.

Westerink, L. G., trans. *The Greek Commentaries on Plato's Phaedo.* Amsterdam: North-Holland Publishing Company, 1977.

## Secondary Sources

Altenburger, Margarete, and Friedheim Mann, eds. *Bibliographie zu Gregor von Nyssa.* Leiden: E. J. Brill, 1988.

Anastos, Milton. "Basil's *Κατὰ Εὐνομίου*, A Critical Analysis." In *Basil of Caesarea,* ed. Paul J. Fedwick, 1:67–137. Toronto: Pontifical Institute of Mediaeval Studies, 1981.

Balàs, David L. "Eternity and Time in Gregory of Nyssa's *Contra Eunomium.*" In *Gregor Von Nysse und die Philosophie,* edited by H. Dörrie, M. Altenburger, and U. Schramus, 128–53. Leiden: E. J. Brill, 1976.

Baldry. "Plato's 'Technical Terms,'" *Classical Quarterly* 31 (1937): 141–150.

Balthasar, Hans Urs von. *Présence et pensée: essai sur la philosophie religieuse de Grégoire de Nyssa.* Paris: Beauchesne, 1942.

Bardy, Gustave. *Didyme l'Aveugle.* Paris: Gabriel Beauchesne, 1910.

Barnard, L. W. "The Antecedents of Arius." In *Studies in Church History and Patristics.* Thessalonka: Analekta Blatadon, 1978. First published in *Vigiliae Christianae* 24 (1960): 172–88.

Barnes, Michel René. "The Background and Use of Eunomius' Causal Language." In *Arianism after Arius: Essays on the Development of the Fourth Century Trinitarian Conflicts,* ed. Michel R. Barnes and Daniel H. Williams, 217–36. Edinburgh: T. & T. Clark, 1993.

———. "De Régnon Reconsidered." *Augustinian Studies* 26: 2 (1995): 51–79.

———. "Eunomius of Cyzicus and Gregory of Nyssa: Two Traditions of Transcendent Causality." *Vigiliae Christianae* 52.1 (1998), 59–87.

———. "One Nature, One Power: Consensus Doctrine in Pro-Nicene Polemic." *Studia Patristica* 29 (1997): 205–23.

Bata, Henri. "Plotinisme et théologie de Saint Basilé de Cesarée", Diss., Université de Strasbourg, 1974.

Beare, John I. *Greek Theories of Elementary Cognition from Alcmaeon to Aristotle.* Oxford: Clarendon Press, 1906.

Bethune-Baker, J. F. *The Meaning of Homoousios in the 'Constantinopolitan' Creed.* Cambridge: The University Press, 1901.

Bianchi, U. and H. Crouzel, eds. *Arché e Telos: L'antropologia di Origene e di Gregorio di Nissa.* Milano: Universita Cattolica del Sacro Cuore, 1981.

Biard, Pierre. *La puissance de Dieu.* Paris: Bloud and Gay, 1960.

Bidez, J. *La Cité du monde et la cité du soleil chez les stoïciens.* Paris: Societé d'Éditions, 1932.

de Boer, S. *De anthropologie van Gregorius van Nyssa.* Assen: Van Gorcum & Comp. N. V., 1968.

Borchardt, C. F. A. *Hilary of Poitiers' Role in the Arian Struggle.* The Hague: Martinus Nijhoff, 1966.

Bostock, D. G. "Medical Theory and Theology in Origen." In *Origeniana Tertia,* edited by R. P. C. Hanson and H. Crouzel, 191–99. Rome: Edizioni dell'Ateneo, 1985.

Boularand, Éphrem, S. J. *L'Hérésie d'Arius et la "foi" de Nicée.* 2 vols. Paris: Éditions Letouzey et Ané, 1972.

Bourgey, Louis. *Observation et experience chez les médecins de la collection hippocratique.* Paris: Librairie philosophique J. Vrin, 1953.

Braun, René. *Deus Christianorum: Récherches sur la vocabulaire doctrinal de Tertullien.* Paris: Études Augustiennes, 1977.

Bréhier, Emile. *Chrysippe.* Paris: Librairie Félix Alcan, 1970.

Brent, Allen. *Hippolytus and the Roman Church in the Third Century.* Leiden: E. J. Brill, 1995.

Brentlinger, John A. "The Divided Line and Plato's Theory of Intermediates." *Phronesis* 8 (1963): 146–66.

———. "Incomplete Predicates and the Two-World Theory of the *Phaedo.*" *Phronesis* 17 (1972): 61–79.

Brunschwig, Jacques, ed. *Les stoïciens et leur logique: actes du colloque de Chantilly. Septembre. 1976.* Paris: Librairie Philosophique J. Vrin, 1978.

Brunschwig, Jacques, and Martha C. Nussbaum, eds. *Passions and Perceptions.* Cambridge: Cambridge University Press, 1993.

Burkert, Walter. *Lore and Science in Ancient Pythagoreanism.* Cambridge: Harvard University Press, 1972.

Burnet, John. *Early Greek Philosophy.* 1892. Reprint, London: A. and C. Black, Ltd., 1930.

Bussanich, John. *The One and Its Relation to Intellect in Plotinus.* Leiden: E. J. Brill, 1988.

Callahan, John F. "Greek Philosophy and the Cappadocian Cosmology." *Dumbarton Oaks Papers* 12 (1958): 29–58.

Canévet, Mariette. *Grégoire de Nysse et l'herméneutique biblique. Étude de rapparts entre le langage et la connaissance de Dieu.* Paris: Études Augustiniennes, 1983.

Cavalcanti, Elena. *Studi Eunomiani.* Rome: Pont. Institutum Orientalium Studiorum, 1976

Cherniss, Harold F. *The Platonism of Gregory of Nyssa.* 1930. Reprint, Berkeley: B. Franklin, 1970.

Claghorn, George Stuart. *Aristotle's Criticism of Plato's Timaeus.* The Hague: Martinus Nijhoff, 1954.

Colish, Maricia L. *The Stoic Tradition from Antiquity to the Early Middle Ages.* 2 vols. Leiden: E. J. Brill, 1985.

Cornford, Francis M. *Plato and Parmenides.* Reprint, Indianapolis: Bobbs-Merril Company, 1977.

———. *Plato's Theory of Knowledge.* Reprint, Indianapolis: Bobbs-Merrill Company, 1957.

Corsini, Eugenio. "La polemica contro Eunomio e la formazione della dottrina sulla creazione in Gregorio di Nissa." In *Arché e Telos: L'antropologia di Origene e di Gregorio di Nissa,* edited by U. Bianchi and H. Crouzel, 197–216.

Daniélou, Jean. *L'Etre et la temps chez Grégoire de Nysse.* Leiden: E. J. Brill, 1970.

———. "Eunome l'Arien et l'exégèse néoplatonicienne du *Cratyle.*" *Revue des études grecques* 69: (1956), 412–32.

———. *Gospel Message and Hellenistic Culture,* ed., trans., and with a postscript by John Austin Baker. Philadelphia: Westminster Press, 1973.

———. *Platonisme et théologie mystique: Doctrine Spirituelle de Grégoire de Nysse.* 2nd ed. Paris: Aubier, 1953.

Dillon, John. "Logos and Trinity: Patterns of Platonist Influence on Early Christianity." In *The Philosophy in Christianity,* edited by Godfrey Vesey, 1–14. Cambridge: Cambridge University Press, 1989.

———. *The Middle Platonists.* Ithaca: Cornell University Press, 1977.

Dodds, E. R. The *Parmenides* of Plato and the Origin of the Neoplatonic 'One'." *Classical Ouarterly* 12 (1928): 129–42.

———, ed. *Les sources de Plotin.* Entretiens sur l' antiquité, Tome V, Geneva: Vandoeuvres, 1957.

Dörrie, H., M. Altenburger, and U. Schramus, eds. *Gregor von Nysse und die Philosophie.* Leiden: E. J. Brill, 1976.

Dörrie, H., ed. *De Iamblique a Proclus.* Geneva: Fondation Hardt, 1975.

Edelstein, Ludwig. *Ancient Medicine: Selected Papers of Ludwig Edelstein.* Edited by Owsei and C. Lilian Temkin. 1967. Reprint, Baltimore: Johns Hopkins University Press, 1987.

Ellis, John. "The Trouble with Fragrance." *Phronesis* 35 (1990): 290–302.

Esbroeck, Michel. "L'aspect cosmologique de la philosophie d'Eunome pour la réprise de l'Hexaemeron basilien par Grégoire de Nysse." In *El "Contra Eunomium I" en la Produccion Literaria de Gregorio de Nisa,* edited by L. Mateo-Seco and J. Bastero. Pamplona: Ediciones Universidad de Navarra, S. A. 1988.

Fabricius, Cajus, and Daniel Ridings. *A Concordance to Gregory of Nyssa.* Studia Graeca et Latina Gothoburgensia 50, 1989.

Fedwick, Paul J., ed. *Basil of Caesarea: Christian, Humanist, Ascetic.* 2 vols. Toronto: Pontifical Institute of Mediaeval Studies, 1981.

Festugière, A. J. *La révélation d'Hermès Trismégiste.* 4 vols. Paris: Société d'Éditions des Belles Lettres, 1949–1954. Reprint, Paris: Société d'Editions des Belles Lettres, 1983.

Findlay, J. N. "The Logical Peculiarities of Neoplatonism." In *The Structure of Being: A Neoplatonic Approach,* edited by R. Baine Harris, 1–10. Norfolk, Va.: International Society for Neoplatonic Studies, c1982.

Florovsky, George. "The Concept of Creation in Saint Athanasius." *Studia Patristica* 6:4 (1962): 36–57.

Fossum, Jarl E. *The Name of God and the Angel of the Lord.* Tübingen: J. C. B. Mohr, 1985.

Frede, Michael. "On Galen's Epistemology." In *Essays in Ancient Philosophy,* 279–300. Minneapolis: University of Minnesota Press, 1987.

———. "Philosophy and Medicine in Antiquity." In *Essays in Ancient Philosophy,* 225–42. Minneapolis: University of Minnesota Press, 1987.

Furley, David J. *Cosmic Problems. Essays on Greek and Roman Philosophy of Nature.* Cambridge: Cambridge University Press, 1989.

Furth, Montgomery. "Aristotle's Biological Universe: An Overview." In *Philosophical Issues in Aristotle's Biology,* edited by Allan Gotthelf and James G. Lennox. Cambridge: Cambridge University Press, 1987.

———. *Substance, Form, and Psyche: an Aristotelian Metaphysics.* Cambridge: Cambridge University Press, 1985.

Gadamer, Hans-Georg. "Hegel and the Dialectic of the Ancient Philosophers." In *Hegel's Dialectic,* translated by P. C. Smith. New Haven: Yale University Press, 1971.

Gersh, Stephen. *From Iamblichus to Eriugena.* Leiden: E. J. Brill, 1978.

Ghellinck, J. de. "Quelques appreciations de la dialectique et d'Aristote durant les conflicts trinitaires du IV siecle." *Revue d'histoire écclesiastique* 26 (1930): 5–42.

Gilson, Etienne. *Being and Some Philosophers.* 2d ed. Toronto: Pontifical Institute of Medieval Studies, 1952.

Goodman, Lenn E., ed. *Neoplatonism and Jewish Thought.* Albany: State University of New York Press, 1992.

Gould, Josiah B. *The Philosophy of Chrysippus.* Albany: State University of New York Press, 1970.

Grant, Robert M. "The Book of Wisdom at Alexandria: Reflections on the History of the Canon and Theology." *Studia Patristica* 7 (1966): 462–72.

Greer, Rowan A. *The Captain of Our Salvation.* Beiträge zur Geschichte der Biblischen Exegese, vol. 15. Tübingen: J. C. B. Mohr, 1973.

Gregg, Robert C., ed. *Arianism: Historical and Theological Reassessments.* Patristic Monograph Series, no. 11. Cambridge: Philadelphia Patristic Foundation, 1985.

Gregg, Robert C., and Dennis Groh. *Early Arianism: A View of Salvation.* Philadelphia: Fortress Press, 1981.

Grundmann, W. "δύναμαι/δύναμις." *Theological Dictionary of the New Testament,* vol. 2, 284317.

Gwatkin, H. M. *Studies of Arianism.* 2d ed. Cambridge: Deighton and Bell, 1900.

Hadot, Ilsetraut, ed. *Simplicius: Sa vie, son oeuvre, sa survie. Actes du Colloque International de Paris (28 Sept.–1er Oct. 1985).* Berlin: Walter de Gruyter, 1987.

Hankinson, R. J., ed. *Method, Medicine and Metaphysics.* Edmonton: Academic Printing and Publishing, 1988.

Hanson, R. P. C. *The Search for the Christian Doctrine of God.* Edinburgh: T. & T. Clark, 1988.

———. "Who Taught ΕΞ ΟΥΚ ΟΝΤΩΝ?" In *Arianism: Historical and Theological Reassessments,* edited by Robert C. Gregg, 7984. Patristic Monograph Series, no. 11. Cambridge: Philadelphia Patristic Foundation, 1985.

———, and Henri Crouzel, eds. *Origeniana Tertia.* Rome: Edizioni dell'Ateneo, 1985.

Harnack, Adolph von. *History of Dogma.* Translated by Neil Buchanan. 4 vols. Reprint, New York: Dover, 1960.

Harre, Romano, and E. H. Madden. *Causal Powers.* Totowa: Rowman and Littlefield, 1975.

Harris, R. Baine, ed. *The Significance of Neoplatonism.* Studies in Neoplatonism, vol. l. Norfolk: Old Dominion University Press, 1976.

———, ed. *The Structure of Being: A Neoplatonic Approach.* Norfolk, Va.: International Society for Neoplatonic Studies, c1982.

Haykin, Michael A. G. *The Spirit of God: The Exegesis of 1 and 2 Corinthians in the Pneumantomachian Controversy of the Fourth Century.* Leiden: E. J. Brill, 1994.

Heidel, William Arthur. *Hippocratic Medicine.* New York: Columbia University Press, 1941.

———. "Περὶ Φύσεος: A Study of the Conception of Nature Among the Pre-Socratics." In *Selected Papers,* edited by Leonardo Tarán, 79–133. New York: Garland Publishers, 1980.

Heine, Ronald. *Perfection in the Virtuous Life.* Patristic Monograph Series, no. 2. Cambridge: Philadelphia Patristic Foundation, 1975.

Hippolyte. *Genesis and Structure of Hegel's Phenomenology of Spirit.* Translated by Samuel Cherniak and John Heckman. Evanston, Ill.: Northwestern University Press, 1974.

Inwood, Brad. *Ethics and Human Action in Early Stoicism.* Oxford: Clarendon Press, 1985.

Jaeger, Werner. *Two Rediscovered Works of Ancient Literature: Gregory of Nyssa and Macarius.* Leiden: E. J. Brill, 1954.

Joly, Robert. *Christianisme et Philosophie.* Bruxelles: Éditions de l'Universite de Bruxelles, 1973.

Jones, W. H. S. *Philosophy and Medicine in Ancient Greece.* Baltimore: Johns Hopkins Press, 1946.

Kahn, C. H. *Anaximander and the Origins of Greek Cosmology.* New York: Columbia University Press, 1960.

———. "Anaximander's Fragment: the Universe Governed by Law." In *The Presocratics,* ed. A. P. D. Mourelatos. New York: Anchor Press, 1974.

Kannengiesser, Charles. *Athanase d'Alexandrie: évêque et écrivain.* Paris: Beauchesne, 1983.

———. *Holy Scripture and Hellenistic Hermeneutics in Alexandrian Christology: The Arian Crisis.* Berkeley: The Graduate Theological Union and the University of California, 1982.

Kees, Reinhard Jakob. *Die Lehre von der Oikonomia Gottes in der Oratio Catechetica Gregors von Nyssa.* Leiden: E. J. Brill, 1995.

Kelly, J. N. D. *Early Christian Creeds.* 3rd ed. London: Longmans, 1972.

Kinzig, Wolfram. *In Search of Asterius.* Göttingen: Vanderhoeck, 1990.

Kirk, G. S., J. E. Raven, and M. Schofield, eds., trans., comms. *The Presocratic Philosophers.* 2d ed. Cambridge: Cambridge University Press, 1983.

Kopecek, Thomas A. *A History of Neo-Arianism*. 2 vols. Cambridge: Philadelphia Patristic Foundation, 1979.

———. "Neo-Arian Religion: The Evidence of the *Apostolic Constitutions*." In *Arianism*, edited by R. C. Gregg, 153–80.

Lebreton, Jules. "ΑΓΕΝΝΗΤΟΣ dans la tradition philosophique et dans la littérature chrétienne du II$^{e}$ siecle." *Recherches de science religieuse* 16 (1926): 431–43.

Lienhard, Joseph. "The 'Arian' Controversy: Some Categories Reconsidered." *Theological Studies* 48 (1987): 415–36.

———. "*Contra Marcellum:* the Influence of Marcellus of Ancyra on Fourth-Century Greek Theology." Habilitationsschrift, Albert-Ludwigs-Universität, 1986.

Lloyd, A. C. "Activity and Description in Aristotle and the Stoa." *Proceedings of the British Academy* 56 (1970): 227–40.

———. "Neoplatonic Logic and Aristotelian Logic." *Phronesis* 1 (1955–56): 58–72 and 146–60.

Lloyd, G. E. R. *Polarity and Analogy*. Cambridge: Cambridge University Press, 1966.

———. "Who Is Attacked in *On Ancient Medicine*?" *Phronesis* 8 (1963): 108–26.

Logan, A. H. B. "Origen and Alexandrian Wisdom Christology." In *Origeniana Tertia*, edited by R. P. C. Hanson and Henri Crouzel, 123–29. Rome: Edizioni Dell'ateneo, 1985.

Lossky, Vladimir. *Essai sur la théologie mystique de l'église d'orient*. Paris: Aubier, 1944.

———. *Mystical Theology*. Reprint. London: James Clark and Co., Ltd., 1973.

Long, Anthony A. *Soul and Body in Stoicism*. The Center for Hermeneutical Studies, vol. 36. Berkeley: The Graduate Theological Union and the University of California, 1979.

———. "The Stoic Distinction between Truth (ἡ ἀλήθειᾳ) and the True (τὸ ἀληθές)." In *Les stoïciens et leur logique: actes du colloque de Chantilly*. Septembre. 1976, edited by Jacques Brunschwig, 297315. Paris: Librairie Philosophique J. Vrin, 1978.

Mateo-Seco, Lucas F., and Juan L. Bastero, eds. *El "Contra Eunomium I" en la Produccion Literaria de Gregorio de Nisa*. Pamplona: Ediciones Universidad de Navarra, S. A. 1988.

Mates, Benson. *Stoic Logic*. Berkeley and Los Angeles: University of California Press, 1953.

Matthen, Mohan. "Empiricism and Ontology in Ancient Medicine." In *Method, Medicine and Metaphysics*, edited by R. J. Hankinson. Edmonton: Academic Printing and Publishing, 1988.

McFadden, William. "The Exegesis of 1 Cor. 1:24, 'Christ the Power of God and the Wisdom of God' until the Arian Controversy." Ph.D. diss., Pontifical Gregorian University, 1963.

McGrath, Charles. "Gregory of Nyssa's Doctrine on the Knowledge of God." Ph.D. diss., Fordham University, 1964.

Meijering, E. P. "Athanasius on the Father as the Origin of the Son." In *God Being History*, 89–102. Amsterdam: North-Holland, 1975.

———. *God Being History*. Amsterdam: North-Holland, 1975.

Méridier, L. *L'influence de la seconde sophistique sur l'oeuvre de Grégoire de Nysse*, Paris, 1906.

Merlan, Phillip. *From Platonism to Neo-Platonism*. The Hague: Martinus Nijhoff, 1960.

Miller, Harold W. "*Dynamis* and *Physis* in *On Ancient Medicine*." *American Philological Association* 83 (1952): 184–97.

Moingt, Joseph. *Théologie trinitaire de Tertullien*. 4 vols. Paris: Aubier, 1966–1969.

Moline, Jon. *Plato's Theory of Understanding*. Madison: University of Wisconsin Press, 1981.

Moonan, Lawrence. *Divine Power: The Medieval Power Distinction up to its Adoption by Albert, Bonaventure, and Aquinas*. Oxford: Claredon Press, 1994.

Moraux, Paul. *Alexandre d'Aphrodise: exégète de la noétique d'Aristote*. Liège: Faculté de Philosophie et Lettres, 1942.

Moreau, Joseph. "Immutabilité du vrai, necessité, logique et lien causal." In *Les stoïciens et leur logique: actes du colloque de Chantilly. Septembre. 1976,* edited by Jacques Brunschwig, 347–60. Paris: Librairie Philosophique J. Vrin, 1978.

Mortley, Raoul. *Connaissance religieuse et herméneutique chez Clement d'Alexandrie.* Leiden: E. J. Brill, 1973.

———. *From Word to Silence.* 2 vols. Bonn: Peter Hanstein Verlag Gmbh, 1986.

Mosshammer, Alden A. "The Created and the Uncreated in Gregory of Nyssa *Contra Eunomium* 1, 105–113." In *El "Contra Eunomium I" en la Produccion Literaria de Gregorio de Nisa,* edited by Lucas F. Mateo-Seco and Juan L. Bastero, 353–79.

Mourelatos, Alexander P. D. "Heraclitus, Parmenides, and the Naive Metaphysics of Things." In *Exegesis and Argument,* 16–48. Assen, Neth.: Van Gorcum and Company, 1973.

Mure, G. R. *A Study of Hegel's Logic.* Oxford: Clarendon Press, 1950.

Mühlenberg, Ekkehard. *Die Unendlichkeit Gottes bei Gregor von Nyssa: Gregors Kritik am Gottesbegriff der klassischen Metaphysik.* Forschungen zur Kirchen und Dogmengeschichte 16. Göttingen: 1966.

Newman, John Henry. *The Arians of the Fourth Century.* 4th ed. London: Basil Montagu, 1876.

Norris, Frederick. *Faith Gives Fullness to Reason: The Theological Orations of Gregory of Nazianzus.* Translated by Lionel Wickham and Frederick Williams. Leiden: E. J. Brill, 1990.

Norris, Richard A. *Manhood and Christ.* Oxford: Clarendon Press, 1963.

Nutton, Vivian, ed. *Galen: Problems and Prospects.* The Wellcome Institute for the History of Medicine: 1981.

Nuyens, Francois. *L'evolution de la psychologie d'Aristote.* Louvain: Éditions de L'institut superieur de philosophie, 1948.

Otis, Brooks. "Cappadocian Thought as a Coherent Systemn." *Dumbarton Oaks Papers* 12 (1958): 95–124.

———. "Gregory of Nyssa and the Cappadocian Conception of Time." *Studia Patristica* 15 (1976): 327–57.

Papageorgiou, Panayiotis. "Plotinos and Eunomios: A Parallel Theology of the Three Hypostases." *The Greek Orthodox Theological Review,* 37 (1992), 215–31.

Patterson, Lloyd G. "*De libero arbitrio* and Methodius' Attack on Origen." *Studia Patristica* 14 (1976): 160–66.

———. "Methodius, Origen, and the Arian Dispute." *Studia Patristica* 17:2 (1982): 912–23.

Phillips, E. D. *Greek Medicine.* Southhampton: Thames and Hudson, 1973.

Pollard, T. E. *Johannine Christology and Arianism.* Cambridge: Cambridge University Press, 1970.

———. "The Origins of Arianism." *Journal of Theological Studies* 9 (1958): 103–11.

Pottier, Bernard. *Dieu et le Christ selon Grégoire de Nysse: Étude systematique du "Contre Eunome" avec traduction inedité des extraits d'Eunome.* Bruxelles: Culture et Vertité, 1994.

Pouchet, Robert. *Basile le Grand et son univers d'amis d'après sa correspondance.* Rome: Institutum Patristicum 'Augustinianum', 1992.

Quasten, Johannes. *The Ante-Nicene Literature After Irenaeus,* vol. 2 of *Patrology.* Westminster: Newman Press, 1953.

de Régnon, Théodore. *Études sur la sainte trinité.* 4 vols. bound as 3. Paris: Victor Retaux, 1892–98.

Reynolds, P. L. "The Essence, Power and Presence of God: Fragments of the History of an Idea, From Neopythagoreanism to Peter Abelard." In *From Athens to Chartres—Neoplatonism and Medieval Thought: Studies in Honour of Edouard Jeauneau,* edited by Haijo Jan Westra. Leiden: E. J. Brill, 1992.

Ricken, Friedo. "Nikaia als Krisis des altkirchlichen Platonisme." *Theologie und Philosophie* 44 (1969): 321–41.

Ringgren, Helmer. *Word and Wisdom: Studies in the Hypostatization of Divine Qualities and Functions in the Ancient Middle East.* Lund: Hakan Ohlssons Boktryckeri, 1947.

Rist, John M. "Basil's 'Neoplatonism': Its Background and Nature." In *Basil of Caesarea,* edited by Paul J. Fedwick. Toronto: Pontifical Institute of Mediaeval Studies, 1981. 1:137–200.

———. *Plotinus: The Road to Reality.* Cambridge: Cambridge University Press, 1967.

———, ed. *The Stoics.* Berkeley and Los Angeles: University of California Press, 1978.

Roberts, Louis. "Origen and Stoic Logic." *Transactions of the American Philological Association* 101 (1970): 433–44.

Robinson, Daniel N. *Aristotle's Psychology.* New York: Columbia University Press, 1989.

Robinson, T. M. *Plato's Psychology.* Toronto: University of Toronto Press, 1970.

Rousseau, Phillip. *Basil of Caesarea.* Berkeley and Los Angeles: University of California Press, 1994.

Sagnard, F. *Clément d'Alexandrie Extraits de Théodote.* Sources Chrétiennes, vol. 23. Paris: Éditions du Cerf, 1948.

Sallis, John. *Being and Logos.* Pittsburgh: Duquesne University Press, 1975.

Sambursky, Samuel. *Physics of the Stoics.* London: Routledge and Kegan Paul, 1959.

Segal, Alan F. *Two Powers in Heaven.* Leiden: E. J. Brill, 1977.

Siegel, Rudolf E. *Galen: On Psychology, Psychopathology, and Function and Diseases of the Nervous System.* Basel: S. Karger, 1973.

Smith, Andrew. *Porphyry's Place in the Neoplatonic Tradition: A Study in Post-Plotinian Neoplatonism.* The Hague: Martinus Nijoff, 1974.

Smith, Wesley D. *The Hippocratic Tradition.* Ithaca: Cornell University Press, 1979.

Solmsen, Friedrich. *Aristotle's System of the Physical World.* Ithaca: Cornell University Press, 1960.

Souilhé, J. *Étude sur le terme Δύναμις.* Paris: Librairie Félix Alcan, 1919.

von Staden, Heinrich. *Herophilus: The Art of Medicine in Early Alexandria.* Cambridge: Cambridge University Press, 1989.

Stead, G. Christopher. *Divine Substance.* Oxford: Clarendon Press, 1977.

———. "The Freedom of the Will and the Arian Controversy." In *Platonismus und Christentum,* edited by Horst-Dieter Blume and Friedhelm Mann. Münster: Aschendorffsche Verlafbuchhandlung, 1983.

———. "The Platonism of Arius." *Journal of Theological Studies* 15 (1964): 16–31.

———. "The *Thalia* of Arius and the Testimony of Athanasius." *Journal of Theological Studies* 29 (1978): 20–52.

Stevens, Annick. *Postérité de l'être: Simplicius interprète de Parménide.* Brussels: Éditions Ousia, 1990.

Stritzky, Maria-Barbara von. *Zum Problem der Erkenntnis bei Gregor von Nyssa.* Münsterische Beiträge zur Theologie, vol. 37. Münster: Aschendorffsche Verlafbuchhandlung, 1972.

Tarán, Leonardo. *Parmenides.* Princeton: Princeton University Press, 1965.

Taylor, A. E. "Forms and Numbers: A Study in Platonic Metaphysics." In *Philosophical Studies.* London: Macmillan and Company, 1934.

———. "The Words Εἶδος/Ἰδέα in Pre-Platonic Literature." In *Varia Socratica,* 178–267. Oxford: James Parker and Company, 1911.

Teloh, Henry. *The Development of Plato's Metaphysics.* University Park: Pennsylvania State University Press, 1981.

Temkin, Owsei. *Galenism.* Ithaca: Cornell University Press, 1971.

Untersteiner, Mario. *Parmenide.* Firenze: La Nuova Italia, 1958.

Uthemann, Von Karl-Heinz. "Die Sprache der Theolgie nach Eunomius von Cyzicus." *Zeitschrift für Kirchengeschichte,* 104 (1993), 143–75.

Vaggione, Richard P. "Aspects of Faith in the Eunomian Controversy." Ph.D. diss., Oxford University, 1976.

———. "Οὐχ ὡς ἕν τῶν γεννημάτων: Some Aspects of Dogmatic Formulae in the Arian Controversy." *Studia Patristica* 17 (1982): 18187.

Vandenbussche, E. "La part de la dialectique dans la théologie d'Eunome le technologue." *Revue d'histoire ecclésiastique,* 40 (1944–45): 47–72.

Venema, Cornelis P. "Gregory of Nyssa on the Trinity." *Mid-America Journal of Theology* 8 (1992): 72–94.

Verbeke, Gerard. *L'evolution de la doctrine du pneuma du stoïcisme à s. Augustin.* Paris: Desclée de Brouwer, 1945.

Vesey, Godfrey, ed. *The Philosophy in Christianity.* Cambridge: Cambridge University Press, 1989.

Vizgin, V. P. "Hippocratic Medicine as a Historical Source for Aristotle's Theory of the dynameis." *Studies in History of Medicine* 4 (1980): 1–12.

Voelke, André-Jean. *L'idée de volonté dans le stoïcisme.* Paris: Presses Universitaires de France, 1973.

Wakefield, Paul. "Why Justice and Holiness Are Similar: *Protagoras* 330–331." *Phronesis* 32 (1987): 267–76.

Wallis, Richard T., ed. *Neoplatonism and Gnosticism.* Albany: State University of New York Press, 1992.

Watson, Gerard. *Stoic Theory of Knowledge.* Belfast: Queen's University Press, 1966.

Weiss, Paul. "The Dunamis." *Review of Metaphysics* 40 (1987): 657–74.

Weiswurm, A. *The Nature of Human Knowledge According to St. Gregory of Nyssa.* Washington, D.C.: Catholic University of America Press, 1952.

Whittaker, John. "ΕΠΕΚΕΙΝΑ ΝΟΥ ΚΑΙ ΟΥΣΙΑΣ." *Vigiliae Christianae* 23 (1969): 96–104.

Wickham, Lionel."The Syntagmation of Aetius the Anomean." *Journal of Theological Studies,* 19 (1968): 532–69.

Widdicombe, Peter. *The Fatherhood of God from Origen to Athanasius.* Oxford: Claredon Press, 1994.

Wiles, Maurice. "The Doctrine of Christ in the Patristic Age." *Working Papers.* 1968.

———. "Eunomius: Hair-splitting Dialectian or Defender of the Accessibility of Salvation?" In *The Making of Orthodoxy: Essays in Honour of Henry Chadwick,* ed. Rowan Williams. Cambridge: Cambridge University Press, 1989.

———. "The Philosophy in Christianity: Arius and Athanasius." In *The Philosophy in Christianity,* edited by Godfrey Vesey, 41–52. Cambridge: Cambridge University Press, 1989.

Williams, Daniel H. *Ambrose of Milan and the End of the Nicene-Arian Conflicts.* Oxford: Claredon Press, 1995.

———. "Polemics and Politics in Ambrose of Milan's *De Fide.*" *Journal of Theological Studies* n. s. 46 (1995): 519–31.

Williams, Rowan. *Arius: Heresy and Tradition.* London: Darton, Longman, and Todd, 1987.

———. "The Logic of Arianism." *Journal of Theological Studies* 34 (1983): 56–81.

———. "The Quest of the Historical *Thalia.*" In *Arianism: Historical and Theological Reassessments,* edited by Robert C. Gregg. Cambridge: Philadelphia Patristic Foundation, 1985.

Williams, Rowan, ed. *The Making of Orthodoxy: Essays in Honour of Henry Chadwick.* Cambridge: Cambridge University Press, 1989.

Winslow, Donald F. *Dynamics of Salvation.* Cambridge: Philadelphia Patristic Foundation, 1979.

Winston, David. *Logos and Mystical Theology in Philo of Alexandria.* Cincinnati: Hebrew Union Press, 1985.

Witt, R. E. *Albinus and the History of Middle Platonism.* Cambridge: Cambridge University Press, 1937.

Wolfson, H. A. "Albinus and Plotinus on Divine Attributes." *Harvard Theological Review* 45 (1952), 115–30.

# General Index

# Scripture Index

# Index of Greek and Latin Terms

*The Power of God: Δύναμις in Gregory of Nyssa's Trinitarian Theology* was composed in Minion by Graphic Composition, Athens, Georgia; printed on 60-pound Glatfelter and bound by Sheridan Books, Ann Arbor, Michigan; and designed and produced by Kachergis Book Design, Pittsboro, North Carolina.